C000174119

COMPLETE PATTERN *Designing*

COMPLETE PATTERN *Designing*

Ann Ladbury

SIDGWICK & JACKSON
LONDON

Book design: Alan Chalk

Line drawings: Jil Shipley

Photography: Dave Yorath

Models: Christina Jansen, Kate Whenray

First published in Great Britain in 1989
by Sidgwick & Jackson Limited
1 Tavistock Chambers, Bloomsbury Way
London WC1A 2SG

ISBN 0 283 99814 8

Photoset by Rowland Phototypesetting Limited,
Bury St Edmunds, Suffolk
Printed in Great Britain by
The Bath Press Limited, Avon

CONTENTS

Introduction 7; How to Use this Book 7; Abbreviations 8; Measurements 8; Lines of Illusion 8; The Elements of Design 12; Principles of Pattern Cutting 14; Blocks, Drafts and Patterns 19; Equipment 22; Fabric Grain and Weave 22; Measuring 24; Table of Standard Body Measurements 26

THE BASIC BLOCKS 27
Skirt Block 27; Bodice Block 29; Sleeve Block 32; Trouser Block 34

FITTING 37
Skirt Block 38; Bodice Block 39; Sleeve Block 40; Trouser Block 41

SKIRT DESIGNS 44
Straight skirts 44; A-line skirts 54

BODICE DESIGNS 62

COLLARS, NECKLINES AND YOKES 73
Collars 73; Necklines 90; Yokes 94

DESIGNS USING SEAMS AND DRAPING 104

SLEEVE DESIGNS 114

ARMHOLES AND SHOULDER LINES 125

KIMONO, RAGLAN AND BATWING SLEEVES 132

DRESS AND TROUSER DESIGNS 150
Dress Designs 150; Trouser Designs 153

OPENINGS, FASTENINGS AND WAIST FINISHES 160
Openings and Fastenings 160; Waist Finishes 168

PATTERNS FROM MEASUREMENTS 172

PATTERNS FOR UNDERCLOTHES, OUTERWEAR, MATERNITY CLOTHES AND SPECIAL FABRICS 188
Underclothes 188; Outerwear 191; Maternity Clothes 201; Special Fabrics 208

How Much Fabric? 213; Supplies 214; Glossary of Technical and Fashion Terms 214; Index 222

INTRODUCTION

It is exciting and very satisfying to be able to design as well as make your clothes. For most people the initial reason for wanting to find out how to make patterns is a desire to take sewing a stage further: to be able to copy quickly the latest fashion or experiment with different collars, sleeves, and so on.

This book contains all you need to know: the basic rules, the equipment required and how to set about it. You will find it's not a bit mysterious; in fact, it is so logical that once learnt it is never forgotten and no matter what the fashion you can always call on your acquired knowledge.

At last you can express your own style and individuality; try your own combinations of line with colour and texture. On a more down-to-earth level you can make the pattern to fit the piece of fabric instead of the other way round.

Pattern cutting ought not to be learned in isolation so I have tried to show how the factors normally associated with sewing all have some bearing on the final results and should therefore be considered while designing the pattern. You will find information on the effect of various outlines on your figure; on designing for velvet, taffeta and lace; on maternity clothes and lingerie; on fastenings, openings, interfacings and lining as well as on working out how much fabric your design will take.

The title *'Complete' Pattern Designing* is not meant to imply that all the styles imaginable have been included. But what I have done is go beyond the purely technical explanations and include in addition to the topics mentioned above, photographs of made-up outfits to give you an idea of the limitless range of styles and features you can design for yourself.

HOW TO USE THIS BOOK

It helps if you have some sewing experience but you need no special knowledge to be able to start cutting patterns.

If you are an experienced dressmaker familiar with techniques and fabrics, you will probably want to make your own blocks and go straight on to select a design. The skirt block is a good starting point as it produces the quickest results.

If you haven't done much sewing and find the idea of blocks a bit daunting, start with a simple skirt from the Patterns from Measurements chapter (page 172) and then do a few practice designs in small scale.

The pattern illustrations in this book are all drawn to scale, the illustrations of the blocks being somewhat less than quarter scale.

The block instructions are for women's shapes but all the information on how to draft features can be applied to men's and children's designs, working in conjunction with a set of bought basic patterns.

Whatever your sewing experience, read about the Principles of Pattern Cutting and use a little time to familiarize yourself with how the book is arranged and where to find everything. Then assemble the equipment and you are ready to start transforming your wardrobe.

ABBREVIATIONS

The following terms are used often and are abbreviated as follows in the text and on the illustrations.

CF	Centre front
CFF	Centre front – place to fold
CB	Centre back
CBF	Centre back – place to fold
CBS	Centre back seam
CFS	Centre front seam
SG	Straight grain
RS	Right side (of fabric or pattern)
WS	Wrong side (of fabric)
cm	Centimetres
in	Inches
m	Metre
yd	Yard
SS	Side seam
SP	Shoulder point
NP	Neck point

MEASUREMENTS

Measurements are given in centimetres followed by an approximate conversion to inches. Use either one system or the other for accuracy. However, the measurements are mainly a guide; it is the basic principles that you are learning, not the amounts. If the instructions say, for instance, add 13mm, it really won't matter if you add 12mm or 14mm or even 15mm; your finished pattern relies much more on your imaginative designing than on your mathematical skills.

LINES OF ILLUSION

Whether you plan to copy a design or sketch one of your own, it will help to show you what the design lines will do for your figure if you draw them on top of the sketch to show the overall illusion. Try to balance any out-of-proportion areas of the figure with an opposing design line. A design with lines that follow the figure closely from top to bottom will serve to emphasize every feature.

Y-line *(see opposite)*

1. Adds height, lengthens the neck. Good for short-waisted figures.
2. Adds height; slimming for large bust. Pockets would emphasize broad hips and thighs.
3. Lengthens neck, would add width to narrow shoulders, good for wide hips and thighs and for short-waisted and thick-waisted figures. In addition, the plain V-neck with contrast constantly draws the eye up and away from the rest of the figure.

T-line *(see opposite)*

1. Adds height, emphasizes waist.
2. Adds height, widens narrow shoulders, good top for large busts. Contrast yoke draws the eye up to the shoulders and neck.
3. Reduces height, good for thick waist.

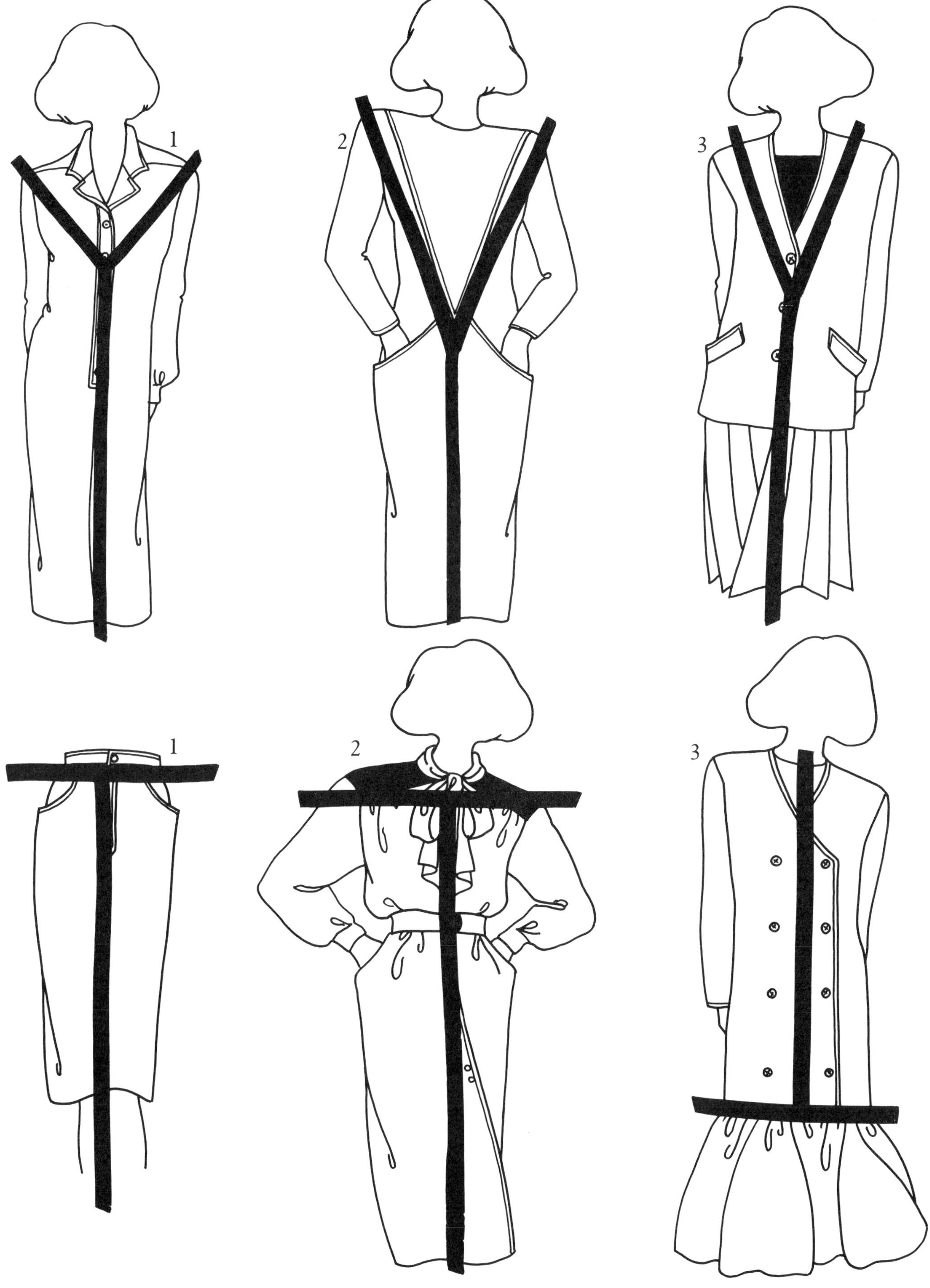
1
2
3
1
2
3

Triangle

1. Emphasizes waist and hips, good for large thighs. Better without contrast for thick-waisted figure.

2. Light colour and decoration draws the eye to bust and neckline, good for small top figures and for broad shoulders.

Wedge *(see opposite)*

1. Good for narrow shoulders, large bust, thick waist. The contrast bow draws the eye constantly up, which makes it suitable for wide hips but pockets should be omitted. Not good for short square figures.

2. Good for narrow shoulders and small bust and would add shape to a square figure.

Rectangle *(see opposite)*

1. Good for large bust or thick waist. Would add height if made all in one colour.

2. Would have a widening squaring effect, therefore not for short or wide figures.

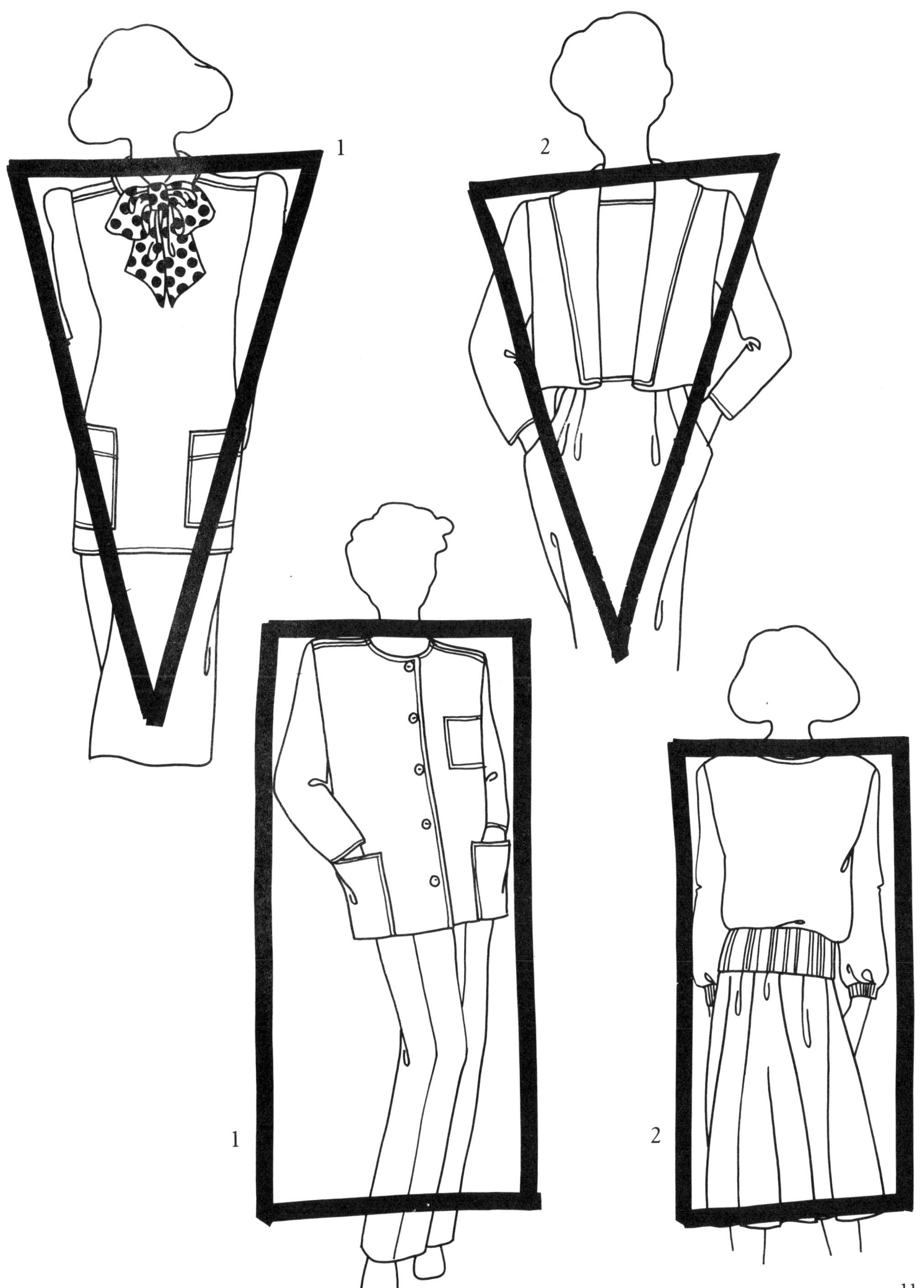
1
2
1
2

Figure of eight

1. Not for short-waisted figures; emphasizes the bust and shortens the neck.

2. Emphasizes the waist especially using contrast fabric. Has a bulging effect so not for the large busted or curvaceous.

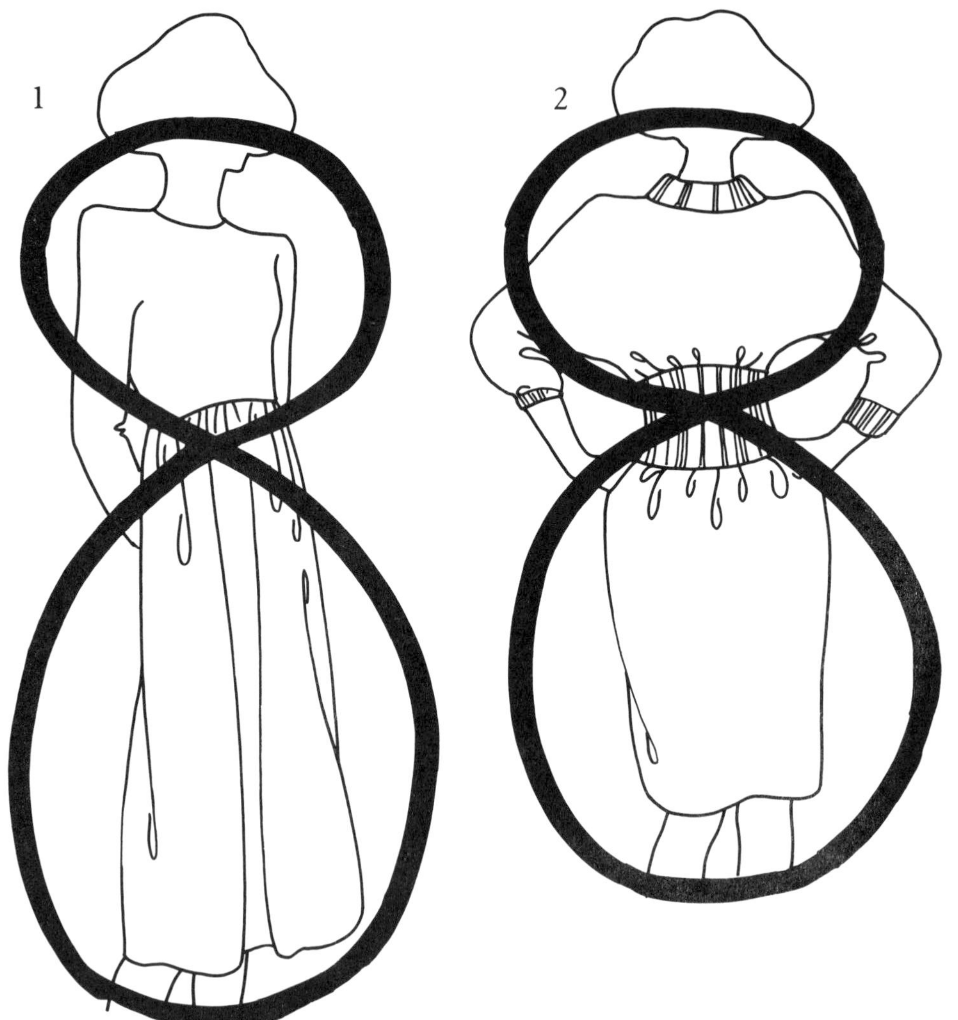

THE ELEMENTS OF DESIGN

Not many people possess average measurements or a perfect figure so designing your own patterns provides the opportunity to emphasize good points and correct any imbalance: to create an illusion. It is a chance to indulge your fancy: to wear waisted dresses, straight dresses, tight trousers, loose trousers, tailored jackets, frilly blouses, shirts or what you choose, whether or not they are in or out of fashion. It is your chance to have your preferred feature where you want it: back buttons, front buttons, no buttons at all; long zip, short zip, pockets, cuffs, fitted waistband and so on.

Most of us can recall a garment that we loved and then when we went to buy another it had been discontinued or gone out of fashion and disappeared. And we can all recall something we loathed because it was too full or too tight or the opening was too short or it kept falling off the shoulders – that sort of thing.

The question of comfort also comes into designing. There are people who cannot wear raglan sleeves, drop waists, front fastenings and so on.

Designing your own patterns can put an end to all this and at the same time you can express your own individuality and fashion sense. Assuming that you know what you like, there are a few other points to consider.

Shape

Consider the shape of the pattern and therefore the finished garment in relation to your own shape. Try to visualize the silhouette or outline in relation to your basic outline. If you are triangular – i.e. narrow shoulders and wide hips – design patterns with wide or padded shoulders, or full sleeves. If you are rectangular, try fitted waists and belts. If you are tall, avoid plain straight unbroken designs.

Proportion

The relationship between the proportion of one part of a pattern and another and the way it will later look and feel when you wear it, is something that can only be learned by experience. At first you are almost bound to make mistakes: a yoke line too high, a pleat too shallow, a panel or a collar too wide. Get into the habit of looking at the latest designs in ready-made clothes; even carry a tape measure and make a note of the length, width, fullness and so on of any new fashions.

Your errors of judgement only need to be small to make a disappointing design instead of a snappy one.

Style of dressing

Even though this is your opportunity to be an individualist beware of making your patterns too bizarre, especially at first. Design patterns that will fit in with your life's activities and your current style.

Sewing skill

Don't get carried away; remember that the pattern has to be made up. Consider your level of sewing skill as well as your likes and dislikes. It will spoil your enjoyment as well as produce a less than perfect garment if you, say, plan a jacket with lots of buttons and loops if you dislike making rouleau or if you have yet to master it.

SELECTING A DESIGN

Copying a picture

If the picture is a photograph it will tell you most of what you want to know. If it is a drawing it may not give much away. You will probably have a front view only so the back must be planned to correspond.

Features

Begin by identifying decorative or added features and this will leave you with those that have to be integrated into your pattern.

Such features will include tabs, ties, bows, belts, straps, loops, pockets and loose folds and drapes or fly-away sections. All these and more can be partly or wholly stitched in with the garment during construction or added at or near the end. While you are new to pattern cutting the latter is the wisest course to take.

Main seams

Look at the position and number of the main seams, shoulder seams, side seams, yokes and panels, so that you know how much sewing as well as pattern drafting will be involved.

Shaping

Decide how each section of the garment is shaped; look for the gathers, darts and tucks that might be providing the main shape. Identify the position of the shaping. Decide where it is coming from to accommodate the body's bulges and hollows, particularly on the bodice front where so much variation is possible. Look at each area in this way and decide whether the darts in the basic blocks will be enough to provide the shaping or whether more will be needed in the skirt, in the bodice, in the sleeve and so on.

Take note of the fullness of the skirt to give

you an idea of the hemline width you will be aiming for. Look at the skirt length compared with its width. Decide which skirt block you will use and whether to use the bodice to waist or hip length.

Techniques

Finally list the techniques involved in making up the pattern: how many buttons, how the neckline is finished, which areas will require interfacing, where is the opening and what sort of fastening will be best.

By this time you should have a clear idea of how to set about making the pattern and constructing the garment and you should also have a firm idea of what fabric will be suitable for the design.

Sketching

Before long you will want to plan your own design, which is very exciting but not as easy as it may sound. You must produce a detailed sketch for a garment of good design and proportion that you can examine and analyse as set out above.

Use an outline of a figure, similar to that shown on page 25, and cut it out in card for ease of copying. It may not look much like you but if you omit the head and hair and add shoes, it could be you.

When you start designing it helps to cut styles of skirts, trousers, blouses and so on from magazines and put them on the body, building up an 'identikit' picture of your design. This is always helpful for features that you have difficulty in drawing. Always make a sketch, however inartistic you feel it is. The practice is good for you and you must have something identifiable to store with the pattern pieces.

Practice

Learn the principles of pattern designing by practising in small scale as explained in the following section but proportion can only be seen in the full-size pattern.

Use your personal blocks even for practice and you will soon build up a library of pattern pieces from which to select when required.

PRINCIPLES OF PATTERN CUTTING

Points of fashion emphasis come and go but the principles of pattern cutting never alter. Patterns are always cut following the same rules and methods, no matter what the current length and looseness may be. Practise the following in small scale.

MOVING DARTS

This is one of the most satisfying things you will learn. Nothing you do later will match the thrill of doing this the first time.

Pivot principle

The bust dart, initially in the shoulder, can be moved to any position provided it runs from an outer edge to the bust point.

Make a copy of the front bodice block to waist level and cut away the shoulder dart. Draw a series of lines to indicate other dart positions, in armhole, from side seam, from neckline, from CF and from waist, where it will join the existing waist dart. Cut along these lines to BP. A piece of sticky tape will keep the pieces together. Close the shoulder dart edges together and allow the block to open at each of the other positions in turn. Outline the block each time and re-draw each dart shorter, to reach either outer or inner BP circle.

The dart can also be divided, with part in one position and the remainder in another. Try experimenting.

Having moved the dart to where you want it you may find that, although the shaping produced is exactly the same as it was, because the dart is never as long as it is from the shoulder,

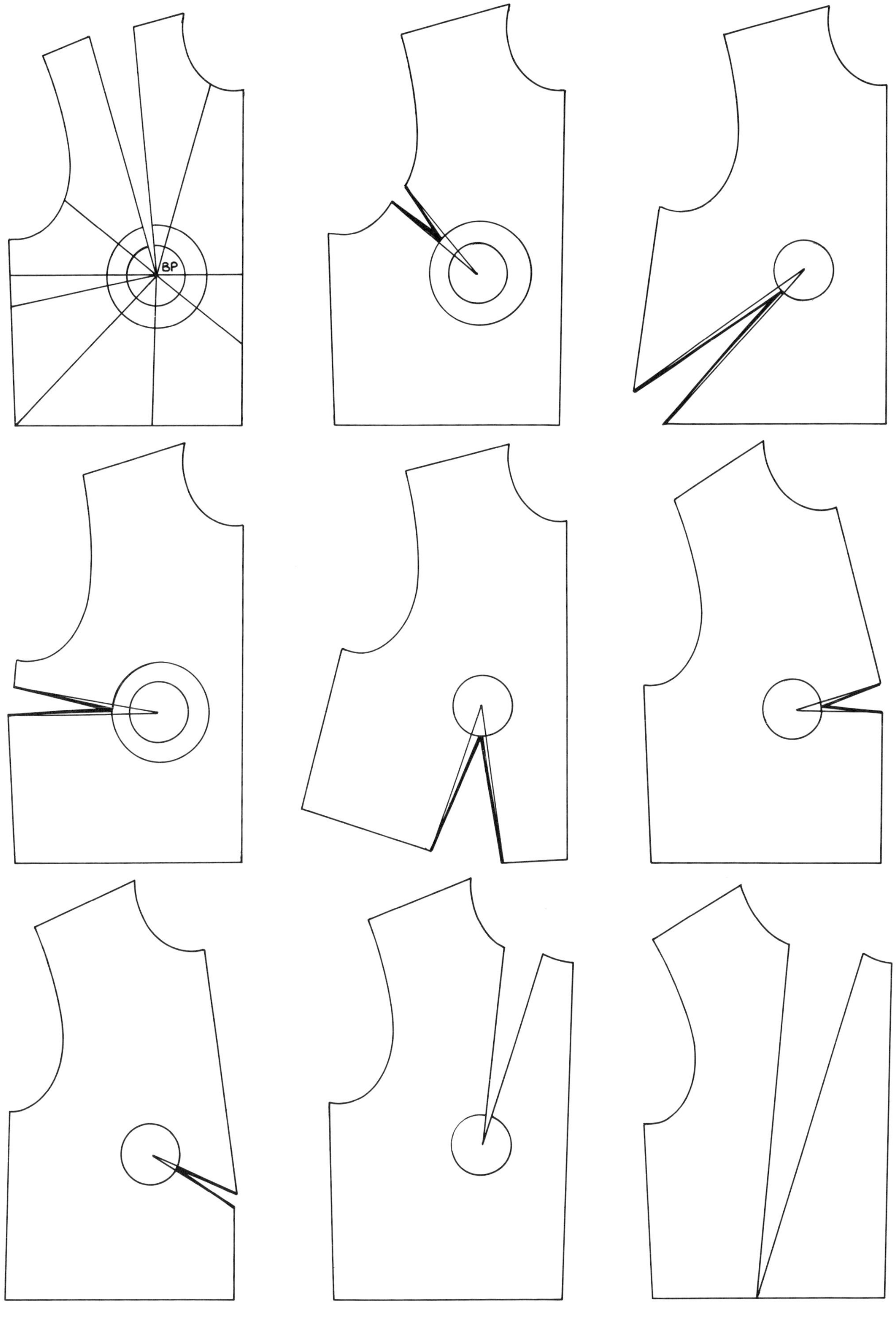
BP

there is not enough of it left to look good decoratively. If this is the case the pattern can be cut through to the opposite edge and additional space opened up.

All the darts shown can be stitched as tucks or even as gathers if preferred; the shaping produced for the bust will remain the same.

Transfer principle

It may be necessary to move darts but keep them on the same pattern edge, or to move a dart when there is no pivot point. Simply cut along a line in the new position, cut from the end to the point of the old dart and close the old dart. Draw new dart to required length.

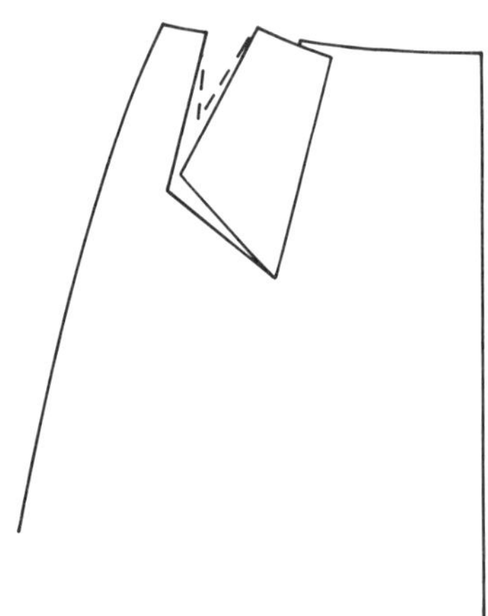

Dart ends. No matter where a dart is placed or what its length on the final pattern piece, the edge must be correctly drawn before cutting along it. Cut all edges except those with darts, fold each dart and flatten it to face the direction it will be after sewing. Either cut the pattern edge or run a tracing wheel through the layers, open it out and cut.

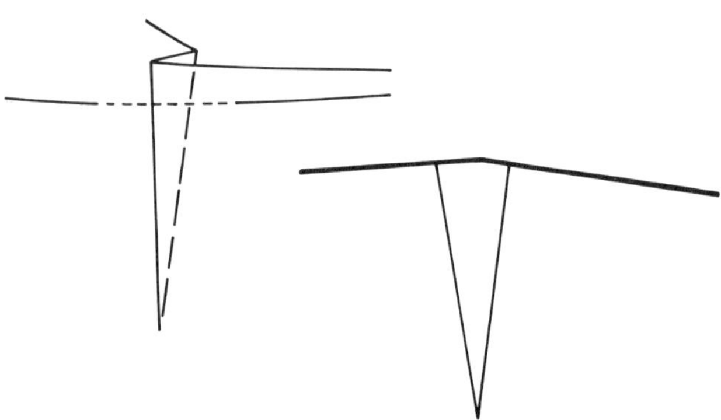

Gathered edges. Gathers form general shaping and take more length. After adapting the pattern gently curve the edge, clipping sharp edges but keeping the new line in the main outside the original block edge.

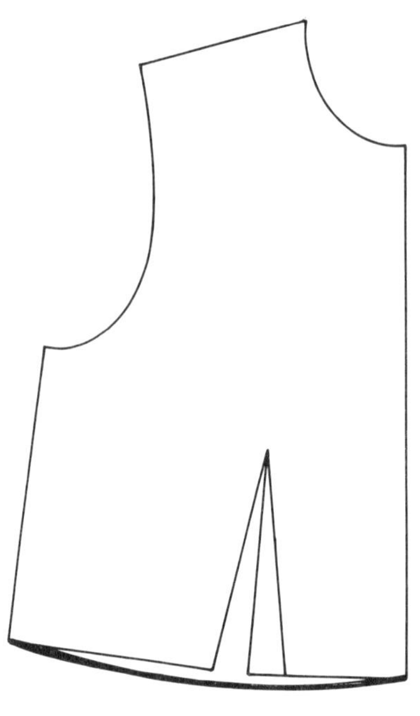

CUT AND SPREAD

Additional width can be introduced by cutting the piece of pattern or the copy of the block and spreading it to the required width.

Even insertions. When adding an even amount right through it helps to rule a horizontal line as a guide and also, if you have decided on the amount required, perhaps for a pleat, mark the distance.

Wedge-shaped insertions. These may be required to add flare and as it can be difficult to keep track of how much you are adding it helps to outline the pattern piece first. To make the insertion cut from one edge to the other but leave paper attached; match the pattern to the shape beneath at this point and swing out as required. Outline new shape drawing gentle curves and clipping off sharp corners. Cut in several places if insertion is required evenly right across.

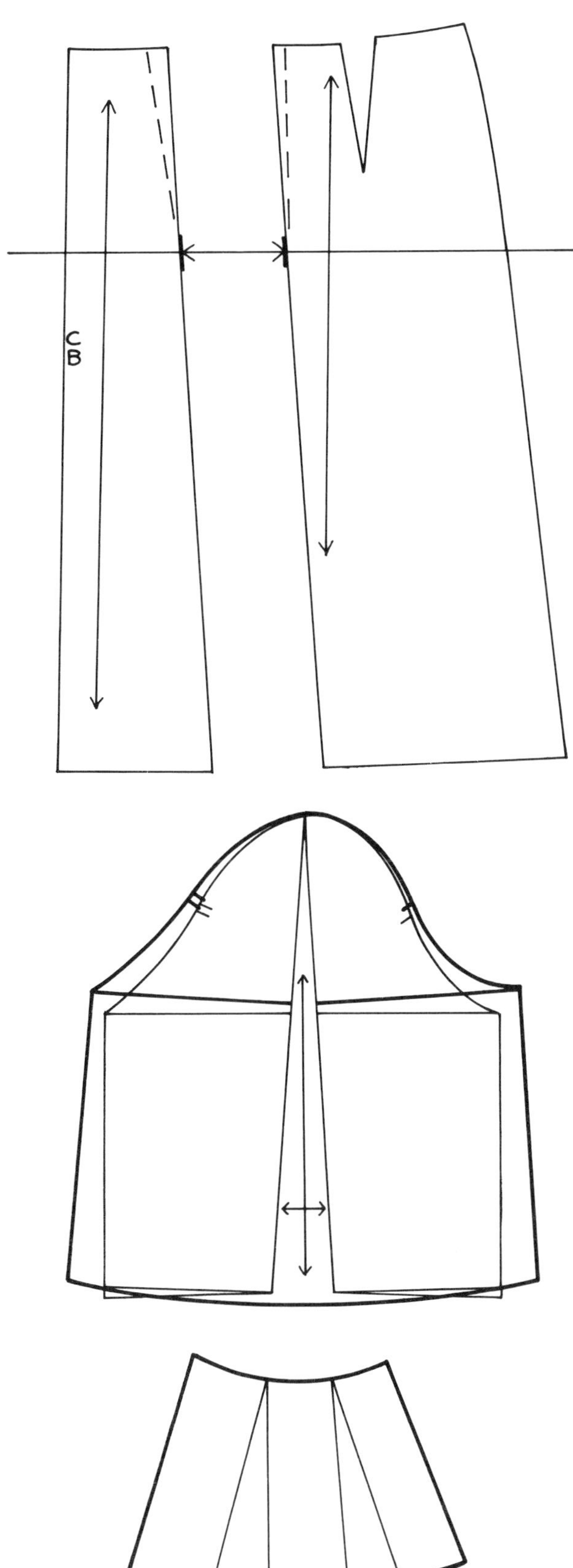

INTRODUCING SEAMS

Additional functional or decorative seams can be added simply by cutting the pattern. However, these seams may lack style especially if they are straight. Make seams slightly curved and if possible introduce some shape by putting a dart or part of a dart into one end. Always make panels slightly wider at the hem or, if horizontal, deeper at CF.

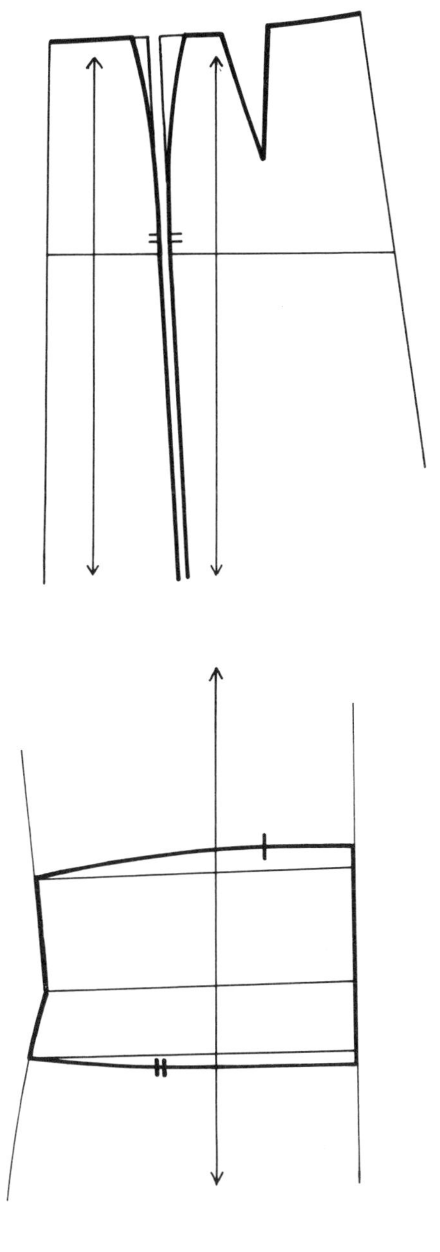

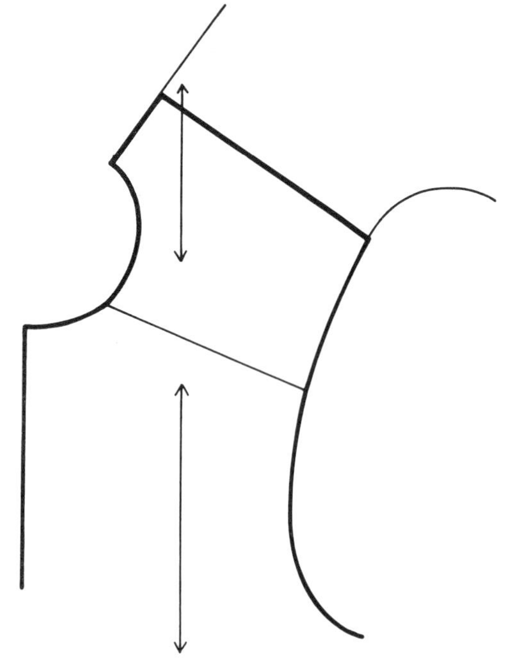

Always insert balance marks across a new seam line before cutting the paper. Rule the grain line before cutting; rule the line on both halves even if one or other is eventually moved. Being vertical the grain line acts as a guide line to keeping pattern pieces upright.

ELIMINATING SEAMS

Straight pattern edges can be put together to make one pattern piece provided the grain on the final shape is acceptable. There would often be a new seam inserted not too far away. If there is any shaping between the two edges it can be made into a dart.

REDUCING FLARE OR WIDTH

A pattern edge can be reduced in length by cutting to the far side and overlapping to remove a wedge shape. As before it helps to outline the original so that you can keep a check on what you are doing.

If this reduction is going to remove essential width the pattern can be cut part-way and then horizontally to each edge. Overlap as before and outline new shape curving the edges and maintaining the same grain as on the original.

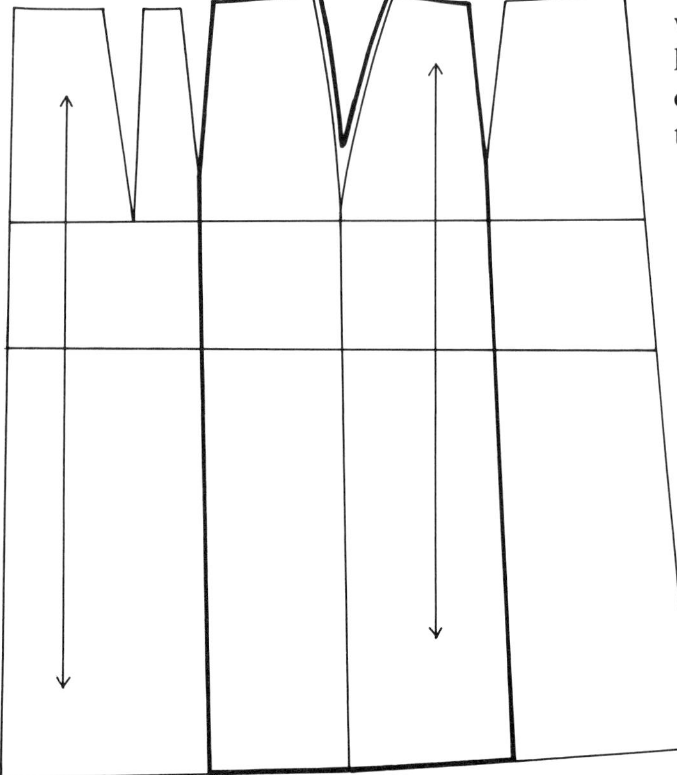

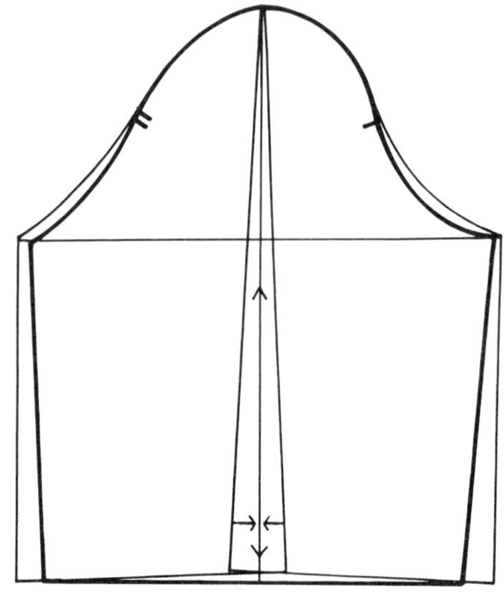

BLOCKS, DRAFTS AND PATTERNS

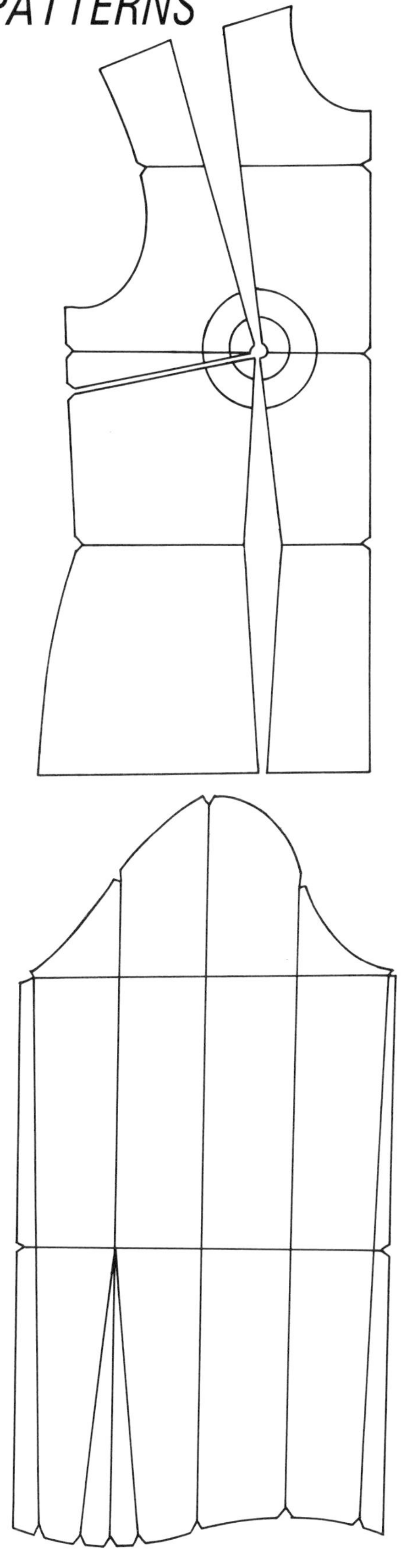

These are the three stages involved in producing a pattern: the block provides the starting point; the draft is all the stages of cutting and folding and probably experimenting too; the pattern is the final piece of paper ready to place on the fabric. Sometimes there is very little drafting to do, especially if you are making basic trousers or a skirt. Some shapes can be marked directly on to the fabric and so the final stage is omitted. Making the blocks is time-consuming so you may prefer to skip this stage and buy a basic pattern instead: most pattern companies produce one.

BLOCKS

The block is an outline of the shape of the body. It is a shell with edges shaped where the body changes shape. It has darts to make it fit the bumps and hollows but it has no other features. The benefit of using it as a starting point is that it is your size and given that fabrics behave differently, it is probably the nearest you can get to a perfect fit.

Having made your blocks, never cut them or mark them; always make a copy instead when you need one. The most convenient system is to make the blocks in durable card which can be quickly outlined. Punch a small hole at the bust point and make nicks in the edge of the card to correspond with construction lines to be marked in pencil and drawn after removing the card. Cut away the darts on the front bodice, make a hinge on which to pivot the block at the bust point by applying a piece of sticking plaster to the underneath of the card. Prepare all blocks this way.

Blocks have no hem or seam allowances included and you will quickly realize why this is an advantage; in fact it would be impossible to work an accurate draft if they had them. If you decide to buy a basic commercial pattern convert the pieces into blocks by removing seams and hems and making copies in card as described above.

DRAFTING

This is the stage where you convert the block outline into your chosen design, adding the features and information relevant to it. Drafting is done with the paper flat on the table but at any time you can check what you are doing by trying it against you or by putting it on a dress dummy. Work in a logical way as follows:

1. Select the relevant block; you may have made a hip-length as well as a waist-length bodice block; you may have a fitted sleeve as well as a straight one.
2. Outline the block on paper, possibly incorporating the first stage of the draft by moving darts. Transfer all construction lines from the block.
3. Draw design lines on the outline, for example, necklines, yokes. Shorten or make additions such as for fastenings. Insert balance marks across lines to be cut and mark centre front and centre back. Rule straight grain lines from top to bottom.
4. On a fresh piece of paper rule a long horizontal line intersected by a vertical line as a guiding grid to laying down pieces accurately.
5. Cut round the outline and cut up the draft as necessary, pinning or sticking the pieces to the grid.

Drafting in small scale

Learn the principles and practise designing using blocks a quarter of their full size. It not only saves paper, it is quicker and the pieces are easier to handle. Also you can work on A4 paper and keep the results in a normal size book or folder for easy reference.

Make quarter-size copies of all the blocks following the instructions but dividing each measurement by four. You may find a quarter scale ruler or a calculator a help.

Make copies in thin card, adding all the lines and information the same as for full-size blocks. Full-size blocks should be adjusted to fit the figure before making copies in card, but this doesn't matter for the quarter-scale copies.

HINTS ON DRAWING

1. Use a short ruler for short lines and a long one for long lines. This may sound like unnecessary advice but it makes for more accurate and efficient drawing.
2. Draw curves with your hand inside the arc keeping your elbow on the table. In some cases a straight guide line might help. If you find curved lines difficult make it a row of dashes instead of a solid line; they will form a perfect curve.
3. Make use of the edge of the paper as a straight line and also the edge and the corners of the table.
4. Use a pin or the point of a compass to pivot pieces of pattern.
5. When making a repeated measurement such as for tucks or pleats mark off the edge of a piece of paper and use it instead of a tape measure or ruler. It is much quicker and there is no likelihood of error.
6. Measure curves by standing tape measure on edge. Check corresponding edges, e.g. of seams, by folding the paper over or by placing one piece on top of the other.
7. Wherever possible trace for accuracy rather than outline.

THE FINISHED PATTERN

Each piece must include all the information needed for cutting out and making the garment. You can add seam and hem allowances if you wish but if so make a note on the pattern as to exactly what has been added.

Prepare each piece of pattern as follows:

1. Make a fresh outline of each piece to eliminate all construction lines and joins. Smooth out all curves and straighten edges where necessary.
2. Mark straight grain arrows.
3. Transfer balance marks from draft and add such things as gathering points, pleat direction arrows, sleeve head and zip points.

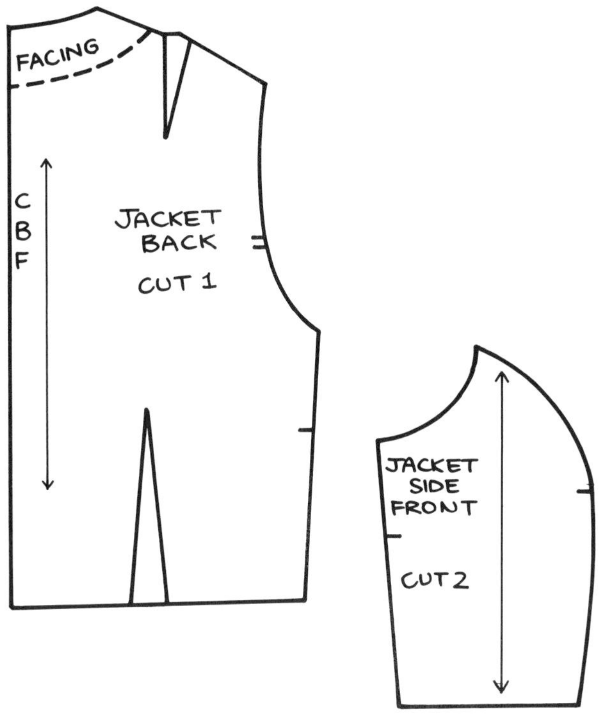

4. Indicate facings with lines of a different colour or thickness if separate pattern is not included.

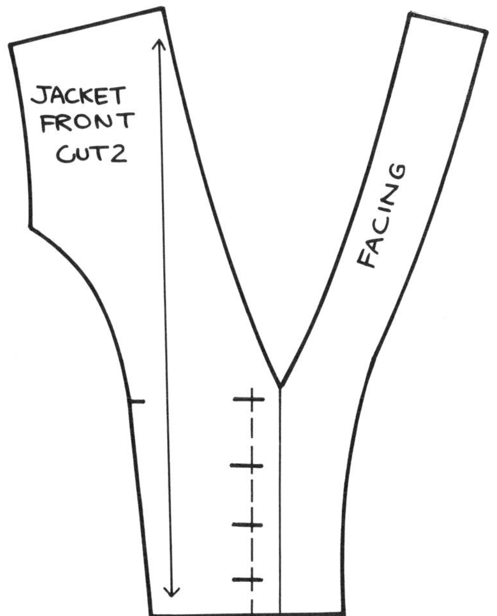

5. Add cutting instructions, for example cut 1, cut 2, cut to fold, and so on.

6. Name each pattern piece; don't assume that you will recognize the shapes when you next use the pattern. Add the size if necessary.

Dart ends and shaped edges

Cut out the pieces that have straightforward outlines. Those that include darts, pleats or extensions should be partially cut and the features folded into the position they will take up when sewn. Cut remaining edges with the paper folded so that you have an accurate pattern edge when opened out.

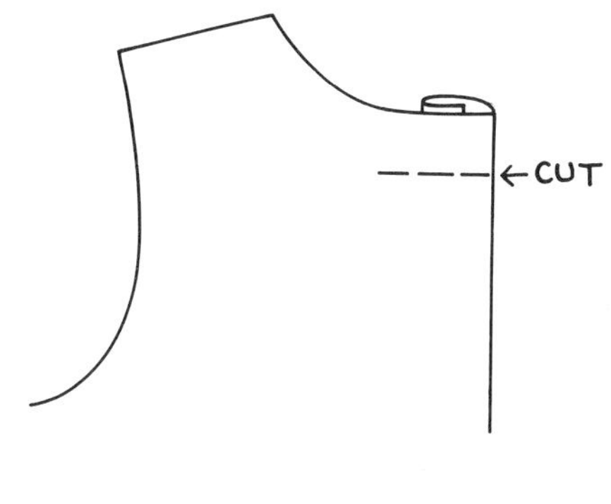

Complete the pattern

Place corresponding seam edges together to check length. Correct by trimming if necessary. Make sure balance marks match; insert them if not already in position.

Draw any additional features for which there was no drafting, for example cuffs, belts, patch pockets; label appropriately and cut out.

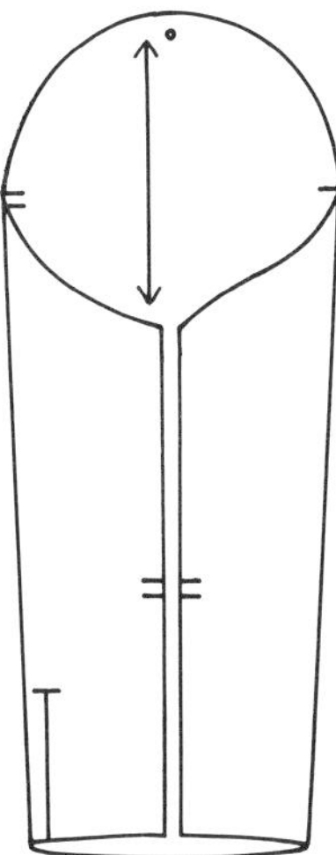

Pin pattern to fabric ready to cut out or fold it neatly and store together with the pieces of draft which will act as a reminder if ever you need a refresher course.

EQUIPMENT

Very little in the way of specialist equipment is required for drafting patterns although in addition to the items listed there are aids for drawing curves which you might like to invest in if you find you need them. For drawing patterns you will need:

Pencils – not too hard
Pencil sharpener
Rubber
Pins
Tape measure
Glue-stick and/or a reel of copier tape
Scissors for cutting paper – not too small
Spiked tracing wheel
Metre rule – wood or metal
Short ruler
Felt tip pen
Set square
Weights; you will find suitable objects around the house – paper weights, small ornaments, even kitchen weights will do.

Card. The blocks are the foundation of almost every pattern so it is worth making copies of them on firm card. Store them flat, under the bed for instance, or punch a hole at one end and hang up with a loop of string. For working in small scale it is useful to make the blocks in thin card as well.

Paper. You will need plenty of paper. It should be substantial enough to endure fitting as well as pinning to the fabric but not so thick you cannot easily fold and cut it. You also need to be able to see through it. You need large sheets of paper; it is irritating and time-wasting to be constantly joining pieces together. Use plain, not squared, paper; it is less confusing and your patterns may be more accurate.

It is worth buying drafting paper. It is specially made for the job, is available in large sheets which can be bought 10, 20, 50 etc. at a time. Alternatively buy a big roll of paper. It is an expensive outlay initially but worth it if you intend to go on with pattern designing.

Small sheets of thin tracing paper are useful and for working in small scale it is worth buying a layout pad – the paper is softer than tracing but you can still see through it.

Table. You need a smooth table top on which to work. If the dining-room table is unsuitable cover it with a cutting board, a folding corrugated cardboard board. One side is marked out in squares, a useful guide for straight lines and angles. Most ordinary tables are too low to work on comfortably so either sit on a stool or have some blocks made with which to raise the table.

STORAGE OF PATTERNS

Work out a convenient method of storage. Large envelopes, polythene bags, or perhaps keep pattern pieces flat in dry cleaners' bags under the bed. Also keep with the patterns, or separately filed, a sketch and the fabric and haberdashery list for easy reference.

FABRIC GRAIN AND WEAVE

One reason why it is best to have a reasonable knowledge of sewing before starting to learn pattern cutting is that it is useful to know something of how fabrics behave. A paper pattern can never be a failure because the principles are laid down and the sequences are logical. A garment made from the pattern will not necessarily be an unqualified success; the final result depends too much on the fabric.

If you can have the fabric before you as you design the pattern, you have a greater chance of success than if you search for something suitable after making the pattern. In any case, always design for a type, if not a specific length, of fabric. Never make up 'any old fabric' to test a pattern. It is a waste of time unless it is very close to the correct fabric and if it is, then the specific fabric might as well be sewn.

Consider the weight of the fabric. Take roughly the amount that will be used: 1.5m/1¾ yd – blouse; 2–3m/2¼–3½yd – jacket; 1m/1¼ yd of wide fabric for trousers and so on, and drape it over yourself. If it feels flimsy and light you might consider designing a pattern with fullness. If the weight of it crushes you it might be wise to design something neat and slim-fitting.

Observe how the fabric falls. Gather it up and see whether it hangs well or whether the gathers remain rigid and puffy. For a wedding or evening gown you might well prefer the latter, but not for a soft blouse to be worn under a jacket.

Fold over a corner of the fabric and hold it against you so that you can see how it looks on the bias. Observe not only the way in which it falls but see what it does to any print or pattern. It may not be suitable for the bias cut or circular skirt that you are planning.

Crush a small area to see whether the fabric creases and look at its behaviour when you open your hand. Does it remain crushed and slowly recover or does it spring right out of your hand?

Finally, examine weave and construction. Is it close, open, tight, smooth, matt, embossed, rough, shiny, hairy? You have, naturally, looked at it before picking it up but how will its qualities affect your design and how will it affect your sewing and the features you are planning?

Weave

Pull the fabric across and down as well as on the bias. How much does it 'give'? Will it need lining? Or even mounting on to a backing fabric?

Consider whether you will have to ensure that all pattern pieces, no matter how small, will have to be cut in one direction, not only because of a nap or design but perhaps because of an unusual amount of give across the width of the fabric. Knit fabrics can normally only be cut running lengthwise because of the appearance of the knitting and the excessive stretch across the width, but test it on the bias too. Pipings and edgings look good on the bias but how will any bias seams behave?

Grain

The warp yarns, running the length, are nearly always stronger in a woven fabric than the weft yarns that run across from selvedge to selvedge. It is therefore safe to follow the rule that the warp should run the length of the pattern piece, to hang vertically when the garment is worn. It provides stability and avoids drooping hemlines and bubbly seams. The rule is often broken for pattern pieces such as waistband or cuffs where the strength is required across the body. The rule may be broken if the pattern on the fabric has to be matched or for items that are out of sight or do not affect the main garment, for example pockets. Sometimes yokes may be cut with the warp running across the body, for a particular effect or for widthways stability. Occasionally pieces of pattern may be moved off the warp grain for economy of fabric but be aware of the possible effect. If the warp and weft yarns are similar you might get away with it but it can spoil a garment to cut the main pieces with the weft threads running vertically. One time when it cannot be avoided is when using border design fabrics but there is no doubt that skirts at least will stand out rather than hang close.

The straight grain arrows on block patterns run parallel with centre front and centre back edges or, in the case of the sleeve and trousers, straight down the middle. Keep the arrows in this position, transferring them to each piece as the pattern evolves. Move them only for the reasons above.

With experience you will be able to cut patterns on the bias i.e. with straight grain arrow at 45 degrees to the original position but experiment first before cutting entire garments. The stretch down the length of the garment will produce uneven hemlines and the pull downwards will make a tighter fit. However, the bias across the body acts like ease so the pattern can be tighter to start with. And where the weaker weft yarns are vertical to the floor the hem will drop more than where the warp yarns lie.

MEASURING

Taking measurements can be tedious but it is best to have a single session at which you record all the body measurements including those you will not be using to start with. Many of the measurements you can perfectly well take yourself; others such as sleeve and trouser lengths will be sufficiently accurate if taken from existing garments. For the remainder you will have to enlist someone's help.

Make a list of the results on something durable like a postcard, add the date, and file it or punch a hole and hang it up with a string loop.

Wear tights and put a T-shirt or body stocking over your underwear; the position of the tape is easier to maintain than when measuring bare flesh and the 6mm/¼in difference it might make is negligible. Stand in front of a mirror. Do not add ease to the measurements. Do not add anything for hems.

Bust. Measure round the figure over the fullest part of the bust, keeping the tape level across the back and not too tight. Best done by helper.

Waist. Pass tape around waist and measure firmly. Afterwards tie a piece of tape or string round the waist to help with remainder of measurements.

Hips. Keeping the tape level, measure round the fattest part of the buttocks at about crutch level or above. An average position is about 20–23cm/8–9in below waist level. See also Measuring Thighs below.

Hip depth. Measure vertically from the point the last measurement was taken up to the waist.

High hip. It is not the round-the-body measurement that is required but rather the depth below the waist, but it is necessary to find the level with the tape. Pass the tape round approximately over the protruding part of the pelvic bone. This will be about 15cm/6in below the waist but it varies with height.

High hip depth. Measure vertically from the point of the last measurement up to the waist.

Buttock depth. Stand sideways on to a mirror and measure from back waist down to where cheek of buttock sticks out furthest. Needed for skirt dart length and trouser crutch size.

Thigh. Measure round the fleshiest part of each thigh about 8cm/3¼in below crutch level.

Knee and calf. Not often needed but useful for calculating openings, as for breeches.

Foot. Measure the length of your foot; required for calculating hem width of narrow trousers.

Centre front length. Measure vertically from hollow (nape) of neck to waist level.

Shoulder to bust point. Measure from mid-shoulder seam to point of bust.

Shoulder to waist. Measure from mid-shoulder seam to waist level with tape over bust point. A useful measurement for those with a large prominent bust.

Centre back length. Measure vertically from top spinal bone down to waist level.

Bust point width. With tape taut and horizontal measure distance between bust points. Record half measurement.

Skirt length. Measure from waist level to below knee. To take the measurement yourself stand in front of the mirror and allow the end of the tape, low numbers, to drop to depth required to enable you to read off the length. Also take an evening dress length to ankle or floor.

Trouser length. As above but measure at side of body so tape passes over hips.

Crutch length. With tape tied round waist measure length of body from CF to CB with tape measure passing between legs.

Inside leg. Crutch to ankle and crutch to knee. Required for trousers and shorts and often more accurately done by measuring seams of existing garments.

Crutch depth. Sit on a table and use a ruler to measure from waist to table at side of body.

Sleeve seam length. Armhole to wrist; another measurement more easily taken from a garment.

Arm length. Measure from top of arm, end of shoulder seam, down the outside of the arm, over a slightly bent elbow, to the wrist. This measurement is needed for drawing the sleeve block and it is easier to take if you put on a blouse or jacket with a basic set in sleeve and measure over that.

Armhole depth. Place a ruler under one arm, keep it horizontal and get someone to measure from the ruler up to the end of the shoulder seam. A measurement not often needed but useful for those with thin arms or square shoulders.

Top arm. Measure round the fleshiest part of the upper arm.

Shoulder length. A difficult measurement to take, from side of neck to the crest of the shoulder bone. You will not know until you fit your bodice block, whether you have got it right so as an alternative the seam of an existing garment can be measured or else take the average measurement for your bust size, from the chart on page 26.

Wrist. A measurement needed for a long fitted sleeve without an opening.

Hand. Measure round widest part. Needed for sleeve openings and pockets.

Chest width. Measure horizontally from armhole to armhole. The position can be located on the flesh as where the crease of the skin of the armhole begins.

Back width. Measure across the back at about mid-armhole level at a position about 14cm/ 5½in down from the top neck bone.

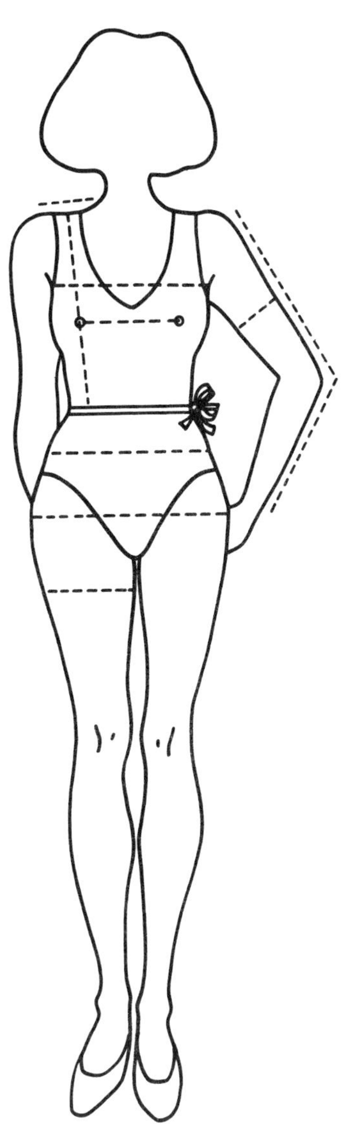

CHART OF STANDARD MEASUREMENTS

SHOWN IN CENTIMETRES WITH AN APPROXIMATE EQUIVALENT IN INCHES UNDERNEATH

SIZE	8	10	12	14	16	18	20	22	24	26	28	30
BUST	80	84	88	92	97	102	107	112	117	122	127	132
	31½	33	34½	36	38	40	42	44	46	48	50	52
WAIST	58	62	66	70	75	80	85	90	95	100	105	110
	23	24½	26	27½	29½	31½	33½	35½	37½	39	41	43
HIP	85	89	93	97	102	107	112	117	122	127	132	137
	33½	35	36½	38	40	42	44	46	48	50	52	54
HIP DEPTH	21	21.3	21.3	21.8	22	22.3	22.5	22.8	23	23.3	23.5	23.8
	8¼	8⅜	8½	8⅝	8¾	8⅞	8⅞	8⅞	9	9⅛	9¼	9⅜
HIGH HIP DEPTH	14.6	14.9	15.2	15.5	15.8	16.3	16.5	16.8	17.2	17.8	18	18.5
	5¾	5⅞	6	6⅛	6¼	6⅜	6½	6⅝	6¾	7	7⅛	7¼
CB LENGTH	38.5	39	39.5	40	40.5	41	41.5	42	42.5	43	43.5	44
	15	15¼	15½	15¾	16	16	16¼	16½	16¾	17	17⅛	17¼
CRUTCH DEPTH	26.5	27	27.5	28	28.5	29	29.5	30	30.5	31	31.5	32
	10⅜	10½	10¾	11	11⅛	11⅜	11½	11¾	12	12⅛	12⅜	12½
ARM LENGTH	55.8	56.5	57.3	58	58.5	59	59.5	60	60.5	61	61.5	62
	21⅞	22¼	22½	22¾	23	23⅛	23⅜	23½	23¾	24	24⅛	24⅜
ARMHOLE DEPTH	20	20.5	21	21.5	22	22.5	23	23.5	24	24.5	25	25.5
	7⅞	8	8¼	8⅜	8⅝	8⅞	9	9¼	9⅜	9⅝	9¾	10
TOP ARM	25	26	27.5	29	30.5	32	33.5	35	36.5	38	39.5	41
	9⅞	10¼	10⅞	11⅜	12⅛	12⅝	13¼	13¾	14⅜	14⅞	15½	16⅛
SHOULDER LENGTH	11.7	12	12.8	12.3	12.5	13.1	13.4	13.7	14	14.3	14.6	14.9
	4⅝	4¾	4⅞	5	5 1/16	5⅛	5¼	5⅜	5½	5⅝	5¾	5⅞
WRIST	15	15.5	16	16.5	17	17.5	18	18.5	19	19.5	20	20.5
	5⅞	6 1/16	6¼	6½	6¾	6⅞	7⅛	7¼	7½	7⅝	7⅞	8 1/16
CHEST WIDTH	29.8	31.2	32.6	34	35.8	37.6	39.4	41.2	43	44.8	46.6	48.4
	11¾	12¼	12¾	13½	14	14¾	15½	16¼	16⅞	17⅝	18⅜	19 1/16
BACK WIDTH	32.4	33.4	34.4	35.4	36.6	37.8	39	40.2	41.4	42.6	43.8	45
	12¾	13⅛	13½	13⅞	14⅜	14⅞	15⅜	15⅞	16¼	16¾	17¼	17¾
ARMHOLE	37.5	39	40.5	42	43.5	45	46.5	48	49.5	51	52.5	54
	14¾	15⅜	16	16½	17⅛	17¾	18¼	18⅞	19½	20 1/16	20⅝	21¼
BUST DART WIDTH	5.8	6.4	7	7.6	8.2	8.8	9.4	10	10.6	11.2	11.8	12.4
	2¼	2½	2¾	3	3¼	3½	3¾	4	4¼	4½	4¾	5
HALF-KNEE WIDTH*	25.8	26.4	27	27.6	28.4	29.2	30	30.8	31.6	32.4	33.2	34
	10⅛	10⅜	10⅝	10⅞	11⅛	11½	11¾	12⅛	12½	12¾	13⅛	13⅜
HALF-HEM WIDTH*	23	23.5	24	24.5	25	25.5	26	26.5	27	27.5	28	28.5
	9 1/16	9¼	9½	9⅝	9⅞	10	10¼	10⅜	10⅝	10⅞	11 1/16	11¼

*For these measure trousers not body

THE BASIC BLOCKS

THE SKIRT BLOCK

The skirt block is drawn within a rectangle that measures half the hip size in width and which, in depth, is equal to the skirt length measurement. The side seam slopes slightly out below hip level making the back and front overlap. Back and front will be traced separately leaving the original drawing complete. For a very slim skirt ignore the extra hem shaping and use the line JK as the side seam for both back and front skirt.

The rectangle

Starting at the bottom left-hand corner measure along the edge of the paper half hip measurement plus 2.5cm/1in. From the same point measure skirt length, hem to waist, up the left-hand edge of the paper. Rule the remaining two lines to complete the rectangle. Mark the vertical edge of the paper on the left, centre back and the vertical line on the right, centre front. The

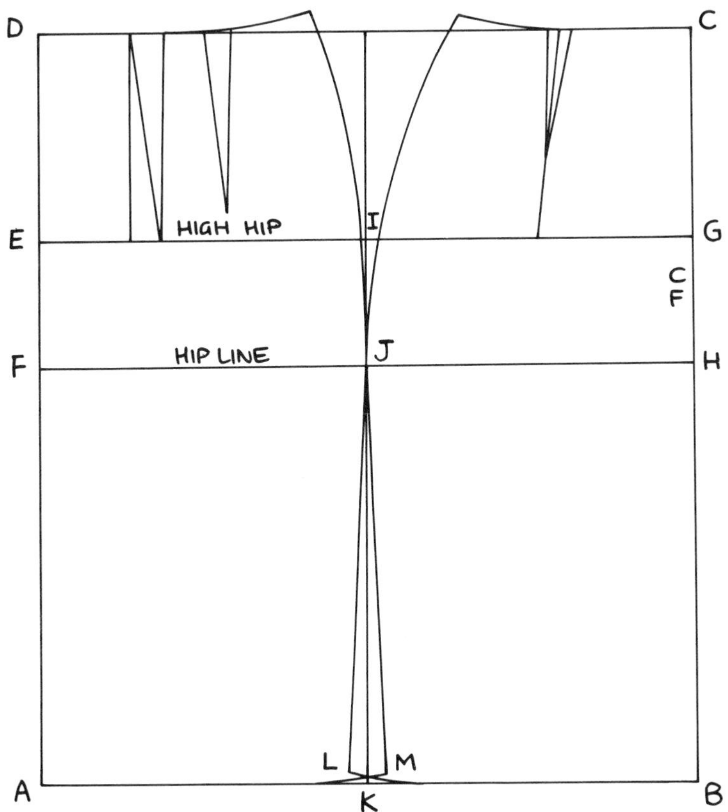

horizontal line represents waist level and the lower edge of the paper is hem level.

Rule two horizontal lines across the rectangle at 15cm/6in and 23cm/9in below waist level. Mark the upper line high hip and the lower one hip line. Alternatively rule these lines to correspond with the personal hip and high hip level revealed when measuring (see Measurements, page 24). Note that the depth of the hip line should be the same as on the bodice block (see Bodice Block, page 29).

Find the centre of the waist line and hemline and rule a vertical line 13mm/½in towards the front. This is the skirt side-seam position. Letter the points as shown in order to follow the block construction more easily.

The skirt

Hem. Measure 13mm/½in each side of point K on the lower edge of the paper. Raise each point 6mm/¼in and mark L and M. From L curve down towards front to meet edge of paper marking the hemline for the skirt front; curve from M in the same way for the back hemline.

Side seam. Rule from L to hip line for front skirt and M to hip line for back.

Back waist. From D measure quarter waist plus 4.5cm/1¾in plus 6mm/¼in ease. Raise the point 2cm/¾in and curve down to waist level. Complete side seam by curving to meet hip line at J.

Front waist. From C measure quarter waist plus 2cm/¾in plus 6mm/¼in and raise the point 1.5cm/⅝in. Curve from there down to waist level. Complete side seam by curving to meet hip line at J.

Back darts. Measure one-third of the way along the waist curve, rule a perpendicular line down to hip line and mark a point 2.5cm/1in to the right. This is the bottom point of the dart. Rule from there to meet the waist line at the top of the perpendicular and for the other side of the dart rule from a point 2.5cm/1in to the right, down to the hip line.

For the second dart measure 3cm/1¼in further towards side seam (for larger sizes 4cm/1½in) and mark a point another 2cm/¾in to the right. From these two points rule a dart at the same angle as the first dart but making it 4cm/1½in shorter.

Front darts. Measure half-way along the waist curve and rule a vertical line down to the hip line. From G measure half waist plus 1cm/⅜in and rule from there to the point on the waist curve. Mark 1cm/⅜in each side of waistline mark for width of dart and rule dart to a point three-quarters of the way to the hip line.

Remember that the position and size of the darts may be changed when the skirt block is fitted. See Fitting, page 37, and pages 16 and 19 for information on shaping dart ends and making permanent blocks.

Check that side seam edges are equal in length. This is difficult to do accurately by measuring and is best left until the first paper copy is made. Adjust at waist level by trimming if necessary.

A-line skirt block

A basic A-line skirt pattern is probably even more useful to most people than a straight one so it is worth making a block that can be quickly outlined as required.

Outline back and front straight blocks. Add 3cm/1⅛in to each at side seam at hem level and connect this point to high hip with a straight line. Take care that the new line runs smoothly into the curve above the hip line, adjusting it if necessary. Curve hemline to meet new side seam, again running it smoothly into existing hem.

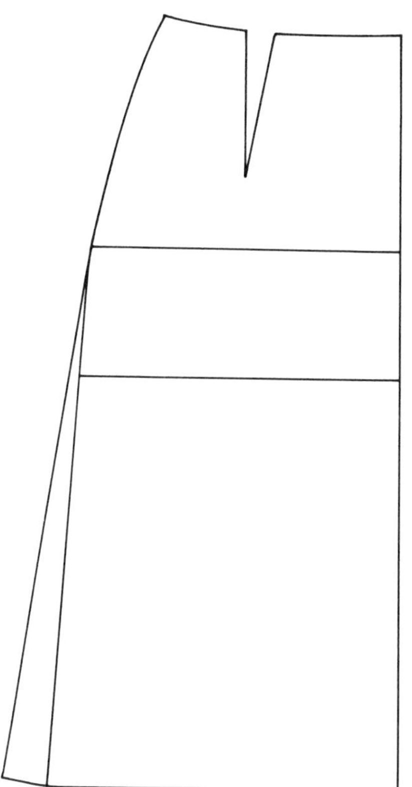

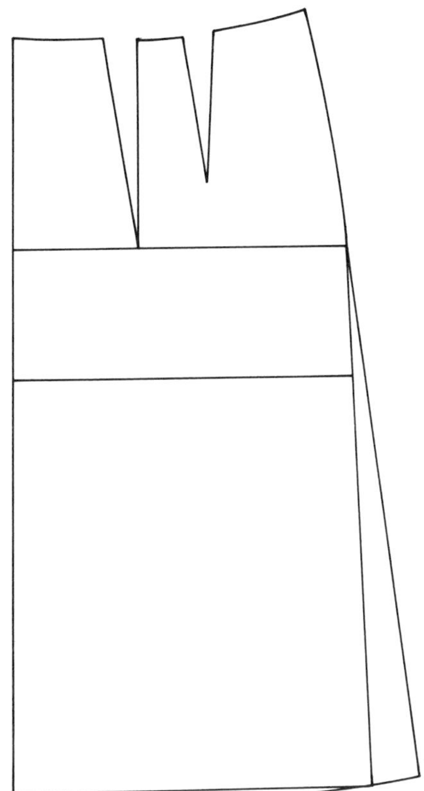

THE BODICE BLOCK

The bodice block is drawn within a rectangle that measures half the bust size in width. Instructions are for a block to hip length as being more useful than one to waist length only. The shaping for the hips will overlap so the back and front will be traced off separately for use, leaving the original drawing complete.

The rectangle

From a point near the bottom left-hand corner of the paper rule a horizontal line half bust plus 2.5cm/1in. From the same point rule a vertical line equal to hip depth and rule a horizontal. Extend left vertical up towards the top of the paper by the amount of back neck to waist measurement. Complete the rectangle.

From the top left corner measure down half back neck to waist plus 3.5cm/1⅜in. Rule a horizontal line from there to the opposite side of the rectangle. Rule another horizontal line quarter back length down from top corner. Label the horizontals as shown. Rule a bust level line 1.5cm/⅝in below underarm line. Divide

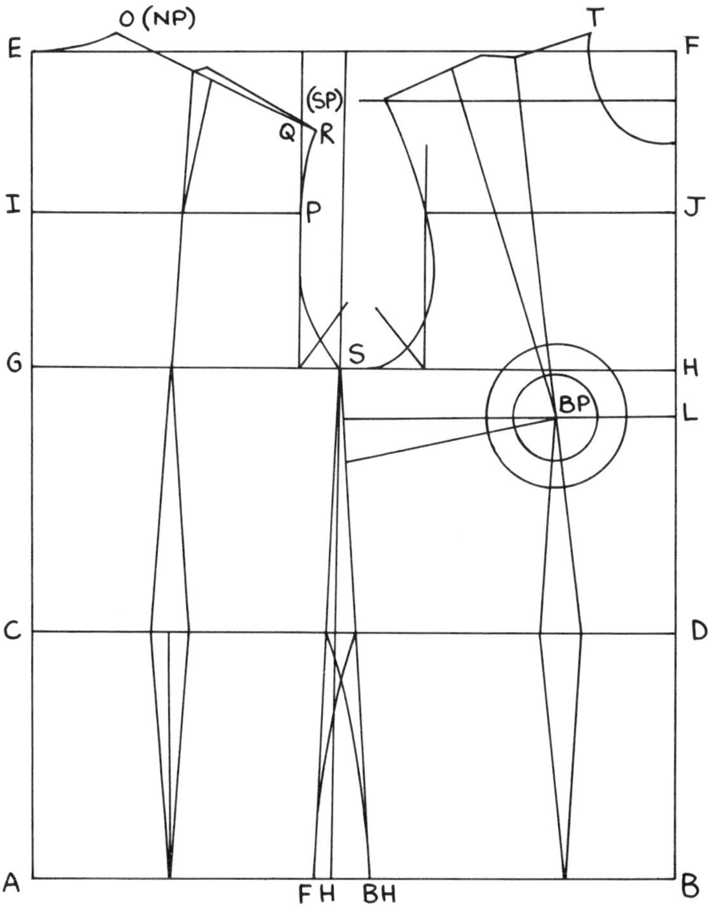

the rectangle with a vertical side seam line quarter bust plus 6mm/¼in from the centre back line.

Letter the points as shown in order to follow the block construction more easily.

Back bodice

This is drawn using the vertical line at far left as centre back position.

Neckline. From E along top horizontal measure one sixth of back width measurement, raise the point 13mm/½in and mark neck point O.

*For sizes above 14 (bust 92cm/36in) raise point O as follows:

Size 16 and 18 1.5cm/⅝in

Size 20 and over 2cm/¾in

Complete back neckline by drawing a curve fairly flat at centre back then curving gently up to O as shown.

Shoulder. From I measure half back plus 6mm/¼in and mark point P. Rule a vertical from P above and below. Measuring up from P mark a point Q halfway between P and top line plus 6mm/¼in.

Rule shoulder line by joining points O and Q. Measure along OQ shoulder length measurement plus 2cm/¾in for ease or dart and mark the point R.

Shoulder dart. It is as well to draw this dart at this stage although often you will be using the back block without it and tracing whichever shoulder line is appropriate for your design. See also Fitting the Bodice Block, page 40.

From O measure 6.5cm/2¼in along shoulder and mark the point.

From C measure along waistline 7.5cm/3in for sizes up to 14 (92cm/36in bust) and 9cm/3½in for sizes above that. Rule a line to connect this point with the one just marked mid-way along the shoulder. At waist level this line forms the left side of the waist dart and at its far end it becomes the left side of the shoulder dart.

To complete the shoulder dart measure 1.5cm/⅝in to the right of the line just ruled. Draw second side of dart to meet in a point on back width IJ.

Waist dart. Measure 2cm/¾in to the right of line just drawn and drop a perpendicular down to AB. At waist level measure another 2cm/¾in to the right, rule from there down to AB and up to GH to complete a double pointed dart.

Side seam. From A measure along AB quarter hip plus 13mm/½in and rule from there to meet underarm line at the vertical line MN. This is a straight side seam for use when required.

Where this side seam crosses CD measure 2.5cm/1in to the left and rule from there to S. From S down to new hip point just marked, rule a straight guide line but then curve it out in a shape to match the curve of the hips.

Armhole. Measure 5cm/2in in from S and rule a perpendicular guide line upwards. Bisect the right angle and rule a guide line. Measure out from the angle along this guide line 4cm/1½in and mark. Draw the armhole with a slight curve from R to P then almost straight for a short distance below P and finally a smooth shallow curve through the point just marked, to S. Do not scoop out too much or it will restrict arm movement and clothes will tear easily.

Front bodice

The vertical line at the far right represents the centre front. The front is made longer than the back to allow for passing over the bust rise. The bigger the bust the longer the front bodice must be: sizes above 14 or those with a full bust who take a bra cup size bigger than D, may need to lengthen the block.

Neckline. From F measure along top line the width of neckline as marked on back bodice. Raise this point 13mm/½in and mark T. Check the length of the block from this point down to waistline CD, compare with body measurement and raise it a little more if necessary.

Add 13mm/½in to neck width and measure from F down centre front line. Draw the neckline in a smooth curve which starts at T and runs more or less flat for a short distance at the centre front.

Shoulder. Rule a construction line 4cm/1½in below EF. Draw shoulder line from neck point to meet this horizontal as follows: Select the dart width for your bust size (see chart page 26) and add it to the shoulder length from your own list of measurements. However, if the size of your bust is more or less than average, (which you know from your bra cup size) select a smaller or larger dart size as appropriate. Swing a line equal to this measurement on to the shoulder level horizontal and mark the point U.

Darts. Check front length from base of neck to waist at D and compare with body measurement. If the block is short mark a new lower point D and re-draw the waist line sloping down from the side seam. From L measure half bust point width and mark BP. From T measure 9cm/3½in along shoulder seam, rule a line from there to BP and extend it down to meet the waist line. This forms the right side of the shoulder and waist darts.

At waist level measure 2cm/¾in to the left of the line just drawn and drop a perpendicular to meet BA. Measure 2cm/¾in to the left of that line at waist and complete a double pointed dart by ruling from waist to hip and from waist to BP.

On the shoulder seam measure width of bust dart as calculated previously and rule a line from there to BP to complete the bust dart.

Side seam. From B measure along BA quarter hip plus 13mm/½in and rule from that point to S to give you a straight side seam when required. You will see that this is where the front and back overlap. To help with tracing off correctly mark the one to the right BH and the one to the left FH. At waist level measure in 2.5cm/1in and rule from there to S. Complete side seam below waist by ruling a straight construction line and then a curved line to match the shape of the hips.

Armhole. From J measure across half front width measurement plus width of dart at that point. Mark the point V. From S measure towards H 7.5cm/3in and rule a short perpendicular. Bisect the right angle and measure 3.2cm/1¼in. Draw the armhole as a fairly straight line from U to V and just beyond. Curve a deep sweep through the point in the right angle and, as it comes round to join the back armhole smoothly, the front armhole can drop a little below the bust line.

Check the complete armhole shape and re-draw if it looks uneven. If you are unsure of the accuracy of the shape place a bought paper pattern on top and run a tracing wheel over it to mark the armhole on to your block. Remember that it is only shape not size that you are transferring.

Underarm dart. Many designs will have the main bust shaping in a dart under the arm rather than in the shoulder. Mark the position on the block by measuring 6.5cm/2⅜in down the side seam from S and rule from there to BP.

Please see pages 16 and 19, for information on shaping ends of darts and making permanent blocks.

Bust point area. The bust point marked on the block will be used as a point for manipulation but no dart could ever extend to that point or there would be no room for movement. For a close fit darts would stop 2.5cm/1in from BP; for a looser fit the distance is 5cm/2in. Draw two circles this size with BP as the centre to use as guide lines.

SLEEVE BLOCK

The sleeve block is simple to draw starting with a rectangle that is the length of the arm and as wide as the widest part of the arm. The tricky part is drawing the shape of the sleeve head which later will have to fit the armhole of the bodice block.

The rectangle

Starting 5cm/2in above the lower edge of the paper rule a horizontal line equal to the measurement taken round top arm plus 3cm/1³⁄₁₆in. Rule a vertical line equal to sleeve length and complete the rectangle. Cut out but without cutting off the margin at the bottom.

Fold the paper lengthways into four and crease. Open out and rule a horizontal underarm line 16cm/6¼in below the top edge. This is an average depth; the variation in size comes with the width of the block but if your size falls outside the range 10–14 you may need it either deeper or shallower. The measurement should be approximately one third of the bodice block armhole size. If it is an area where you normally have fitting problems you may prefer to use that measurement.

Rule the elbow line 6mm/¼in above mid-way between the armhole and the wrist line at the bottom. This also can be checked later; the elbow is approximately at waist level.

Mark the point where the central line meets the top edge SP, sleeve head point, which will always be matched to the end of the shoulder seam and must always appear on every pattern.

Rule lines along vertical creases and label them for identification; they will be useful in various ways. There are more basic descriptions but the following allow for no confusion because they coincide with the fingers.

Line at far left: Little finger line. Also the position for openings in long sleeves.

Line at far right: Thumb line. Runs from protruding bone of shoulder down to thumb and is valuable when checking the hang of the sleeve.

Centre line: Middle finger line. Also useful at fitting; runs from shoulder seam to wrist.

Sleeve head outline

Rule guide lines as follows preparatory to drawing the sleeve head curve.

From top of paper measure along thumb line half-way to underarm line. Measure from top along little finger line half-way minus 13mm/½in.

Rule 4 straight lines to connect underarm and SP points mid-way along each of the four lines.

Sleeve head curve. For the curve on the back of the sleeve, between sleeve seam and little finger line, mark a point 6mm/¼in inside the line; between little finger line and SP, mark a point 1.5cm/⅝in out.

For the front sleeve head, between SP and thumb line, mark a point 2.5cm/1in out and on the final section between thumb line and sleeve seam, mark a point 13mm/½in inside the line. Draw the sleeve head, connecting all the points. Initially the shape may not be very good; if you want to check it place your block on a commercial paper pattern, remembering to choose a plain fitted sleeve and look at the shape, not necessarily the size, of the curve.

Balance marks. The sleeve inset points, vital to any pattern right through to the fabric stage, correspond with the points where little finger and thumb lines meet sleeve head curve. Even if you do not transfer all the construction lines when cutting patterns, never omit the sleeve head balance marks.

Wrist. Extend little finger line 13mm/½in. Shorten thumb line 1cm/⅜in and draw a gentle curve through all points. The additional length allows for the elbow and the shortening ensures the sleeve will clear the thumb rise.

Wrist opening. This block will often be adapted but whether adapted or used as it is any opening in a long fitted or cuffed sleeve will lie along the little finger line and will be between 6–10cm/ 2⅜–4in in length.

Sleeve seam balance marks. These will become important when the block is adapted for shaped sleeves. Measure 5cm/2in above elbow line and 8cm/3⅛in below on each seam edge and insert balance marks.

Checking wrist and underarm. Fold sleeve sides to middle so seam edges and balance marks meet. Check the accuracy and smoothness of the wrist and underarm curves and also make sure the sleeve seam edges are precisely equal in length.

Transferring sleeve head points to bodice. Back: Reverse the sleeve and place in position with underarm points together (see dotted outline). Carefully move the sleeve, matching the armhole to the bodice and transfer balance mark to bodice armhole edge.

Front: Reverse the sleeve and place in position (dotted line), measure off sleeve edge against armhole and transfer balance mark.

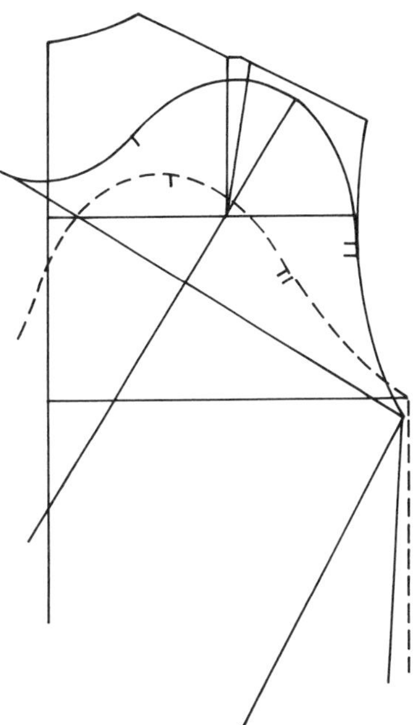

Checking size of sleeve head. Having transferred balance marks check the remaining length of the sleeve head against armhole. With sleeve reversed and balance marks matching, measure off sleeve against armhole. Repeat with front of sleeve. The sleeve should be 2–4cm/

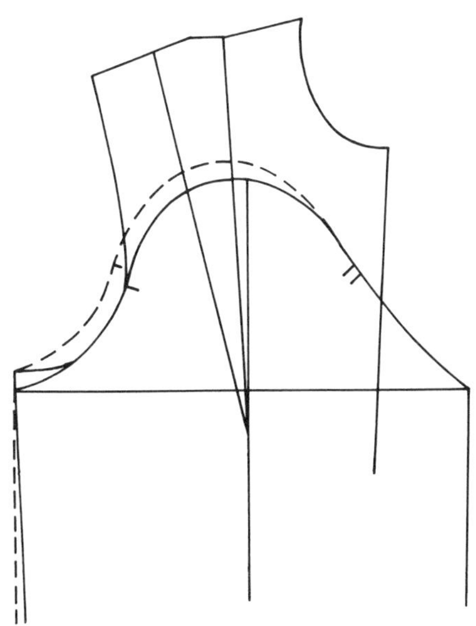

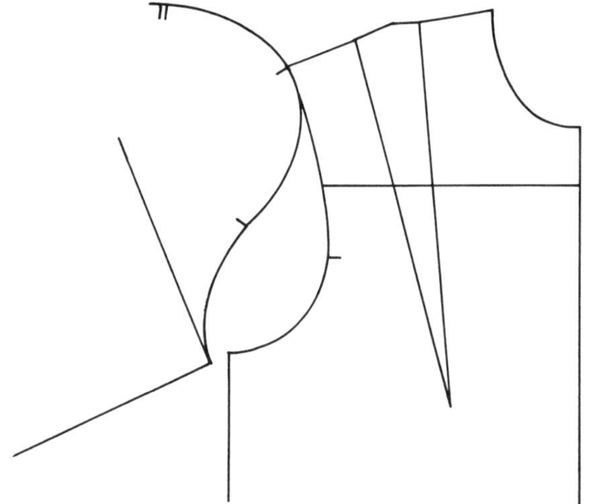

¾–1½in larger than the armhole for ease. In some fabrics that do not ease in it may be necessary to reduce it by lowering the sleeve head a little.

Please see page 16 for information on shaping ends of darts.

TROUSER BLOCK

No amount of measuring can indicate thickness of body or crutch shape and this makes the trouser block the most difficult of all the blocks to draft with any accuracy. Many books on pattern drafting chicken out altogether saying that the whole thing is too difficult. The instructions I have worked out produce a good trouser shape and I have introduced the following innovations which are of particular help in fitting the female figure.

⋆The back is slightly wider than the front, against tradition, but it is more comfortable for walking.

⋆The back crutch seam slopes by the same amount as the side seam. When fitting treat both areas as if they are darts, altering width and length as necessary.

⋆The inside leg seam on the back is shorter than the front. When sewing them together stretch the back edge – it is on the bias – to help reduce bagginess.

⋆The front crease line is marked on the block although at fitting you may find a position that is more slimming for your figure. When you press the trousers, each leg separately before joining the crutch, fold leg and press front crease then keep pressing across leg until the back crease finds its own position.

⋆There is an instruction included for checking the width of the front trouser across the stomach. Wearing trousers or a skirt measure straight across fullest part of stomach from side seam to side seam.

The back and front are drawn within a rectangle half hip size in width with extra added for crutch extensions. I have found this the best system because you can establish the hip width accurately but also make the crutch seam as long as necessary.

The rectangle

Rule a vertical line equal to trouser length, at least 15cm/6in in from right hand edge of paper. Rule horizontal equal to half hip size plus 2.5cm/1in. Complete the rectangle. CF is right-hand line, CB is at left. Measure from CF ¼ hip plus 6mm/¼in and rule a vertical line from waist to hem. Rule horizontal lines at hip and high hip levels.

Front

Waist. Measure along waist from CF to side seam, subtract ¼ waist plus 6mm/¼in and divide the remainder into three parts.

At side seam measure off two parts, raise 1cm/⅜in and mark new waist point. Draw a curve from there to meet waist line.

From CF measure 8.5cm/3⅜in (9–10cm/3½–

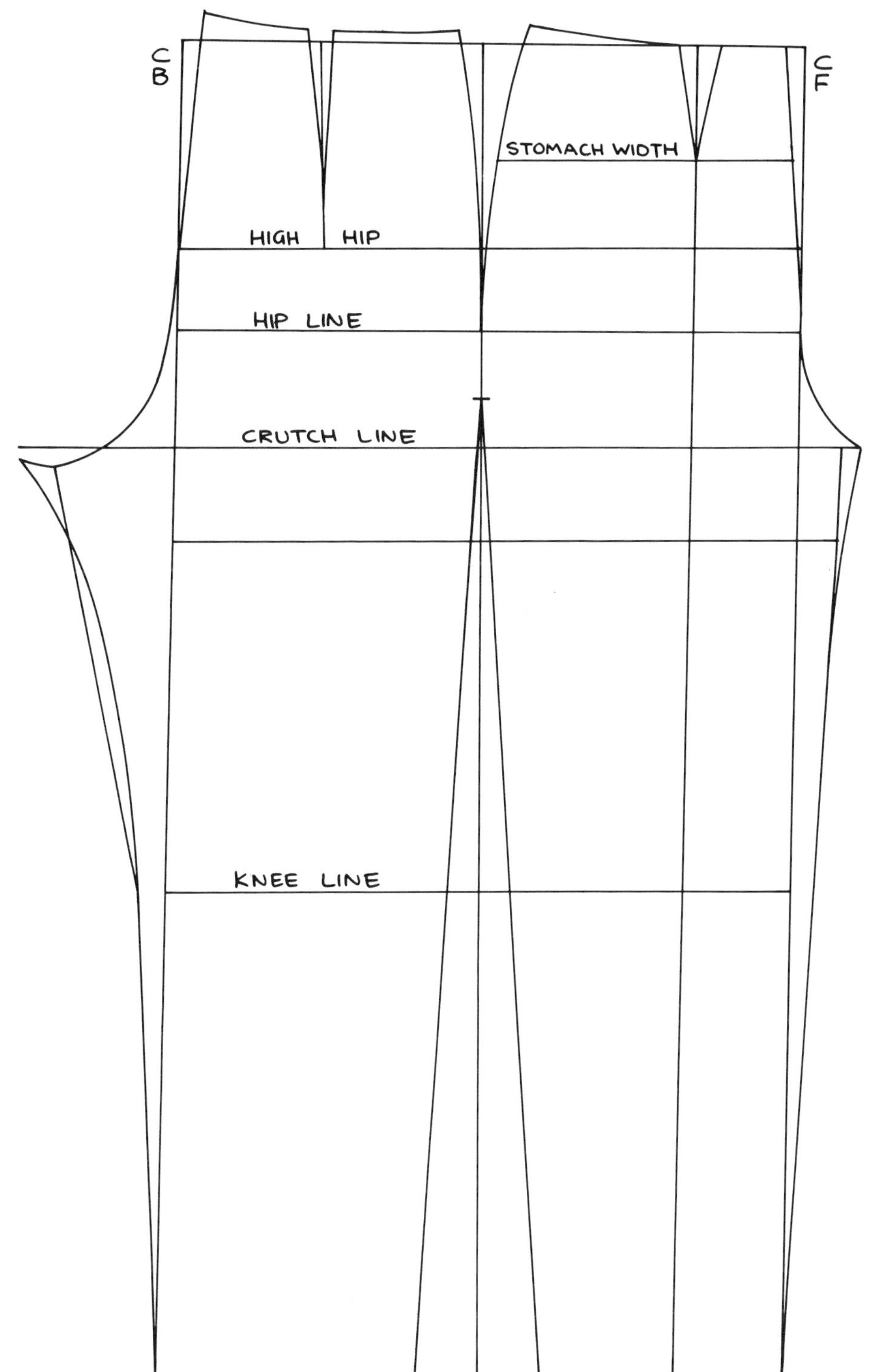

4in for sizes larger than 14) and rule a vertical line from waist to hem. This is the front crease line. At waist use the third part of the waist surplus to make a dart with its central line on the crease line and the point half-way between waist and hip level.

Side seam curve. Rule guide line from new waist point to hip level at side seam. Check stomach width by measuring along high hip line ½ stomach plus 6mm/¼in. If it comes outside the guide line mark the point. Curve side seam from waist to hip, through stomach point if necessary.

Crutch curve. At side seam measure crutch depth plus 6mm/¼in from the waist and rule a horizontal. Calculate ⅕ width of front trouser at hip level and extend crutch line by that amount. From the angle measure up CF the same distance and draw a guide line. Curve crutch seam between these points.

Centre front seam. Measure waist curve (now a longer line than original waist line), subtract dart width and mark off any surplus waist reduction at CF. Rule a line from that point to top of crutch curve. Those who had to extend the side curve to accommodate the stomach measurement would do well to keep the original vertical CF line until after fitting.

Knee depth. Rule a horizontal line mid-way between crutch and hem level.

Thigh depth. Rule a horizontal 7–9cm/2¾–3½in below crutch line, or at whatever level you took the measurement.

Hem width. Divide proposed bottom width into four. At front crease mark measure along hem ¼ hem width minus 1cm/⅜in towards CF and ¼ hem plus 1cm/⅜in towards side seam.

Inside leg seam. Measure in from crutch point 13mm/½in and rule from there to hem point. Complete seam by making a gradual curve from crutch point to line.

Side seam. On side seam mark a point mid-way between hip and crutch depth. Rule a guide line from there to hem point. At knee level mark a point 6mm/¼in inside guide line. Check width at knee level if making a block with narrow hem width. Draw side seam shaping it in from point above crutch level and ruling straight between knee level and hem.

Back

Waist. Measure along waist from CB to side seam, subtract ¼ waist and divide remainder into four.

At side seam measure off one part and raise the point 1cm/⅜in. Curve to meet side seam just below high hip line.

Centre back. Measure one quarter of waist surplus at waist, raise the point 2cm/¾in and rule a line from there to hip level. Curve from new CB to side seam. Halfway between these two rule a vertical line to high hip line and draw a dart equal to the remainder of the waist surplus with the point two-thirds of the way to hip line.

Side seam. From CB at hem level measure half proposed finished hem width and rule from there to side seam at same point where front leg seam joins it.

Crutch curve. Extend crutch line at CB by half the distance from CB to side seam. At crutch point measure down 1cm/⅜in. Draw crutch curve with a slight slope from hip level then a deep curve under the crutch line and up to the new point. It is very unlikely that you will get this right first time so keep it fairly shallow until fitting (see page 43).

Inside leg seam. Measure knee width of front and mark off on back knee line. Rule from there to hem.

At crutch corner measure in 2.5cm/1in and rule to knee line as a guide. Curve from crutch point to knee line.

Fold darts and cut waistline in a smooth curve. Cut out both legs and check side seam edges. Place inside leg seams together. Back seam should be slightly shorter. Lower back crutch point if necessary although you may prefer to wait until fitting before doing it.

FITTING

It is important to understand that the blocks you have made are close-fitting shells shaped to your body and are therefore much tighter than the commercial patterns you may be used to using.

Make sure you add whatever fullness, shoulder width, sleeve width etc., that you need when adapting the blocks to patterns. Check the size of existing garments when in doubt and perhaps also add generous seam allowances when cutting the fabric.

There is nothing quite as good as fitting patterns and clothes on a warm, moving body but a dummy can be a useful additional piece of equipment for the main areas especially if you have to fit yourself with your blocks, patterns and garments.

It is unlikely that the dummy you buy is the same shape as you are even if it has the same measurements. Dummies that adjust do so by means of discs which open up spaces at centre and sides until the appropriate size is reached. If you have one of these you will probably be able to do most fitting on it, though not trousers of course. The areas that may not be adjustable include bust level, bust cup size, hip level and thigh bulges and arms. If your fitting problems lie in these areas fit those in the usual way, using the dummy for the remainder.

If you have the standard, solid, linen-covered dummy that cannot be adjusted either use a combination of fitting methods, some on the figure, some on the dummy or else pad out the dummy to your shape.

For the latter to be successful the dummy must be smaller than you are at the crucial points. To add padding you will need:

soft jersey, not too stretchy, for a new cover
double sided tape
wadding in sheet form
kapok or wadding pieces
thin sheet foam
shoulder pads (for sloping shoulders or a permanent shoulder shape)

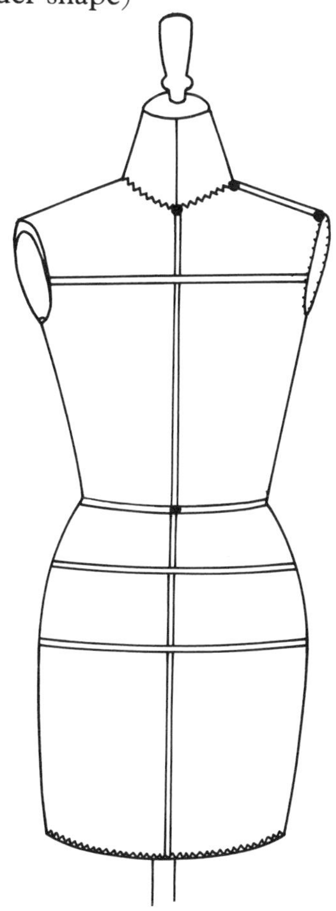

a bra that is adjusted to fit
flexible adhesive

Padding out

1. This can be time-consuming and it must be accurate. Be careful not to over-exaggerate the features. Make sure each area is smooth and check the measurements repeatedly. Put the bra on the dummy and fill with pieces of wadding until bust is filled to correct size and level. Anchor the straps to the dummy with double sided tape.

2. Put shoulder pads in place, adjusting to correct width according to body measurements. Attach with tape.

3. To increase waist or hip size or to add rolls of fat for thighs attach several strips of foam or wadding and cover with a piece of thin jersey to compress the padding and eliminate ridges.

4. Pad shoulder blades slightly if necessary, taping a thin, oval shape of wadding in position.

5. Cover the dummy with a tube of jersey fabric stitched to fit firmly but not so tight as to make the dummy lumpy. Finish edges at the neck, armholes and bottom by trimming with pinking shears and sticking the edge flat to the dummy or fold under the raw edges and hem in place.

Guide lines

Using a felt pen or lengths of tape glued to the dummy, mark as many guide lines as you can to help with designing as well as with fitting. Use your measurements or if average markings are more use to you follow the figures given in the chart on page 26. Alternatively, and this is particularly applicable if you have not padded your dummy, use two colours of felt pen, marking average positions in one and your own in the other.

Guide lines to be marked include waist, hip and high hip levels; CF and CB from neck to bottom of dummy; shoulder seam and shoulder length, marking NP and SP as well; chest width, back width and armhole depth.

Using a dummy for designing

A dummy can be a great help with designing, even if it is not your size or shape.

Mark guide lines on it as described above and use the dummy for checking proportion; for example, depth of yokes, width of panels; for the accuracy of exaggerated features such as low necks and asymmetrical lines; and for the size and proportion of additions such as collars and pockets.

SKIRT BLOCK

A skirt is not usually too difficult to fit and your block should be a fairly good fit if you have taken care with your measurements. However, the darts may need adjusting in length and position to ensure maximum comfort and the most flattering look. The other area requiring attention is the waist edge and any adjustments made here during fitting will affect the length and the general hang of the skirt.

Make a note of all adjustments and transfer them to your basic block, re-cutting the block if necessary. The skirt block, in contrast to the other blocks, can be used as a pattern for a fashionable skirt just as it is without any adaptation, so it is worth taking the trouble to see that it is perfect in every detail.

The width can be checked at this stage but remember that complete accuracy is only possible when the skirt itself is tried on during construction. It is more the shape of the block you are checking than the size.

In most cases it is satisfactory to fit a paper copy of the skirt block, fitting half the pattern to half the body. Where extensive adjustments become necessary or where the figure is lopsided, perhaps one hip noticeably bigger than the other, it would be wise to make a toile of the complete skirt and fit it.

Skirt block in paper

Outline the front and back straight skirt block on drafting paper and mark the high hip and hip lines and SG. Add 2cm/¾in seam allowance to the side seam; fold the darts and pin so that the bulk of the paper is pressed towards CF or CB; cut along waistline with paper folded and continue cutting round the outline.

Which block to fit?

It is best to use the original skirt block because this will reveal the fitting problems. However, those with relatively large hips or thighs who know from experience that they can never wear a skirt with such straight sides, should use the A-line block. Prepare it for fitting as described above.

Skirt toile

To make a complete skirt place front and back blocks on a folded piece of calico or cotton fabric, placing CB and CF against the fold. Outline using a fabric pen, marking darts, high hip and hip lines. Add 2cm/¾in seam allowance to side seam, fold darts and pin so bulk of fabric lies towards CB and CF and cut out the skirt, cutting along the waist with darts still folded. Open out fabric and mark CB and CF with dotted lines.

Fold and stitch all darts and press with bulk towards CB and CF. The crease lines will act as guide lines if alterations are necessary. With back and front RS together, hand or machine baste the side seams leaving an opening 25cm/10in long at the top of the left seam.

Waist fitting aid. The waist is difficult to fit both in size and in level. The position can best be defined by tying a piece of tape or string around the waist and then putting the pattern over it but it also helps to have a guide to place over the top.

Using a length of curved petersham cut it to fit the waist and overlap by 8cm/3in. Attach Velcro to the overlap. The Velcro makes it adjustable: if you fasten it too tight over the paper the pattern will tear; if it is too loose over the calico it will not follow the true waist. This petersham fitting aid can also be used to check the waist level when fitting skirts and trousers at the fabric stage.

Fitting

It is possible to fit yourself with your skirt block provided you can set up two mirrors to give you a view of the side and back.

Wear a thin, short top or jumper and tie a piece of tape or string comfortably around your waist. Wear shoes; bare feet alter your posture and would be tiring.

Have ready within reach, so that you don't have to move and tear the paper, pins, tape measure, felt pen and a hem marker if you have one.

BODICE BLOCK

Several major areas are fitted by the bodice any of which may be the cause of problems. The focal point is of course the bust, which varies in shape and level as well as in size. It appears as the source of many problems not least because the arms, requiring maximum all round movement, are close by.

The shoulders are important because it is from here that every bodice – for a blouse, dress, jacket or coat – is to hang.

The movement of the arms and the act of sitting down, bending or walking affects the back and shoulder blades, other areas to be fitted with care.

The trouble is 'large' does not mean 'comfortable': if it did it would be the solution to it all. It is the shape that is all-important in the bodice block but once you have it right you will have a good base for everything no matter how extensive the adaptation.

Start by fitting the front and back in paper, with shoulder and side seam joined for the second stage. If any major problems appear make a whole bodice in calico for the second stage.

It is perfectly possible to fit yourself if you set up mirrors to give you an all-round view and if you are patient.

Bodice block to hip. The hip-length block as you have drawn it is very convenient for making patterns for items such as blouses, dresses, housecoats, tunics, jackets and waistcoats. To check the fit, however, it is best to copy it to the waist only. Also when you come to practise the principles of dart moving you will use the block to the waist. When using it to learn how to make patterns for collars and bodice designs it is more economical than using the hip-length block.

I suggest the most suitable sequence of events might be as follows:

1. Fit bodice back and front to waist only.
2. Transfer any alterations to hip length block and re-draw if necessary.
3. Fit hip length block to check width at lower edge.

With the exception of long garments like those listed above use the block to waist length for all your practice designs including those worked in quarter scale.

Use the hip length block for all your own patterns where suitable.

Bodice block on paper

Outline back and front to waist level including any darts. Add 2cm/¾in seam allowance to shoulder and side seam and cut out. Mark CF, CB, chest and bust lines. Fold out the darts and pin with bulk of each dart towards CF or CB. Cut round outline with paper folded.

Bodice toile

Half bodice. If it is just a matter of checking length or shape rather than width place back and front bodice on a single layer of calico or cotton fabric. Add 2cm/¾in to side seam and shoulder. Mark darts, CF and CB. Fold darts into position and cut round the outline to waist level.

Stitch all darts and press flat; bust and waist darts meet. Stitch shoulder and side seam and press seam allowances towards back.

Complete bodice. Place back and front block on double fabric and outline to waist level. If you have someone to fit you place CF against fold of fabric and add 2cm/¾in along CB so that it can be overlapped and pinned. If fitting yourself place CB to fold and either leave open the left seam to pin up, or better still add 2cm/¾in to CF to be overlapped and pinned. Alternatively, if you know you have to check bust, chest, neckline or shoulder problems, a front opening allows easier access for re-pinning.

Have ready pins, tape measure, small scissors, fabric pen and the tape or waist fitting aid used on the skirt.

Fitting

Wear your normal bra and a thin short jumper to pin into for the first session using half the bodice. Remove the jumper for fitting the whole bodice. Wear a skirt or trousers with a narrow waistband or a petersham finish. Trousers with elastic or track suit or pyjama trousers are excellent as they can be pulled down clear of the bodice. Unlike when fitting the other blocks you can sit down, at least in the early stages.

SLEEVE BLOCK

There are two aspects to sleeve fitting: hang and fit. Both are affected by the bodice block fit and the shape of the armhole. A certain amount of fitting can be done before the sleeve is attached to the bodice but hang can only be observed and corrected when the sleeve is in the armhole.

The initial unshaped block can be used for fitting the sleeve head and the width but the shaped block with wrist dart will be needed for elbow shaping and length. As you have discovered, the bodice block has a basic fitted armhole and the sleeve head is slightly bigger but must be fitted smoothly into the armhole. All other styles such as raglan, kimono, cap sleeve, square armhole, are a looser, less critical fit and are certain to be fine provided the basic fitted sleeve is correct.

Fit and adjust the bodice before starting on the sleeve.

The fitting of the sleeve can be done and some checks on the sleeve head and armhole can be made, using a paper copy of the sleeve block. Faults in hang can only be seen in fabric so at the second stage you will need a calico toile.

It is usually sufficient to fit just one sleeve, the right one, although as with other blocks, if the figure has severe problems or if it is lopsided each side will have to be fitted separately including the armhole.

Sleeve block in paper

Outline or trace whichever block you decide to fit, marking underarm and elbow lines and all vertical lines. Add 2cm/¾in seam allowance to sleeve seam edges. Cut out adding a small extension at sleeve head and another at one side of wrist dart of shaped block.

Sleeve toile

Using the block or the paper copy place RS up on single calico. If the purpose of the toile is to fit an uneven figure place on double fabric. Outline, adding 2cm/¾in seam allowance to sleeve seam and 1cm/⅜in to sleeve head. Add a little tab to sleeve head and wrist dart as before. Mark all construction lines with fabric pen.

Fold each sleeve and stitch the seam from underarm to wrist; press seam allowances to one side. Insert a line of large machine stitches over sleeve head between front and back construction lines. Pull up the thread a little until the seam allowance folds over at right angles. Do not pull it so tight that gathers form.

Fitting

You should be able to manage the fitting yourself by standing in front of mirrors set up to give you an all-round view. If you are right-handed you might find it easier to fit the left sleeve, leaving your right hand free to pin etc. If you do this make sure you do check both sleeves separately at some point as your right arm and shoulder may be more developed than the left.

Even the second stage, checking the hang, can be done alone although it is tedious and if a friend is available so much the better.

There is a problem with what to wear. The bodice block may be distracting; a thin jumper is fine but it will not have a basic armhole line, neither will a sleeveless blouse. Ideally, mark an armhole line over your shoulder bone using a pen that will easily wipe off your skin. The correct position is the end of the bone, the peak where it appears just to the front of the shoulder. The back follows straight down although if fitting yourself you will not be able to reach to draw that part.

Put on the sleeve pattern, overlap tab at wrist and pin shoulder tab to bra strap with edge of sleeve head level with line on body. Underarm can be pinned to bra provided it does not distort the sleeve.

TROUSER BLOCK

Trouser fitting is not easy but there are several points to bear in mind that will make it a less difficult task.

The block you have drawn is the right size but it may not be the right shape so the adjustments you make will be quite small. It is worth making notes of what you do and altering the block so that each pattern that is developed from the block gives you trousers that are the same basic shape and size.

Remember that it is only a basic block at this stage; don't have it too tight, too loose or too wide. Instead make slight adjustments for fashion when you cut the actual pattern for each pair of trousers that you make. There are several areas to fit but they are closely related. It can happen that correcting one problem may create another nearby so watch the whole trouser as you fit.

The section of the crutch seam that is below waist level at the back is on the bias of the fabric and it is the stretch that is in this seam that allows you to walk and sit down. Don't be afraid to adjust it; the more it is on the bias the more comfortable the trousers will be.

Most of the problems relate to the crutch seam so leave that area until last. Fit one trouser leg only to start with, make any necessary alterations to it and then use it to make up a complete trial pair and then fit the crutch. This eliminates the need for ripping undone the crutch seam at the initial fitting stage simply to get at other problems. Try on right side out to start with but if you have extensive adjustments and re-pinning to do put them on WS out.

Trouser toile

Cutting and making. Place the front and back block on a single layer of calico or cotton and outline using a fabric pen. Add 2.5cm/1in seam allowance at waist edge, side seam and inside leg seam. Mark darts, hip and high hip lines, crutch and crease lines. Cut out each piece, match side and inside leg seam edges and machine or hand baste together. Stitch darts. Press darts flat and press seams towards back; the crease lines from pressing provide useful alteration guide points. Fold and press front crease.

If you have mismatched hips or leg lengths make two leg toiles, marking them right and left. Small differences can simply be noted on the block, for example, 'shorten left leg 1cm/⅜in'. This will then be transferred to each pattern as a reminder when cutting the fabric and marking up.

Fitting

Put on the trouser leg and tuck in a short blouse or thin sweater. Pin the toile to it front, back and side. Wear shoes in the middle of the range of heel heights you normally wear. Bare feet alter your posture and make your bottom stick out which distorts the hang of the trousers. Have ready a length of narrow tape or seam binding to help with locating the waist line; it will also hold up the trouser leg while you fit. A length of curved petersham is useful as a guide for a lower waistline on the block for use when making trousers without a waistband.

Have ready pins, tape measure, small scissors, thread snips or unpicker and a fabric pen. Stand normally; not too erect nor with stomach held in.

SEWING TIPS

★ When sewing the crutch seam of trousers retain as much stretch as possible by using a stretchy polyester thread such as Drima with a triple straight stitch, stretch or zig-zag stitch, a four-thread overlock, or you can even sew the seam in the traditional tailor's way using double thread, waxed, and back stitch.

★ Press open the crutch seam for a short distance down from the waist but not through the curve of the crutch. Never snip the crutch seam allowances; it weakens the seam and destroys the elasticity needed for movement.

★ Women's waists often vary in size: allow for any alteration that might be needed by making the waistband in two halves attaching the pieces to each trouser waist and then stitching across the waistband and on down the crutch seam. It makes it much easier to do an alteration.

Crutch seam

Front. If the crutch is uncomfortably tight or the top of the inside leg seam is too far back, snip the stitches in the seam and ease it forward. Note the size of the gap created; this is the amount to be added to the inside leg edge of the block.

Back. If the crutch seam is too tight and the trousers do not reach up to the waist make a note to lengthen the seam by cutting the block diagonally from crutch curve to side seam and inserting an additional amount. If the trousers hang in loose folds below the buttocks and crutch this indicates that the seam needs re-shaping in order to be able to lift the trousers at the back to remove the excess. Make a note to scoop out the seam on the block. This alteration makes the waist bigger so take in the seam at the centre back to compensate.

Adjust width and length as necessary.

SKIRT DESIGNS

STRAIGHT SKIRTS

BASIC SKIRT

A simple skirt can be made without adapting the block but it requires some preparation. As the hem width is limited make the pattern slightly shorter than the block. Put the zip in the left side seam. The back has a CB seam for ease of fitting and for economy of fabric. Attach a straight or curved waistband and fasten with a button and buttonhole, a flat skirt hook or 3cm/1¼in Velcro.

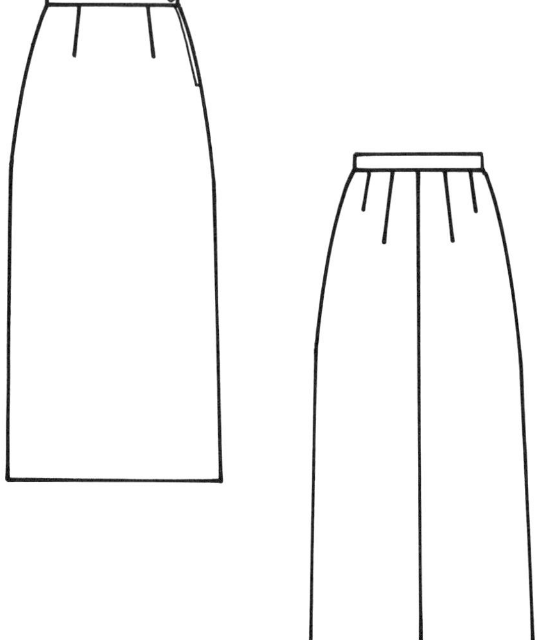

Back. Outline block, shortening it by 6cm/2⅜in or as desired. Mark balance mark on hip line.

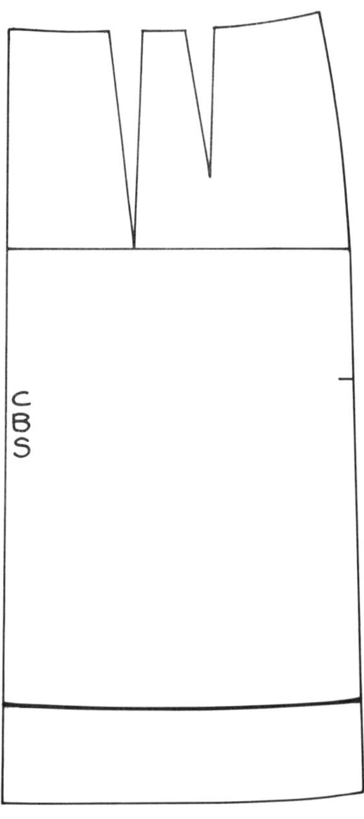

Put zip depth point 20cm/8in below waist, mark SG and cutting instructions. Shape dart ends.

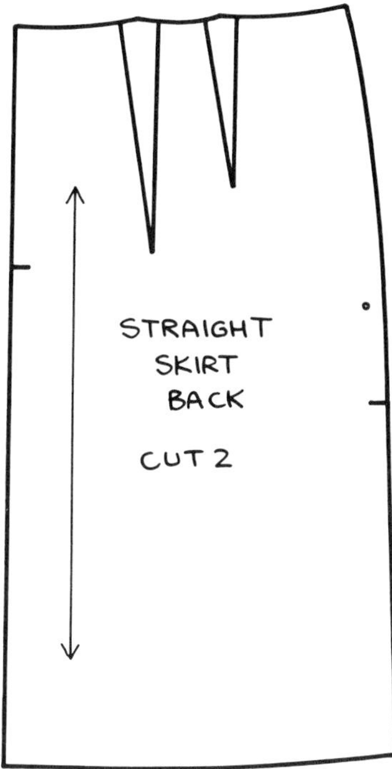

Front. Outline block shortened to match back. Insert balance mark and zip point on seam side to correspond with back. Mark CF FOLD.

Waistband. Draw rectangle 5cm/2in wide and waist measurement plus 2cm/¾in in length. Extend by 5cm/2in for fastening. Mark SG and cutting instructions. For alternative waist finishes for all skirts see page 168.

SEWING TIP

If you wish to line this skirt use the same pattern but leave a slit in the hem at the CB or left seam to allow for movement otherwise the lining will split.

SOFT WAIST SHAPING

Tucks or gathers can be used in the front of the skirt for a more comfortable fit or to lessen the emphasis on the stomach.

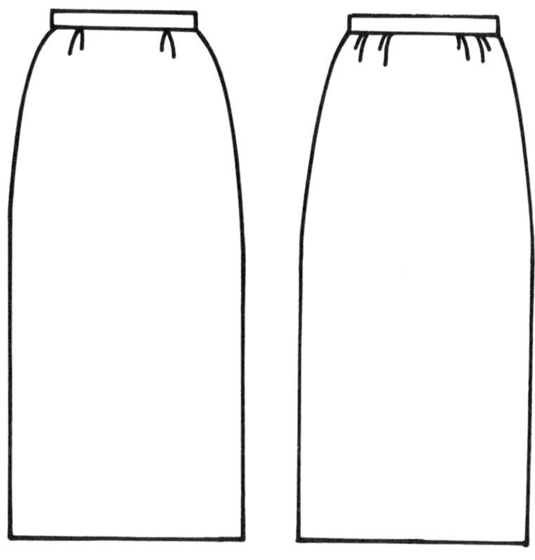

Tucks. Outline front block including dart. Cut out, fold dart towards CF and mark new shape of waist edge. Mark tuck with two short lines.

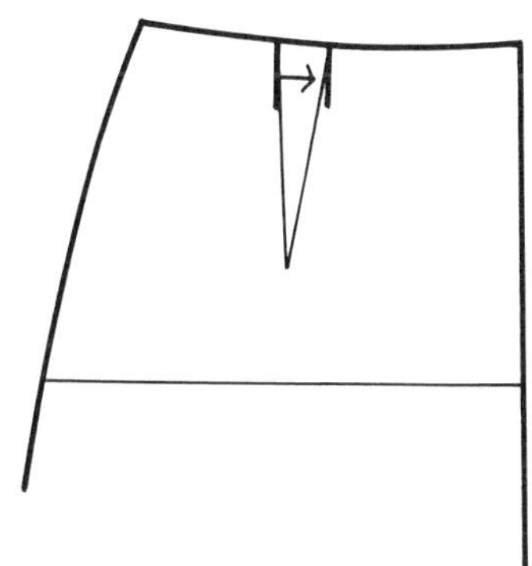

Gathers. Outline front block without dart, complete waist curve and mark gathers to extend for 1cm/⅜in each side of dart area.

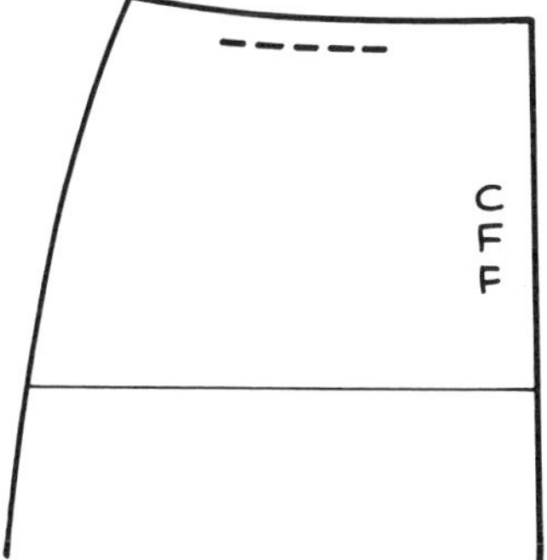

Additional gathers. For a skirt with a more gathered front waist but still pencil slim below the hips, outline block and cut out, cut dart away. Cut from dart point to high hip line and from there to side seam, leaving paper joined. Swing side piece out until an additional 1cm/⅜in is added to the dart gap. Trace around side piece. Draw new waistline curving down from side seam to CF. Indicate gathers.

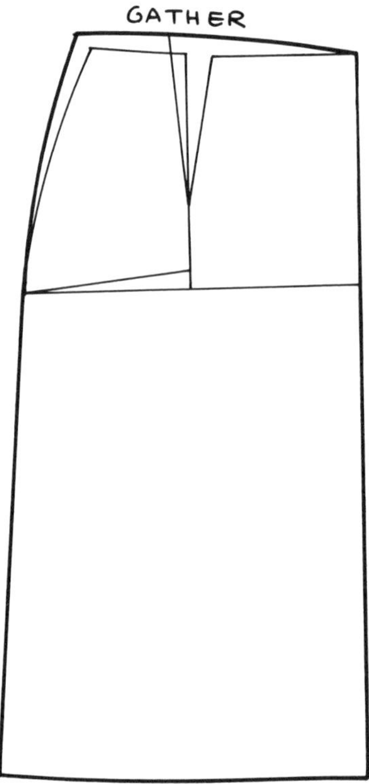

A possible waist finish to use instead of a waistband on a style like this is elastic. Choose wide soft elastic, possibly a ruched variety, perhaps even striped; measure it round the waist and join the ends together to fit. Divide elastic into four sections and mark; mark waist edge of skirt similarly. Attach elastic to skirt waist overlapping one edge onto RS skirt; use a stretch or elastic machine stitch and stretch the elastic to fit the skirt.

Peg-top effect. For pronounced fullness that extends to hip level and below trace the block and draw a curved line from mid-way between dart and side seam to just below hip level. Cut out pattern, cut along curved line and also cut

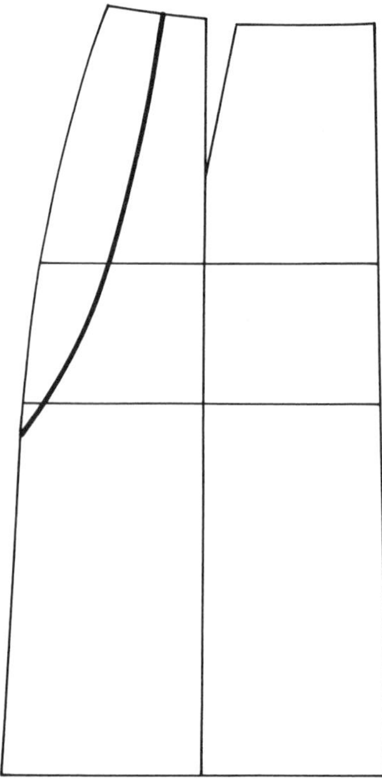

away the dart. Cut from dart to hem and open both pieces until 1.5cm/⅝in, or more if preferred, is inserted at waist. Outline the pieces, remove the angle from the hemline by drawing a

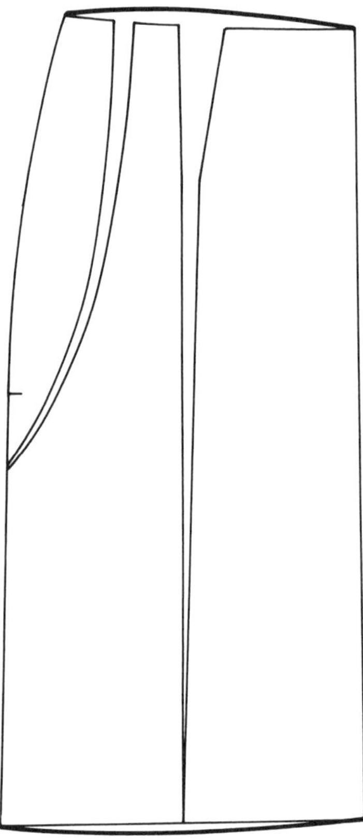

straight line and curve the waistline, adding extra length to the skirt as shown. Indicate gathers at waist or mark the fullness as three small tucks.

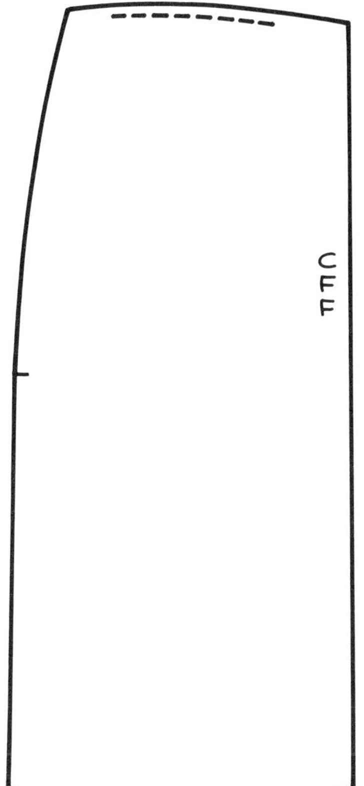

HEMLINE PLEATS AND SLITS

These add room for walking as well as being a style feature so the block can be used full length or even longer. Slits can be at one or both sides or at CB; pleats are usually at CB. The depth is a matter of preference but they tear very easily if not made long enough.

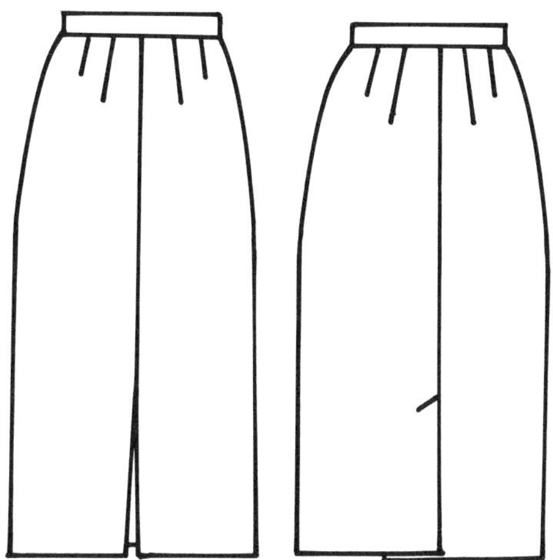

SEWING TIP

Keep to soft lightweight fabrics for full gathers and put zip in CB seam.

Hemline slit. Outline block and mark depth of slit required at CB seam. Add an extension of 2cm/¾in and make it 4cm/1½in longer than the

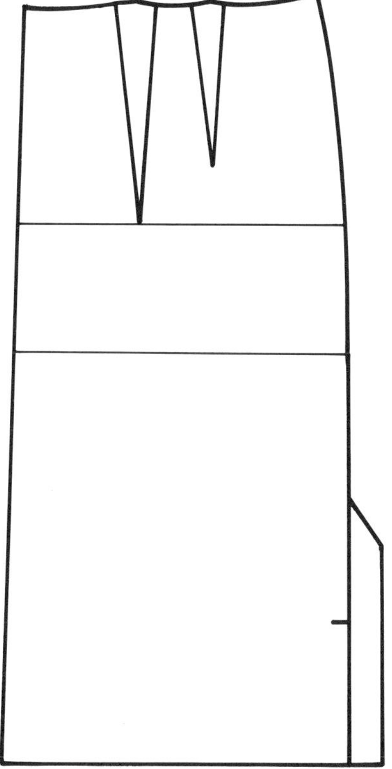

slit. Angle the top as shown to help keep it in place in wear. Make sure the hemline is straight so that the extension folds back evenly. When the seam allowance is added the extension will be wider which will ensure that no edges will be visible in wear.

SEWING TIP

Secure the extensions by placing a strip of Wundaweb between the layers of fabric. Press well.

Hemline pleat. Outline block and mark required pleat depth at CB. Add an extension for

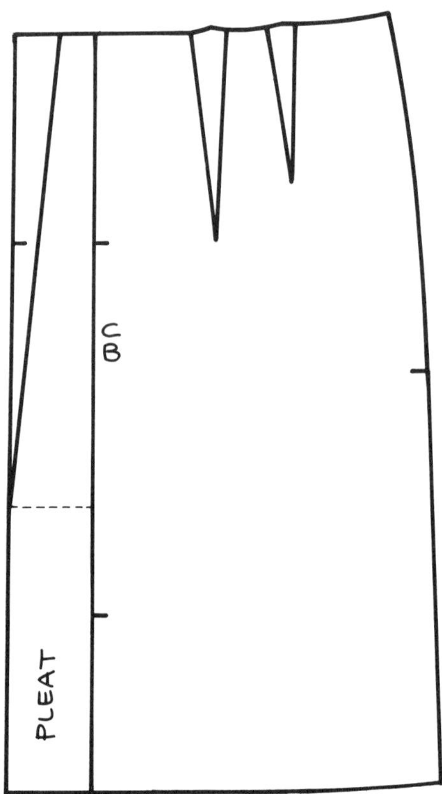

the pleat 5–6cm/2–2¼in wide; anything less will open in wear and remain open. On heavy fabrics reduce the bulk at the waist by drawing a sloping seam from a point 6–8cm/2¼–3in above the pleat depth.

SEWING TIPS

The bulk can be reduced still further by cutting the pleat as far as the dotted line and then attaching a piece of lining fabric at that point. Never have a short pleat extension as shown by the dotted line as it will hang below the hem of the skirt when worn. If you are short of fabric or cannot use lining as described a good substitute is a length of seam tape attached to the upper edge of the pleat extension and caught in with the stitching of the waistband.

POCKETS

Skirt pockets should be small to avoid a bulky look; have the bag extending no lower than the high hip line. Curve corners of bag pieces to prevent them curling over and making a ridge. Suspend the bag to keep it flat by extending pattern to waist where it will be included in the waist seam. See Patterns from Measurements, page 172.

SEWING TIPS

Reduce bulk by using lining material for at least one piece of pocket bag and the underside of flaps.

Prevent pocket bags from rolling up and making a ridge by attaching light iron-on Vilene to WS of inner piece of pocket bag. Do this immediately after cutting out so all edges are enclosed during construction.

PLEATS

In order for pressed pleats to hang well the top must be included in the seam at the waist or alternatively in a yoke. The width of the pleat fold is a matter of choice although the type and weight of fabric may be a consideration. For example, quite fine pleats will stay in place in a light crisp woven polyester but not in a woollen tweed. Also the pleat folds should not overlap at the back in bulky fabrics so either the tops must be tapered or the pleats made narrower. Alternatively the pleats could be spaced further apart. Remember that although pleats provide useful room for movement their main purpose is to make the design attractive so make sure they hang in a closed position in the skirt when you stand still.

The distance you plan to stitch along the pleat from the waist depends on the design but also on the shape of the block. The following designs are adaptations of the straight skirt block and so the pleats should only open below thigh level.

Keep the back of the skirt plain or with a centre kick pleat or the pencil slim line will be lost. Where possible plan a separate pleat backing to be seamed to the skirt front. This will keep the pleats in place better, it nearly always means a more economical use of fabric and it means the bulk can be shaped away at the waist. However, it entails more sewing and beginners especially would be best to cut the front in one piece for the sake of simplicity.

A. Centre front inverted pleat

Outline front skirt block with surplus paper beyond CF edge. Decide on pleat depth and mark stitching point, remembering that it can be raised or lowered if necessary when the skirt is tried on.

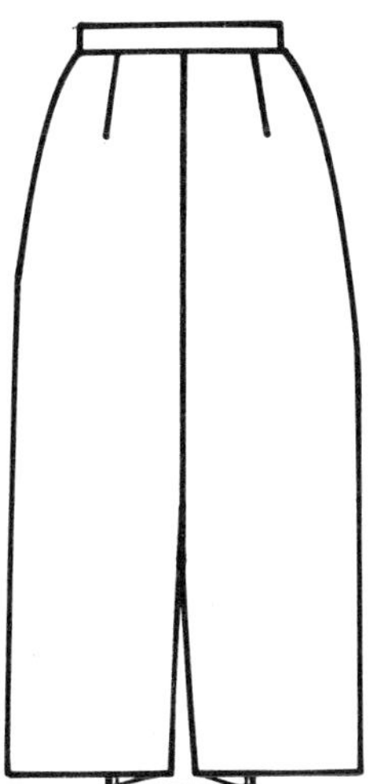

Fold paper under, creasing it along CF line. Decide on pleat width, usually from 4–8cm/ 1½–2½in at waist. Cut along waist and hem with paper still folded; cut along edge of pleat and remainder of skirt with paper opened out.

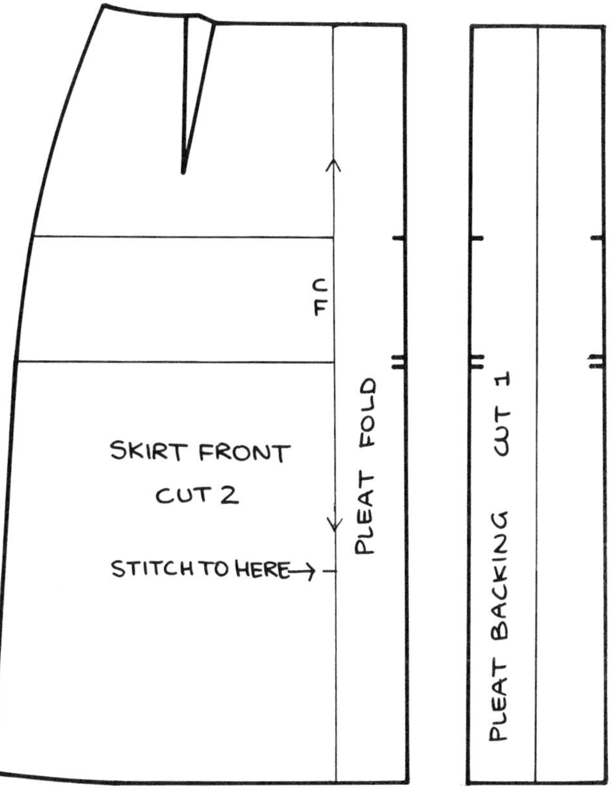

To make pattern for pleat backing fold another piece of paper, mark the crease CF and add grain arrows. Measure or trace from the fold the exact width of the pleat fold which was added to the block at the CF. Cut out pleat backing with paper still folded. Mark two sets of balance marks on skirt and corresponding marks on pleat backing.

B. Beginner's pleat

Outline front skirt block with surplus paper beyond CF edge. Fold paper under, creasing along CF line. Measure 6cm/2⅜in beyond fold and rule a line. Crease paper on this line to bring it back under CF again. Cut through the paper beside CF fold but close to it; mark this edge 'CF fold' or 'CF seam', depending on the width of the fabric to be used. With paper still folded cut along waist and hem edges. Mark CF fold with grain arrows, mark a suitable stitching depth for the pleat and mark pattern 'cut one to fold' or 'cut two', depending on whether the whole pattern can be cut without a CF seam or not.

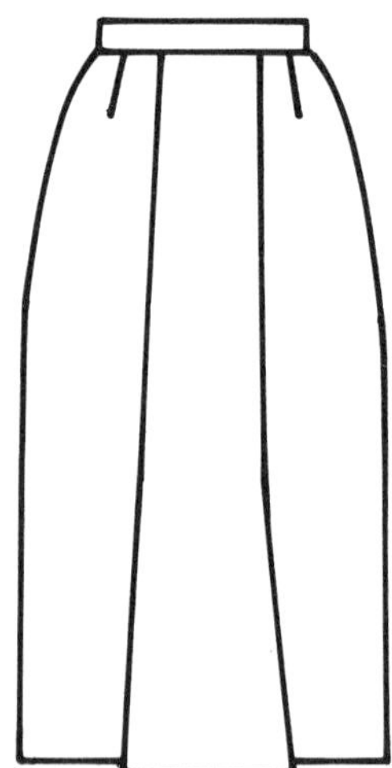

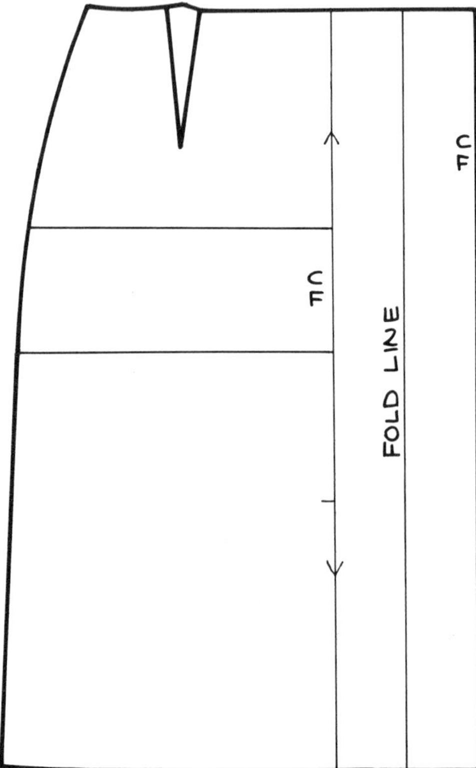

C. Front box pleat

A single box pleat must have seams at the back so that the pleat can be made wider at the hem. Even if you want it to look the same width all the way down, it still must be shaped in this way. Do not allow the pleat folds to meet at the back or the seam allowances on the finished skirt will overlap. Measure 6.5cm/2½in along waist edge from CF and 8cm/3½in along hem, join up with a straight line. Insert balance marks at hip and high hip line and mark pleat stitching point. Cut along line from hem to waist and place both pieces of skirt on new paper with space between for the pleat.

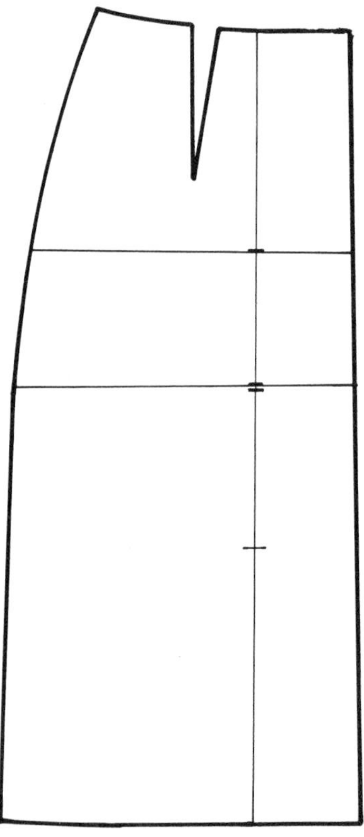

Working on CF section first, fold under the paper along the pleat edge. Mark pleat width 3–5cm/1⅛–2in at waist and 5–8cm/2–3⅛in at hem. With paper folded cut along waist and hem but cut new pleat edge and remainder of skirt with paper opened out. On both pieces of pattern transfer balance marks to pleat edge. On

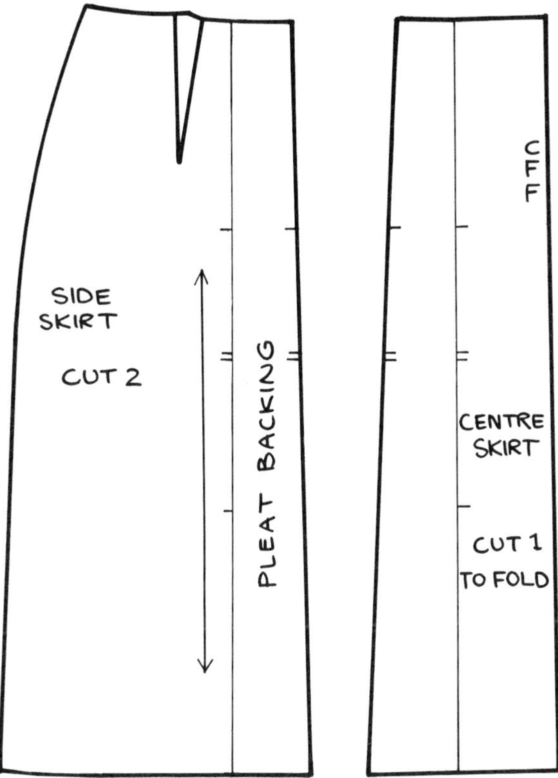

side skirt rule SG line parallel with original CF line on block. Centre skirt section is placed to fold when cutting out.

Check accuracy of pieces by folding pleat into position on centre skirt and placing it on the side skirt pattern, matching balance marks and pleat lines. Pin together and cut along waist and hemlines.

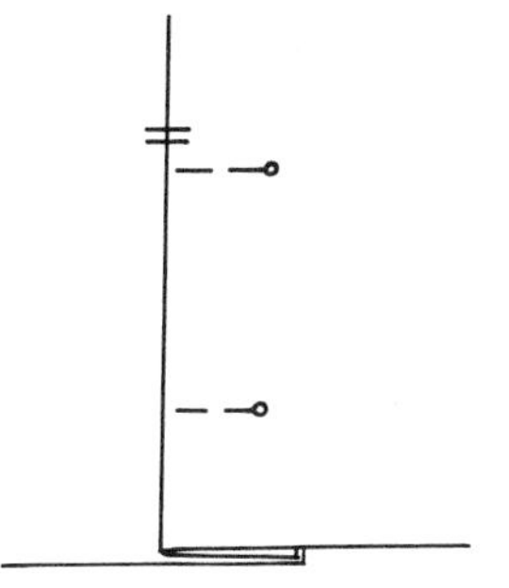

D. Two knife pleats

These are placed in line with the waist dart and the dart width is included in the pleat fold.

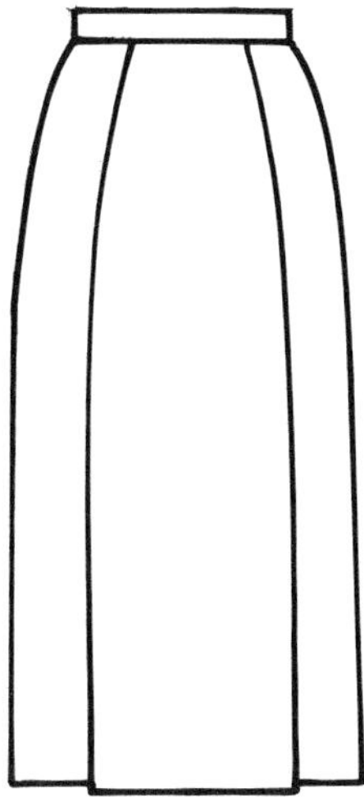

Rule a line from centre of dart to hem, slanting it out a little. Mark pleat depth and balance marks. Trace off each section separately following pleat line but also marking the sides of dart. Outline side section then place centre section

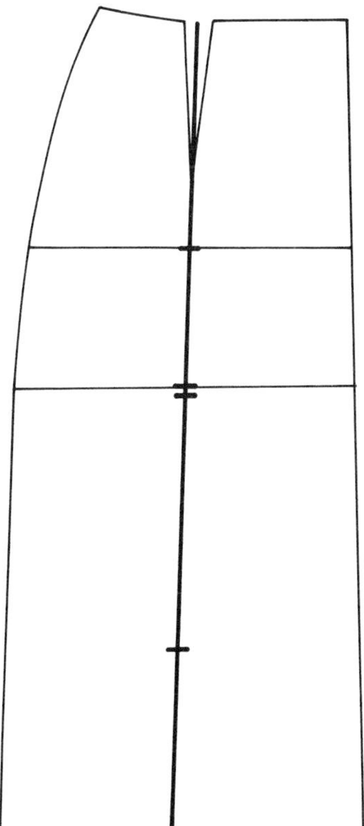

6cm/$2\frac{3}{8}$in away from it at the waist and 8cm/$3\frac{1}{8}$in away at the hem. Re-draw sides of dart

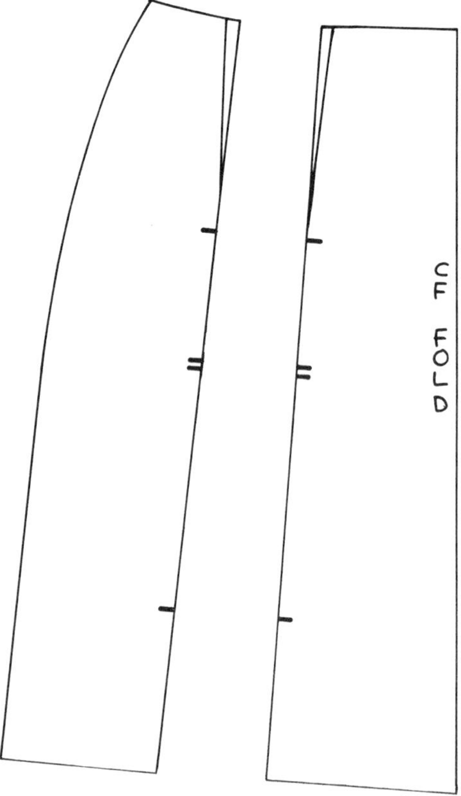

curved into pleat line instead of angled, mark these new lines as the stitching line and erase the straight lines. Fold pattern along pleat line, bring to meet corresponding line, crease pleat into position and cut along hem. Open out and fold from waist for the length of what was the dart and bring pleat lines to meet. Cut along waist and around remainder of pattern.

To make pattern lie flat when pleat is in

SEWING TIP

For a good hem finish mark the hem level with pleats tacked down to lower edge. Work tailor tacks along the hem mark, through all layers of pleat. Snip threads carefully, remove pleat stitching and turn up hem.

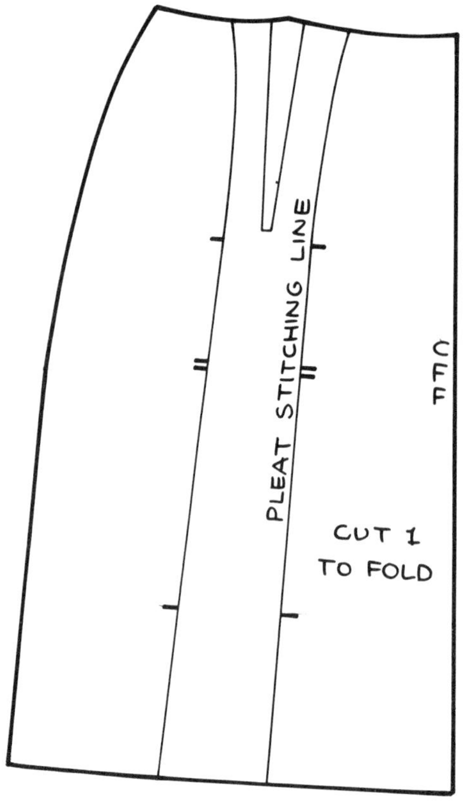

position cut along the edge of the fold on the inside of the skirt. This may be done now, on the pattern, but is probably best left until the skirt is being constructed in case any adjustments to fit or pleat position are required.

E. Single hemline pleat

The illustration shows a panel seam to match the pleat seam as this is more economical of fabric

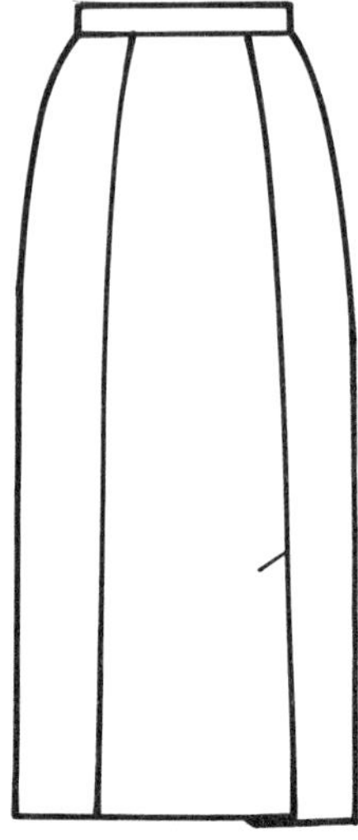

but it could be cut as an asymmetrical design with the right half of the skirt cut in one as far as the pleat and having the original dart at the waist.

On the front block mark the panel and cut out as for previous design remembering to mark sides of dart. Cut out each piece. Outline side skirt and cut out, trimming off paper to dart line. Add balance marks and SG and mark the pattern 'side front right – cut one with pattern RS up'. Reverse this piece of pattern and outline it again marking it 'side front left – cut one with pattern RS up'. Mark pleat depth then add an extension for the pleat. If the pleat is made narrow i.e. no more than 3–4cm/1⅛–1½in, it will not be too heavy so this could be a case for tapering the pleat extension as shown instead of extending it up to the waist.

To make pattern for centre of skirt fold a piece of paper and put the remaining piece of block on it with CF along the fold. Outline the block removing the dart. Open out and mark CF and balance marks. Trace the pleat extension added to the side front pattern, reverse it and add it to centre front against the left-hand edge.

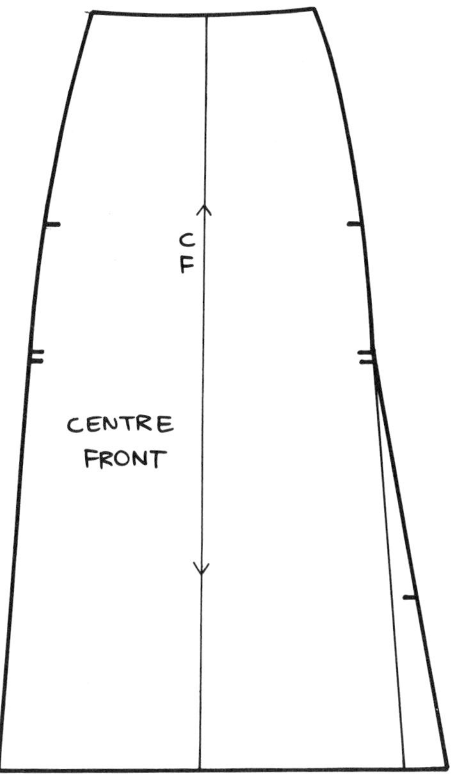

This design could feature a hemline slit as described for the back of a skirt, page 47, although it is less satisfactory because the pleat backing will move when you sit down.

F. Knife pleated panel

This design could have either two panel seams or one seam and one dart as shown.

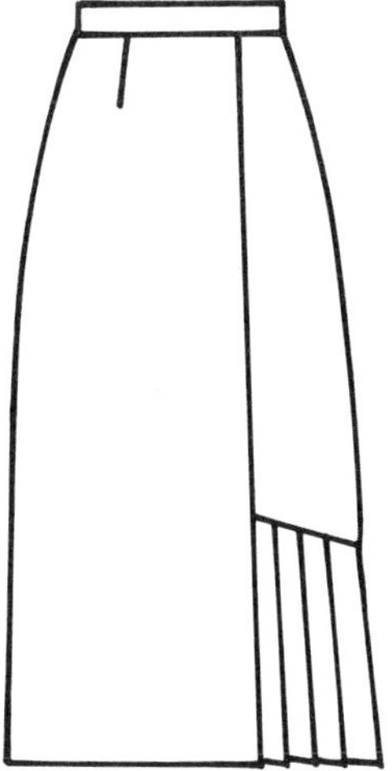

Fold a piece of paper and cut out the skirt block with CF along the fold so that you have a complete skirt front pattern. Draw the panel seam on the left through the dart and mark balance marks and depth of the pleated section.

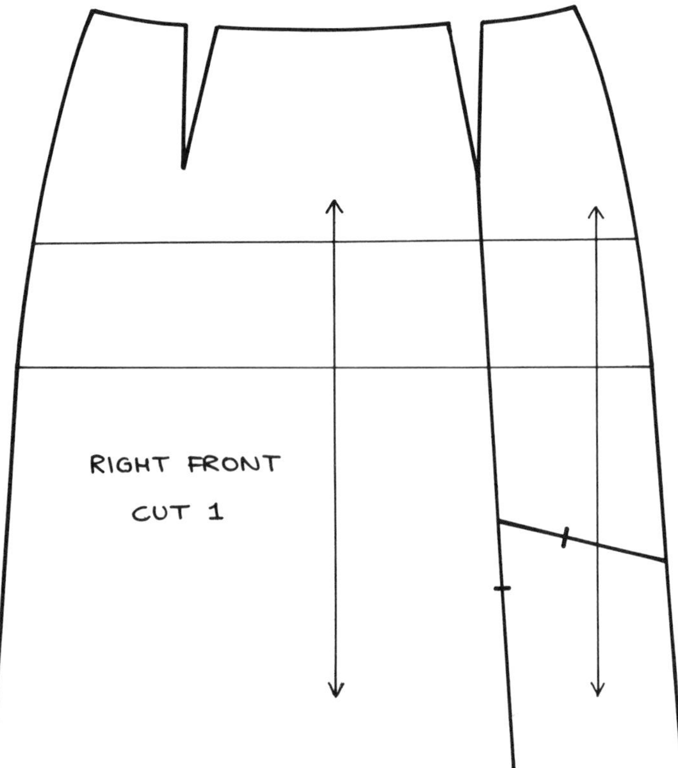

Balance mark each line, cut along each line and spread the pieces using a horizontal line to keep them level and inserting an equal amount between each. The pleats should not overlap or the panel will be too bulky.

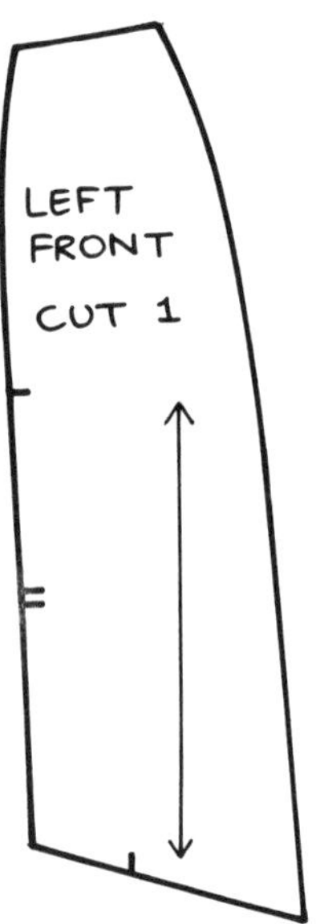

Fold each pleat towards side of skirt and cut out pattern with paper folded. Open out, mark SG and label it 'pleated section'.

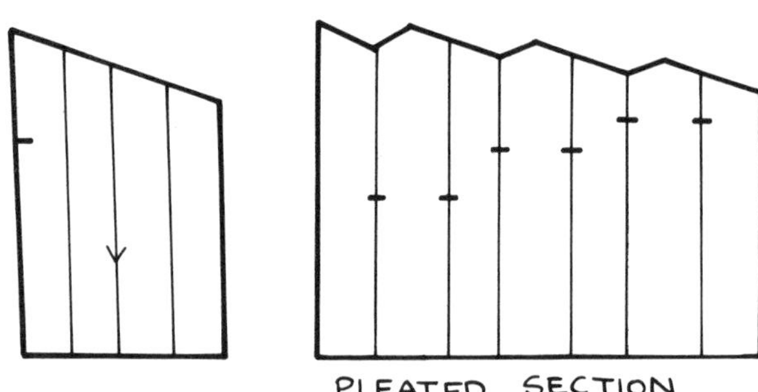

A-LINE SKIRTS

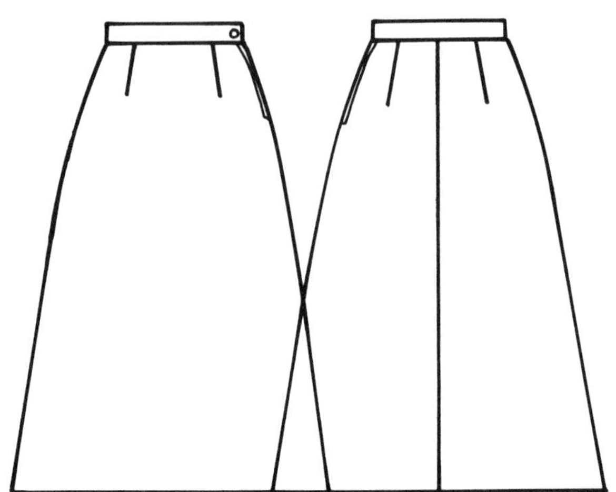

BASIC SKIRT

A simple A-line skirt can be made from the block as it is. No adaptation is required but dart ends must be shaped, straight grain marked parallel with CF and CB and zip position marked. It is always advisable to cut the back with a CB seam; it is more slimming and gives you a point of adjustment if necessary. The zip may be in the side or the CB seam. For the same reasons the front may also have a centre seam if you wish.

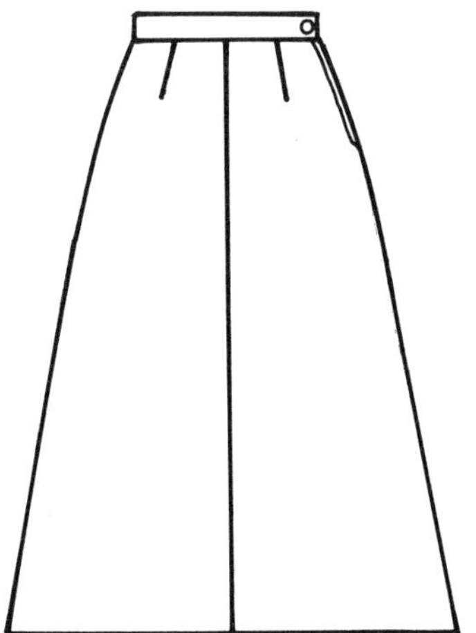

Finish the waist with a straight or curved waistband or with petersham. Fasten at the top of the zip with a button, skirt hooks or 3cm/ 1¼in Velcro.

A. Unpressed pleat

Suitable for almost any fabric. Follow instructions for inverted pleats, page 49.

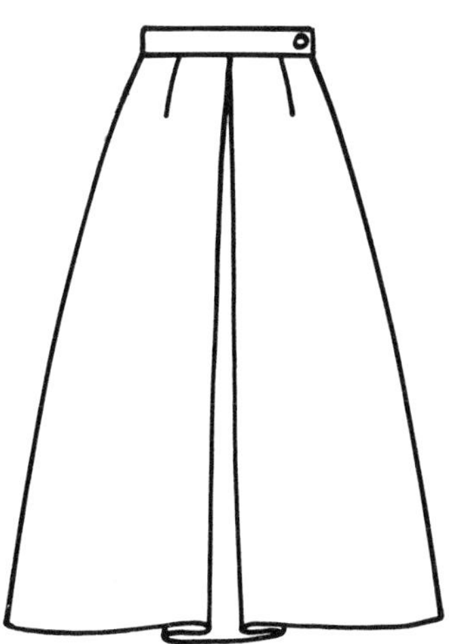

B. Wrap-over skirt

Patterns for wrap skirts are easy to make but the results often lack style unless the skirt is either very long or very short. Wrap skirts fall open

when you sit down so make the under section extend as far as the dart. Alternatively make the pattern to wrap over at the back, extending the

waistband to the far side for a neater look. Fasten the band with two lengths of Velcro. The vertical edge on any version can be held in place with one or two Velcro Spot-Ons concealed under the flap.

Outline the back or front against the fold of a

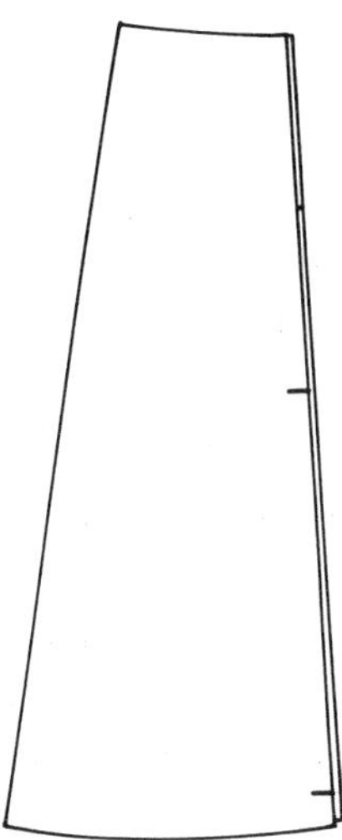

piece of paper. Adjust length. Open out. Draw the edge of the wrap through centre of dart and extend to hem making sure it slopes out towards the hem. Shape hemline if you wish. Trim waist curve to remove remainder of dart. Mark pattern 'cut 2' and add SG along CF. Mark cutting line for left side.

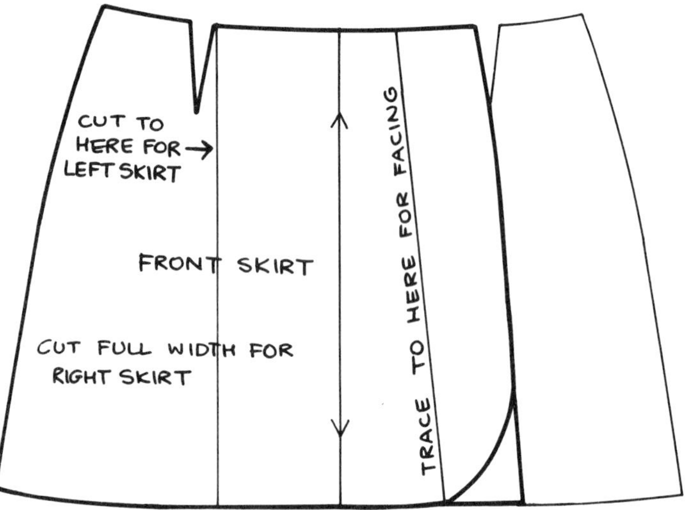

To make waistband measure back waist and add front waist of both pieces. The front skirt pattern is to be placed on single fabric and cut once full width for right skirt. Flip the pattern over before cutting the second piece as far as cutting line for left skirt. The skirt edge and hem can have sufficient seam allowance added to enable you to finish it with a narrow hem. If you prefer to face the wrap edge trace off a section 6–8cm/2⅜–3⅛in wide for facing pattern.

C. Gored skirt

These skirts have 2, 3 or 4 panels at the back and front, the waist darts are usually eliminated by shaping the seams and flare can be added to each seam if desired. Use the A-line block.

In order to make the gored skirts hang correctly the same amount of flare must be inserted into each seam. Some flare has already been added to the side seams and the same must be added to the gore seams. When cut out in fabric the grain will then be exactly the same on matching edges and on all seams.

With all the following skirts it helps to copy the line indicating the amount of flare already added.

Four gores. This is similar to using the A-line block with seams at CB and CF but by eliminating the front dart and part of the back the skirt is given more swing.

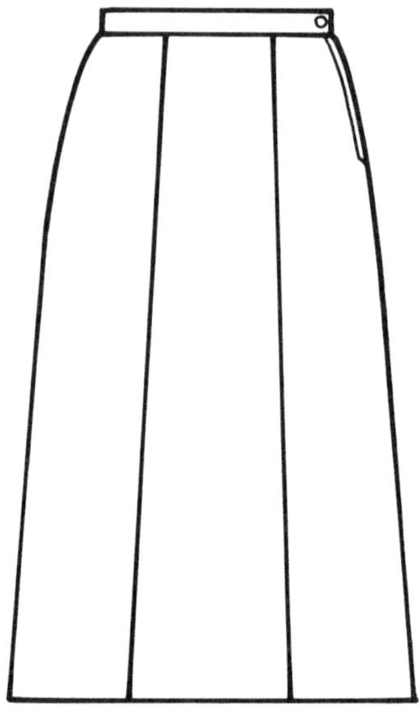

Front: Rule a line through dart to hem and cut to point of dart. Close dart so pattern opens at hem. Cut out and fold through the middle matching CF edge to original block side seam.

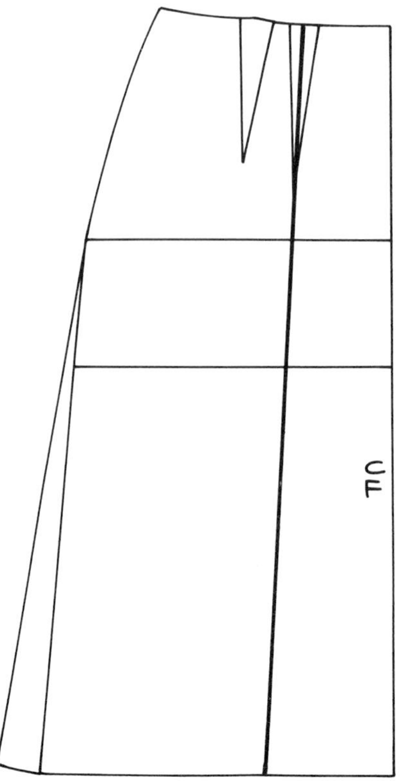

You can now clearly see how much flare must be added to CF to make it correspond with the shaped side seam. Cut out with paper folded, at the same time cutting a good curve at the hem. Retain the curve on the side seam or you will find the pattern will not fit you over the hips. Open out the pattern, mark SG along the central crease, add balance marks to both seams.

Back: Rule a line from mid-waist to mid-hem and cut from hem to high hip line. Measure width of dart nearest CB and mark half of it on

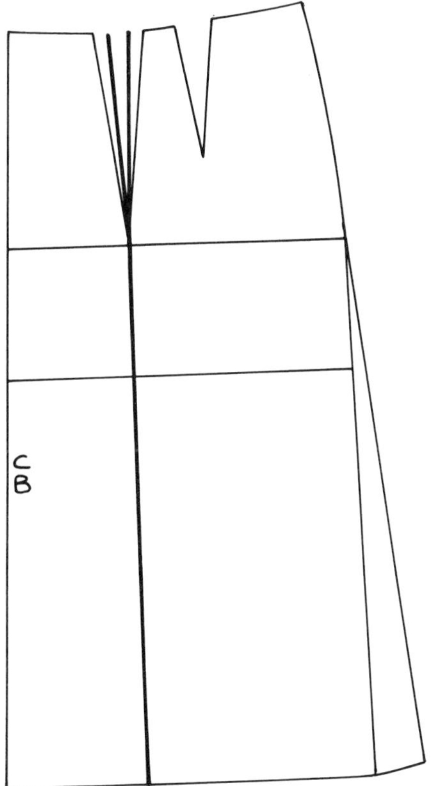

each side of new line. Close dart to allow pattern to open at hemline. Outline and cut out. Fold pattern as for front, add flare to CB edge to correspond with flare already on side seam and re-curve hemline. Mark SG along crease and transfer remaining dart. Add balance marks to both edges to match those on front pattern.

You can see that because the original block was wider at the back than the front the gores are going to be different widths. In small sizes the difference will be very little. On larger sizes you may wish to even them up by taking a little off the back at the side seam and adding a corresponding amount to the front pattern.

Six gores. If the amount of flare you want at the hemline is minimal, remember that whatever is added at the side seam will be repeated on all six gore seams. Use your original skirt block as a starting point, copying the side seam JK. If you are planning a full skirt use the A-line block.

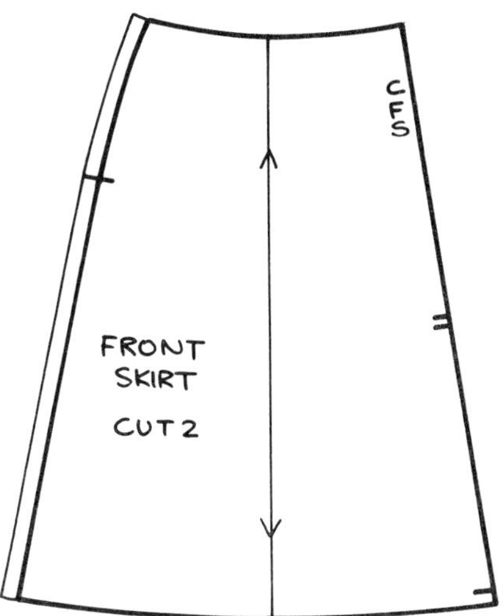

All the darts are eliminated and the gores are all equal in width at the hemline. Remember to retain the shape of the side seam to ensure a good fit over the hips.

Outline back and front, marking flare at side seam if using A-line block. Indicate all darts with dotted lines. Divide high hip line into three and rule vertically lines to hem and waist; use two of the marked sections for side panels and one for centre panel – it will be cut to the fold.

Back: Place half the long dart on each side of panel line. Shorter dart will be retained to ensure correct fit. Trace off each section separately leaving spaces between and putting balance marks at hip and high hip lines. Trace the A-line shape at side seam and add the same amount to each of the gores. Curve the hemlines a little. If the straight block was used, add about 2–4cm/ ¾–1⅝in to each seam edge. Mark CBF, add cutting instructions and number of gores. SG must run down the centre of the side gores. Find correct position by folding and matching original straight construction lines.

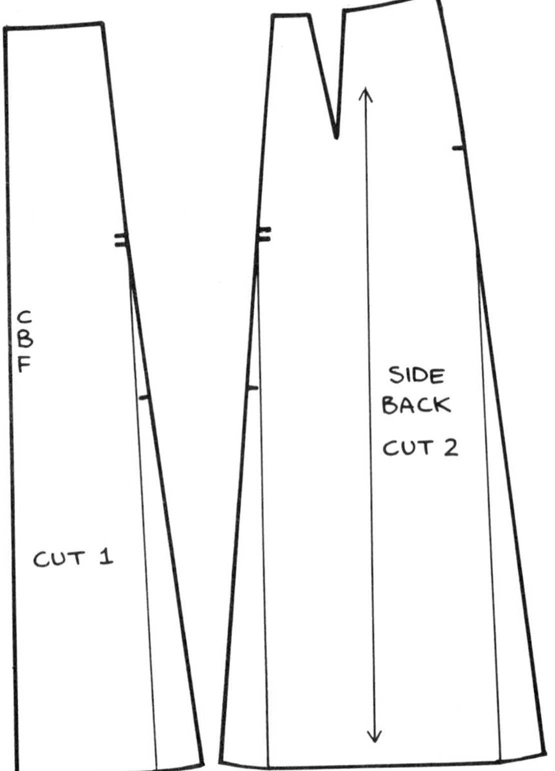

Front: Mark off half the dart on each side of panel line. Trace off each gore separately with space between. Add balance marks. On figures

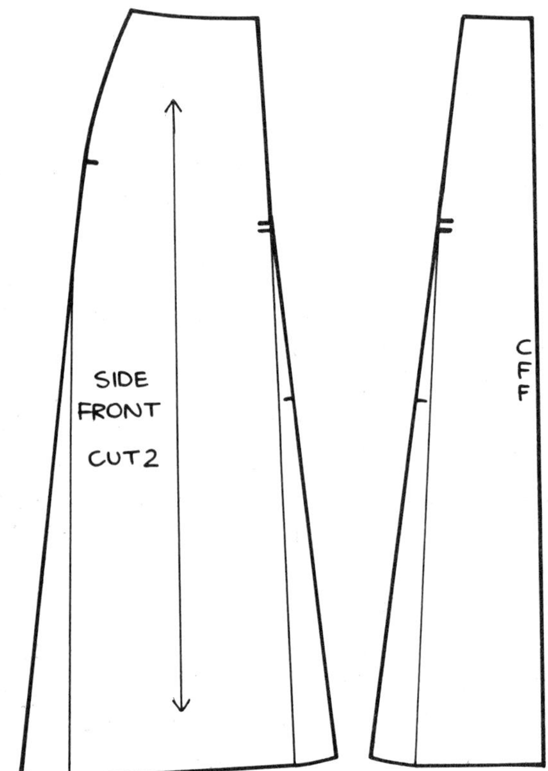

with a large waist compared with hips or with large hips the waist dart is very small and may not provide an attractive panel seam. Even up the gores if necessary by making the waist shaping more pronounced and adding on the same amount at the side seam to compensate.

Gores with flare. Follow instructions for gored skirt above, extend hemline each side of gore

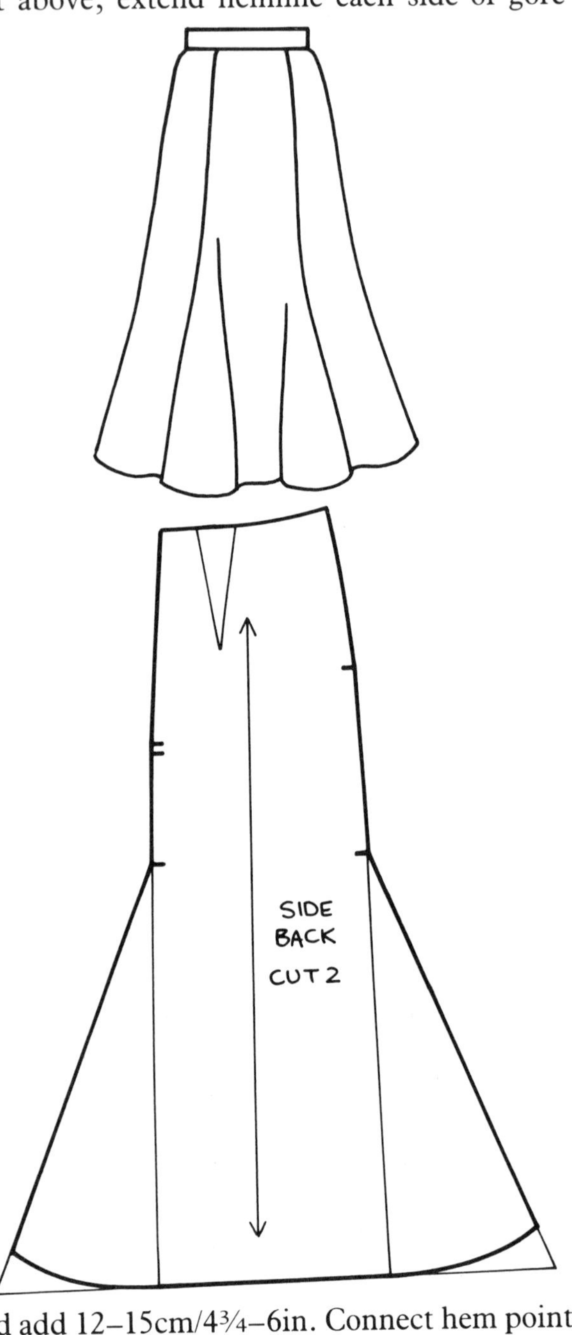

and add 12–15cm/4¾–6in. Connect hem points to hipline. Measure equally from hip and curve hem.

D. Separate godets

The flared sections can be cut separately. This is more economical of fabric and it provides an opportunity to use contrasting fabric.

Prepare the panels as described for previous design, adding the flare required to one panel only. This can be as much as you like now that it is to be a separate piece of fabric. If you want to insert a quarter circle, rule a line at right angles

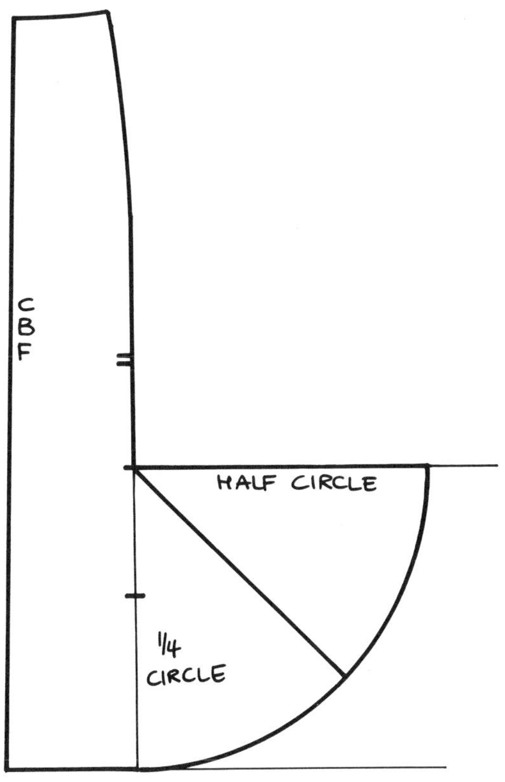

and draw a semi-circle for the hemline. Trace off, fold with straight edges together to find SG.

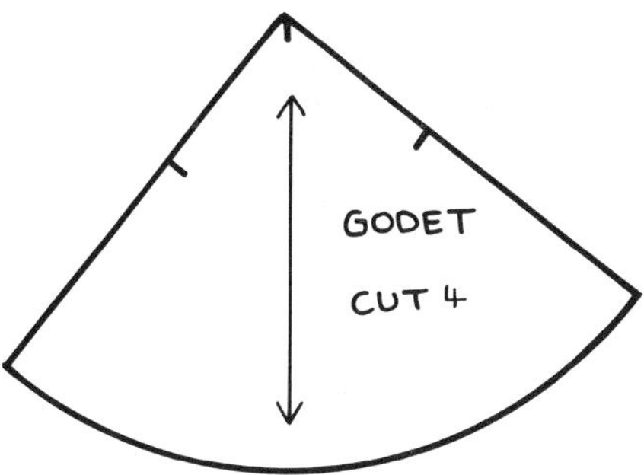

To make a half circular godet outline the quarter against a folded piece of paper. Cut and

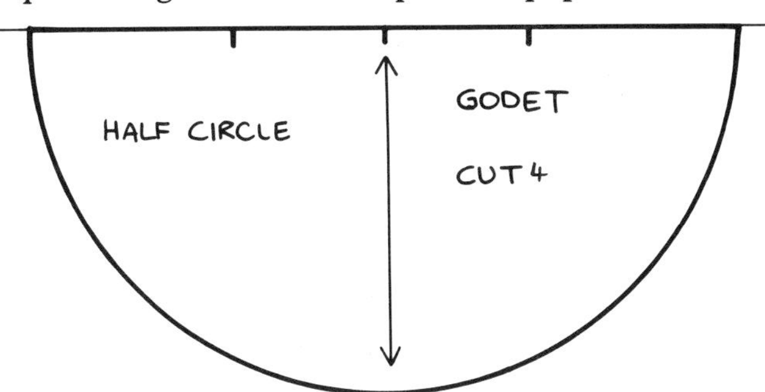

open out. Circular godets could be permanently pleated after cutting.

E. Panel over hip

This style has integrated godets the same as for design C above but the panel seams curve over

the hips. The darts can be transferred into the seam but a little gathering should be allowed at the waist.

1. Outline blocks and draw panel lines to base of dart; from there curve into side seam. Cut

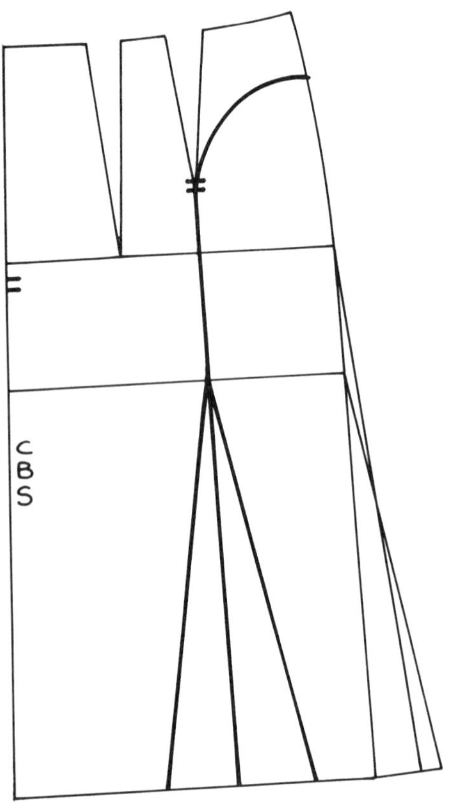

along curve to base of dart. Insert balance marks.

2. Add flare to each panel seam. For soft

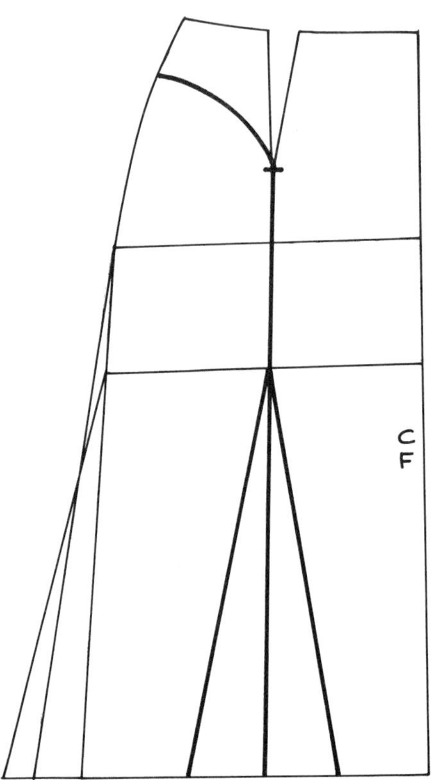

fabric make the flare about twice the amount already marked on the block as A-line flare.

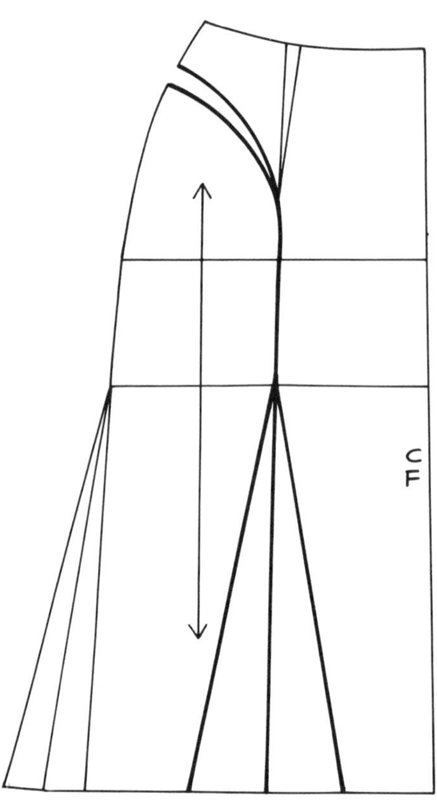

3. On back close dart so shaping transfers into hip curve, leaving inner dart to be gathered. Mark zip position in CB seam.

4. On front skirt transfer half the dart to the hip seam leaving the remainder to be gathered.

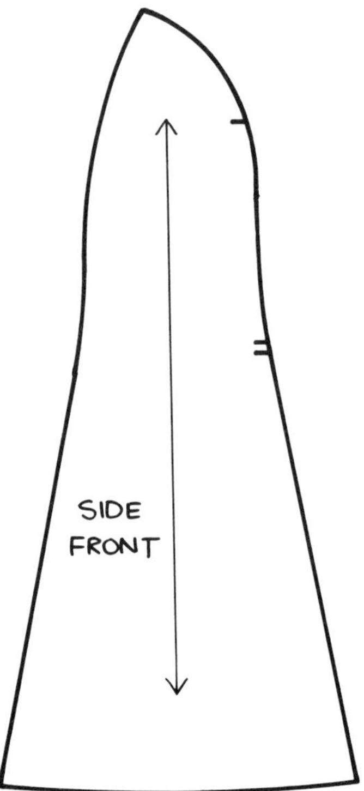

5. Trace off all sections. Mark SG down centre of side panels.

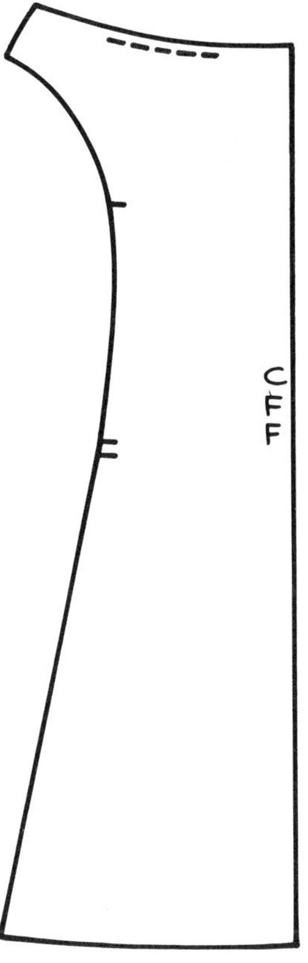

F. Gathered panels

Gored and panelled skirts made in soft fabrics can have gathers inserted as an additional feature. Adapt the block to the required number of sections as described in the preceding examples. Insert extra width in each panel by cutting from mid-waist to mid-hem and spreading apart. The amount inserted will depend on the fabric being used as well as on the effect required. Try gathers in the side panels only or the centre panels only, for a stylish design.

G. Multi-panels

Skirts with 8, 10 or even more gores are made on the same principle as for six, dividing the block into the number of panels required. The style of skirt that is made up of numerous sections, each one often stitched down the centre, can be made using only one pattern piece. Divide waist and hip measurement including ease into 16, 18, 20,

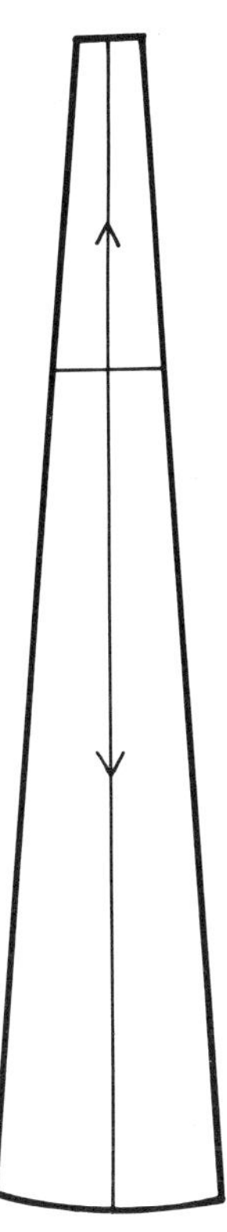

30 or more, and rule two lines that distance apart representing the panel edges. Extend both lines to length required. Curve hemline and complete waist. Mark SG down centre.

This style of skirt looks effective made in woven and knit fabrics of light and medium weight. If it is to be worn beneath a hip-length top, a smoother line can be achieved by making a yoke from waist to high hip line. Detach yoke pattern from block and make the number of panels required to the remaining length and to fit the lower edge of the yoke when joined.

H. A-line skirts with pleats

Follow instructions given for inserting pleats on pages 47–54, but using the A-line block.

BODICE DESIGNS

BUST DART

You have seen that the dart that provides the bust shaping can be moved to various positions (page 15); it can also be divided up so that a small amount appears in several places and it can be combined with the waist dart, putting all the front shaping in the waist. The final alternative is to lose the bust dart altogether (page 71).

The picture that you choose to copy or the sketch that you make should indicate, or at least give a clue, as to where the bust dart is. Begin by deciding on its position, on how it is to be used, for example dart, tucks, gathers. If it is a dart, decide whether it should extend to the inner or outer bust point circle. If it is gathers, decide whether the dart will be sufficient or whether more shaping has to be found, either by including the waist dart or by cutting and spreading the paper.

If you already have the fabric, consider what the effect of your design on the fabric will be. This in turn will change the effect it creates when worn. Stripes, checks and regular patterns will be distorted by all shaping; often basic florals and especially satin are very enlarging to the figure with the bust shaping in some positions.

The following designs show the front bodice. In some cases you will make a similar adaptation to the back block to make the complete pattern, in others the back darts can be used as on the blocks.

In each case outline the front block to required length with bust dart transferred to position and alter basic neckline if necessary.

A. Bust dart in shoulder – tucks. Measure width of dart and draw three equal tucks from shoulder; mark the stitching lines.

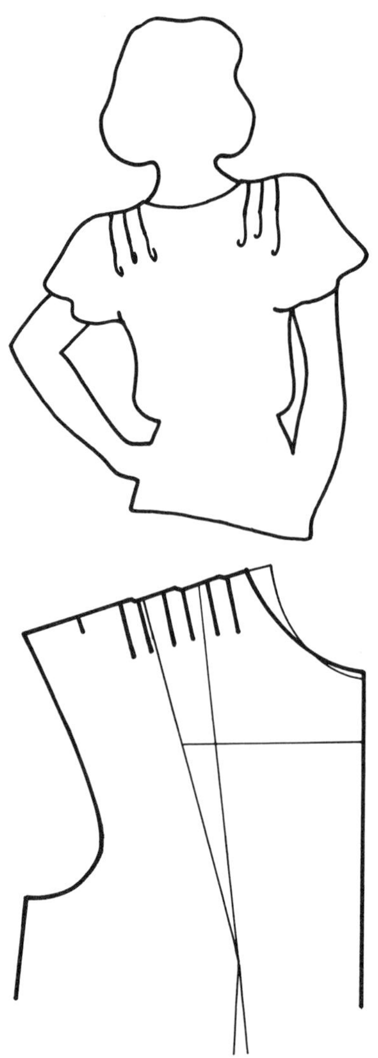

B. Bust dart in shoulder – gathers. There is more gathering in the shoulder seam than could come from the bust dart. The garment is close-fitting at hip level which indicates that additional fullness should be added at shoulder only.

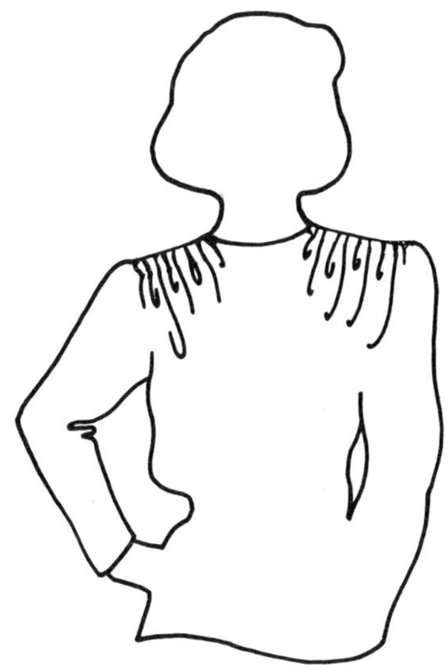

Draw a line from mid-shoulder to mid-hem, cut almost to hem and spread to insert about 7cm/2¾in. Exact amount will depend on type of fabric.

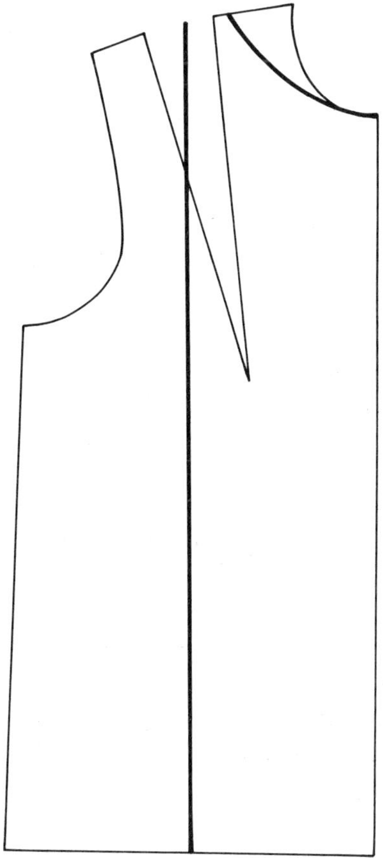

Outline again, straighten hemline and curve shoulder seam raising it at shoulder point to loosen the armhole. Mark CFF, mark SG parallel with CF. When adding seam allowances remember to add 2–3cm/¾–1⅛in for drawstring casing.

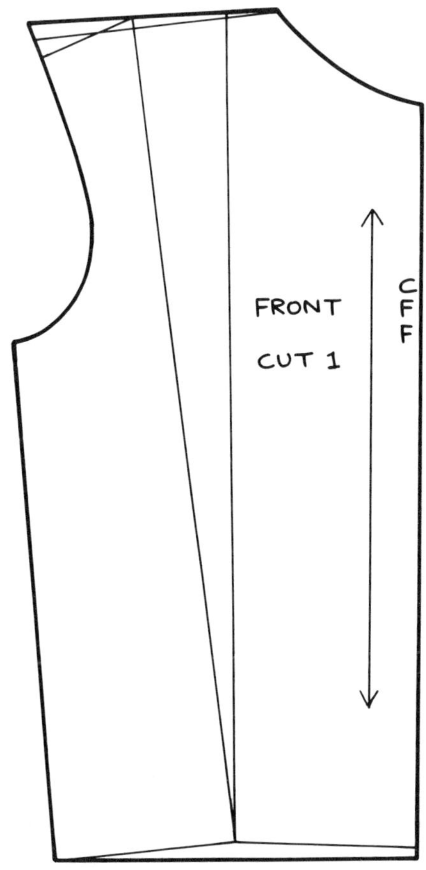

C. Bust dart in shoulder – gathers in yoke.

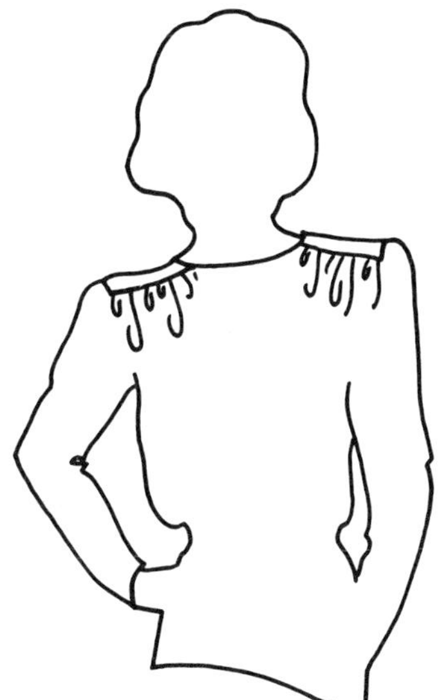

Close shoulder dart and outline neck and shoul-

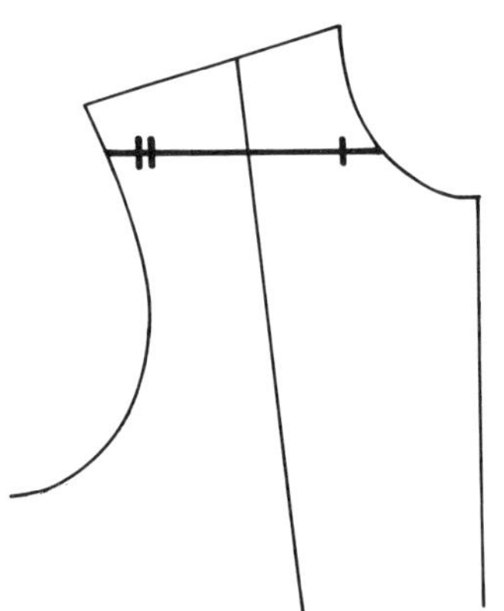

ders. Draw yoke line, add balance marks. Trace yoke pattern, mark SG.

Trace remainder of block to hip level with

dart open. This does not produce sufficient for the gathers shown but it is a slim-fitting dress so

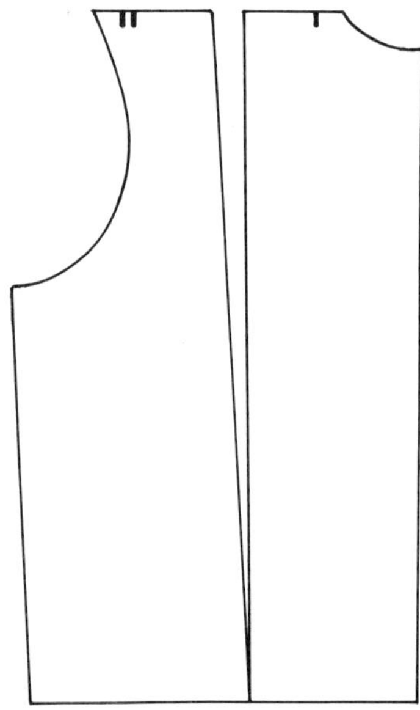

cut from point of dart to hip level and open at yoke.

D. Bust dart, in underarm and neckline – dart and seam. Although, like the armhole position, this has to be a short dart, the edge of the pattern is straight, the shaping is more gentle and the garment can be made looser.

This would be a good choice for large sizes because the bust dart is not to be entirely committed to the underarm position and also some of the waist dart shaping can be taken into the seam. The other benefit of having a seam in the neckline is that gaping can be eliminated.

Draw new neckline and armhole. Trace off. Close underarm dart sufficiently to transfer one third back to the shoulder, letting it open at the side of the neck. Draw panel seam from each side of dart over BP and either side of waist dart down to hip. Extend block to dress length. Draw

SEWING TIP

With low necklines and sleeveless armholes interface the entire area to help keep the garment smooth and supported. On design D, above, interface centre panel to a depth of 5cm/2in; interface strap and armhole almost to the level of the underarm dart.

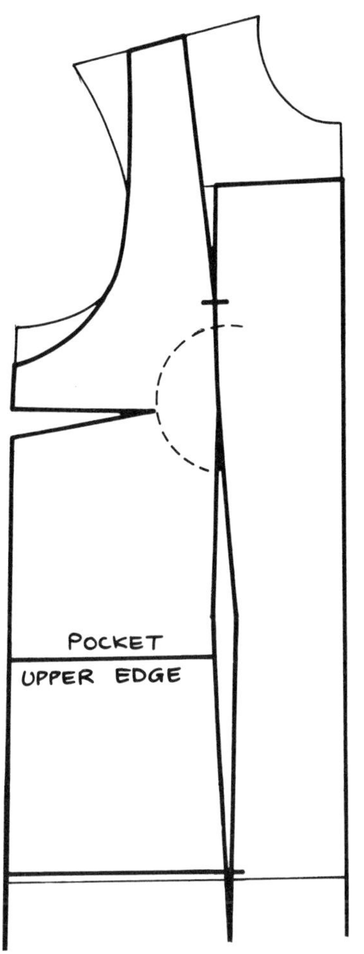

pocket position. Trace and label each section of pattern separately. SG to run parallel with CF on all pieces.

E. Bust dart at underarm – gathers. Please see Patterns for Under Clothes, page 188, with instructions for changes to the block.

Draw upper edge of camisole; mark strap. Extend side in line from underarm to add extra

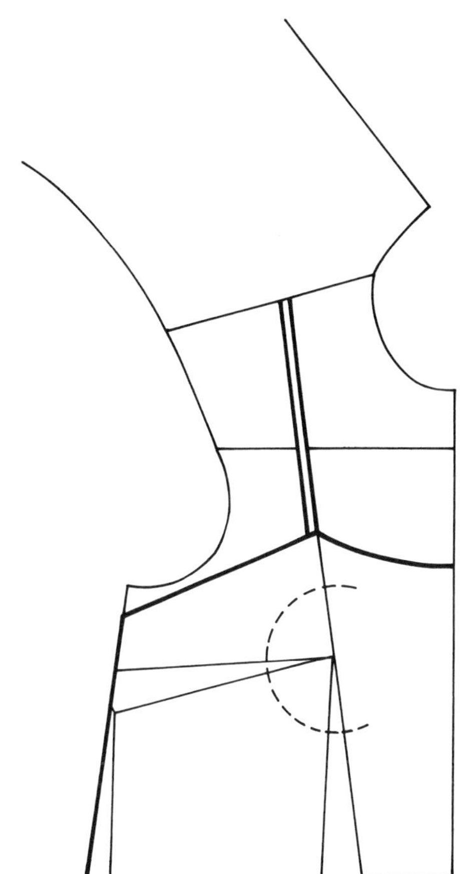

at waist. Trace pattern, mark gathers to cover twice width of dart. Mark CFF and strap position.

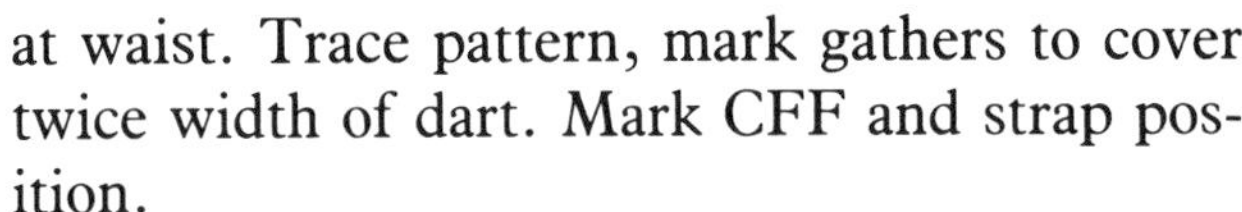

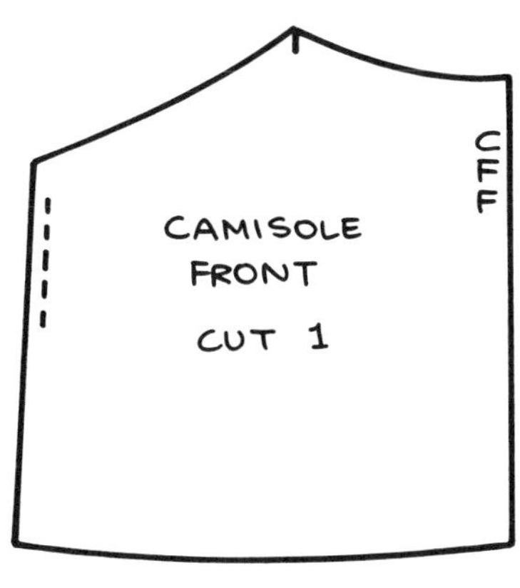

F. Bust dart in waist – eased fullness. Loose fit at armhole indicates an extended shoulder and lowered armhole.

Raise and extend shoulder and lower the armhole. (See page 125 for details.) Draw new neckline and mark depth of band.

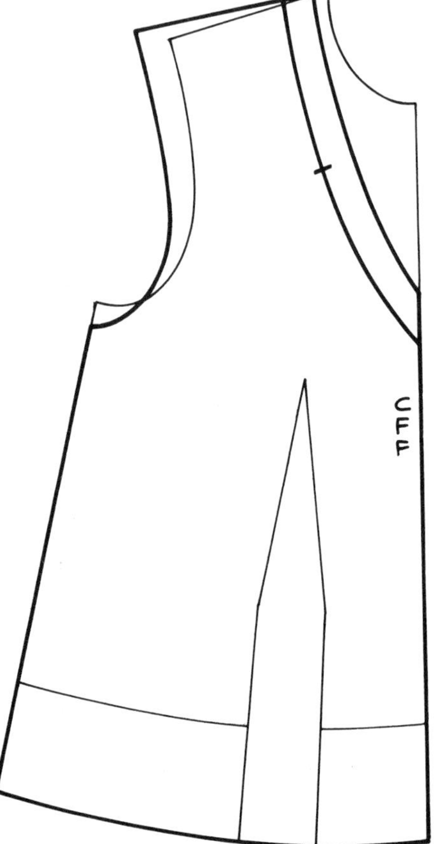

Adjust length if necessary. Draw rectangle for hip band to twice depth required. Length of

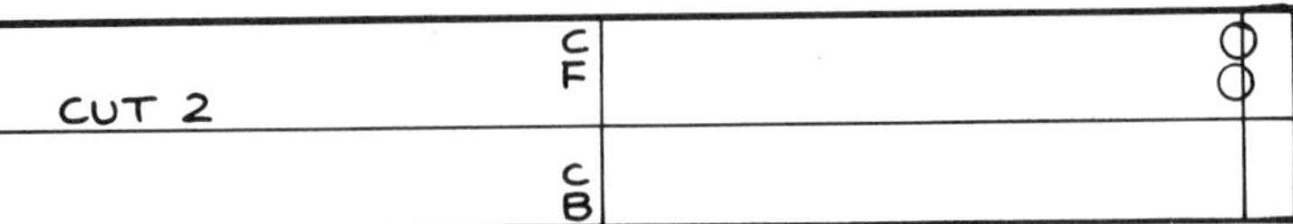

band should equal measurement taken round thighs plus extension for fastening.

G. Bust and waist darts in neckline – gathers. Measure length of neck edge and note it for

length of binding to be cut. Rule two transfer lines from BP into neckline and cut along them.

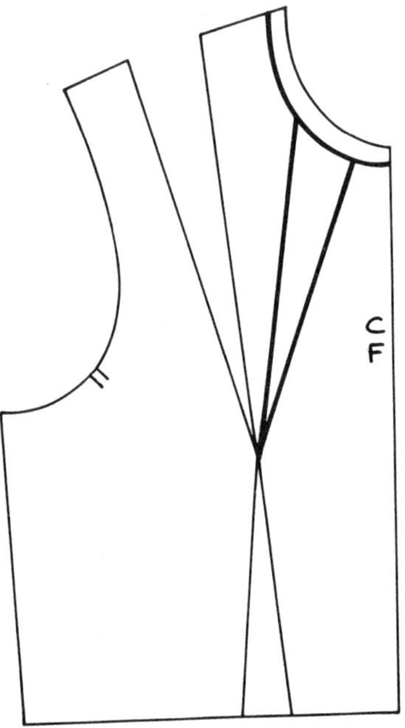

Trace CF edge and waist edge as far as dart. Cut out. Close waist dart; outline remainder of waist, side seam, armhole and shoulder as far as dart. Close shoulder dart; outline remainder of shoulder and first part of new neckline. With final section placed centrally to divide fullness evenly, outline remainder of neckline. Re-draw neckline and waist in smooth curves.

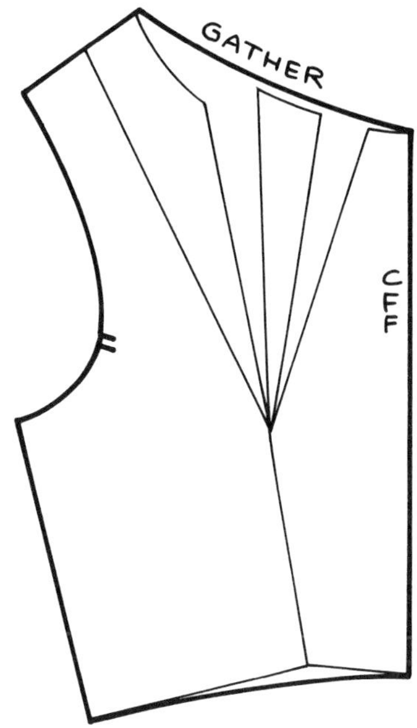

Rule three transfer lines from CF to BP. Insert balance mark 1cm/⅜in each side to indicate area to be gathered. Measure between marks and make a note on the draft as to the amount the seam is to be pulled up. Cut out pattern.

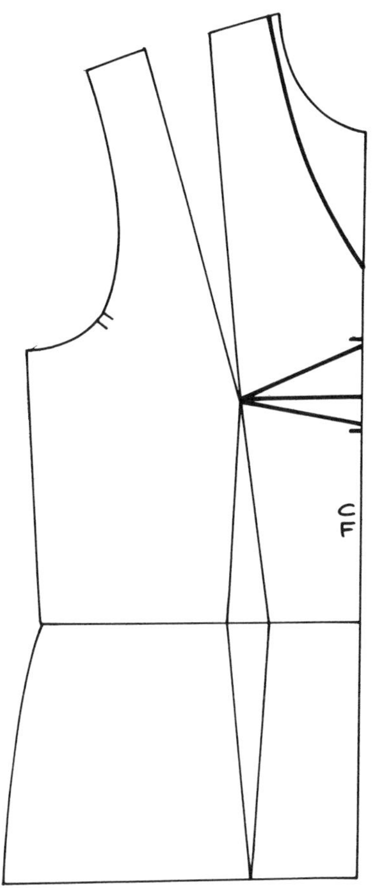

H. Bust dart at centre front – gathers.

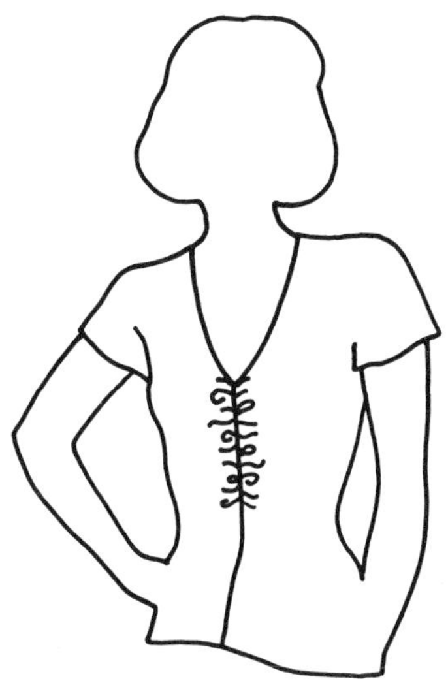

Outline CF and waist edge corner and CF down to hip level. Cut along waistline and darts. Close waist dart to BP; outline waist, armhole and shoulder as far as dart. Close bust dart, outline neckline and corner of CF. Without detaching them at BP arrange sections at CF to distribute fullness into three approximately equal sections. Mark SG parallel with original CF.

To complete hip section close waist dart, match edges at side seam allowing CF edge to swing out. Trace round in this position. You will see that the waist dart has moved into the waist area. Mark hemline, re-draw CF seam in a

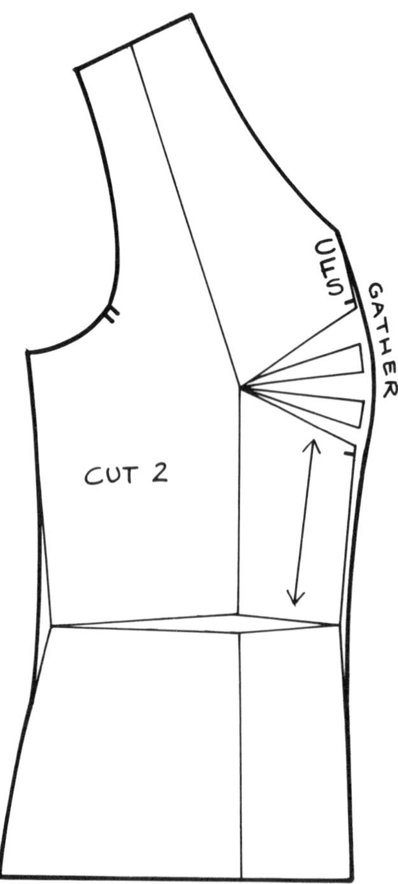

smooth curve to below waist. Curve side seam to remove sharp angle.

I. Bust dart and waist dart in neckline – loose folds. To be cut on the bias so a complete front

pattern will have to be made. Calculate how low you want the neckline to droop by looping a tape measure down from your neck.

Rule two transfer lines from BP to neckline. Transfer waist and bust dart to neckline with

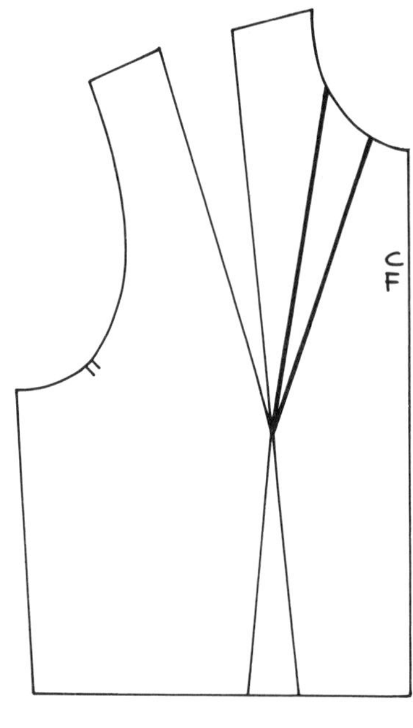

roughly equal amounts between the neck sections. Complete neck edge by extending CF upwards and drawing a line at right angles to meet the neck point. Check the length of the

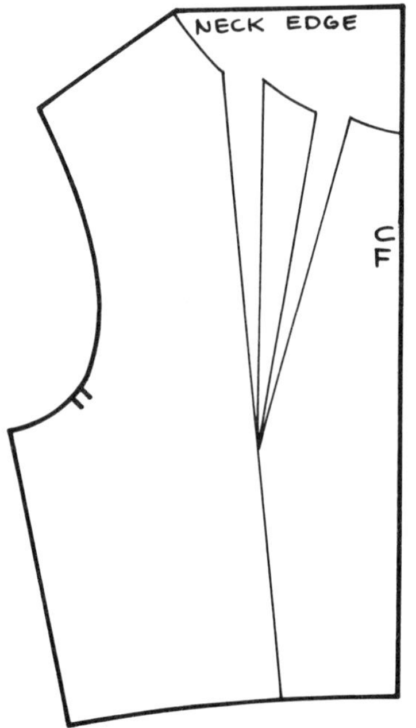

straight edge with your body measurement. Open or close the pattern if necessary.

Cut out the pattern and place it with CF on a folded sheet of paper. Outline the shape re-

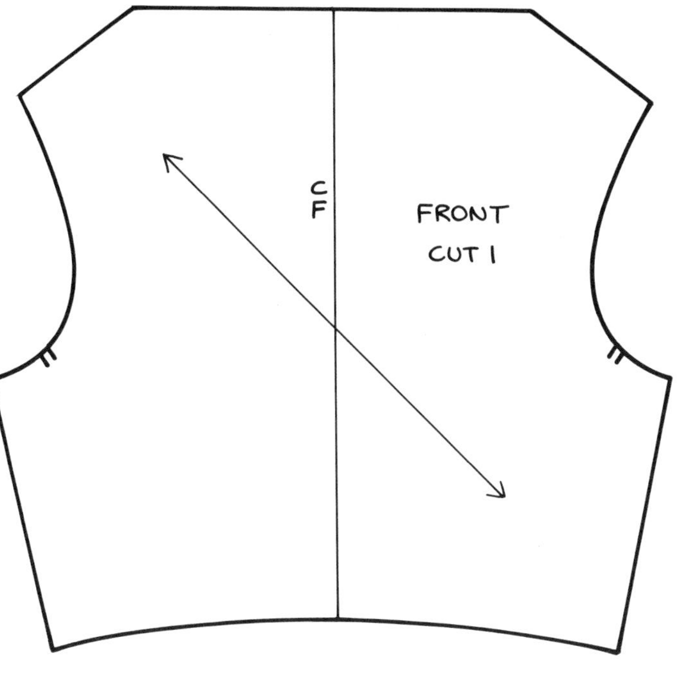

curving the waistline. Cut out the double paper, open out and mark SG at 45 degrees to crease.

J. Bust dart in shoulder – funnel neck, seam. Cutting the cowl section separately enables the main part of the garment to remain fitted and it is also more economical of fabric as only the cowl need be cut on the bias. However, raising the neckline so that it hugs the sides of the neck means back neckline must also be raised to make shoulder seams equal in length.

1. On a copy of the back bodice rule a vertical line from mid-neck to hem. Cut and open to insert 1cm/⅜in. At the same time transfer shoulder dart to neck.

2. Extend CB and mark height of funnel required, about 4–5cm/1½–2in. Rule a vertical line from neck point parallel with CB and curve new neckline measuring evenly to same depth as CB. Measure length of CB curve below as it was after inserting the 1cm/⅜in, omitting dart width. Measure this distance from CB on new

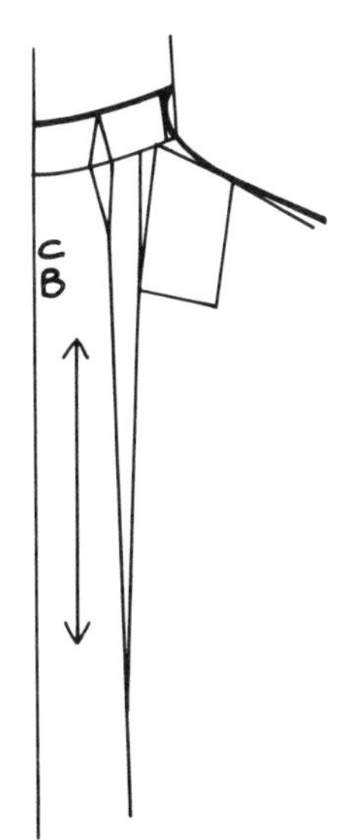

neckline and rule shoulder seam from that point to neck point. Remove the angle from shoulder seam and mark small double-ended neck dart. Trace pattern, mark CB fold or seam, SG is parallel with CB.

3. On a copy of front bodice draw slightly curved V, insert seam and balance mark it. Cut along line to CF and from CF to BP. Do not allow paper to detach.

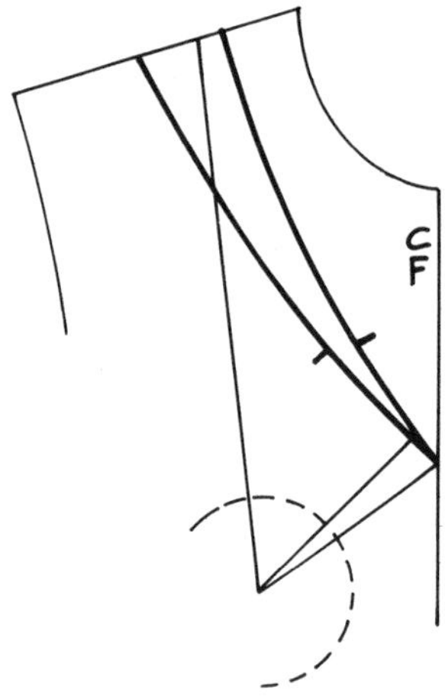

Close bust dart and outline pattern. Trace off main bodice front and mark CF, SG and cut 2. Trace off V inset, extend CF and shoulder seam.

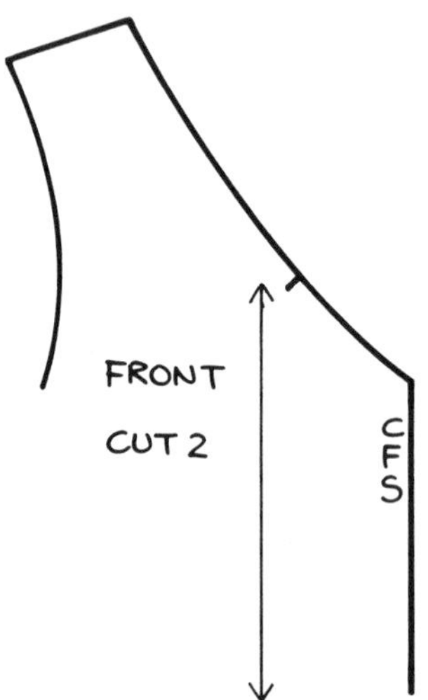

Raise neckline at CF if you wish, but not necessarily. Mark depth of funnel along extended shoulder seam and curve from that point to CF.

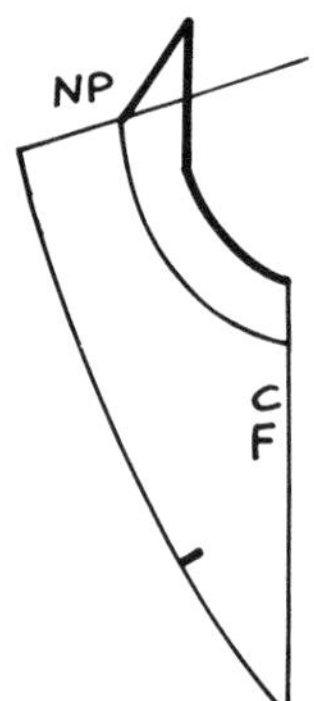

Measure size of original neckline and measure this amount round the curve from CF. Join new neck point to original one.

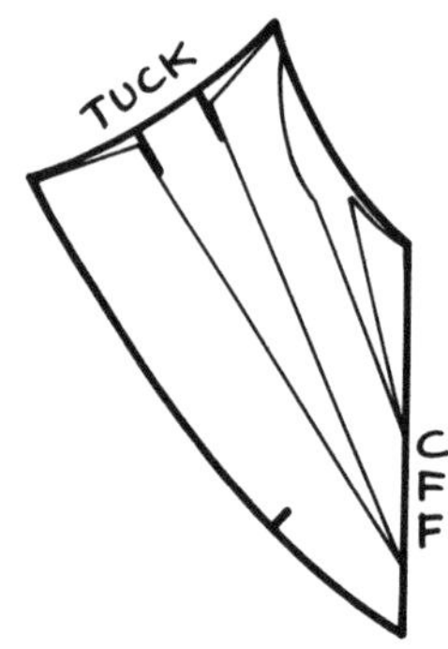

4. Trace inset. Rule lines from neck and shoulder to CF, cut along lines and open out. Curve shoulder seam to remove angle and draw neckline less curved.

SEWING TIP

It is best to make a cowl wide enough to get it over the head; an opening is not very satisfactory in a soft style. Check your head measurement and open the neckline slash in the pattern sufficiently. If using a knit fabric make it tighter.

K. Bust dart in shoulder – wide neckline. Folds produced by making the front neck wide.

Keep the back neck fitted or the garment will fall off the shoulders. The bust dart is taken into a fold in the seam. See page 137, Raglan sleeves, for first stage of draft.

1. On simple raglan outline draw new neckline.

2. Trace centre section of bodice allowing dart to open in shoulder position. Mark dart width as a folded tuck.

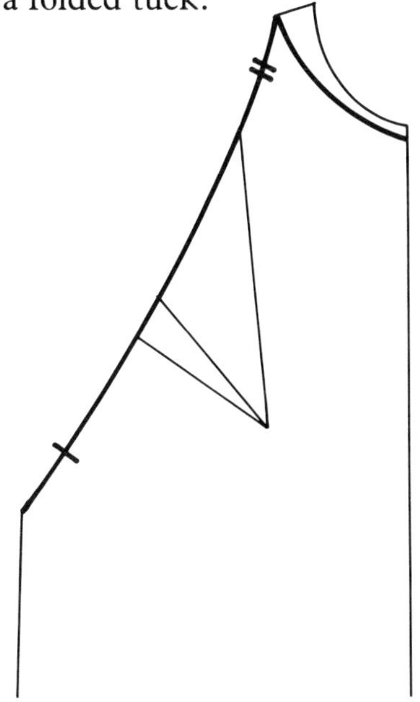

3. Rule three lines between neckline and CF. Cut along lines leaving paper joined at edge and spread to insert even amounts at neck edge. Keeping CF edge vertical outline for final pattern. Draw straight neck edge by extending CF and ruling a line at right angles from shoulder point.

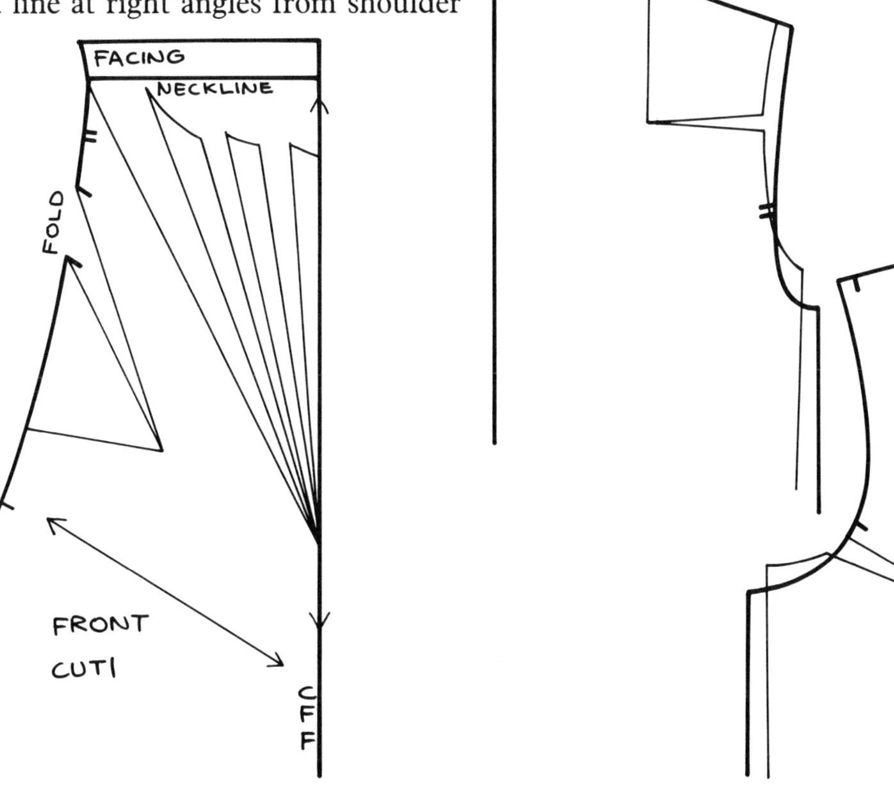

It would be sensible to add a facing at this stage instead of having a separate facing.

BODICE WITHOUT DARTS

Some designs are so loose as to make it possible to dispense with the darts in the block. When this line is in fashion it would be worth making a dart-less block. Sizes above 16 or 18 should consider always including a bust dart, or a portion of a bust dart in every design.

Many designs with deep or loose fitting armholes as described on pages 127–129 can be made without darts and in fact part of the adjustment to eliminate the darts is the same.

Back: Rule a horizontal from point of shoulder dart to armhole, close dart and outline block. Extend shoulder by 1cm/⅜in. Waist dart is ignored.

Front: Rule a line from armhole to BP and cut. Arrange block to have 1cm/⅜in of dart in shoulder position 1cm/⅜in in armhole and the remainder in waist. Extend shoulder to match length of back shoulder. Waist dart is ignored.

Widen and lower the armhole by 1.5cm/⅝in the same as for deep armhole (see Armholes and Shoulder Lines, page 125). Adjust sleeve as described on the same page. Rule vertical seams to length required on front, back and sleeve. Redraw armholes.

COLLARS, NECKLINES AND YOKES

COLLARS

You will know from your sewing that attaching a collar can be tricky because the neckline is one shape – round, V, square – but the edge of the collar to which it is to be attached is often a quite different shape. The only time it is easy to attach a collar is when it is curved like the neckline, for example a Peter Pan collar. The straighter the collar edge the harder it is to attach.

This gives you a clue to one of the principles that lie behind cutting collar patterns.

Collar neck edge. The neck edge of the collar may be any shape from very curved or slightly curved to straight or even curved in the opposite direction. But the length of this neck edge must equal the length of the neck edge on the garment. It must remain that length no matter what shape you make it.

Garment neck edge. The shape of the garment neck edge can be whatever you wish, front and back the same or different – low, high etc. Simply draw the shape you wish it to be then make the neck edge of the collar the same length (but not necessarily the same shape).

Shape of collar outer edge. The outer edge of the collar may be any shape you wish. It is this edge that gives it style; it is this which changes with fashion.

Length of collar outer edge. The length of the outer edge varies with the style of the collar. As the collar falls over chest, back and shoulders an excessively long outer edge will flute, a short one will cause the collar to rise and fold against the neck and one which is the same size as the garment will lie flat.

Width or depth of collar. The width of the collar can be as you wish; same width all round, narrow at back, wide at front etc. The height above garment neckline is to a certain extent limited by the human neck although if it is made very wide it will simply double over which is a type of collar in itself. One point you must bear in mind is that if the outer edge is so short that the collar rises and folds against the neck, allowance for this must be made by making the collar wider to start with.

Designing

The very set and style of a collar depends on the relationship between the five points described above. You can design any collar you wish keeping this in mind. Experimenting is fun and if you create a horror it takes but a few minutes to try again. When cutting a collar for a garment always cut the whole collar, not just half, in paper or Vilene and try it on a dummy or on yourself before adding seam allowances and finalizing the pattern.

As indicated above, styles of collars come and go with fashion changes but as with all pattern drafting the principles remain the same. The collar designs that follow illustrate the main methods of achieving various styles. Provided you understand the points made earlier you will be able to use these methods for any collar you design.

Preparation

Always begin by transferring the bust dart, outlining the front and back blocks and altering the neckline to the shape you want. Add any features to the bodice such as yoke and raglan seams, then outline and trace off the collar. The remainder of the bodice adaptation is then completed and you work separately on the collar shape.

While you work consider how the nature of the fabric might help and what type and weight of interfacing you might use. Always try the interfacing on a scrap of fabric, particularly iron-on varieties, before making up the collar.

Folding out and cutting and spreading will, as usual, produce stepped edges but they will seem more exaggerated on such small pieces of pattern. Remember to re-shape edges of final pattern to a smooth line before adding seam allowances.

SEWING TIPS

1. Collar points. To ensure perfectly matching collar ends place your original draft, without seam allowances, on the fabric and mark using chalk or fabric pen before stitching the collar.

2. Interfacing, e.g. iron-on Vilene. When cutting out interfaced part place pattern on Vilene and cut out then press the Vilene to WS fabric with grain correct as indicated on pattern. Cut out round edge of Vilene. This ensures an accurate collar and it also prevents getting adhesive on the iron or ironing board.

FLAT COLLARS

A. This collar lies flat on the garment. A child's Peter Pan collar might be attached to the basic

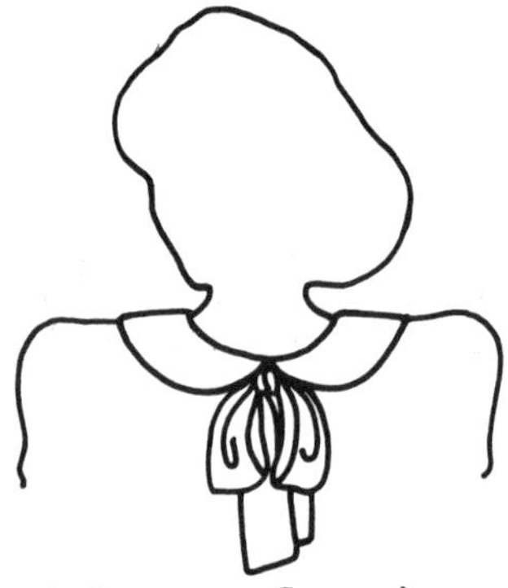

neckline but it is more flattering, especially on adults, if the neckline on the block is lowered and widened. A flat shoulder-width design is often called a Bertha collar.

1. Outline back block; place front block against it with neck points together and shoulder

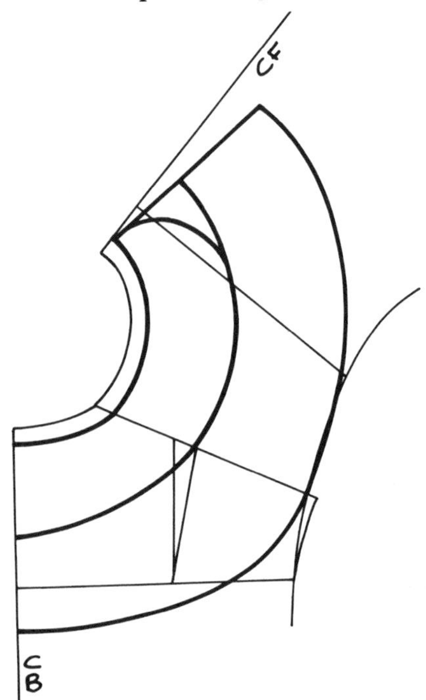

edges meeting. Lower neckline all round.

2. Mark width of collar and measure evenly from neckline all round. Curve CF corners.

Collar can be cut in one piece with CB pattern to a fold or it can be in two parts. The latter is necessary if garment has a back neck opening.

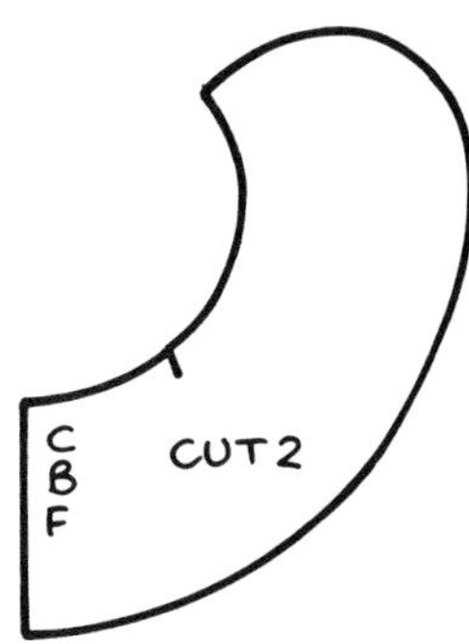

The collar described above would be extremely flat, even liable to curl up, so it is preferable to overlap the shoulder seams by about 2cm/¾in at armhole and to shorten the

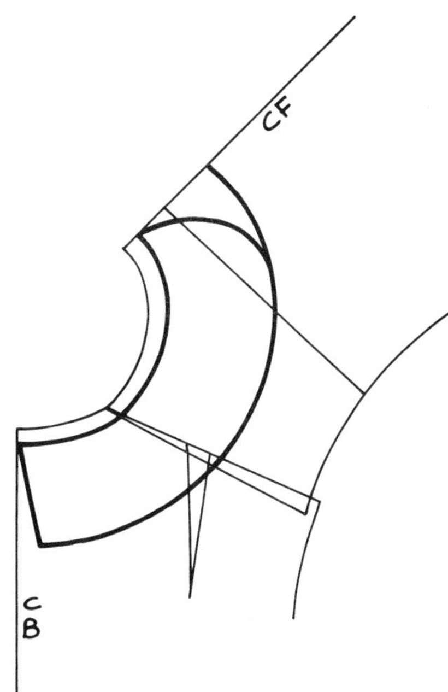

outer edge a little. Trace collar, insert balance mark level with shoulder seam, mark SG parallel with CB, mark CB, cut 2 or 4, as appropriate.

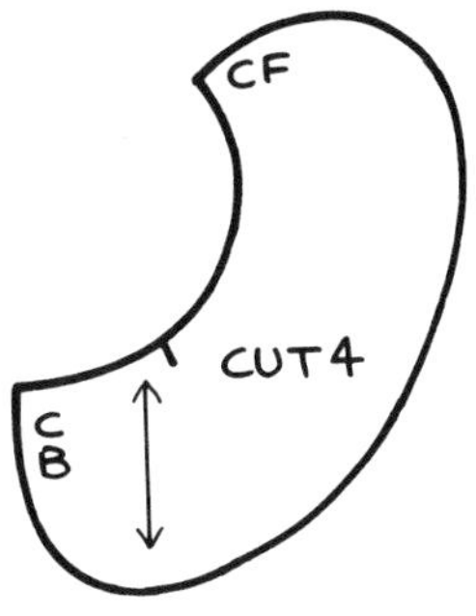

B. The combination of a flat collar at the front and one slightly re-shaped to hug the neck at the back. There is room under the collar for a narrow tie. Alternatively, the tie ends could be

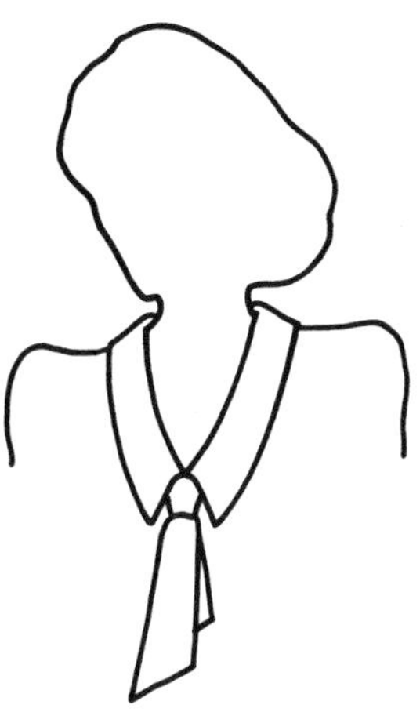

made short and fasten to the bodice using a Velcro Spot-On just out of sight under the collar.

1. Outline back and front block overlapping shoulders. Draw shape of new neckline.

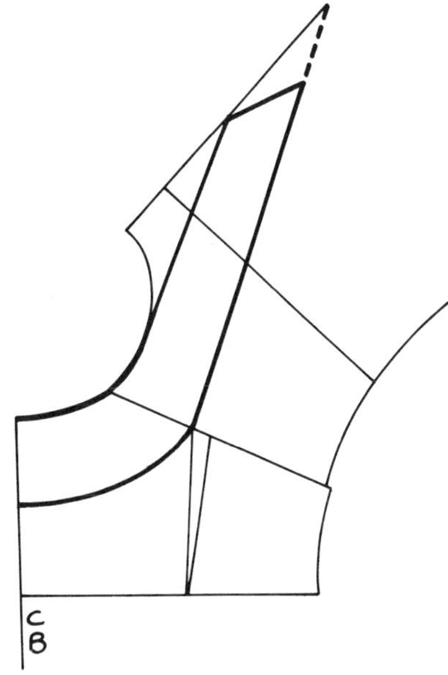

2. Mark width of collar making it wider round back of neck to allow for the stand. Shape collar ends. Trace collar and cut out.

3. Reduce length of outer edge between shoulder and CB by removing 6mm/¼in at CB,

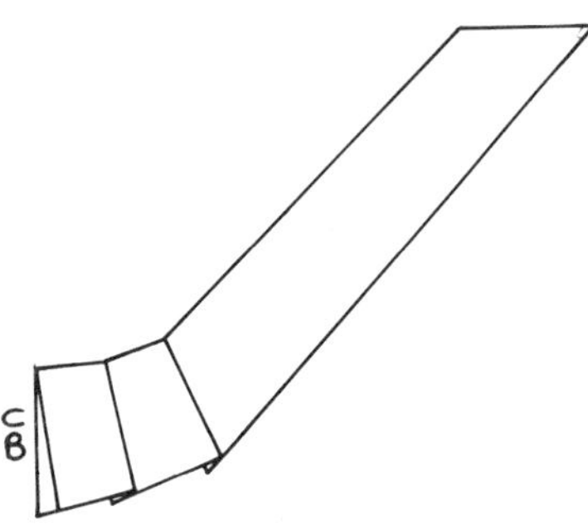

1cm/⅜in at shoulder and 1cm/⅜in mid-way between shoulder and CB. Outline again, mark CBF, cut 2.

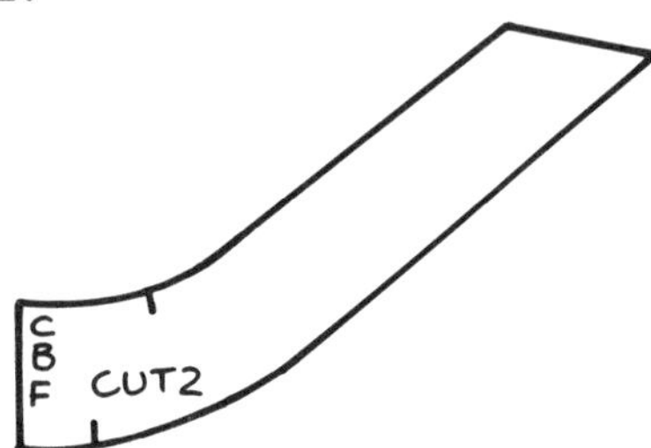

COLLARS WITH STAND

These are collars that rise against the neck and then fall with no part lying flat on the bodice. The outer edge must fall far enough to cover the neck seam.

A. The neckline is lowered a little at CF but raised at CB to provide the back neck stand. The stand at the front is necessary to take the tie.

1. Outline blocks overlapping shoulders as for previous designs. Raise back neck by 10–12mm/⅜–½in and re-draw neckline. Lower

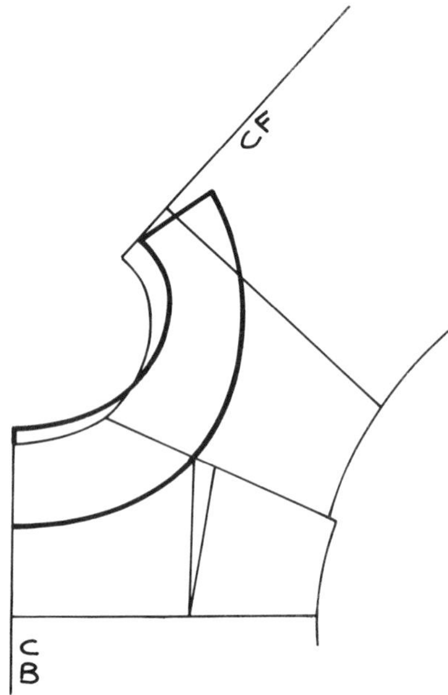

front neck and complete the neck. Mark depth of collar evenly all round; shape CF point.

2. Trace collar. Divide collar into six and reduce outer edge. When you test this by cutting a complete collar check that the collar has a small amount of stand at shoulder reducing to nothing at CF. Thin line indicates position of roll line.

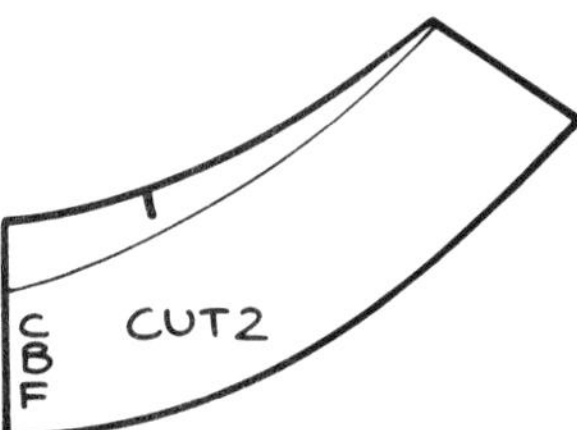

B. This collar has stand all round but it does not hug the neck which indicates that the outer edge is reduced considerably to make the collar stand away along the roll line.

1. Outline blocks, raise back neck 2cm/¾in and draw new neck as far as shoulder seam. Draw collar width an even distance from block neckline and draw CF point.

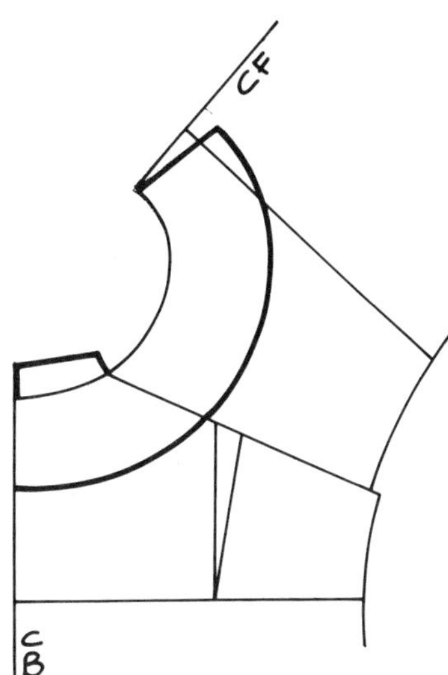

2. Trace collar and cut out. Reduce outer edge by 6mm/¼in at CB. Divide remainder into 10 or 12 segments and cut from outer edge almost to neck edge. Overlap each section evenly

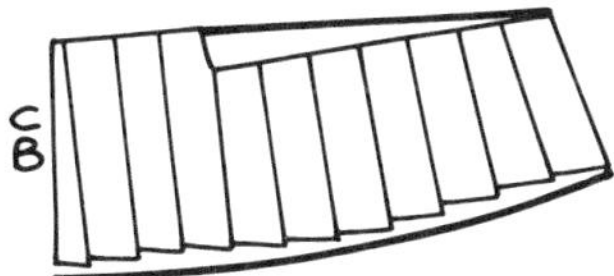

until outer edge is almost straight, i.e. the same length as the neck edge. Outline collar, complete remainder of neck stand from shoulder gradually reducing to nothing at CF.

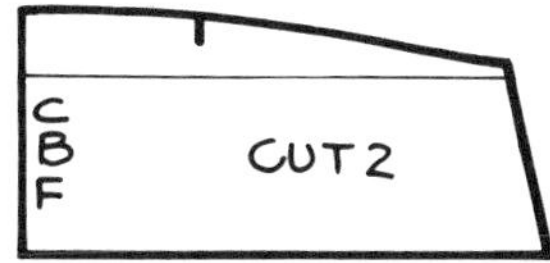

The collar pattern you made in the previous exercise was almost a rectangle. Now that you can see how it was arrived at you can eliminate the initial stages of tracing the block and start with a rectangle.

This style of collar is also used with simple revers. Make a wide facing for the CF edge extending up to shoulders. Fold back the revers and adjust collar pattern to fit neckline and lie flat at the front.

STRAIGHT STAND COLLARS

The collars in this section all have the outer edge equal or shorter than the length of the neck edge. You can begin with a rectangle to save having to trace the block but you must measure the neck edge to obtain the measurement for the collar length.

To practise you could use an average size but when making your own patterns there is no alternative but to measure your adapted neckline each time.

It is important to make the pattern for the garment first, at least as far as establishing the neckline so that it can be measured accurately. In fact if there is any doubt about the style or fit of the garment it is safest to construct and fit the bodice before returning to the pattern to cut the collar.

Carefully measure the established neckline, adding front neck to back neck and holding the tape on edge. Decide on the depth required and rule a rectangle making one end the CB.

A. Often referred to as a classic Mandarin collar, this is a narrow stand that meets edge to edge

or with a gap. Alternatively, on a wider neck it may be one piece. The basic neckline should be lowered so that the collar stands away from the neck.

1. Lower the neckline on back and front by 6mm/¼in. Measure total neck length and draw a rectangle making it 3cm/1⅛in deep. Shape CF end.

2. Trace collar, mark CBF, cut 2.

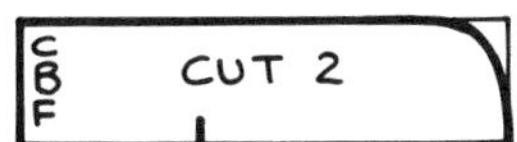

B. A similar shape to A but the ends extend beyond CF to fasten.

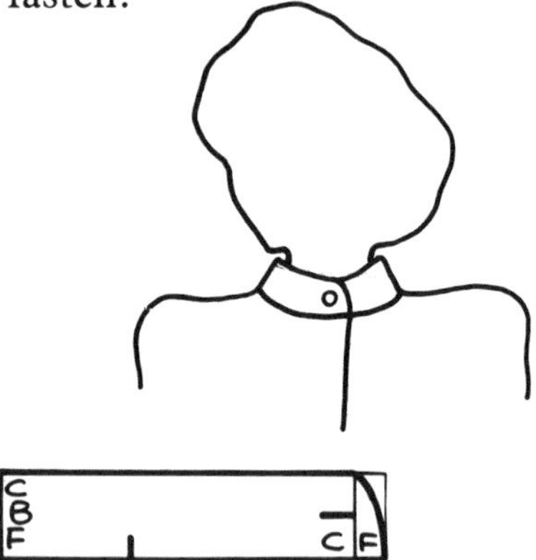

C. A collar to illustrate the principle of making the outer edge any length while keeping the neck edge the same. A shaped Mandarin collar that has the outer edge reduced so that it curves round the neck. It has more style than a straight collar and is more often used. In this instance the collar meets edge to edge above a zip or slit at CB.

1. Draw rectangle to length and depth required. Draw CF shape.

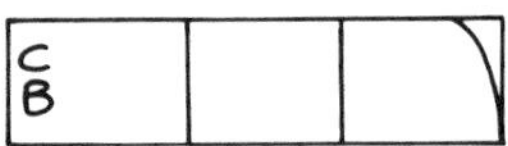

2. Trace collar and cut out. Divide into three and cut along lines from outer edge down towards neck edge but leaving pieces attached. Overlap each slit by 5–10mm/¼–⅜in.

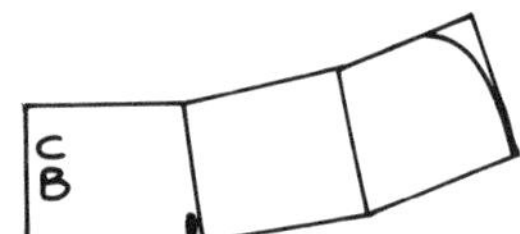

3. Re-draw with smooth outline and trace. Mark CB, cut 4.

D. All the collars so far have required a seam along the outer edge. The collar now shown, set on to a lowered neckline, is deep and straight and can therefore be cut in one piece.

1. Rule rectangle to length and depth required against a folded piece of drafting paper.

2. Cut out and open out the paper.

3. Mark CBF, cut 1 and mark shoulder balance mark on each edge. Add CF and buttonhole positions.

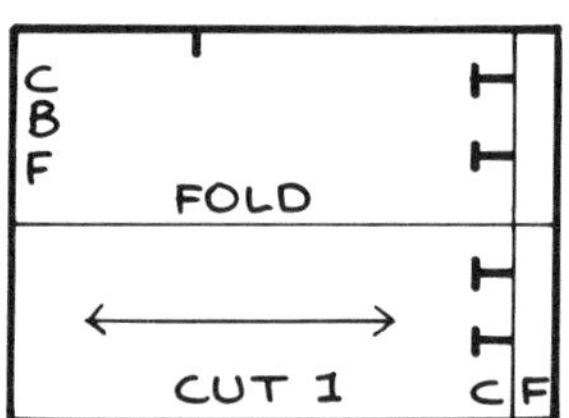

E. All the collars so far have had the SG position parallel with CB. You can add a further dimension to your pattern cutting by using the bias of the fabric to produce a longer outer edge without

shaping the pattern. The collar illustrated fastens end to end above a back neck opening.

1. Lower the back and front neckline and measure the total length. Draw a rectangle four times the finished collar depth. Mark each end CB and mark CF at centre. Cut out.

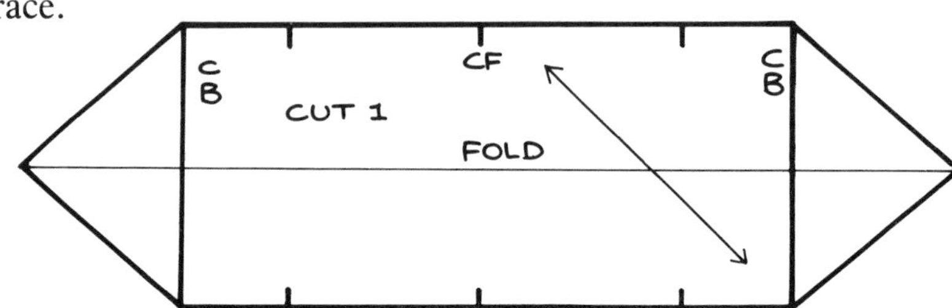

2. To place central fold line on the bias fold over one corner of the pattern until short end lies on top of long edge. Mark SG along crease. Mark collar cut 1. To give it a loose cowl effect lengthen central line and draw angled ends.

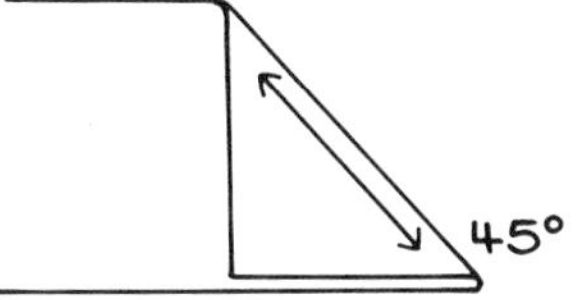

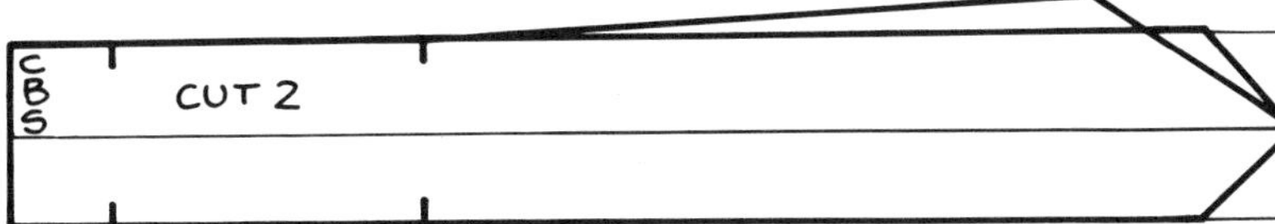

F. Simple neckband with tie ends. This is a straight piece of fabric that can be on the straight grain up to a depth of 4–5cm/1½–2in; more than that and it will have to be a bias strip that will shape to the curve of the neck.

Lower basic neckline by 1.5cm/⅝in at front, or shape to V if required. Mark buttons and add extension and fold-back facing if required. Measure total length of neck edge and draw a rectangle, marking CF and shoulder point as well as CB and grain.

The tie ends may be made wider if required. Also a narrow collar could be made with a seam

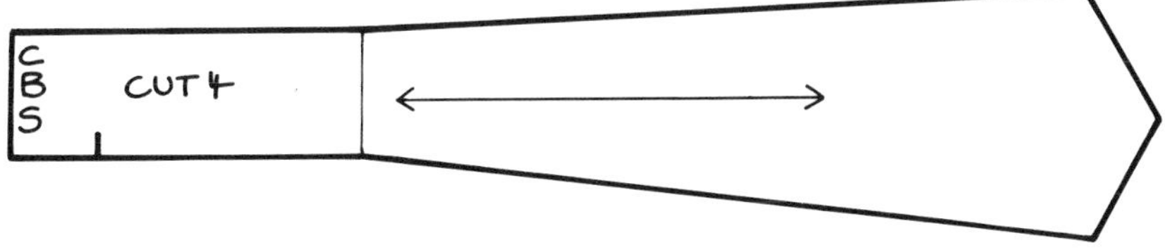

along the upper edge. The edge may be made shorter so that it hugs the neck more closely although the grain is then at an angle on the tie ends. If an exaggerated shape is required at the ends make a seam along the outer edge. Alternatively make a mandarin collar shape and insert shaped ties into the CF ends.

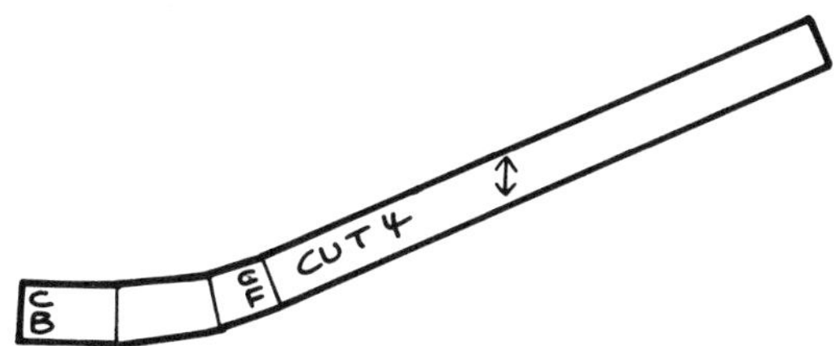

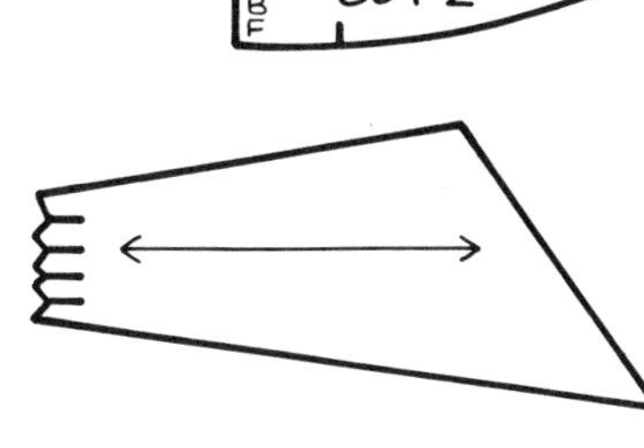

FLUTED COLLARS

If the outer edge of a collar is lengthened to an exaggerated degree and the pattern is cut from a single layer of soft fabric it will fall into attractive flutes. Return to the bodice blocks to begin with to obtain the initial shape.

A. Flute on V-neck.

1. Outline blocks with shoulders meeting; shape the neckline. On the garment illustrated

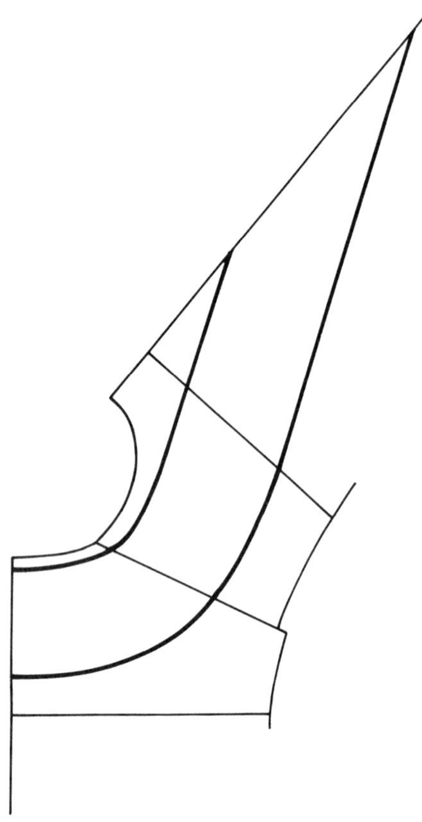

the back, or front, is widened and the front, or back, lowered to a deep V. As always with a low neck fold a small dart between neck and bust point to tighten. Mark collar width required; it need not be the same width back and front.

2. Trace collar, fold to divide into 10 or 12 segments and cut along each line towards neck

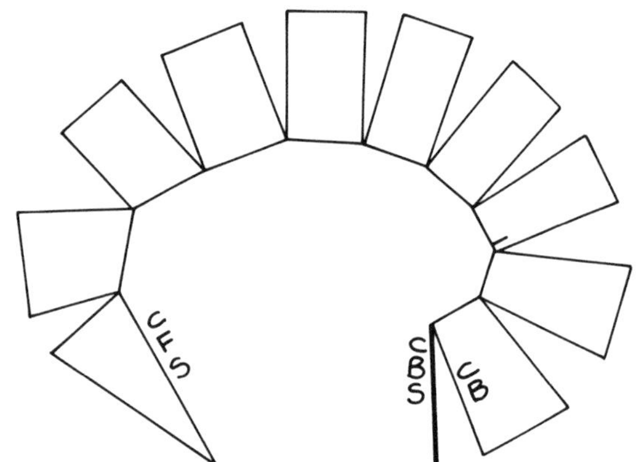

edge. Starting at CB outline each segment inserting extra width at outer edge. Extra can also be added at CB. The segments could be spread even more bringing CF point round almost to meet CB.

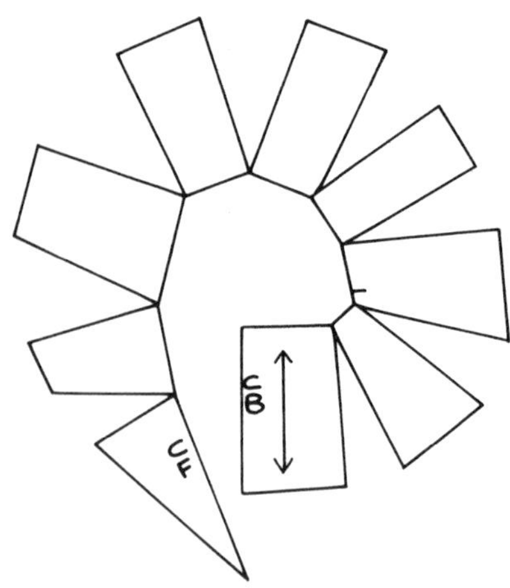

3. Re-draw neck and outer edges to a smooth curve. Mark CB seam and CF seam. SG may be parallel with CB or with shoulder seam. Mark the pattern cut 2.

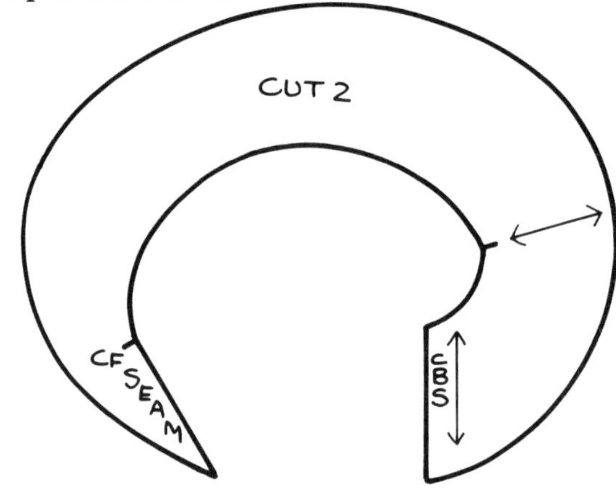

This is an illustration of the principles that the neck edge can be any shape provided it is still the right length and that the outer edge can be any shape or length.

As you can see the collar neck edge forms a circle so why not simply draw a circle? To do this

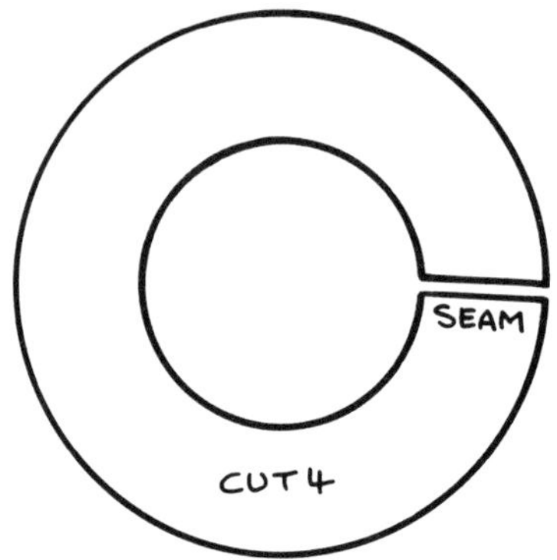

measure the neck edge and draw two or four circles the inner edges of which total the garment neck edge. Alternatively, as it is extremely difficult to handle circles without stretching, you can cut six or eight circles big enough to gather up to fit the neckline.

B. Combination of stand and flat collar. The cape front is cut on the flat collar principle. Use the same method if the cape is preferred at the back.

1. Make pattern for bodice front and collar (see Stand Collars, page 76) including the front band.

2. Trace the blouse front but use your block to transfer the bust dart to the neckline as shown in the illustration. Draw outer edge of cape.

3. Trace cape and rule lines from outer edge to neck where flare is shown. Cut on lines

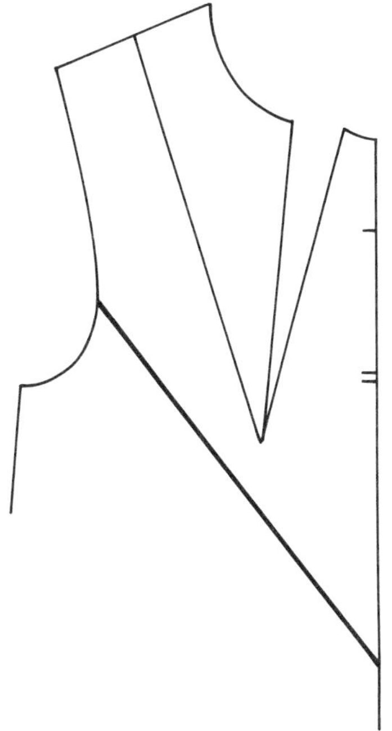

and spread at outer edge. Re-draw shoulder seam straight, curve armhole and outer edge smoothly, mark tuck and label pattern cut 2. SG

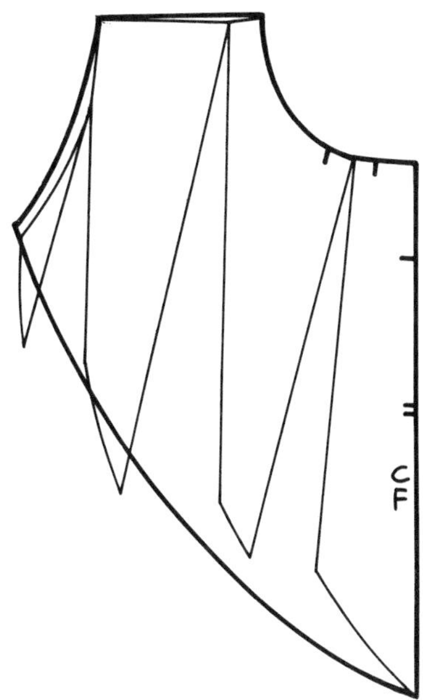

may be parallel with original CF or you may wish to cut the collar on the bias. The decision would depend largely on the type of fabric to be used.

SHAWL COLLARS

The description covers all collars that have a rever that extends round the back of the neck. The under collar is cut in one with the bodice and the top collar is cut in one with the front facing. Designs nearly always have a front opening. There is a slight limitation on the use of this type of collar as the only seam is at the CB by which time the grain of the fabric is very much on the bias. This is one reason for the snug comfortable fit of the collar but the effect on striped and check fabric would not always be acceptable. A plain contrast fabric could provide the solution.

With a full-length garment such as a dressing gown or even a dress, the front facing is a very long piece of pattern that is quite wasteful of fabric, partly because of its shape at the top. The solution to this is to make a join in the facing just below the top button or wrap-over point. If you do this it gives you the opportunity of moving the grain on the upper section to make the CB seam fall accurately on the bias.

The shawl collar perfectly illustrates the principle that the outer edge of a collar can be any shape you wish.

There is more than one method of drafting shawl collars but they all begin with the bodice block. Prepare the block each time by transferring the bust dart as appropriate and adapting CF for the buttons, wrap-over, and so on. Outline the block at this stage with plenty of paper to the right but do not cut it out.

A. Fold-back rever. Not really a shawl because it falls on the front only, but it is a good first-

stage collar on which to learn. The front edge of the bodice is folded back to form a small rever.

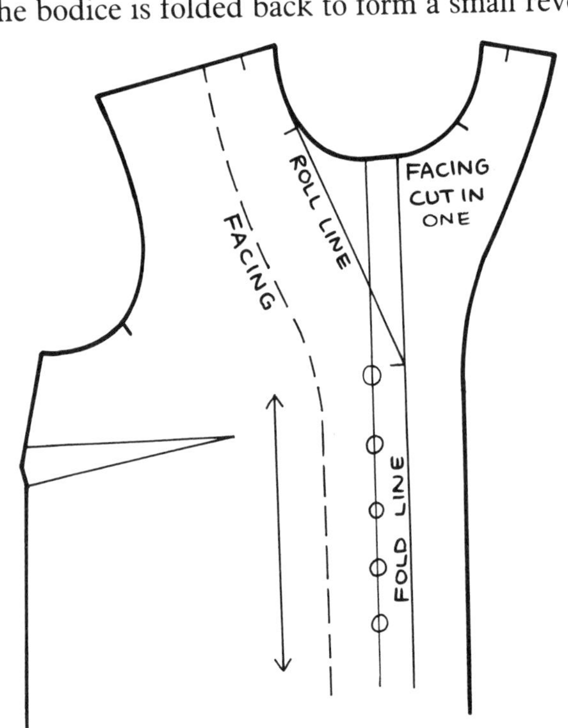

CF edge is straight; the front facing could even be cut all-in-one and the revers simply pressed back. However, more style would usually be required so the CF edge may be shaped:

1. Outline front block; draw buttons and rule the rever fold line from top button to neck point. Insert balance mark on neck edge.

2. Draw required shape of rever and trace off. Reverse the rever, match balance mark and outline it against roll line. Outlining may be done with a tracing wheel or you can cut out the shape and outline it. Copy again for final pattern.

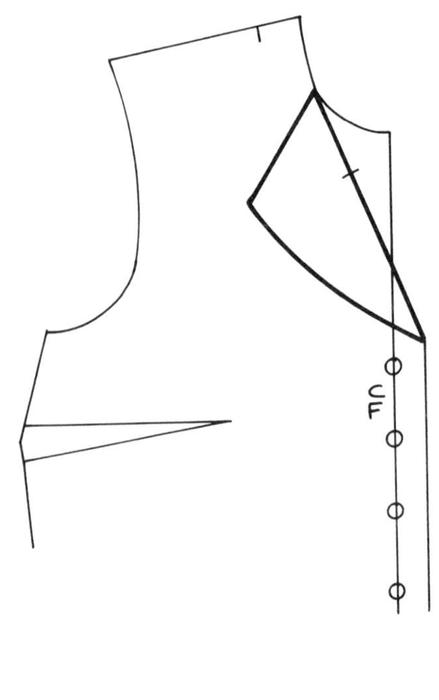

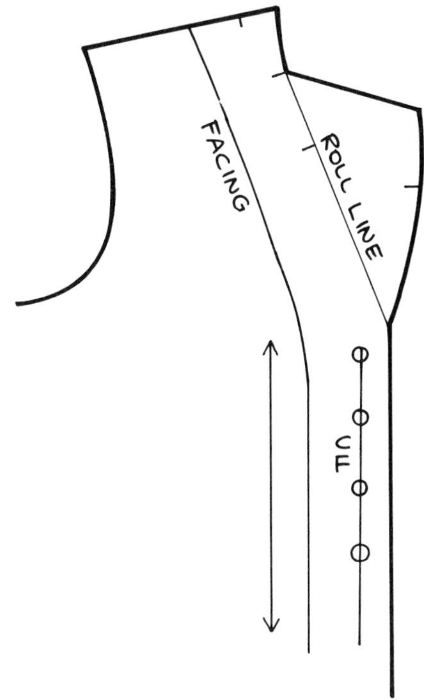

3. Mark width of front facing on shoulder seam and draw facing to hemline. Do not make facing too narrow along roll line or it may pop out in wear. Trace off top collar/facing pattern.

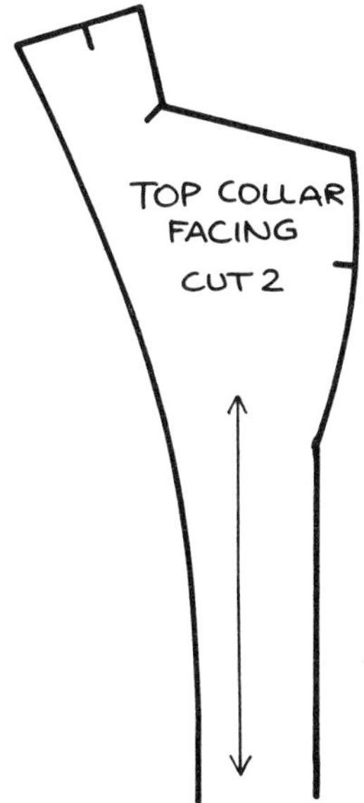

B. A long fairly flat collar based on the same method as the first collars in the book, page 74.

1. Outline back and front blocks with shoulder seams overlapping by 1cm/3/8in and add extension for wrap. Draw roll line from CF edge to neck point. Insert balance marks on back neck and roll line.

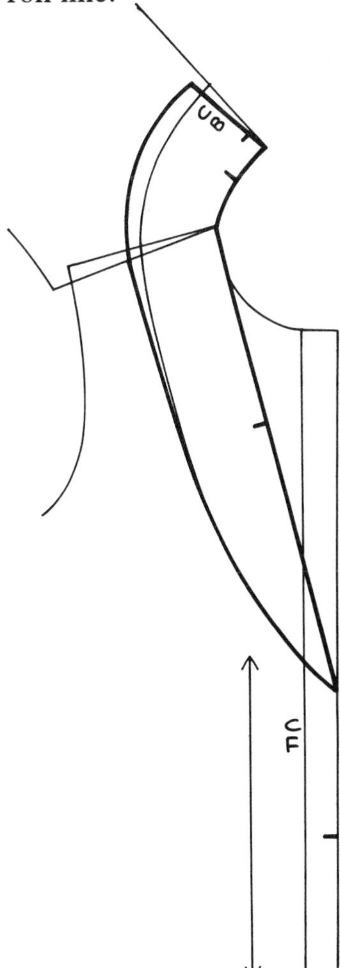

SEWING TIP

A shawl collar covers quite a distance without a seam: prevent it bubbling or the facing popping out by inserting small pieces of Wundaweb between facing and garment. Hold collar back in its folded position and insert the Wundaweb between the roll line and the edge of the facing.

Another solution is to stitch the edge of the facing to the garment, a technique often used on wrap-over dressing gowns which have no fastenings to hold the facing in position.

2. Draw outer edge of collar on front and back making it slightly wider at the back. Reduce length of outer edge by removing a wedge shape from CB.

3. Trace collar, reverse and place with roll lines matching; outline. Insert balance mark on CB seam. Outline again for final pattern.

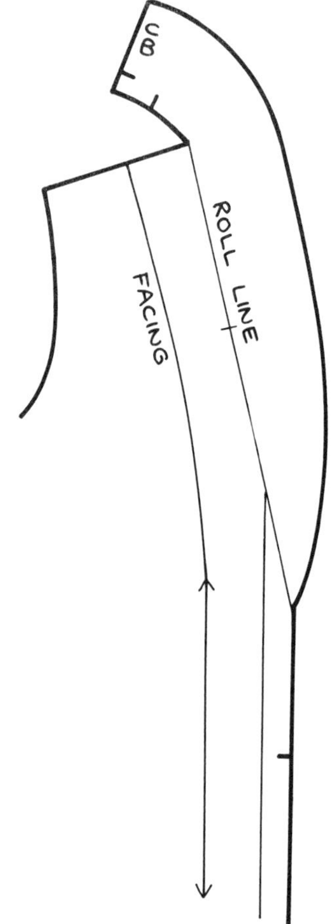

4. Measure width of front facing along shoulder seam and draw facing width to hem. Trace

top collar/facing. The above illustration shows how facing might be cut in two pieces with grain moved to 45 degrees to CB seam.

SEWING TIP

Shawl collars require only soft interfacing so that they roll softly against the neck. The use of soft interfacing, such as stretch Vilene, will allow the outer edge of the collar to give a little which also contributes to a soft line.

The next illustration shows the pattern pieces for cutting collar and facing in contrast fabric, with under collar detached from front bodice.

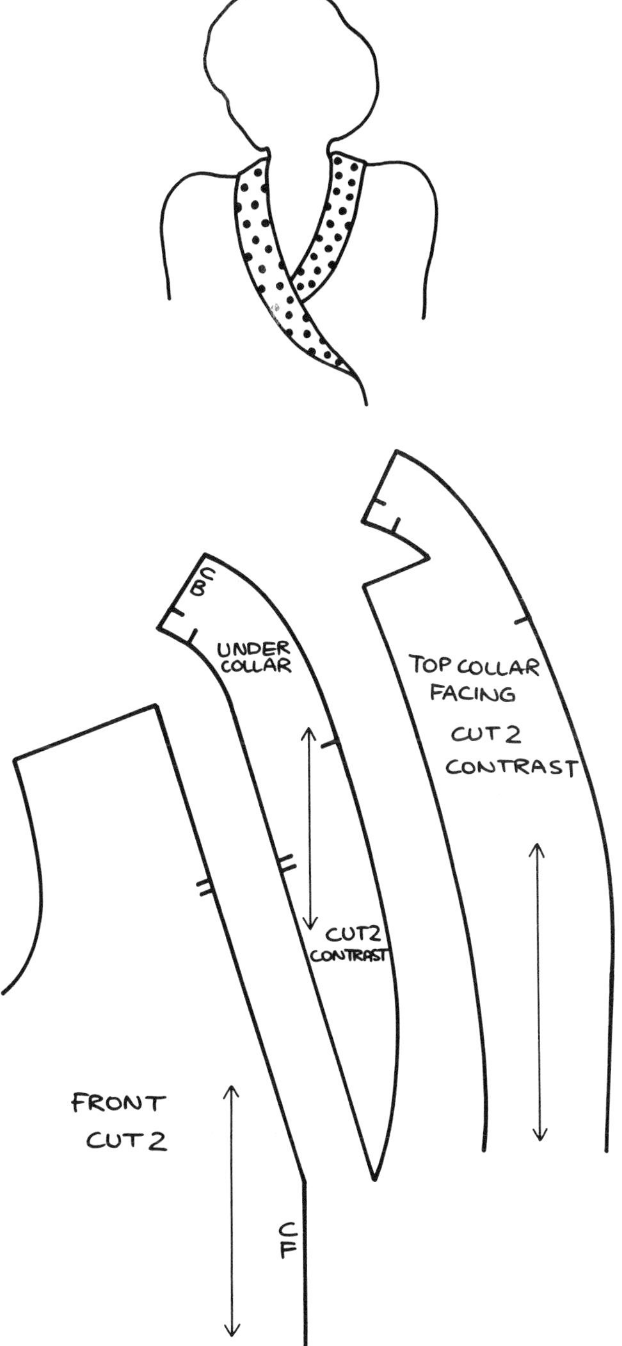

C. Close fitting collar with short revers. It is obvious that this is less casual than the previous designs and this is achieved by having a stand at the back of the neck.

1. Outline back and front blocks overlapping shoulders by 13mm/½in. Draw roll line and outer edge of collar in the same way as for previous design. Trace, reverse and add collar to roll line as before.

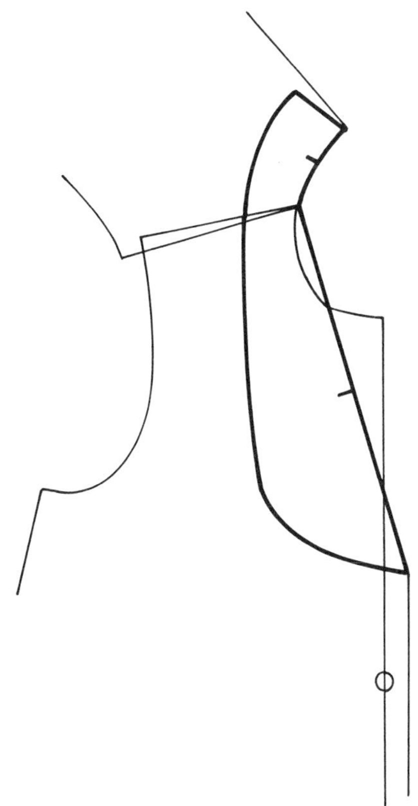

You will remember from the early flat collars that the outer edge must be shortened still further if the collar is to hug the neck. Divide back neck section into three, cut from outer edge and

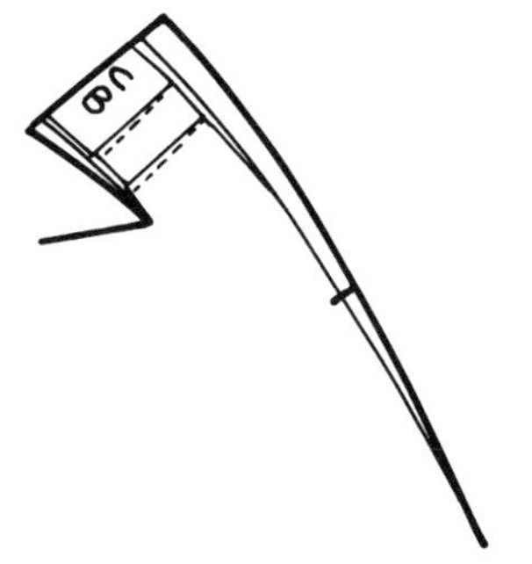

overlap. The exact amount will depend on the effect you want but try removing 3mm/⅛in from each cut. Outline new shape.

2. Outline the overlapped sections with a smooth line. The pattern needs a further adjustment because although the straighter neck edge will bring the collar closer to the neck, there will probably be insufficient depth to roll over and cover the neck seam.

Extend CB seam line by 1–2cm/⅜–¾in on both edges and re-draw outer and neck edge. Experiment to discover the amount of adjustment; it will depend on the weight of the fabric to be used.

3. Mark width of facing along shoulder seam and draw facing. Trace top collar/facing pattern and insert SG and balance marks.

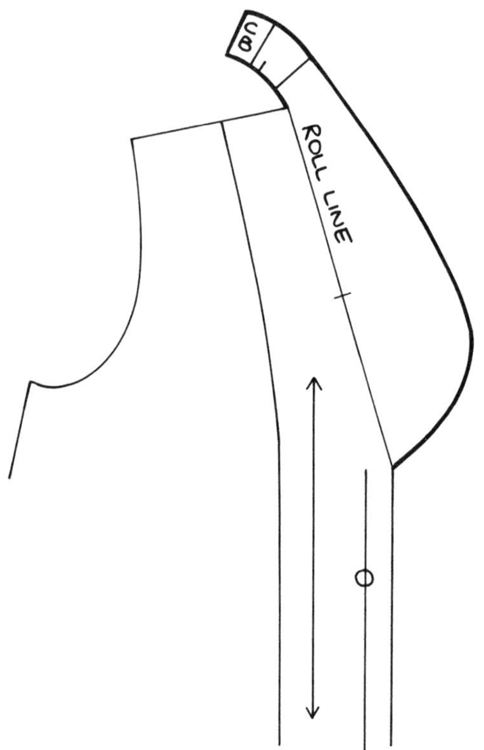

When the previous pattern finally emerged the back section bore little resemblance to the back block. You can see that the neck edge is straight and the outer edge almost so.

The next exercise shows how the initial stages shown previously can be short-circuited.

D. A shawl collar extending to garment hem.

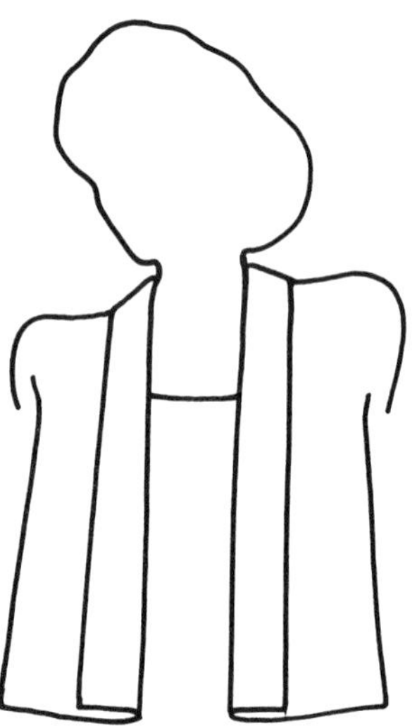

1. Outline front block only, draw new front edge inside edge of block. This is also the roll line. Draw width of collar and trace off.

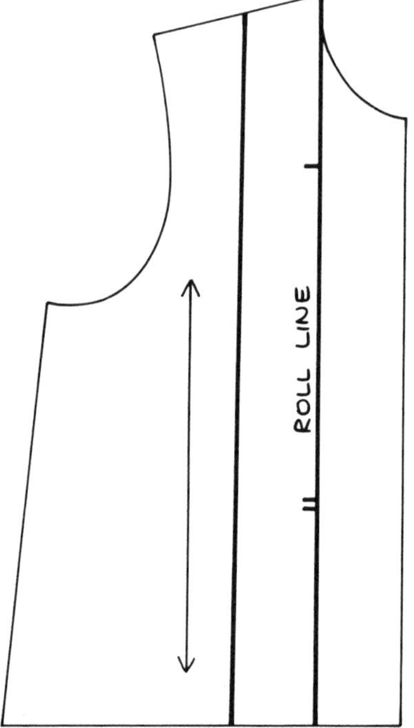

2. Reverse collar and outline against roll line. Extend roll line and outer edge above shoulder. Place back bodice block against roll line with neck points together and mark off the size of the back neck on the line. Also outline CB for a short distance. Reduce outer edge by removing a wedge shape, taking out 1cm/⅜in.

3. Measure width of facing along shoulder seam and draw facing to hem. Trace pattern and trace top collar/facing separately. Adjust hemline to make sure collar will not rise where it folds back. Fold pattern along roll line and cut along hem with paper folded.

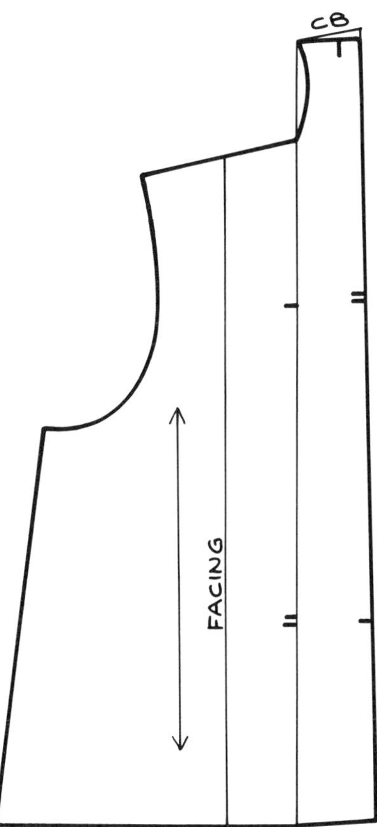

The next refinement is to add some neck stand to the bodice itself before beginning the collar draft. Decide on final width of collar allowing for ⅓ stand and ⅔ fall so that neck seam will be hidden. Extend shoulder seam and mark depth of collar stand on the line. Rule a line from that point to top button and that is the roll line, taking up a position much higher on the neck than in previous designs (see next page).

SEWING TIP

Prevent fraying at the angle of the notch by pressing a small piece of Bondaweb to WS fabric before stitching and trimming. Also use a small stitch around the angle.

E. Notched shawl collar. This is half-way between a soft dressmaker collar and a tailored collar with lapels. There is more shaping at CB and the under collar is cut separately.

1. Outline block, mark button positions and add extension for fastening, in this instance double breasted. Extend shoulder seam. Measure along this line from neck point amount of neck stand required and also mark full width of collar fall. Rule lines from button position to neck point and new neck point: this is the roll line. Extend roll line above shoulder. Using back block measure back neck width along this line. Rule CB collar at right angles.

2. Cut out leaving surplus paper around front. Fold paper along roll line. Draw outer edge of collar including notch, through point marked at shoulder.

3. At CB of collar curve the seam line in 6mm/¼in at roll line to tighten the collar against the neck. To make under collar seam, rule a line

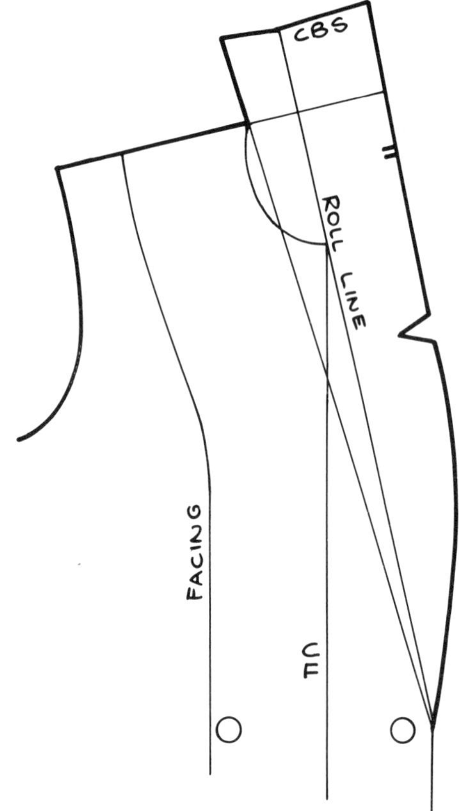

from original neck point to button position on front edge. Curve from notch to line. Trace off

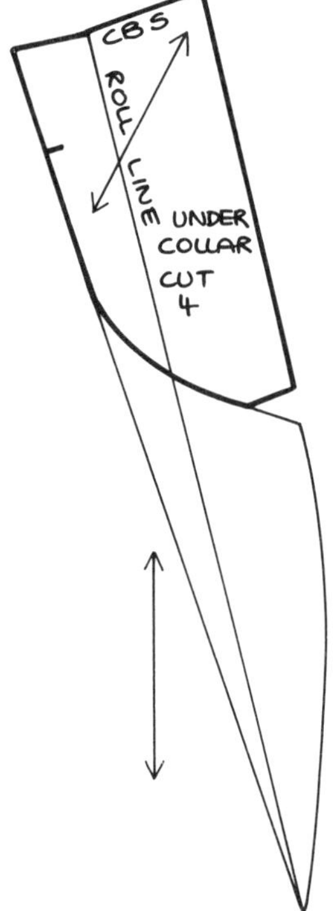

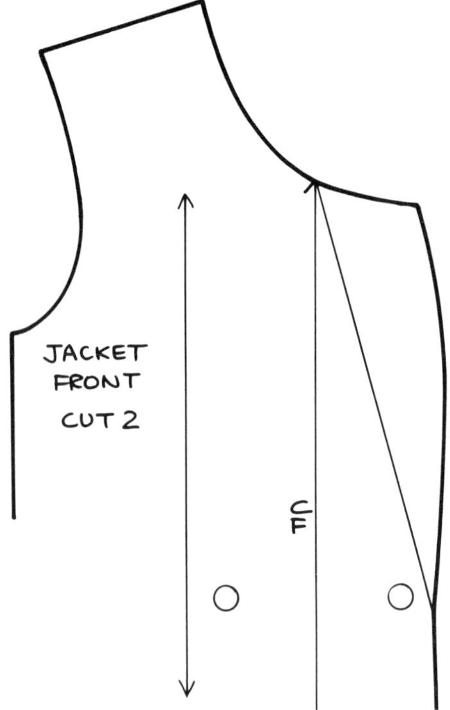

under collar. Mark balance marks, roll line and CB and mark SG at 45 degrees to outer edge. Trace remainder of front jacket and trace top collar/facing pattern in one piece.

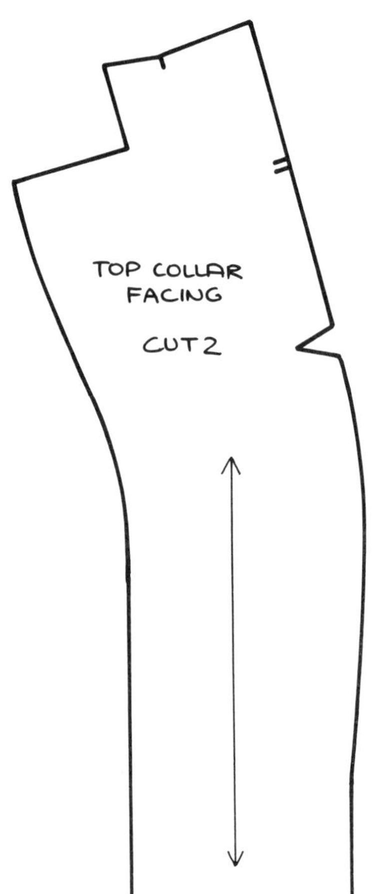

F. Tailored collar and lapels. Please see page 191, Patterns for Outerwear, Coats and Jackets.

SHIRT COLLARS

Used on other things besides shirts, this is the type of collar that has a stand almost equal in depth to the fall of the collar and the whole is firmly interfaced so that a conventional tie can be kept in place.

The stand section must hug the neck closely all round and fasten at CF while the fall section is only sufficiently far out to allow for the thickness of the tie. The simplest way to regard this collar is as a shaped stand collar as described on page 78, design (C), attached to a pointed collar similar to design (B) on page 76, collar with stand. If you look at the collar of a man's shirt you will see that this is so.

From now on the stand section will be referred to as the collar band, to avoid confusion.

A. Classic shirt collar buttoned to neck and with seam along top of collar, illustrated closed. Entire collar is interfaced with additional pieces at collar points and an extra layer or a firmer interfacing in collar band.

1. Lower front neck of block 1.5cm/⅝in.
2. Measure neck edge, adding back and front together. Draw rectangle to size, making it 2–3cm/¾–1¼in deep. Rule a line across at shoulder seam position and mark a point three-quarters of the way from CB to CF.

3. Leaving the quarter nearest CF untouched divide remainder of collar into four, cut from upper edge, leave attached at neck edge and overlap the sections. Raise the neck edge at CF by 2–2.5cm/¾–1in or until upper edge equals neck measurement plus ease.
4. Draw shirt button at CF. Extend neck edge in a straight line for 1–1.5cm/⅜–⅝in and curve from there back to upper edge. Outline for

new pattern with smooth curves. Collar band may be 6mm/¼in deeper at CB if desired. Mark CBF, cut two.
5. Draw a second rectangle for pointed section of collar equal in length to that drawn initially for collar band. Mark shoulder seam point two thirds of the way from CB to CF.

6. To shape neck edge extend CF line downwards for 13mm/½in and rule a line from there back to shoulder seam point. To add shape to collar point extend CF line at outer edge of collar upwards and horizontally. Draw the shape and size of point required connecting the outer edge with two-thirds point previously marked. Mark CBF, cut two.

B. In this version the seam along top of band is eliminated and the collar and band cut all in one.

It does not give such a close fit as the previous design but is perfectly acceptable for blouses and dresses and for jackets requiring a softer look.

Rule a vertical line, mark it CBF, and outline the pointed collar against it, re-drawing the point to the shape desired. Place collar band against CB line, sliding it towards pointed section until collars meet at CF. You can now see that it was the dart-like shape between the two collars that makes classic collars like design (A) such a good fit.

Outline collar for final pattern marking it CBF, cut two.

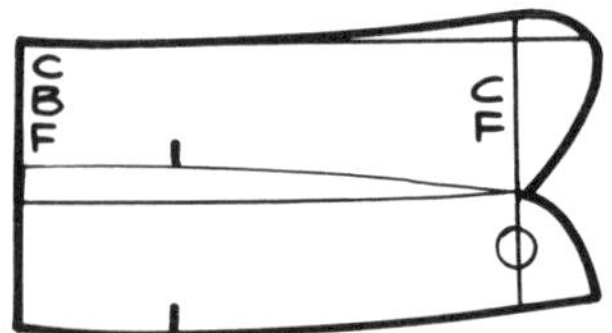

NECKLINES

Round, square or V-necks that are cut low at the front will be liable to gape whatever the type or style of the garment. After drawing the new neckline, remove 1cm/⅜in by folding out a dart from the neck edge to BP and allowing it to open in the waist. Re-draw neckline if necessary.

On the back bodice gaping is prevented by retaining the shoulder dart and transferring it to the new low neckline. Sometimes there may be a seam conveniently close so that the 1cm/⅜in can be taken out in the seam.

Sleeveless bodices

On the same principle as described above, the armhole of a sleeveless garment with low neck will be liable to gape at the front. After transferring dart to required position fold out a 1cm/⅜in dart from armhole to BP allowing it to open at waist. Large sizes may need to transfer more than 1cm/⅜in. Raise the underarm point 13mm/½in. Reduce length of shoulder seam if required. Adjust back to correspond, transferring 1cm/⅜in from armhole to waist dart.

Edge finishes for necklines

For a conventional hem finish, add whatever is appropriate when cutting out. Shaped edges require different treatments, depending on the design and the fabric.

The choice rests between a facing, on inside or outside: a band of matching or contrast fabric which is made double, or a binding, in which case no pattern is required. If the garment is to be lined, the lining can be brought to the garment edge. The decision depends on the fabric and on the effect required. In all cases the blocks should first be outlined and the edges altered to shape.

It is not absolutely necessary to make patterns for facings although space has to be allowed when laying out on the fabric. The alternative to a pattern is a line on the main pattern. A pattern piece for a binding strip is not necessary either but it will help you later if you at least have a note of the length required.

If a back shoulder or neckline dart is being used on the bodice this should be folded out before drawing the facing otherwise the facing will not lie flat.

Facings

A. A slightly lowered back neck and V-front.

1. Outline blocks with shoulder dart folded out and shoulders together.

2. Lower back neck and draw front V. Remove 6mm/¼in at CF and rule new line. Mark width of facing shaping to a curve at CF.

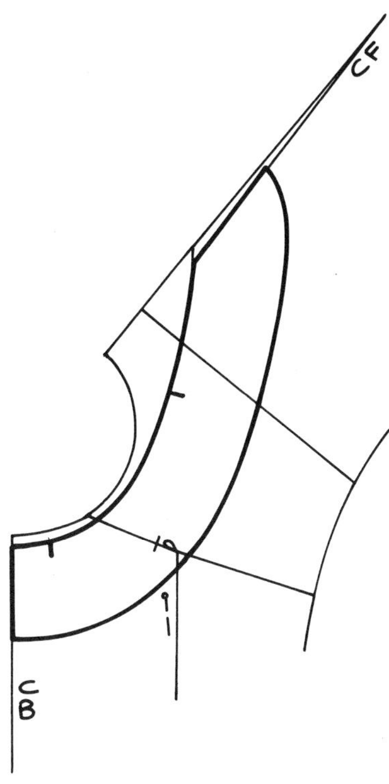

3. Insert balance mark across shoulder seam and also on neck edge of front and back. Trace

back and front facings separately, mark CFF and CBF, cut 1.

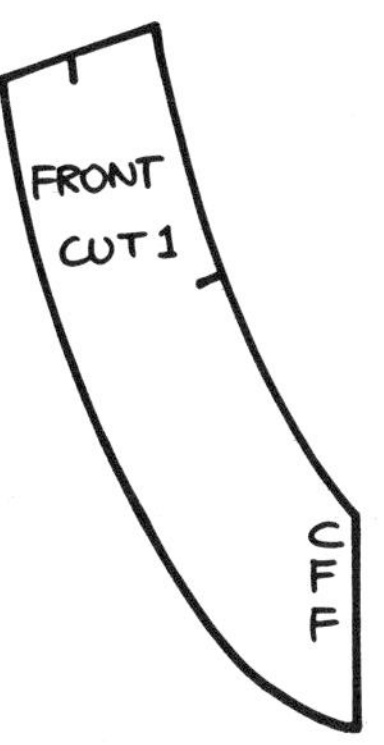

B. Scooped and scalloped neckline which could be lined to the edge with chiffon or net. In opaque fabric a separate facing could be used; the neck would also require interfacing. With an intricately shaped edge like this draw the scallops on the pattern as a stitching line to be transferred to the fabric but do not trim the paper to shape.

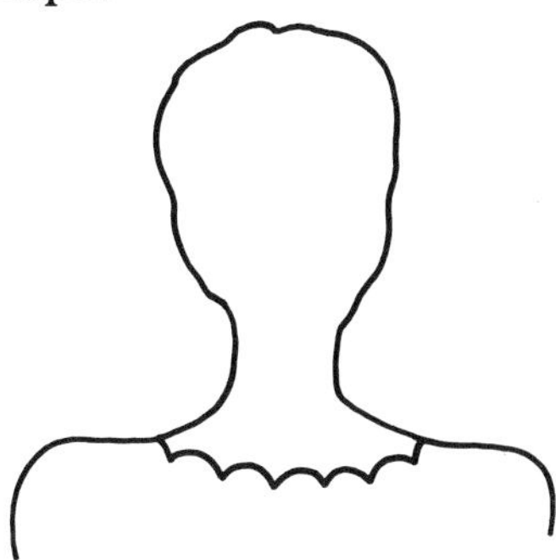

1. Outline blocks with shoulders meeting, ignoring the dart. Scoop out back neck and shoulders and raise the front neck a little if necessary to make a good shape.

2. Using spare paper work out size of scallop. To do this measure new neckline and cut a piece of paper to length. Fold it until you can draw one scallop the size you want. Cut out one only and

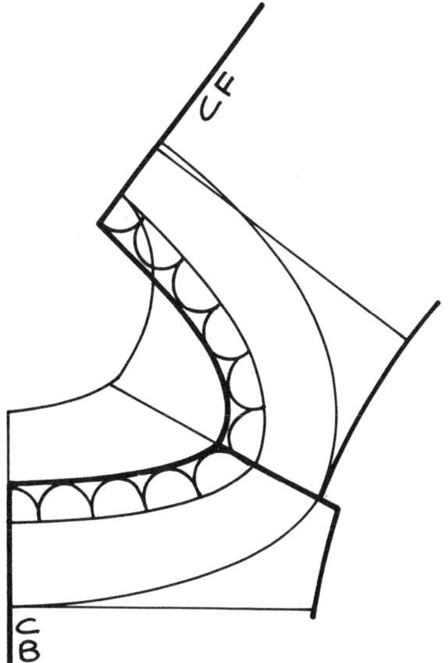

outline the shape repeatedly along the neck edge, keeping remainder of strip for reference.

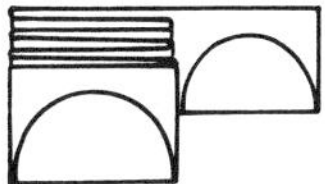

3. Mark facing edge and trace if required, otherwise mark finished pattern line to edge. Do

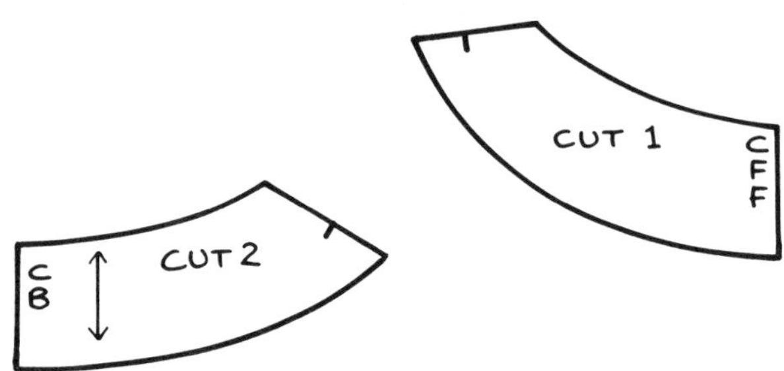

not draw the scallops on the lining or on the facing pattern. When making up mark scallops on WS fabric and stitch from that side.

Shaped bands

A. Scooped neck finished with double band of contrast fabric, retaining the back neck dart for a neat fit. Requires CB opening.

1. Outline blocks and draw new neckline. Mark depth of band. Insert balance marks on both edges and at shoulder.

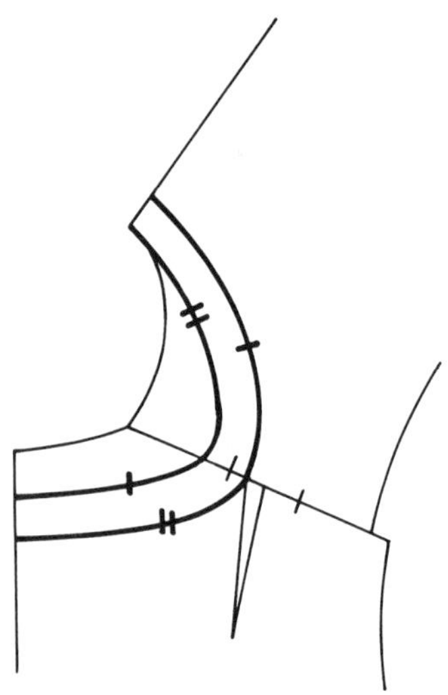

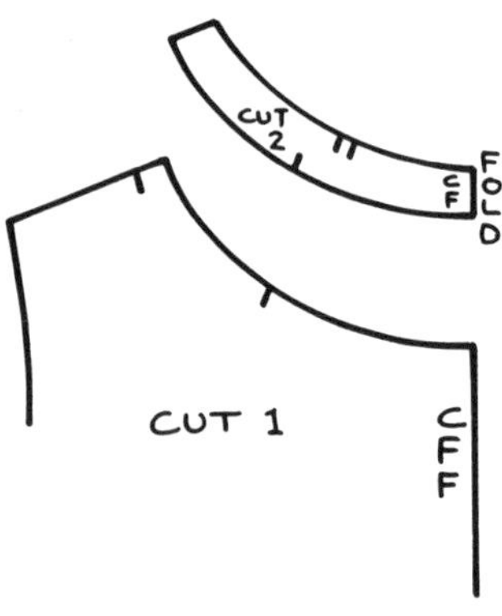

2. Trace back and front bands. Mark front band CFF cut 2 and back band cut 4.

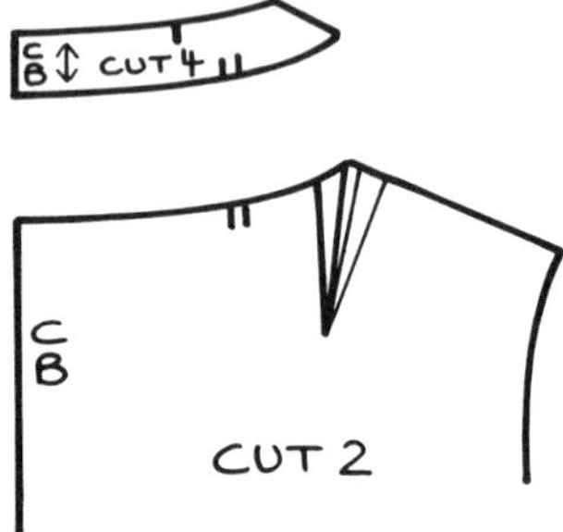

3. On back bodice transfer dart so that it runs into the neckline instead of the shoulder seam.

B. The deep V-neck has a wide double band of fabric, so wide that the seam runs from mid-shoulder over the bust. This is an opportunity to conceal the bust dart and the back shoulder dart in the seam.

1. Outline back of block, place front against it and outline neck and CF. Draw neckline. Draw depth of band on back neck, curve neck edge of garment to meet band leaving a gap equal

to the width of the dart. Insert balance mark where curves meet.

2. On front bodice draw width of band. Transfer half the shoulder dart to the waist leaving half in the shoulder. Mark width of dart at shoulder and curve a line to meet band at CF. Insert balance marks.

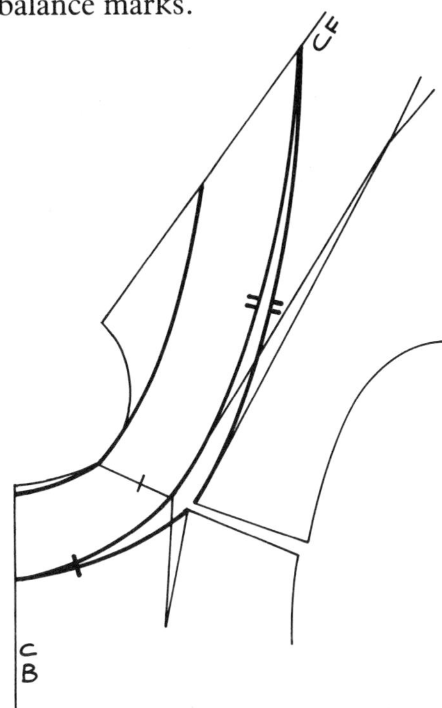

3. Trace back and front bodice, mark CFF, CBF, cut 1. Trace back and front bands, mark cut 2, CFF and CBF. SG runs along centre fold on each piece.

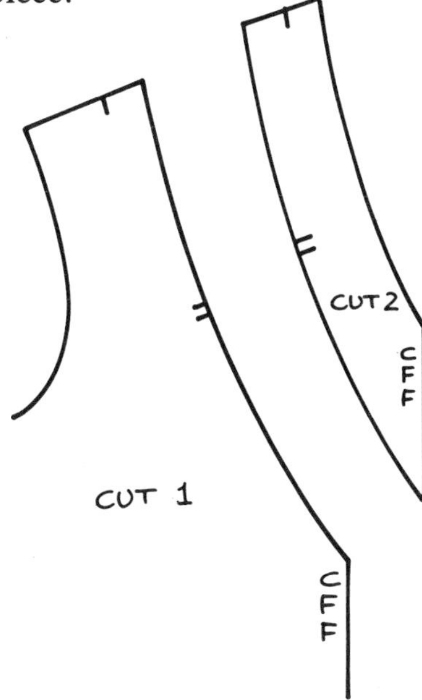

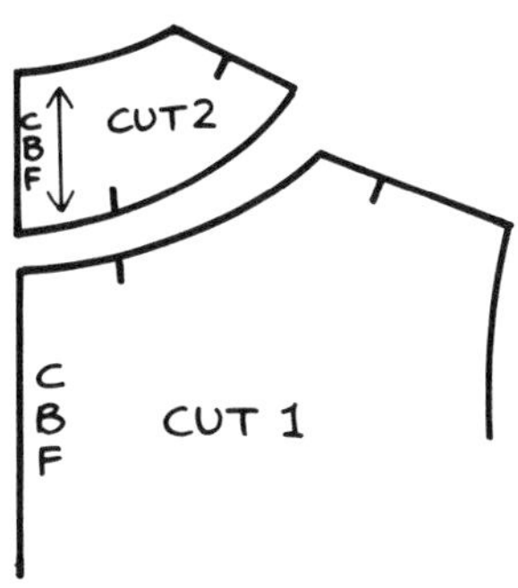

C. This jacket hangs straight from the shoulder so part of the bust dart should be transferred into the armhole and the remainder to the waist. The

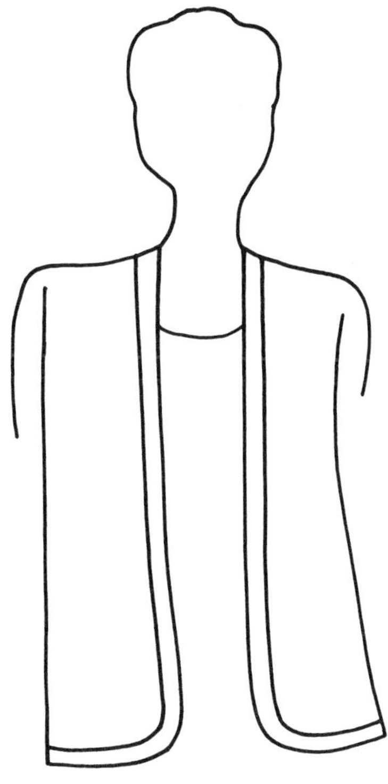

band is shown cut in one from CB to side seam but if you use a fabric with nap or a design that would be distorted, seams will have to be made in the band to correspond with the jacket shoulder seams.

1. Outline back block to hip. Place front block beside it with one third of the shoulder dart transferred to armhole and the rest to the waist dart. Outline to hip level. Lower back armhole to correspond with front.

2. Adjust length at hip if required. Draw jacket neckline removing a little from CF edge but adding to shoulder and back neckline to make a straighter edge and curve hem edges. Draw required width of band. Insert balance marks. Trace band in one from CB to side seam. Mark CB, cut 4. Place SG parallel with CF jacket.

3. Trace back and front jacket patterns. On back transfer dart to neckline to help keep jacket neatly on the shoulders.

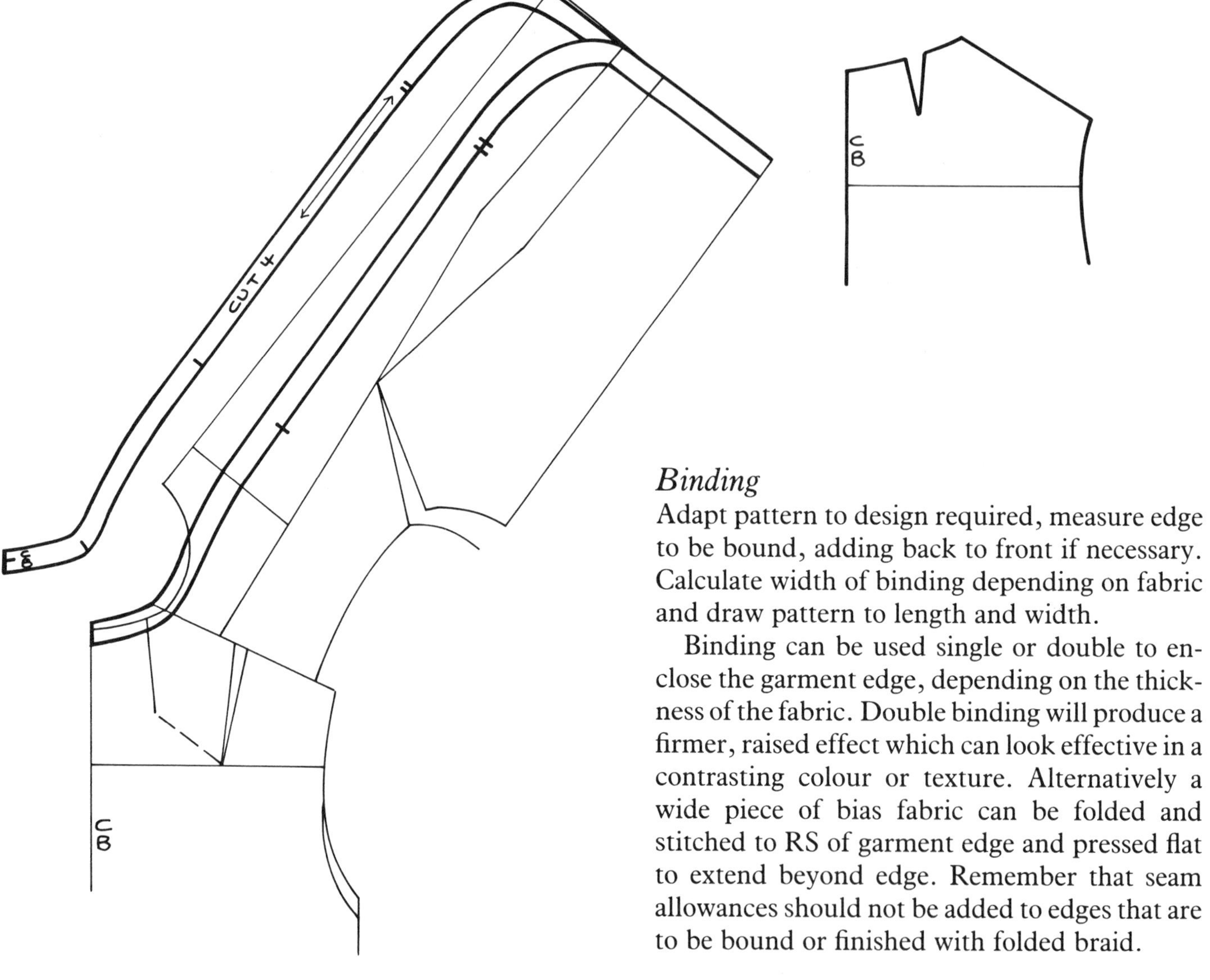

Binding

Adapt pattern to design required, measure edge to be bound, adding back to front if necessary. Calculate width of binding depending on fabric and draw pattern to length and width.

Binding can be used single or double to enclose the garment edge, depending on the thickness of the fabric. Double binding will produce a firmer, raised effect which can look effective in a contrasting colour or texture. Alternatively a wide piece of bias fabric can be folded and stitched to RS of garment edge and pressed flat to extend beyond edge. Remember that seam allowances should not be added to edges that are to be bound or finished with folded braid.

YOKES

In addition to being a style feature a yoke provides an opportunity for adding fullness, for altering the direction of the grain and also for the bust dart to be concealed in the yoke seam.

The yoke may be at the front and at the back in which case the shoulder seam can be eliminated. Or it may be at the front only or even at the back only. Take care when positioning the yoke seam: the lower it is the more fullness can be used. Fullness on a high yoke makes an unattractive profile. A back yoke that is too high gives a round-shouldered look.

A. Front yoke with gathers.

1. Add button extension, adjust neckline if appropriate, and cut out block. Close bust dart and draw yoke seam; add balance marks. Cut off

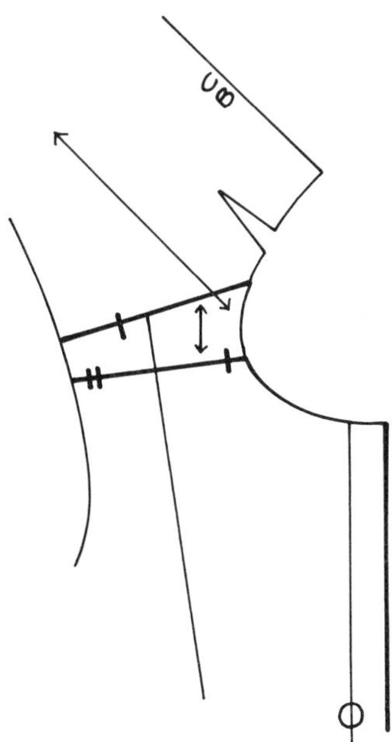

yoke and mark 'cut 2' or 'cut 4' if it is to be lined. Alternatively a shallow yoke may be cut in one with the back bodice in which case SG will be marked parallel with CB. Check the appearance of the yoke before you do this in case the angle of the grain looks wrong for your fabric.

2. On lower part of bodice open bust dart in shoulder position and outline. Copy balance

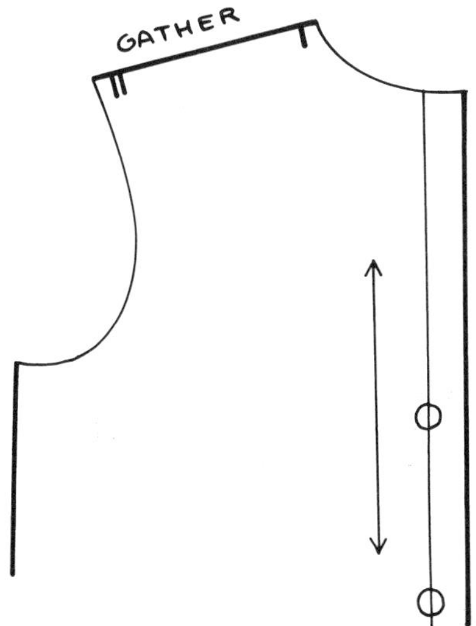

marks on to yoke edge. On an average size this will provide 4cm/1⅝in of gathers. This is sufficient provided the yoke is high and the remainder of the garment is loose fitting.

3. Facing. If there is a shoulder seam trace a facing to extend to the shoulder, otherwise take

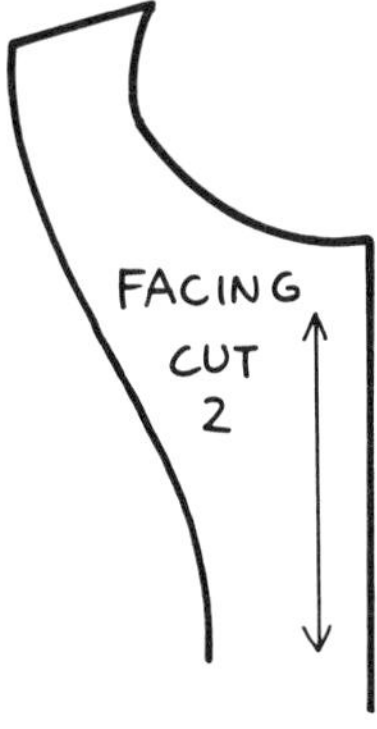

it only as far as the yoke seam but keep it quite narrow so that it will leave the bust gathers free.

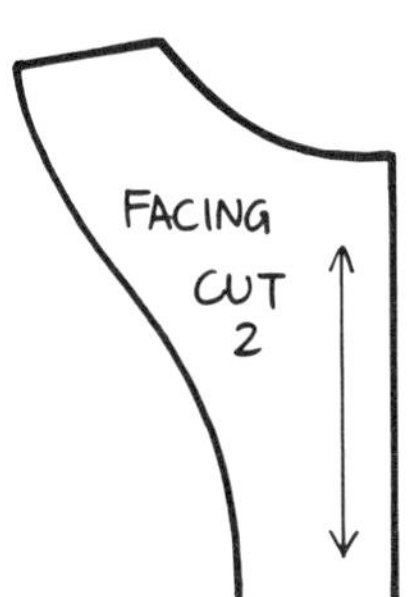

B. Front and back yoke; additional gathers. Design shows more fullness than could come

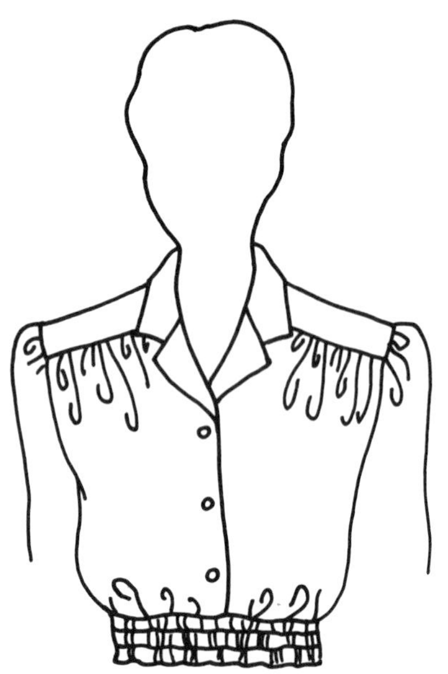

from the bust dart and combined with the waist fullness it indicates extra width right through the pattern.

1. Add button extension to block outline, close bust dart and draw yoke. Place back and front together at shoulder, close back dart, draw back yoke and outline complete, or saddle, yoke.

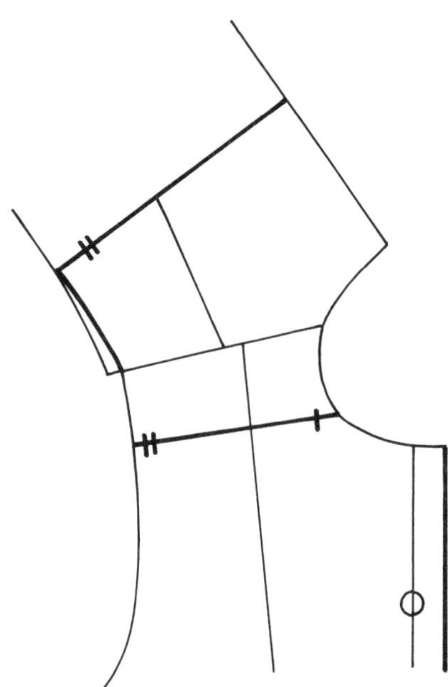

2. Trace yoke, insert balance marks, CBF and cut 2. Cut out, trimming off the small overhang at back shoulder.

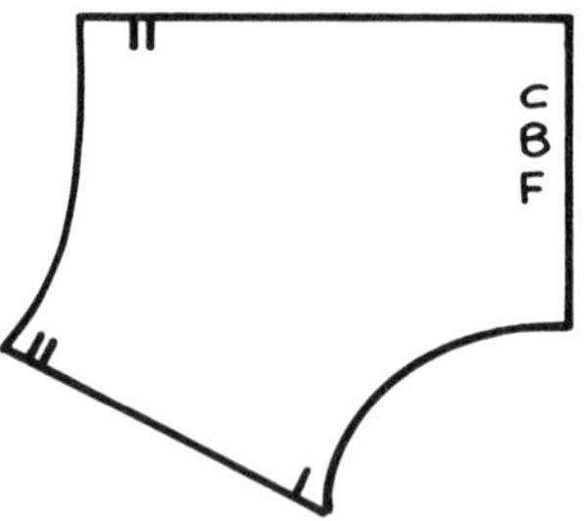

3. On lower part of bodice front open bust dart and cut from BP to hem. On the back cut through waist dart to yoke edge. Spread front and back and insert extra paper until required fullness is reached. Remembering that you already have the width of the bust dart in the front you may wish to insert more in the back to make it a corresponding width. Shorten to length. Complete the yoke edges, curving the front and transfer SG and balance marks.

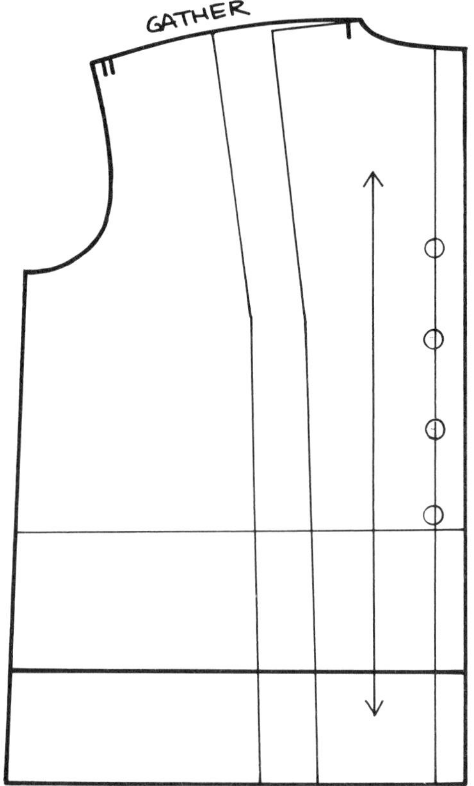

C. Yoke back and front without gathers. High yoke with strap fastening.

1. Copy front block with bust dart temporarily in the armhole. Cut off front band, mark and detach yoke and make pattern as for design A.

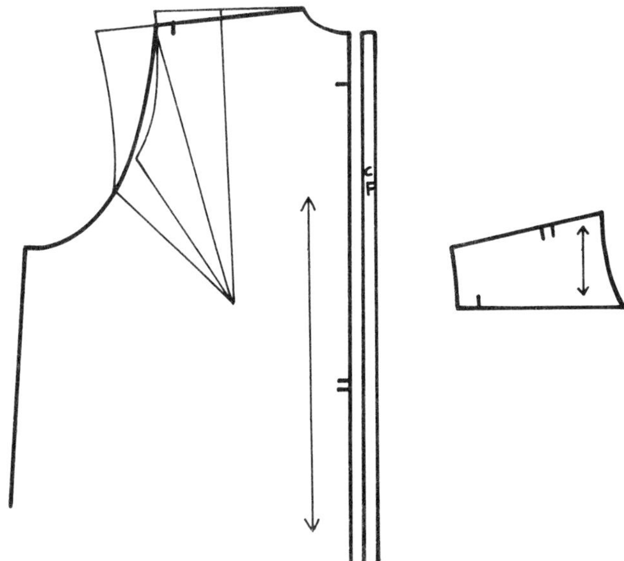

2. On lower part of bodice close armhole dart keeping BP in same position (this can be done with the point of a pin or compass), allowing the bodice to swing and the yoke edge to dip at the armhole. Outline new yoke edge slope. Copy pattern, add SG and balance marks.

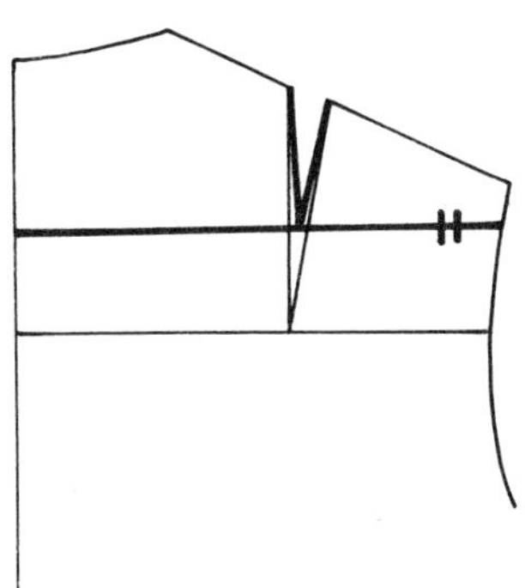

3. Back dart can be transferred to yoke seam in the same way. On a copy of the block draw yoke seam. Insert balance marks. Re-draw dart to that level. Cut along seam, close dart and outline yoke. Trace lower part of bodice. Re-draw shoulder seam straight and reduce the acute angle on the yoke by adding a little to the edge and removing the same amount from the lower bodice so that both edges are gently curved.

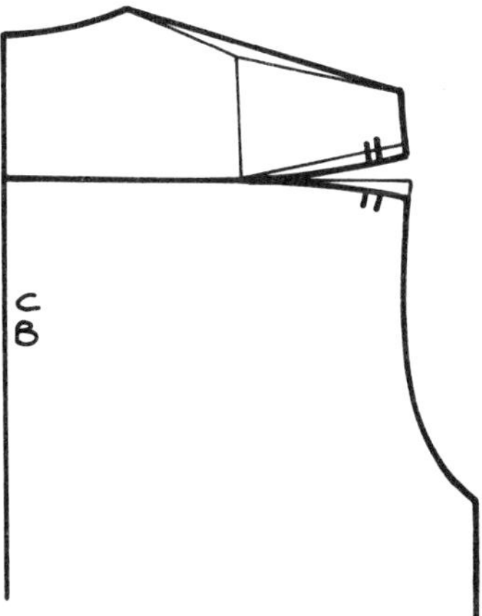

SEWING TIP

Illustration B shows the use of wide web elastic stitched in the hemline. Measure the elastic round the body without stretching, cut off and measure the piece. The elastic will stretch to one and a half times its length. Divide that figure by four and you have the maximum width of the pattern piece. If this is insufficient make a separate hem band twice the length of the elastic and thread the elastic through.

D. Deep yoke and flared skirt

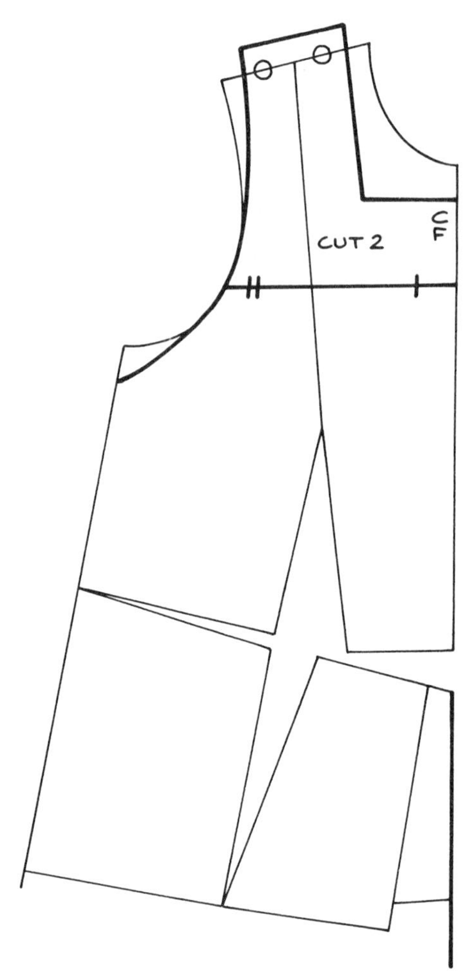

1. Outline block with dart at waist. Draw new neckline and armhole. Draw yoke and trace, adding button extension.

> ### SEWING TIP
>
> Yokes often require to be interfaced especially when supporting a full-length garment. Press a suitable weight of iron-on Vilene to WS yoke, with an additional strip along fastening edge.

2. On lower section pivot the pattern on BP as for previous design, closing the bust dart at the waist. You will know when you have moved it far enough as the CF edge below the waist will once more be vertical. Draw new yoke edge

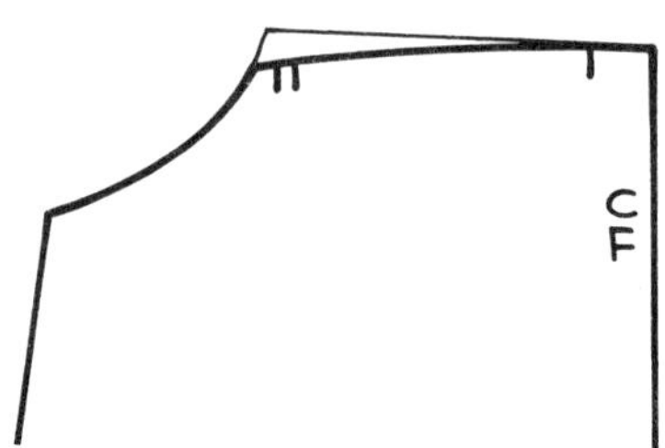

slightly curved but keeping it the same length as it was originally.

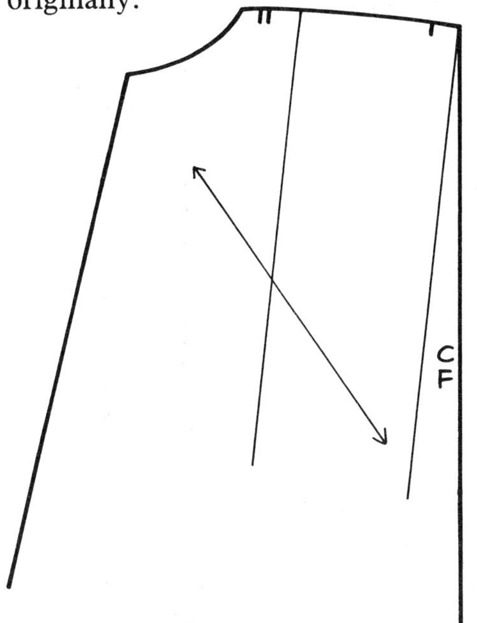

You can see that additional shape was added to the side seam when the dart was put in the waistline and by manipulating the pattern in this way the width has been retained. To convert the lower section to a flared skirt and CF seam on the bias, fold pattern in half matching CF to armhole, and add the same amount of flare to CF edge. Mark SG at 45 degrees to original CF line.

E. Shaped waist yoke. Shaped, fitted midriff with gathers under the bust; additional fullness is needed or it will look a tight fit.

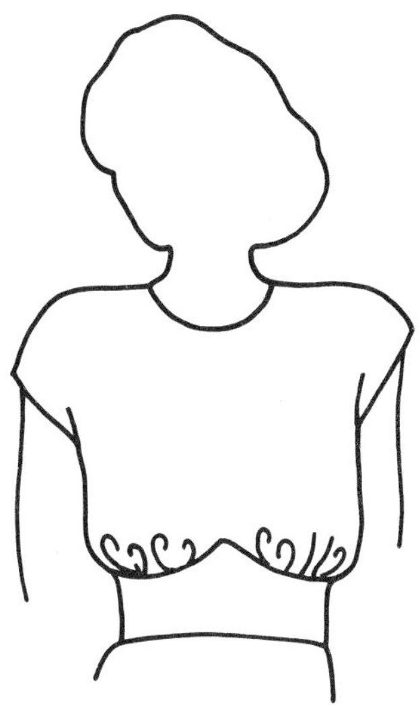

1. Outline front block to waist level, draw seam under bust using outer BP circle as guide. Lower the neckline. Cut out, cut off lower

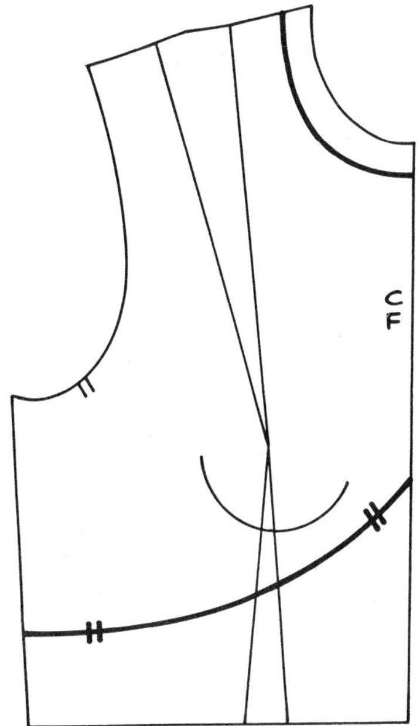

section, close waist dart and outline. Re-curve upper and lower edges smoothly and tighten the waist by taking 1cm/⅜in off the side seam.

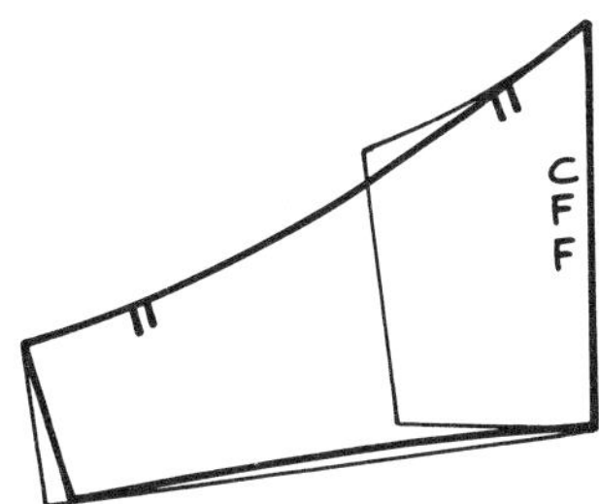

2. On upper section close shoulder dart and transfer so that it joins top part of waist dart. Cut from BP to armhole and open up the under bust

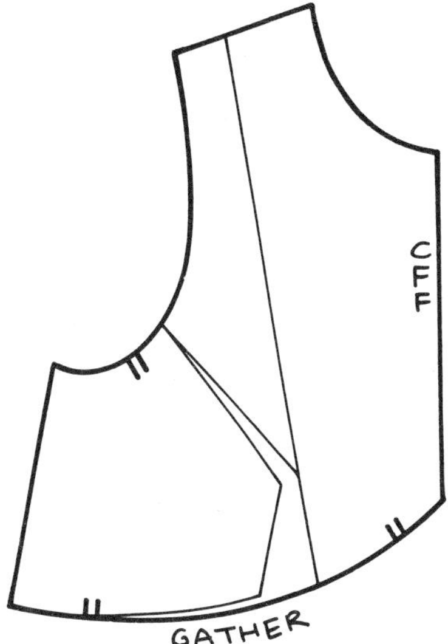

seam to add an extra 2cm/¾in. Re-curve seam line and check that armhole edge is smooth.

F. Centre panel and side yokes. Shaped seams from side of neck, curved under the bust and into the side seam. Gathers cover a small area directly under bust.

1. Outline front block to waist level; draw panel seam using outer BP circle as guide, insert two sets of balance marks on seam. Trace. Cut off CF section, close waist dart and outline new shape. Re-curve edges where dart was removed.

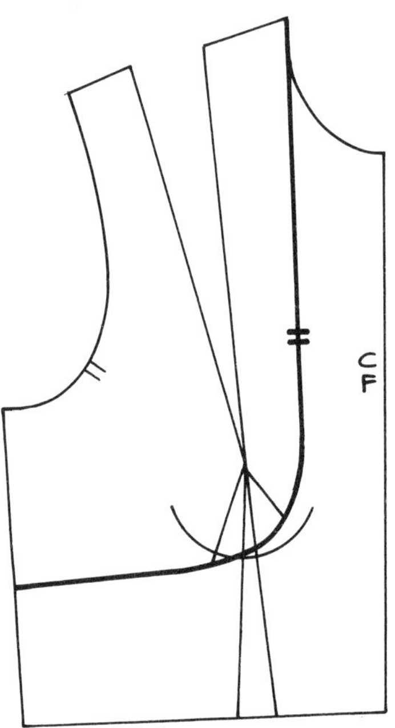

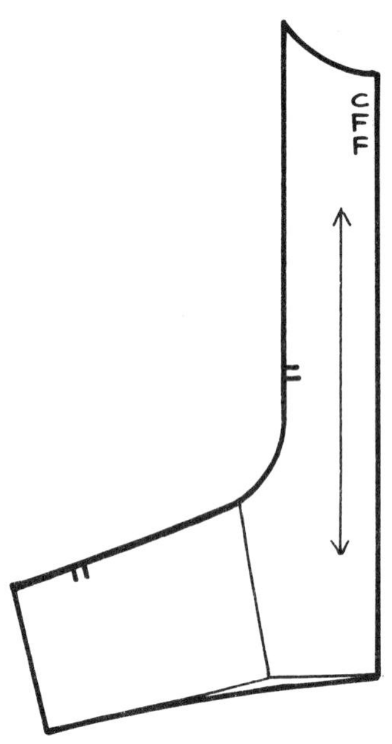

2. On side section draw a transfer line from BP on each side of waist dart and cut. Close shoulder dart and position waist sections to divide the fullness. The section of waist dart will be included in the gathers but as the seam is so close to the bust it will look a tight fit unless additional fullness is added. Trace the side section, cutting from armhole through BP to seam and open up at the seam edge to add an extra 2cm/¾in. Re-draw smooth curves at armhole

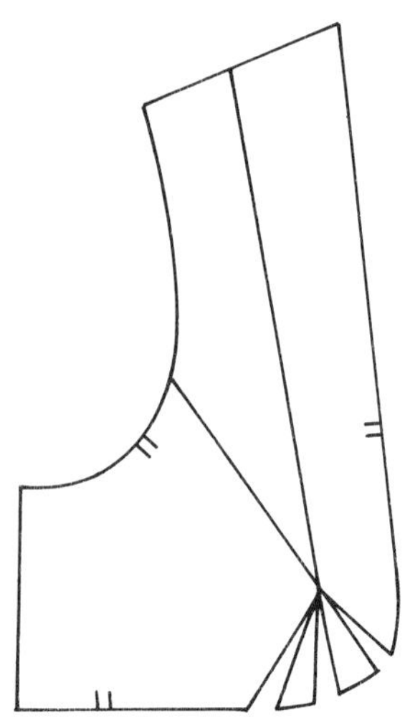

and under bust. Mark SG parallel with original position on block.

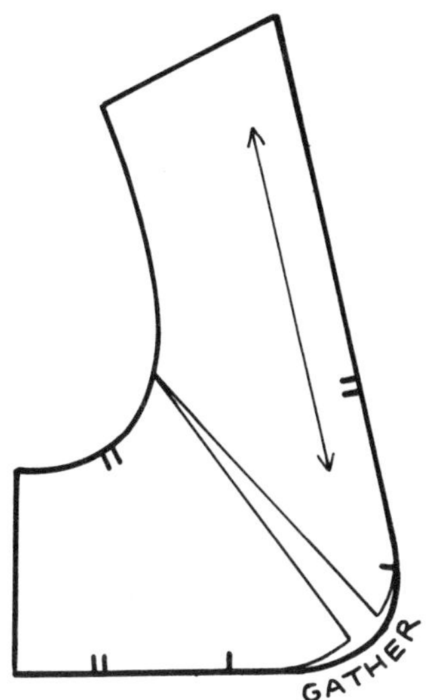

G. Yoke with pleats. Inverted pleats extend from yoke to hip at the front; the back could have a matching yoke and also pleats if you wish.

1. Draft stand collar as described on page 78.
2. Draw yoke line on back and cut off. Transfer shoulder dart to yoke and outline, straightening shoulder seam and also reducing the angle on lower edge of yoke.

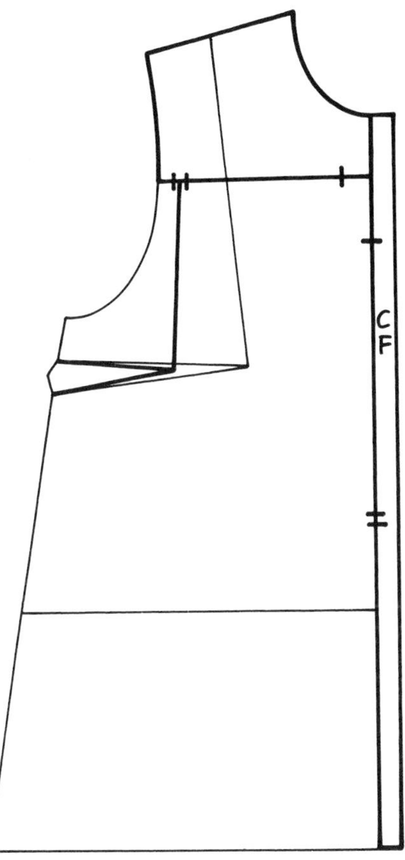

3. Outline front block with bust dart at underarm. Detach front band. Draw yoke and trace off. Trace main part of bodice and transfer bust dart to vertical position as shown, keeping it clear of where you plan to put the pleats.
4. Draw pleat line and cut and spread on a horizontal line to insert sufficient for pleat. The

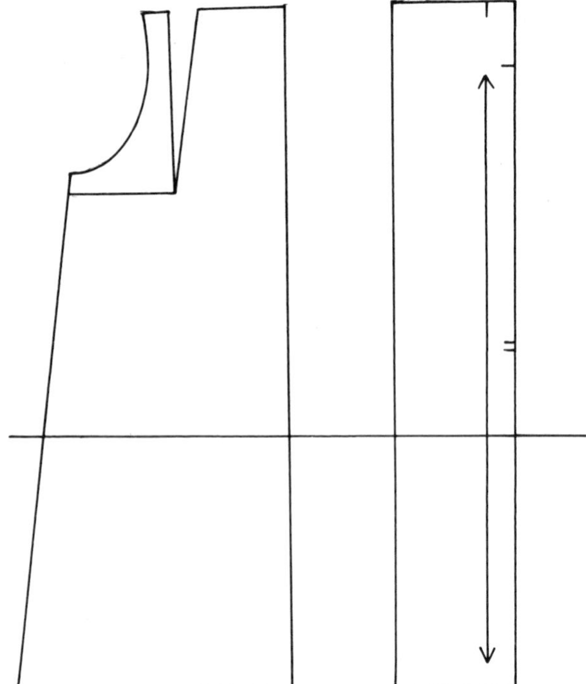

dart can be eased or gathered on to the yoke if fabric is suitable. If you prefer a plain front transfer the dart to the pleat, placing half on each side and drawing a sloping pleat fold line. Remember the grain will run parallel with CF so this last alternative might be unsuitable for check or striped fabric.

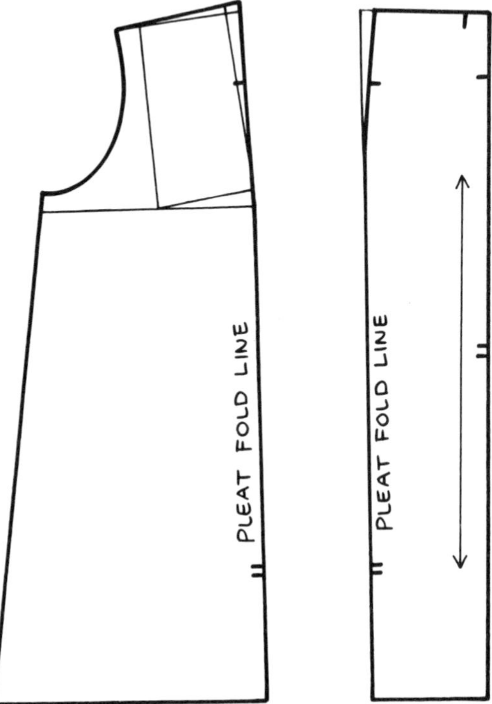

Compensate for the extra length in the pleat when transferring the dart by removing a wedge the same size from yoke edge. Mark pleat fold lines.

H. Asymmetrical yoke. Fullness on one side only. Make collar as for deep stand (page 78).

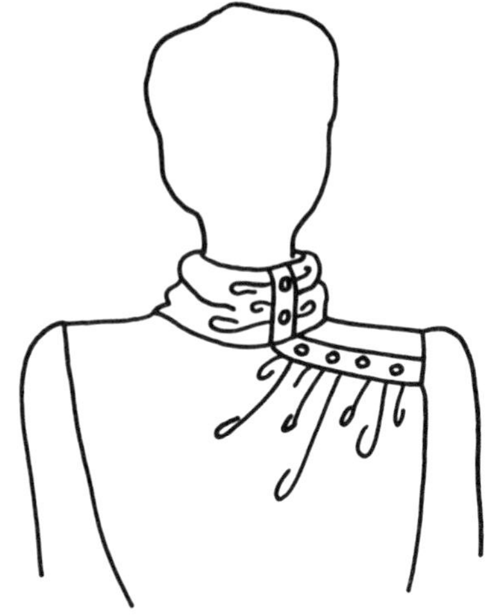

1. Fold a piece of drafting paper and outline front block against the fold with dart in armhole.
2. Mark yoke, insert balance marks and detach. Mark SG parallel with CF.

3. Draw band pattern, measuring yoke edge and adding twice the depth you want the collar drawn to. Make the band 6cm/2⅜in wide to take Fold-a-Band.

NECK	BAND	CUT 2
	FOLD O O	O O O O

COLLAR – YOKE EDGE

SEWING TIPS

The band opening could be fastened with Velcro Spot-Ons with buttons sewn on the outside.

Use soft Fold-a-Band to interface strip.

4. Rule four lines from yoke to hem and cut without detaching at hem. Open sections and insert sufficient to make four folds at the yoke edge. Outline for final pattern curving yoke edge and hem. Mark SG following original CF line.

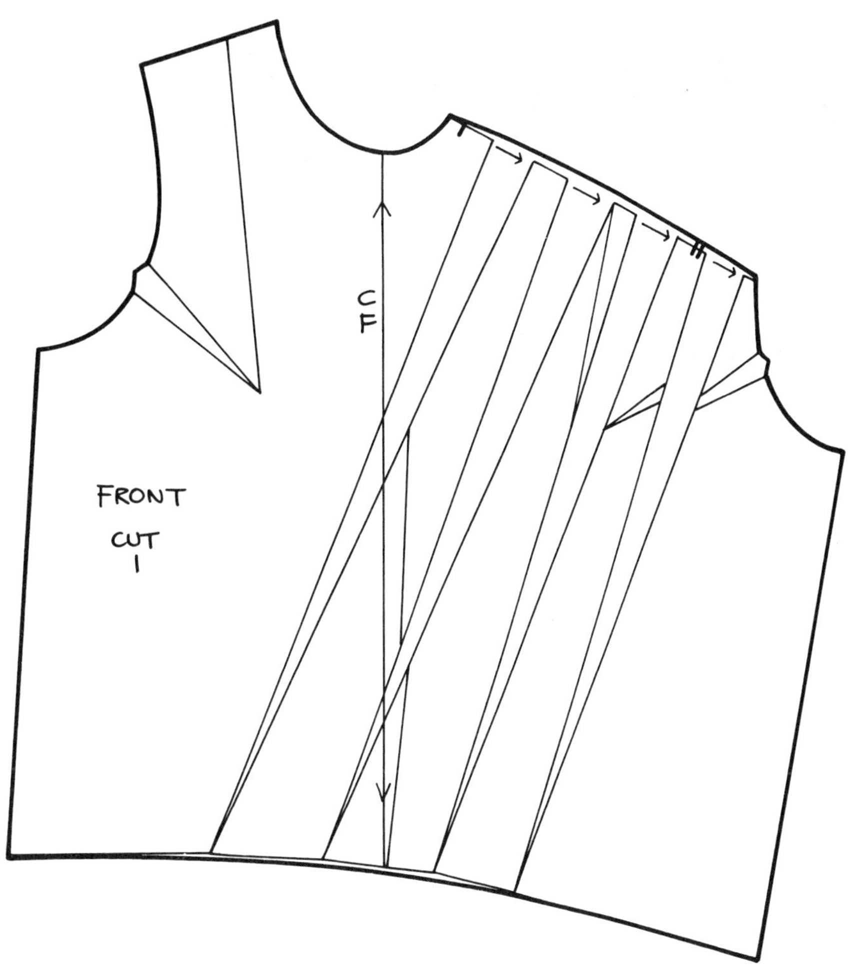

DESIGNS USING SEAMS AND DRAPING

The use of seams allows greater freedom in designing. Interest can be added, slimming lines emphasized and flare can be inserted without throwing out the grain of the main pieces. In addition, seams allow more shape and a closer fit, and where jersey, knit and other stretch fabrics are concerned in which darts should be eliminated, seams can be used to avoid a loose, bulky look.

Seams can be shaped to include existing darts or they can be used in conjunction with darts, depending on the design.

PRINCESS SEAMS

These run from mid-shoulder to hem passing through the bust point; back and front are usually the same style. Princess seaming is an excellent aid to fitting for large or problem figures. It would be worth making a permanent Princess block in cardboard if it is a style that suits you or which you find useful.

Converting the basic bodice block

(see opposite)

On the back rule a straight line from shoulder along left side of dart to top of waist dart and on to the waist (one of the bodice construction lines). This is the seam line for a centre panel, running from waist to hip line along dart. The other side of this seam is angled, so when tracing it for use soften the corners. Also mark with balance marks across the seam.

On the front block the panel lines already exist, running along each side of all the darts from shoulder, through BP and waist, to hem. Again all corners should be softened when tracing the panels. Mark SG lines parallel with CF and CB although they may be moved later.

To turn these bodice blocks into dress length or ankle length basic outlines simply extend the dart lines at the same angle to the length required. Each panel must be traced separately for use. Slightly curve the hems. To balance the flare introduced in the panels add the same amount at the side seam, ruling the line straight to meet the original seam line at hip level.

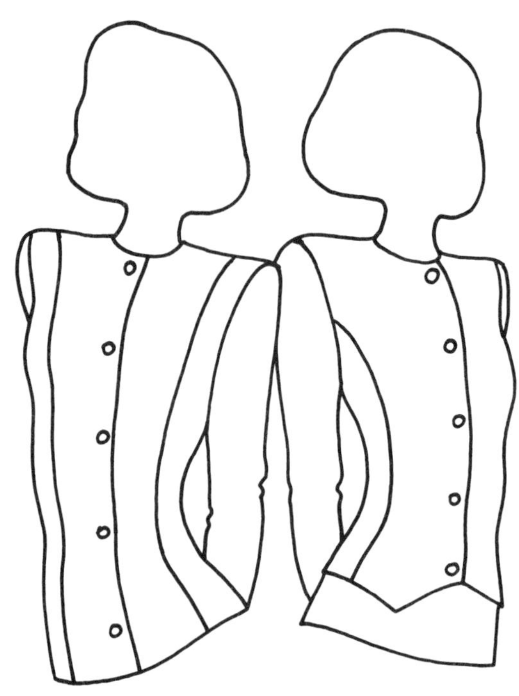

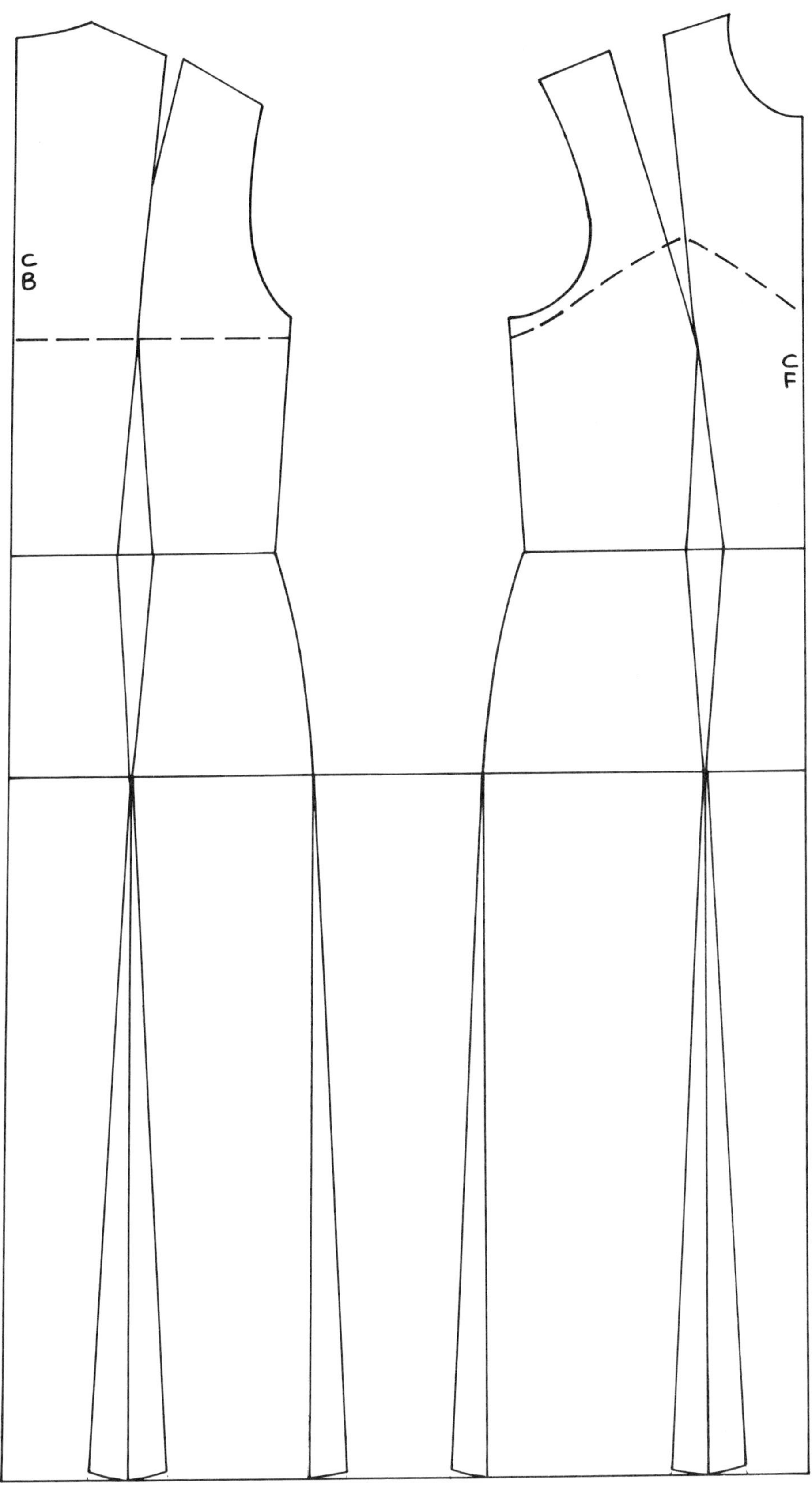
CB
CF

Princess designs

A. Bias-cut petticoat. Follow the instructions on page 104 including lengthening and adding flare to Princess seams and side seam. Draw upper edge of petticoat across the back level with top of waist dart and at the same level at side seam on the front. Shape upper edge of front (see dotted line on block on previous page). Trace off each panel separately including balance marks at bust and hip line. Draw SG at 45 degrees to original grain lines.

For strap add measurements from front and back together from upper edge of petticoat to shoulder. For length of bias strip to finish upper edge measure pattern.

B. Button-through sundress. Use bodice block converted for lingerie for a closer fit (see page 188); insert Princess seams. Extend to hip length and from there to full length required. Extend Princess seams from hip adding 8cm/3⅛in at hem. Extend side seams by the same amount. Draw upper edge of sundress at underarm, curving the front down to required level at CF (see opposite). Reduce width of dart by 1cm/⅜in. Check length of seam edges from BP to upper edge. At CF opening draw front strap and trace onto folded paper for final pattern. Draw strap. Trace off each panel separately and include balance marks and SG on all pieces.

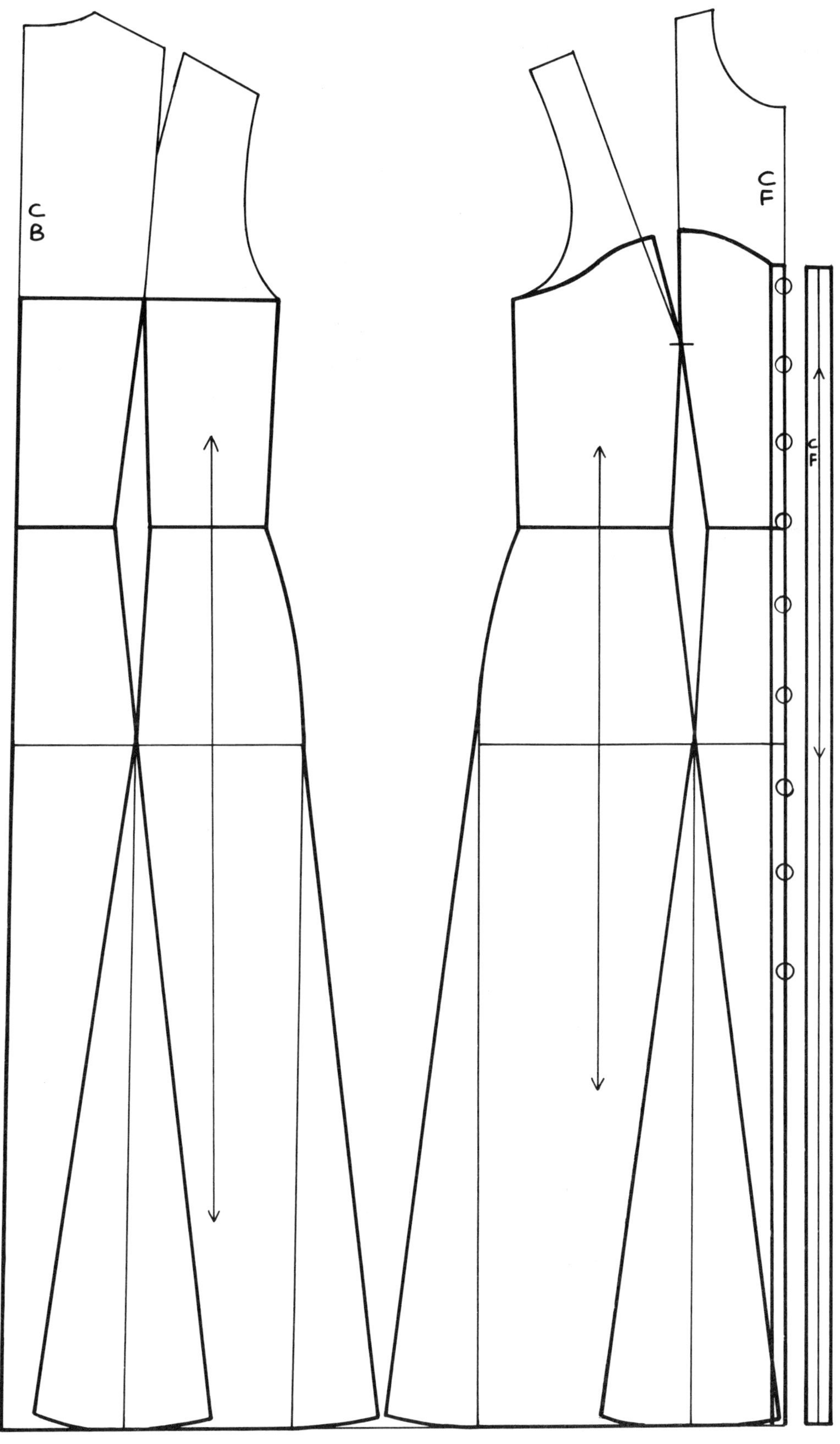
CB
CF
CF

C. Strapless bodice. Use Lingerie block (see page 188). Draw upper edge and panel seams and trace each section separately to waist level. When making up tighten upper edge of bodice at side seams if necessary.

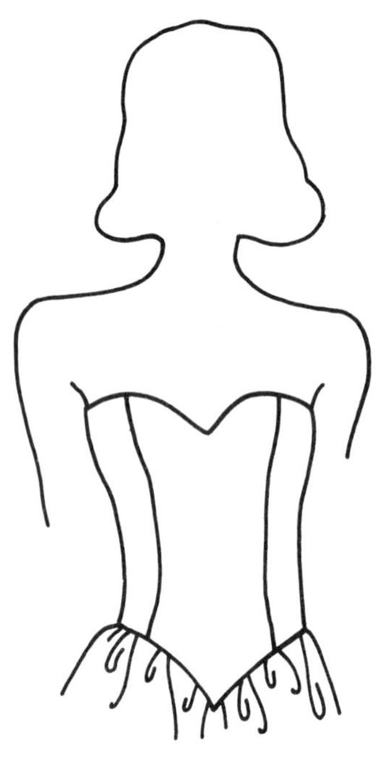

PANEL SEAMS

These seams usually run from the armhole, approximately at balance mark level, curving round to run into the waist dart. The shoulder and bust darts are transferred into the seam and below that the seam runs along each side of the waist dart. These seams are useful for people who find that armholes often gape.

Panel seams are a favourite choice for tailored jackets and fitted coats, as a smooth fit can be achieved. Also, a one-piece underarm panel can be made eliminating the side seam.

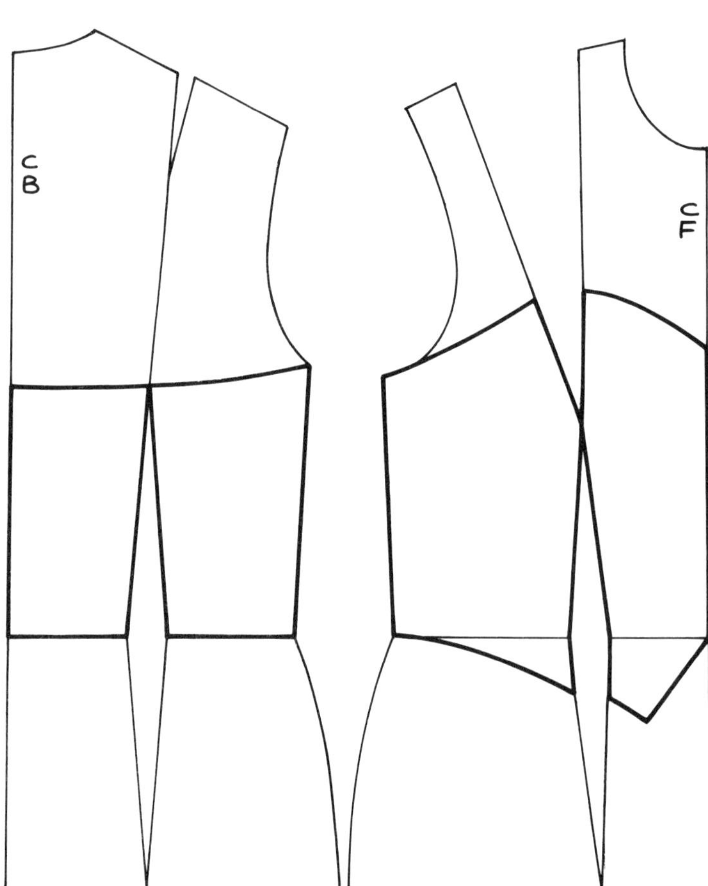

Converting the basic bodice block

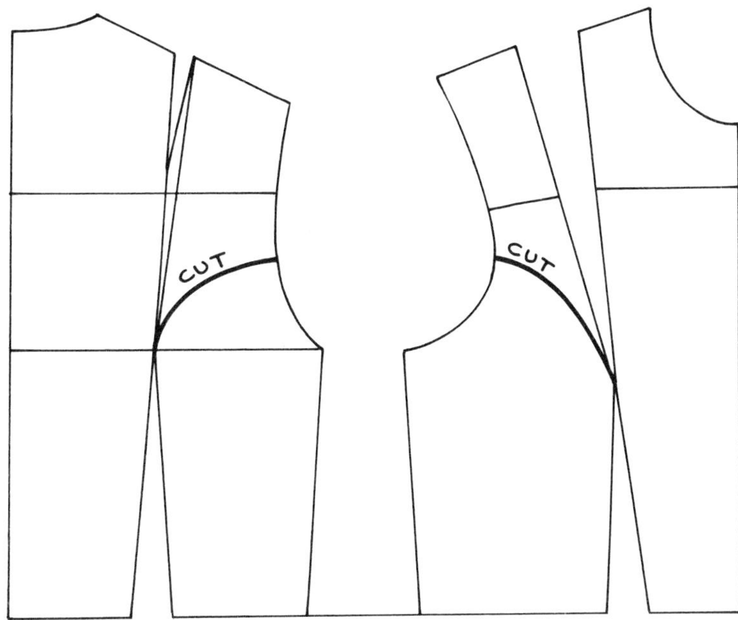

Outline back and front to waist level. Draw curved lines from armhole to run smoothly into top of waist dart. On the back rule a straight line from top of waist dart to side of shoulder dart. Cut along curved line to point of waist dart and close shoulder dart to allow it to open in armhole. On front cut along curved line to BP, close shoulder dart to allow it to open in armhole.

Outline each piece separately adding balance marks and eliminating any sharp corners. Check that shoulder seams match.

For hip-length pattern add lower section of original bodice block. For full-length garments extend panel lines and add flare as described for princess line.

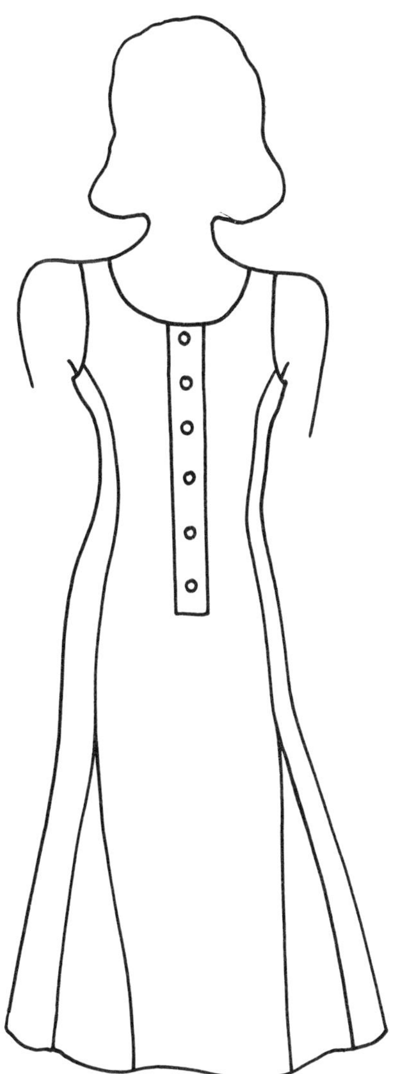

Panel designs

A. Sleeveless dress with front buttons and godets. Outline panel seam block to hip level. Take 1.5cm/⅝in off shoulder seam on back and front and re-curve armhole. Lower back neckline by 3cm/1⅛in; lower front by 4cm/1⅝in at CF and 3cm/1⅛in at NP. Rule strap opening 1.5cm/⅝in wide to just above hip line and trace off on paper folded double for final pattern. Mark off neck facing width or measure total neckline for binding length.

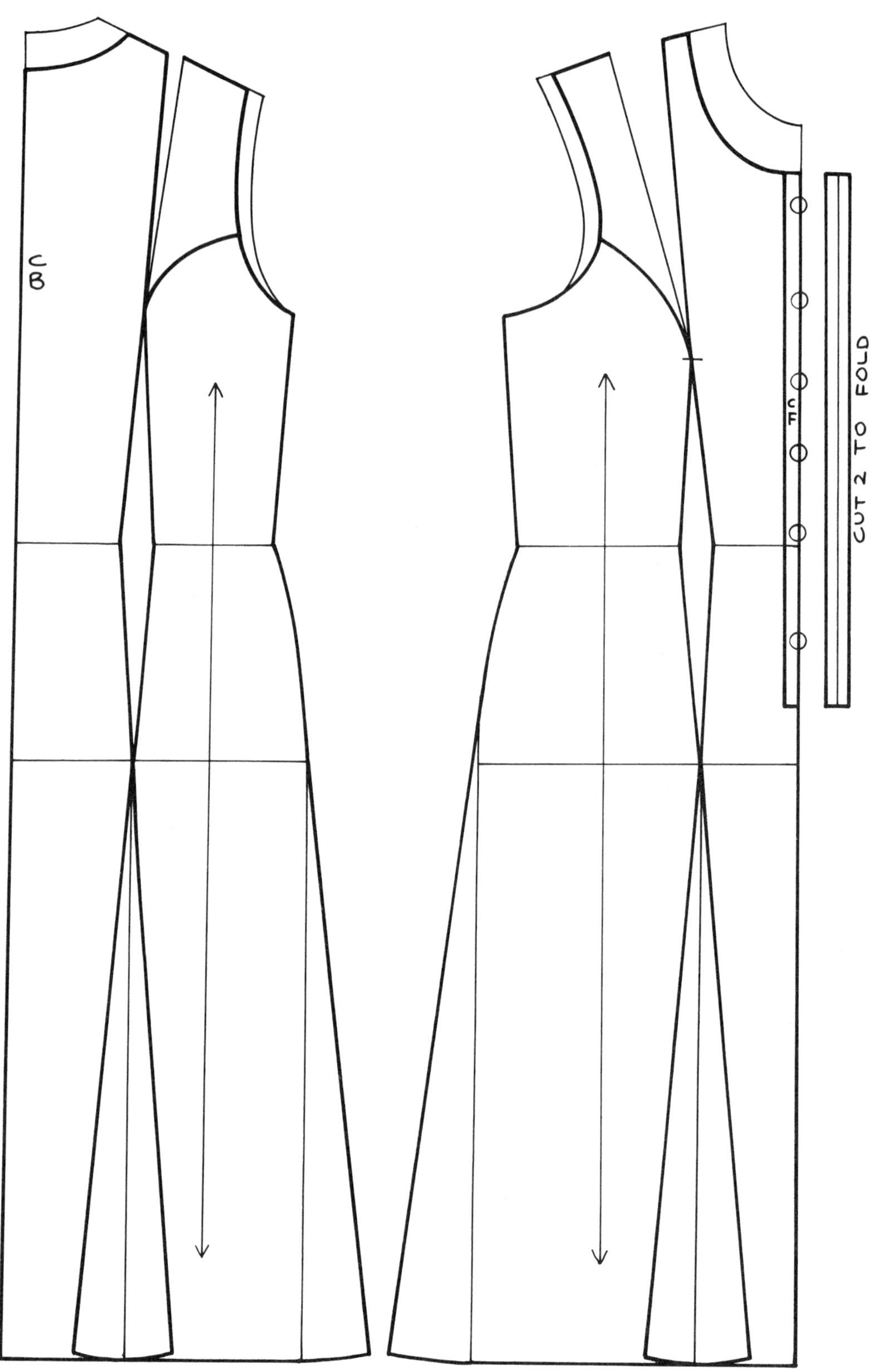
CB
FC
CUT 2 TO FOLD

At hip line extend panel lines to required length, adding flare at hem. For godet pattern rule a vertical line equal to hip to hem length,

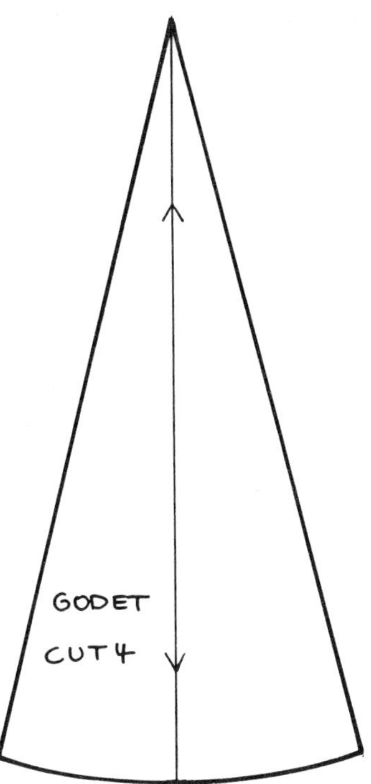

fold paper along line and measure out 12cm/4¾in at hem. Swing a line from the top making it equal to length of fold and draw curved hem to complete. Add flare at side seam equal to half of one godet, i.e. 6cm/2⅜in, and rule new side seam to hip level.

B. Jacket with peplum. Outline back and front panel seam block to hip line. Shorten hip section

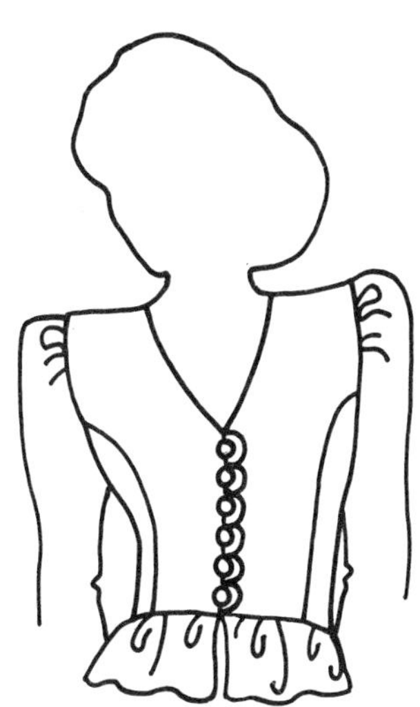

to required length. Draw new neckline on front, mark positions of rouleau loops; alternatively, extend CF to include fabric scallops. Mark facing if not lining garment to edge. Trace separately all bodice sections including below waist.

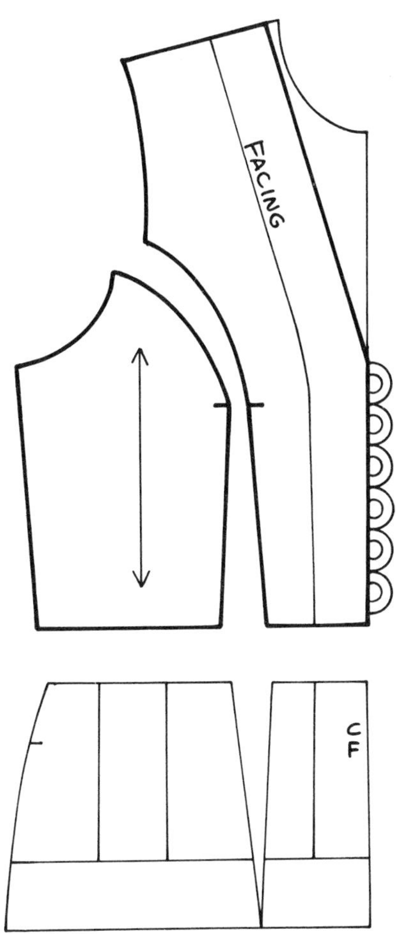

To make gathered peplum cut each piece vertically into four or five, using dart as one slash. Spread sections inserting 2cm/¾in in each gap at waist and spreading at hem until almost quarter circle.

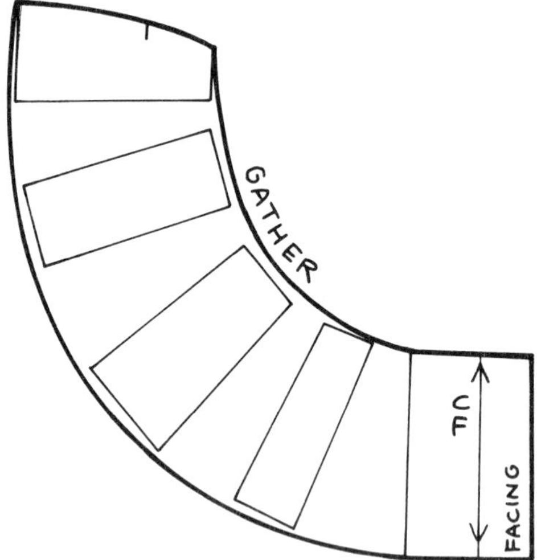

Re-draw outer edges in smooth curves checking seam and CB and CF length. Add facing to CF if not lining. For a circular peplum measure waist edge of jacket and cut circle from measurements. See page 180, Making Patterns from Measurements. See also page 116, Sleeve Designs, for sleeve pattern.

SWATHES AND DRAPES

You will guess that the cutting and spreading technique is used to achieve draped styles. With experience you will learn to estimate how much fullness is involved but at first it is wise to experiment. With special items such as bridal gowns it is worth buying a piece of cheap fabric – chiffon or georgette, for example – of similar weight and thickness to the garment fabric to make sure you get it right.

With fitted styles make a plain base adapted from the block to hold the swathes in place. For the outer section cut off any areas of block that will be used as they are. Remaining areas will be cut and spread as required.

You will find it easier to copy designs to start with rather than draw your own: cut and spread precisely where the folds are shown. Remember too that fitted swathes will not remain in place without anchorage so make good use of seams.

A drape could be defined as a loose swathe with at least one edge attached to the garment. With these also it is not easy to estimate how much to spread the pattern.

A. Swathed bodice on drop waist base. Lingerie block used; base fitted with vertical seam

incorporating darts. Section to be swathed cut and spread vertically.

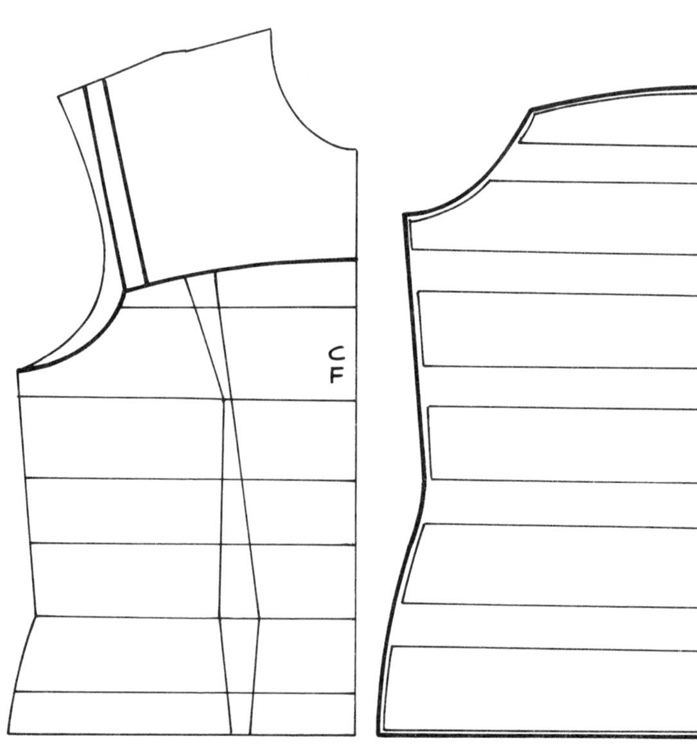

B. Asymmetrical swathe with beaded panel. Use a complete front and back lingerie block side by side; bust dart is reduced by 1cm/⅜in. Draw applied beaded panel and shoulder strap on back and front shortening distance to shoulder by 1cm/⅜in. Trace off right and left sides separately. Close remainder of bust dart and transfer to waist on beaded panel. On back beaded panel close waist dart and re-curve waist edge.

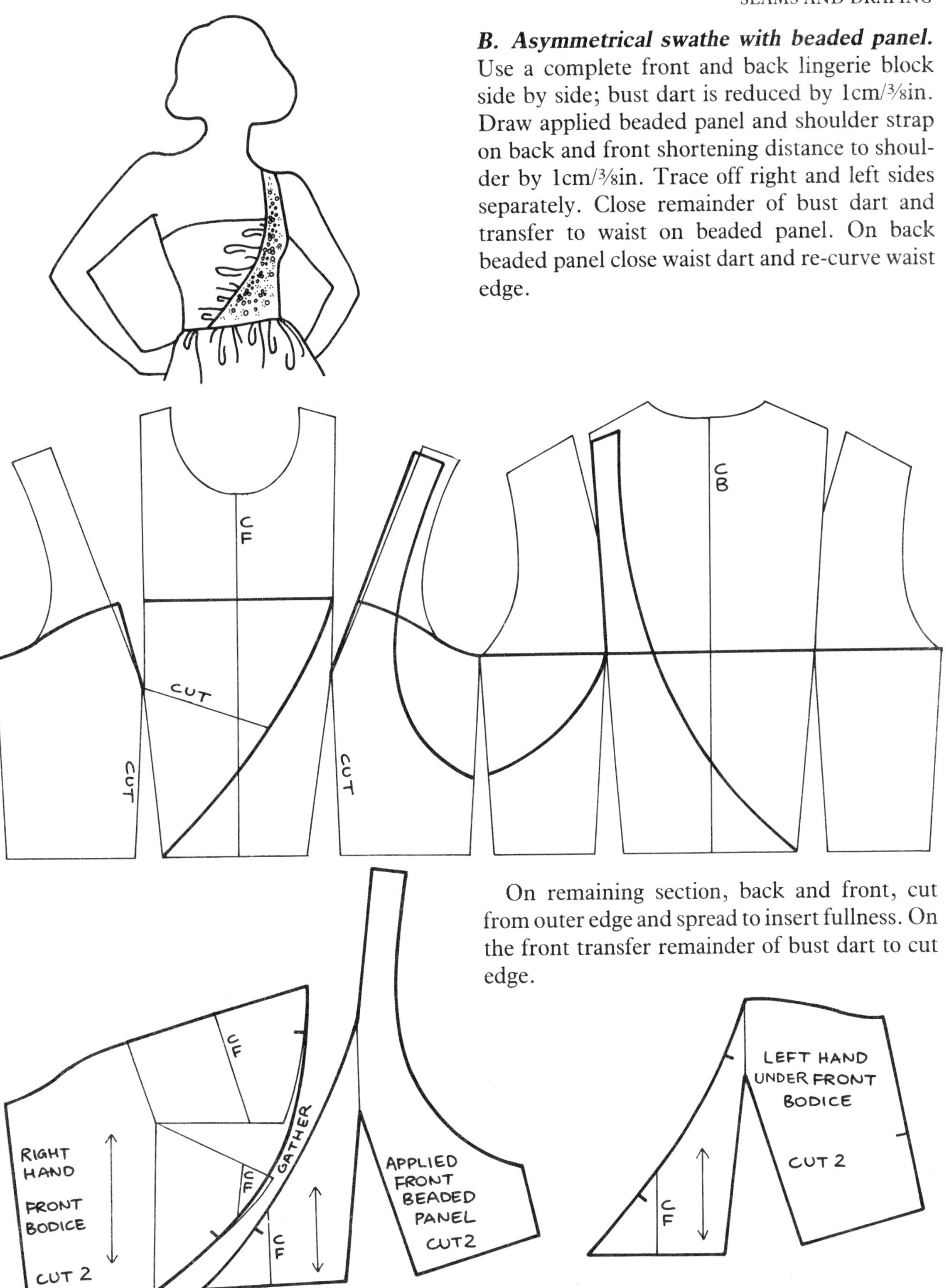

On remaining section, back and front, cut from outer edge and spread to insert fullness. On the front transfer remainder of bust dart to cut edge.

SLEEVE DESIGNS

Styles of sleeves vary like all the other aspects of fashion and will be affected by changes in shoulder line. Please see page 125, Armholes and Shoulder Lines, including adjustments for shoulder pads.

There are three main basic sleeve shapes. The first uses the sleeve block with shaped head that fits the basic armhole. The others, raglan and kimono sleeves, involve combining the sleeve with the bodice block before making the pattern for the sleeve, and are described in a separate chapter (see page 132).

All the basic principles of pattern cutting apply: cutting and spreading, adding extra length where fullness is introduced, and so on. Always begin by ruling horizontal and vertical guide lines. Always transfer the sleeve head point and balance marks through every stage of developing the pattern. When outlining for final pattern make sure all curves are smooth and check seam edges are equal in length.

SLEEVES FROM BASIC BLOCK

Straight sleeve

A. The block may be used as it is, with straight sides and to wrist length.

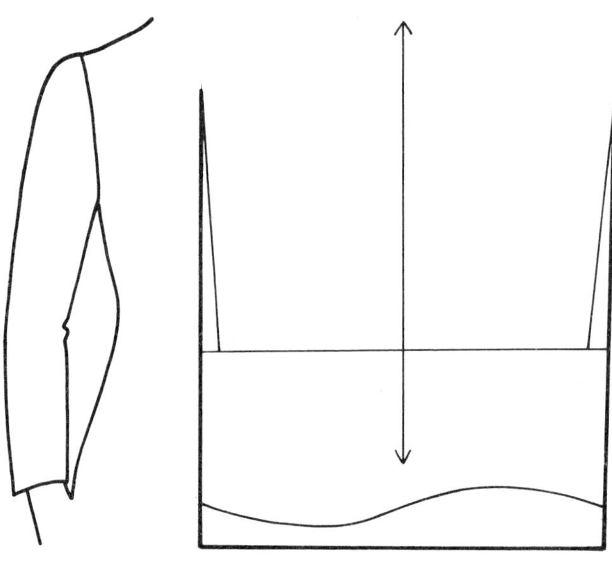

B. If you wish to gather or tuck it into a cuff, mark an opening 10cm/4in long on the little finger line. Decide on depth of cuff and make

pattern to wrist measurement plus 6mm/¼in plus overlap. Reduce length of sleeve by half depth of cuff.

CUT 2

FOLD

CUFF CUT 2

C. For a roll-back cuff use the block full-length so that it may be worn with or without the cuff.

However if the roll-back is part of its style it is best to shape the seam in by 1cm/⅜in at three-quarter length to ensure that the sleeve remains rolled back. To shape the cuff leave additional paper below wrist, straighten lower edge and fold back and trim the seam edges.

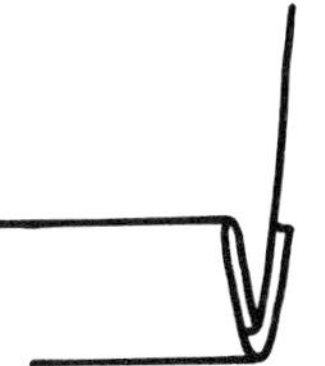

Fitted sleeves

A. Slight fitting. Shape the seam edges at the wrist 2–3cm/¾–1⅛in to reduce wrist size. Do not make it too tight or there will be insufficient elbow room. It is worth making a cardboard block for future use as this shape can be used for many sleeves of all lengths.

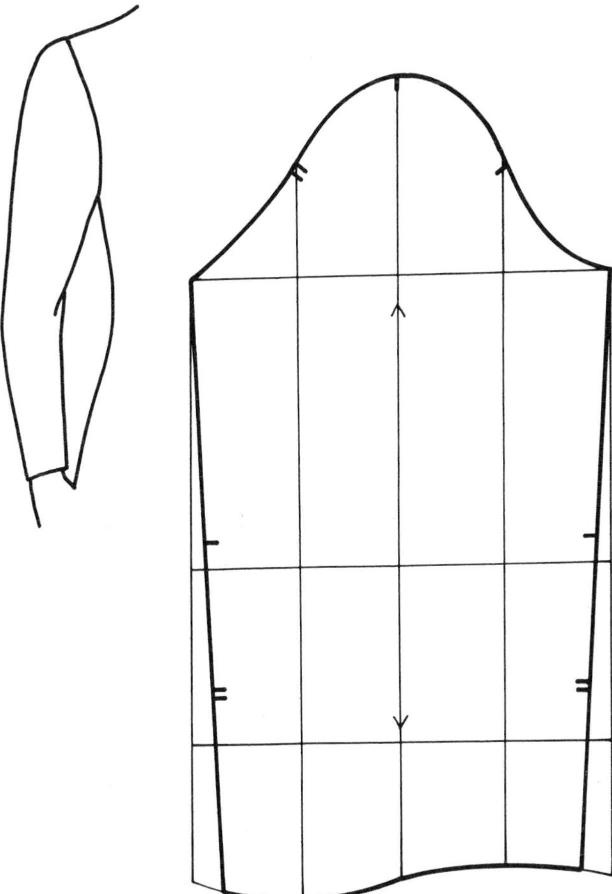

B. Semi fitted. Reduce wrist as above but in addition make dart 5cm/2in wide and 15cm/6in

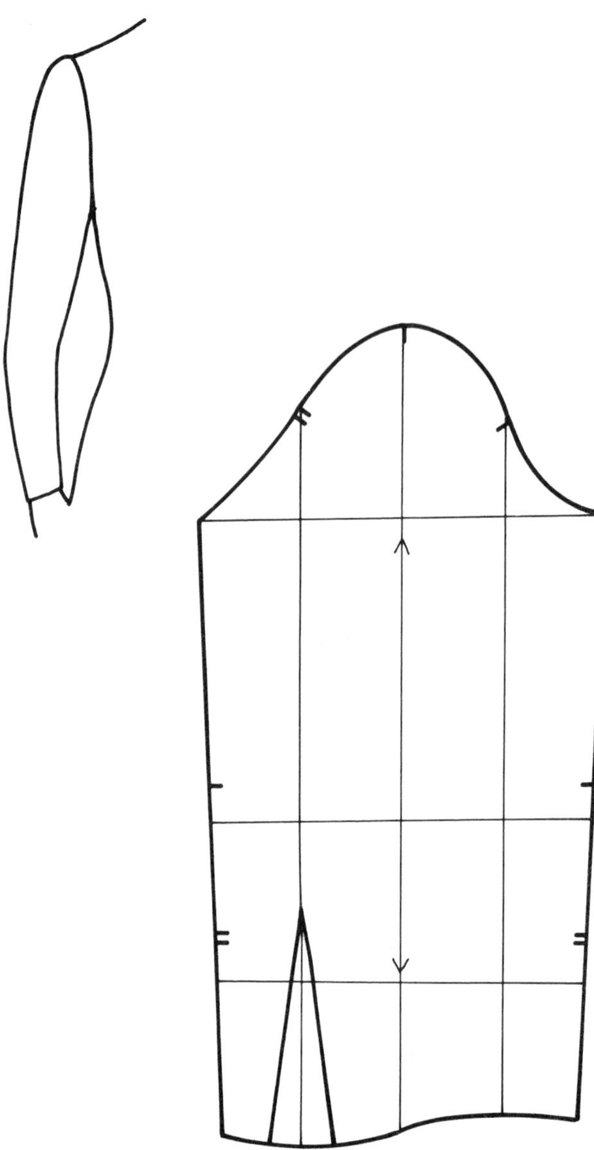

long on the little finger line. This can be sewn as a fold-over opening, fastened with press studs or Velcro Spot-Ons, or it can be cut out, bound and fastened with buttons and loops or with press studs.

An alternative for unyielding fabrics is to cut the block along elbow line to the little finger line, cut from wrist to elbow line on little finger line and overlap at wrist to remove 5cm/2in. Draw a dart at the elbow and mark an opening at the wrist on little finger line – now sloping.

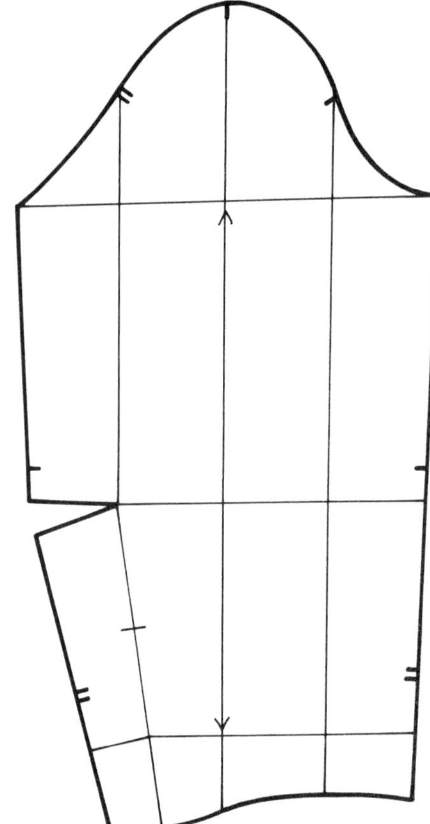

C. Tight sleeves. On the whole if a sleeve is tightened at the wrist it has fullness introduced at the head. This not only supplies room for movement, it also tends to balance the design.

At the same time as you narrow the wrist by overlapping, gathers can be inserted in the sleeve head by opening the pieces. Slope seam edges by 2cm/¾in at wrist; cut along finger lines and open at head.

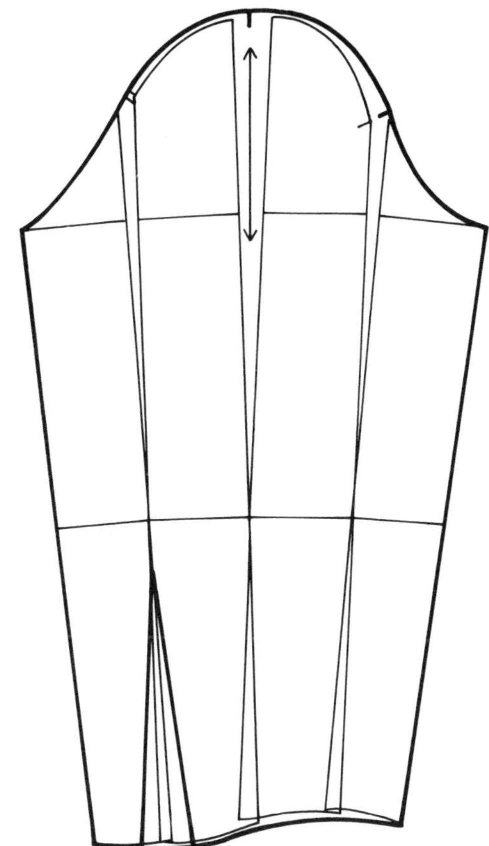

Cut along all three vertical lines from wrist to sleeve head and manipulate so that wrist is reduced and 6–8cm/2⅜–3¼in are inserted on sleeve head. Do not allow paper to open at elbow line. At wrist make a 5cm/2in dart (or whatever is required to reduce wrist to size) to within 2cm/¾in of elbow line and cut it out and mark as an opening.

D. Tucks. For the same fitted sleeve but with tucks, reduce seam edges by 2cm/¾in, shape the lower part of the sleeve by cutting along elbow line to thumb line and overlap on little and middle finger line. Draw a line across sleeve head and mark tuck positions from sleeve head to line. Cut out centre section, cut along sleeve head line, raise centre section and pivot side sections to insert 2–3cm/¾–1⅛in in each space. The elbow shaping can be sewn as a dart or on soft fabrics it could be eased in when seam is stitched. Mark wrist opening parallel with new seam edge.

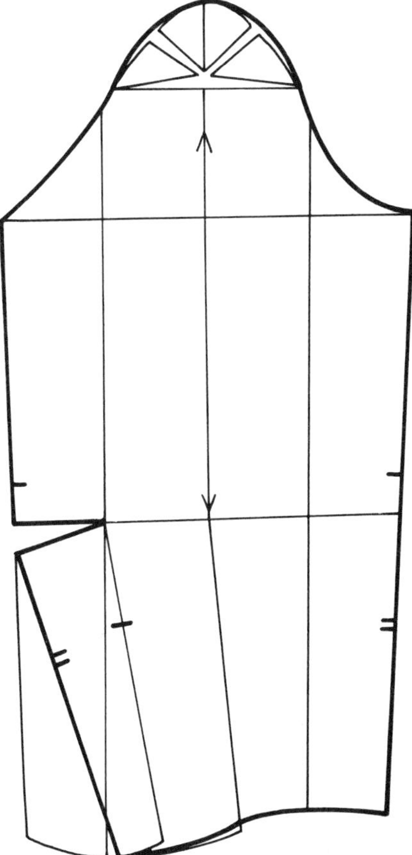

E. Combination full and fitted sleeve. Slope seam edges 3cm/1⅛in, cut across sleeve below

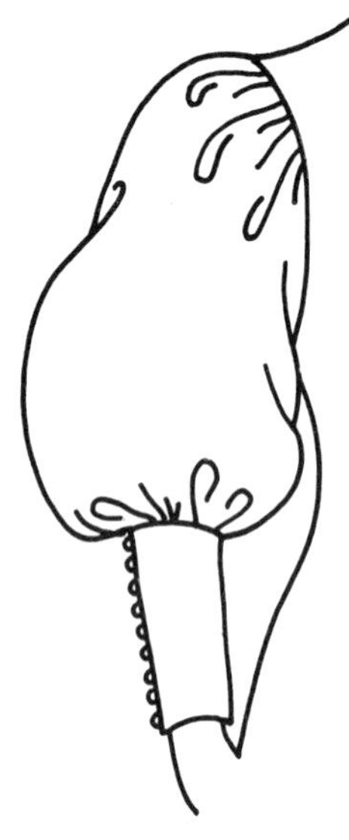

elbow line, cut along all finger lines and overlap at wrist. Mark opening parallel with new seam edge, and full depth of section. Check wrist measurement and cut out a small dart if necessary to make it fit. Finally check size of arm where upper edge will come and reduce side

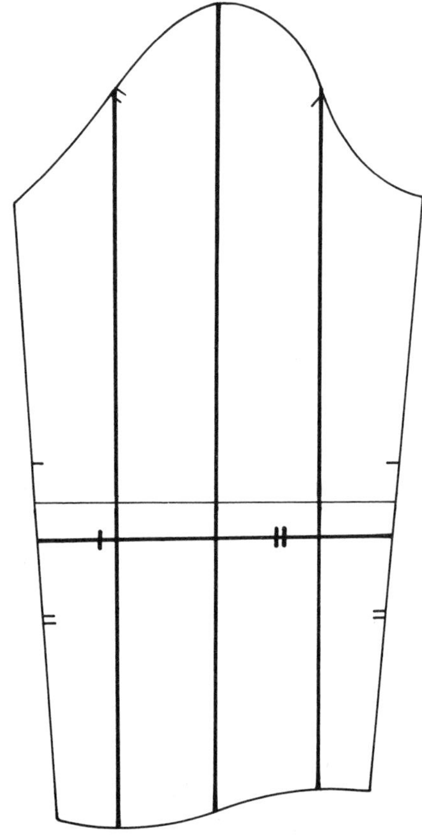

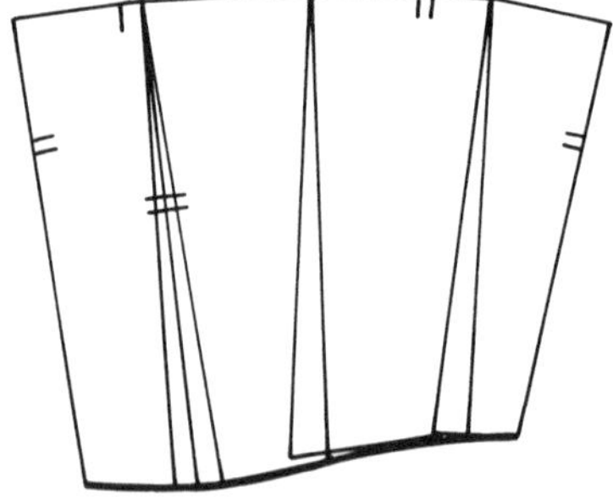

edges if necessary. Sections could be placed together and re-drawn to eliminate the seam.

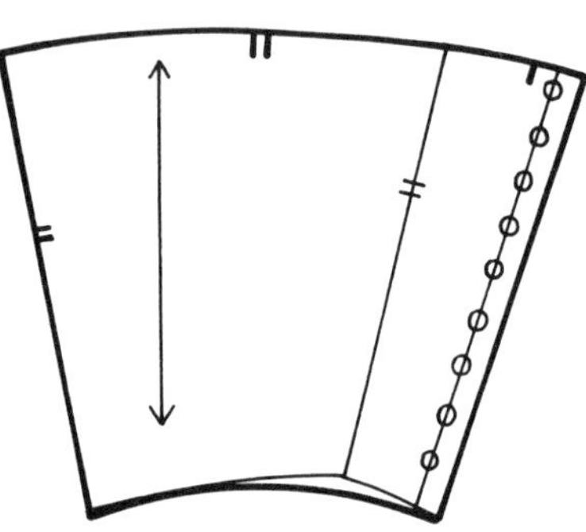

Trace upper sleeve section, cut along all three vertical lines and spread to insert amounts for gathering, depending on type of fabric. These inserts can be an even width or, as in the case of the design illustrated, the sleeve is fuller at the bottom edge. Outline both parts of sleeve for final pattern.

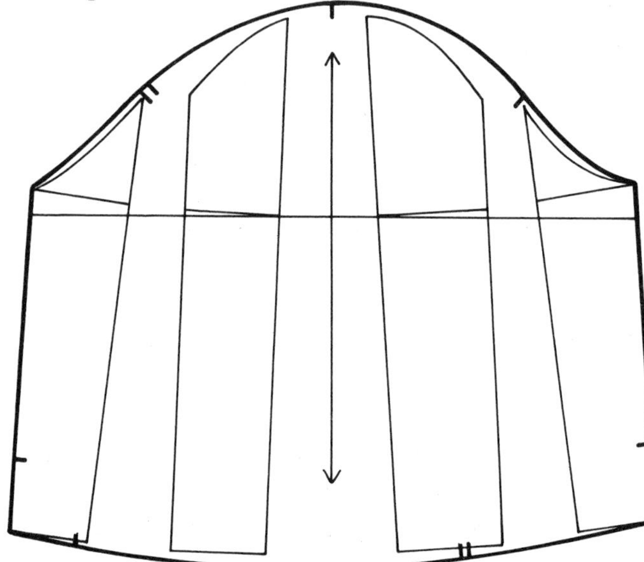

VARIATIONS

A. Full gathered sleeve. Draw cuff pattern. Reduce length of sleeve by half depth of cuff.

Trace remainder of sleeve and cut along all finger lines. Open to insert fullness at head and wrist as required. Mark opening in centre of gap at little finger line. Outline for final pattern adding length at head and wrist when drawing curved pattern edges.

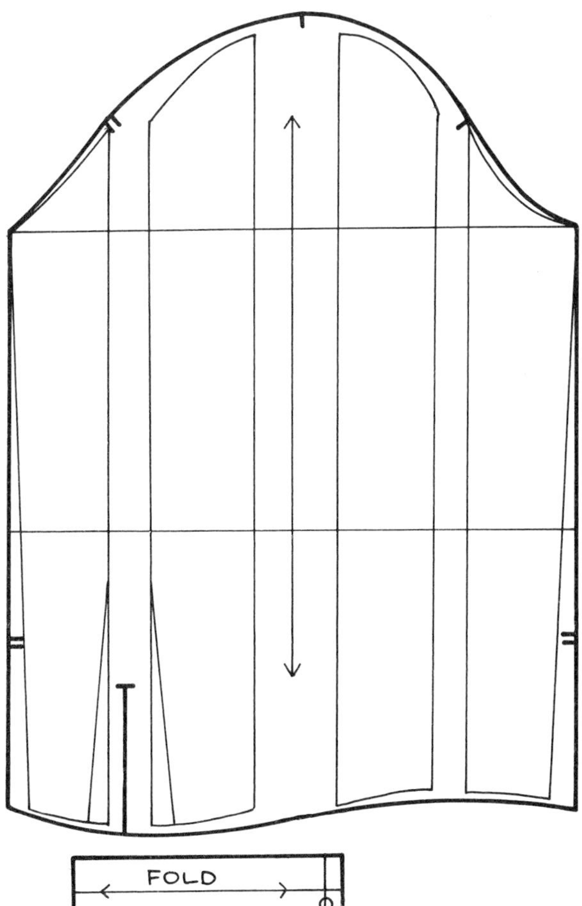

B. Shaped cuff on fitted sleeve. Adapt block to fitted sleeve by cutting along elbow line and

overlapping on middle and little finger lines. Outline and mark opening and elbow shaping.

Mark depth of cuff parallel with wrist edge.

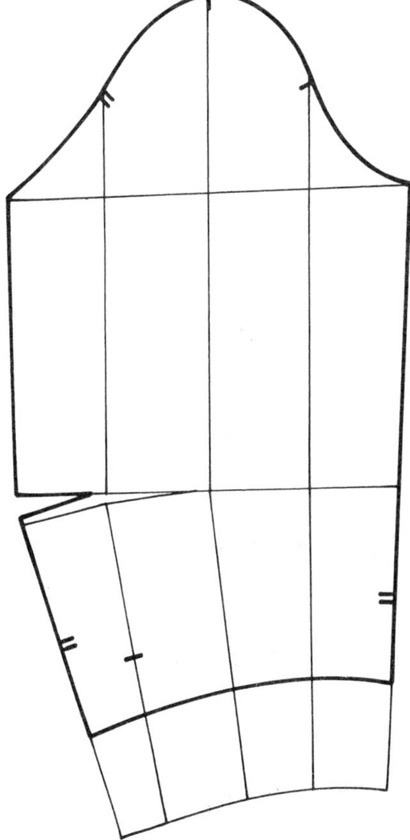

Trace cuff including opening position. Cut out, cut along opening and re-draw with seam edges together but inserting a little extra at upper edge and a little at the opening in addition to the overlap. This will help the cuff stand clear of the sleeve. If cuff is to have both ends extending as illustrated, draw buttons and extension at both ends. SG position may need adjusting: fold cuff end to end to check.

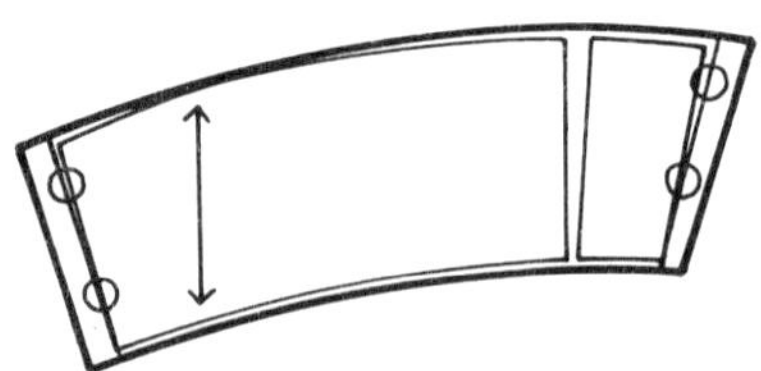

C. Shirt sleeve with pleated head. Slope seam edges 2cm/¾in. Draw cuff and reduce sleeve

length by half depth of cuff. Cut from head to below elbow along all finger lines and cut from there to side edges. Open all pieces as shown inserting sufficient at sleeve head to make six deep pleats. Outline sleeve, curving seam edges. Mark pleats evenly over sleeve head and fold before cutting final pattern. Mark wrist opening.

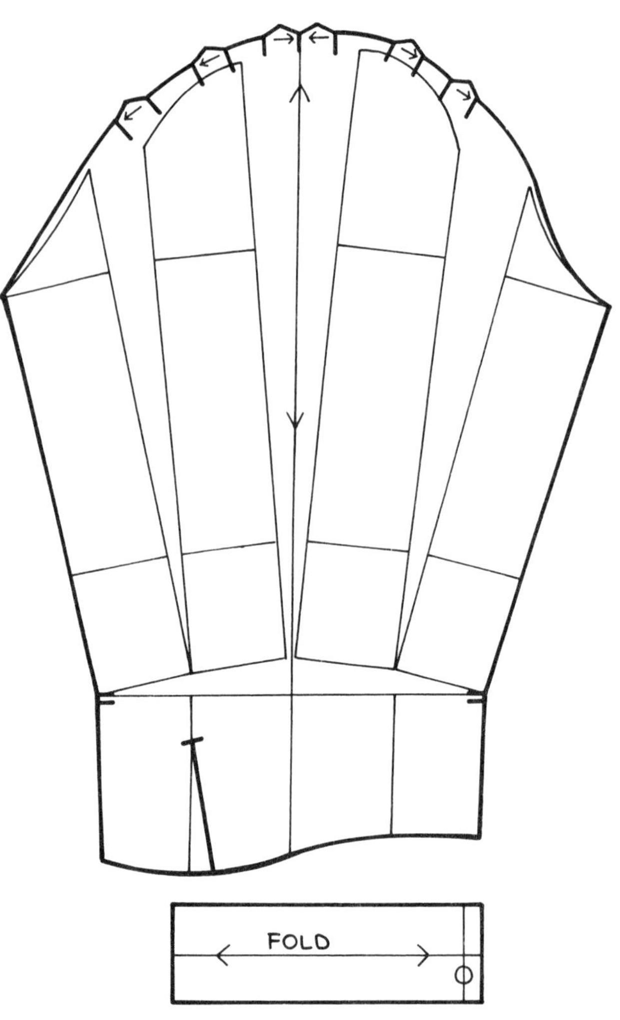

Short sleeves

A. Basic. Rule horizontal line across block quarter to half-way between underarm and

elbow line. Slope seam edges in 13mm/½in at hem. Cut up centre line from hem to sleeve head and overlap at hem 13mm/½in. Draw curved hemline; mark grain down centre.

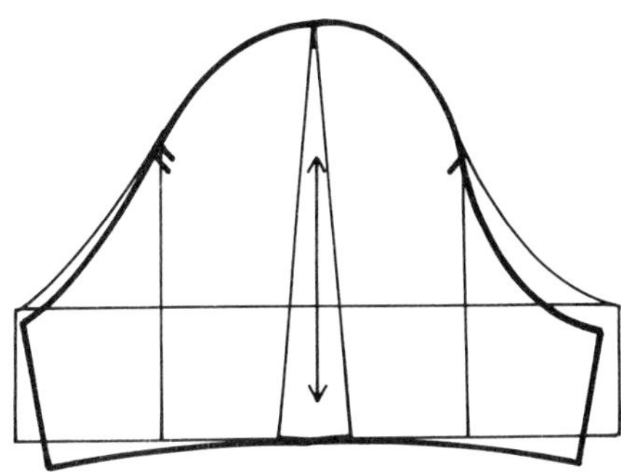

B. Gathers at head. Using short basic sleeve A above – lengthen if required – cut along middle finger line and open sleeve at head. Re-draw sleeve head slightly higher to allow depth for gathers.

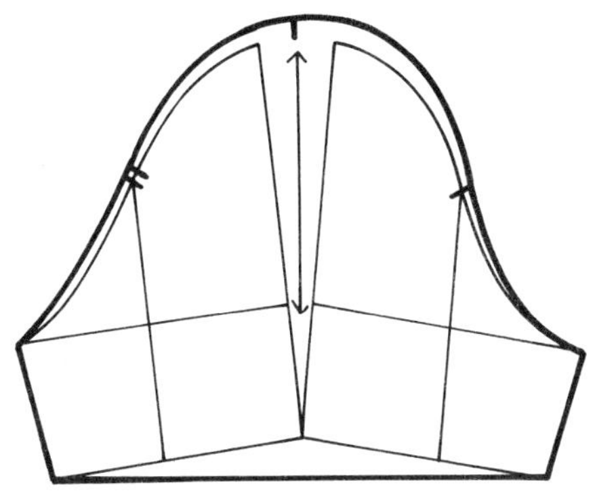

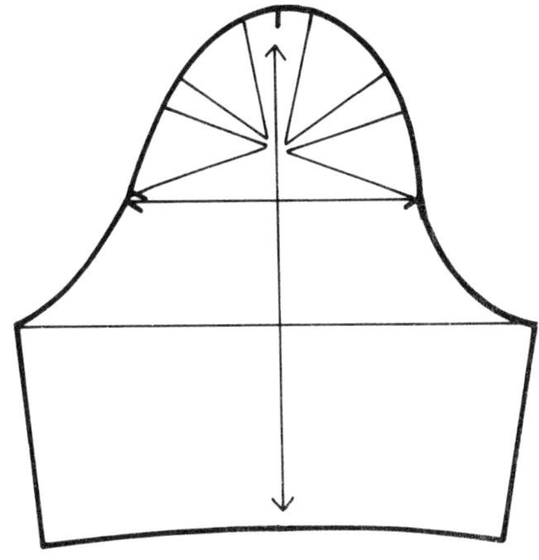

If the sleeve is required fitted to underarm but fully gathered over the head, rule a line between the balance marks and cut, then cut from sleeve head three times and open to insert fullness. Re-draw sleeve head.

C. Tucks at hem. Trace block to above elbow line and using sloping seam. Cut up the three vertical lines and spread sleeve at hem to insert sufficient for five tucks. Draw the tucks making each slightly bigger than allowed so that sleeve is not too loose. Re-draw hemline.

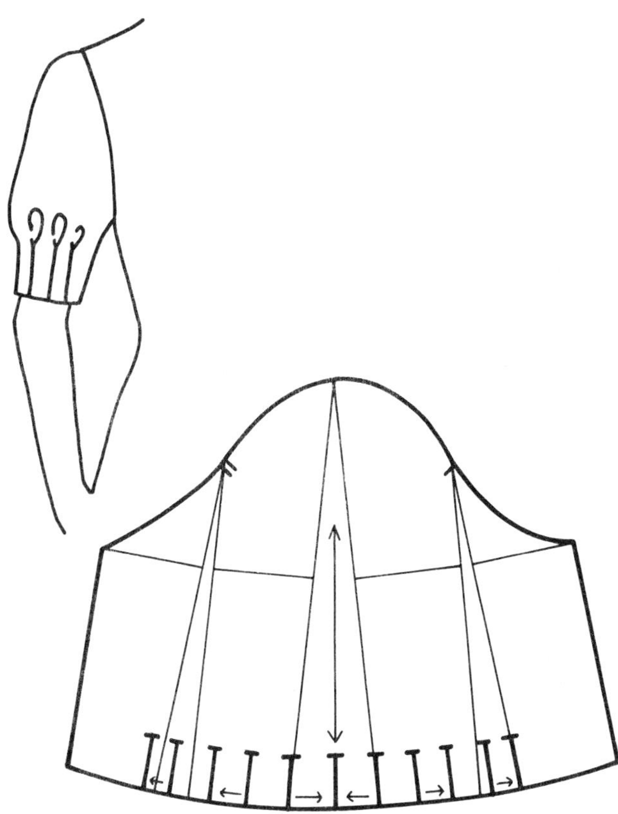

D. Hemline dart. For a long hemline dart, slope the seam edges and cut and open the sleeve

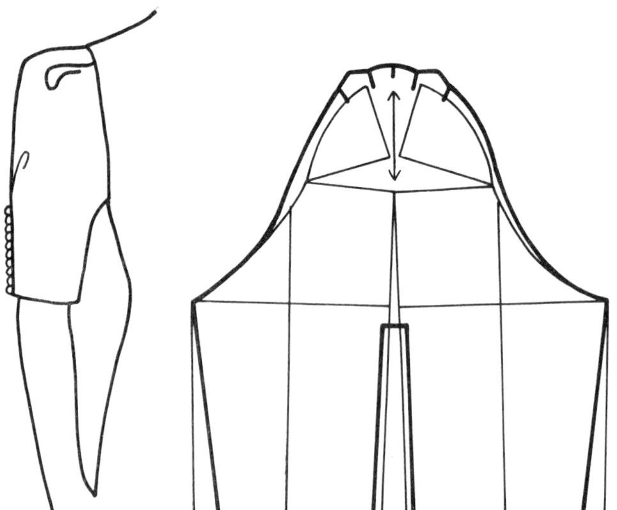

to insert half the amount needed. The remainder will be taken from sleeve width to tighten it.

E. Keyhole sleeve. Open sleeve head to allow for gathers, outline and trace. Cut along central

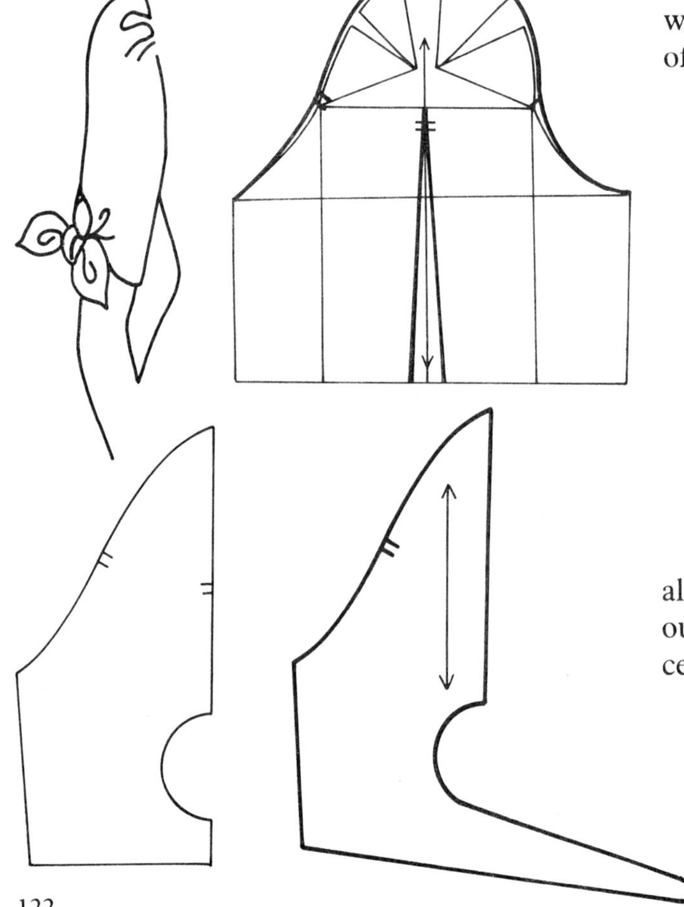

line and shape a little. Outline each half separately, draw keyhole and extension for tie.

F. With cuff. Use shaped short sleeve as described in A above and make a copy of it. Cut

along middle finger line and arrange the pieces with seam edges together. Draw size and shape of cuff extending it 3mm/⅛in beyond sleeve to

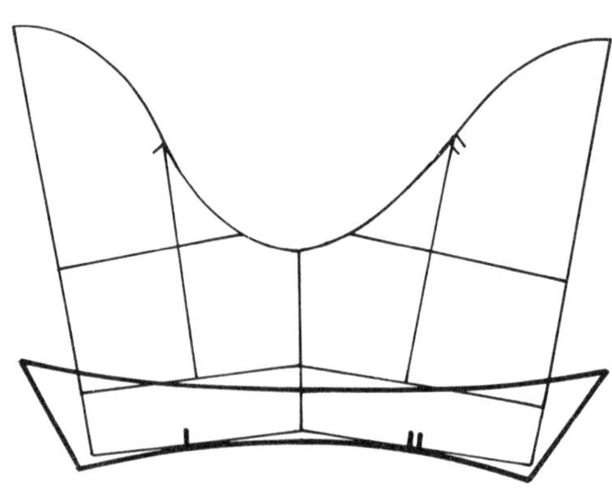

allow for it being double and fitting over the outside of the sleeve. Trace cuff, mark grain in centre.

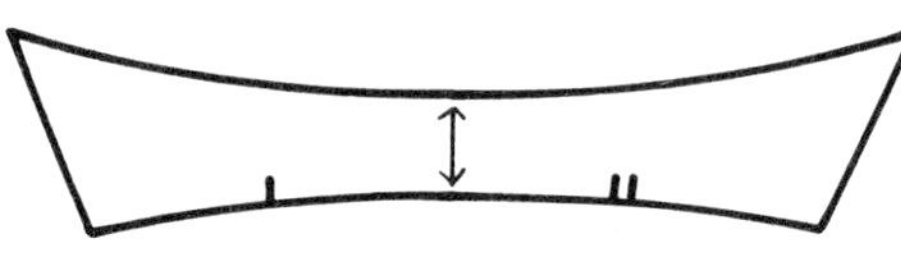

G. Puff sleeve. A classic sleeve with lower edge bound or with a band attached. Measure arm at

appropriate level and draw pattern for band or binding. Trace sleeve block to 2.5cm/1in lower than that level. Cut along all vertical lines and spread at the head and the hem. The sleeve is often fuller at the bottom than the top.

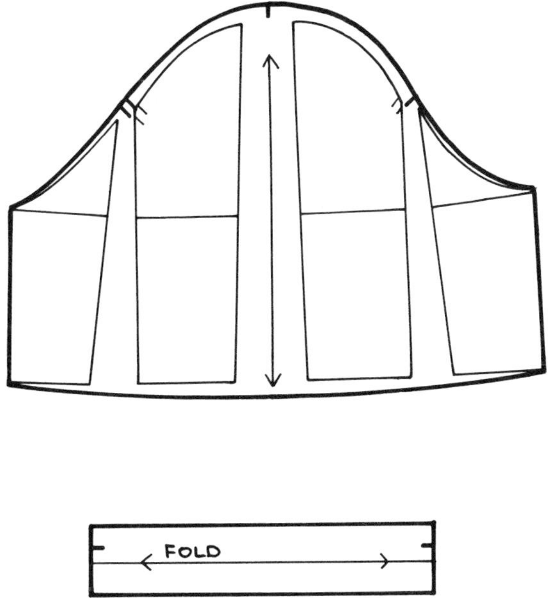

Three-quarter sleeves

A. Full. Trace basic block to mid-way between elbow and wrist level; a three-quarter pattern

needs to be made longer than you might think, especially if full. Re-draw sleeve head and curve hemline. Add extension for casing if required. Either add a deep hem when cutting out or make a facing. If fullness is required at hem spread pieces at lower edge only.

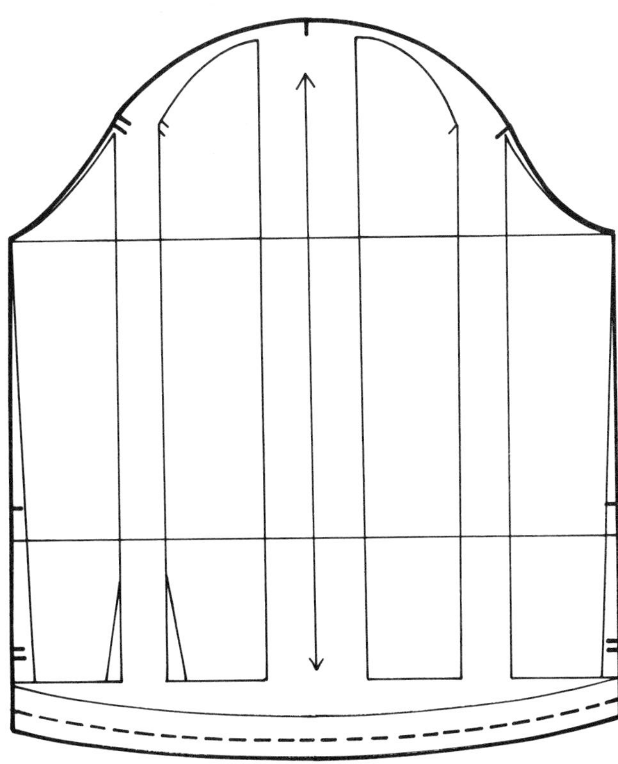

B. Fitted. An elbow dart is essential especially if the sleeve head is smooth. Adapt block to

semi-fitted sleeve on page 116, design B, sloping side seams and reducing wrist size. Cut to length which will be about half-way between elbow line and wrist, the exact position being a matter of choice. Shape the edge so that it is parallel with the hem edge. Draw dart on elbow line as far as little finger line. Cut along middle finger line to underarm and out to the sides. Overlap sections at sleeve hem, but keeping sleeve head flat. The amount you overlap will depend on how tight the sleeve is to be. If you reduce it to fit the arm, allow at least 13mm/½in ease so the sleeve can move when your arm bends. Mark an opening.

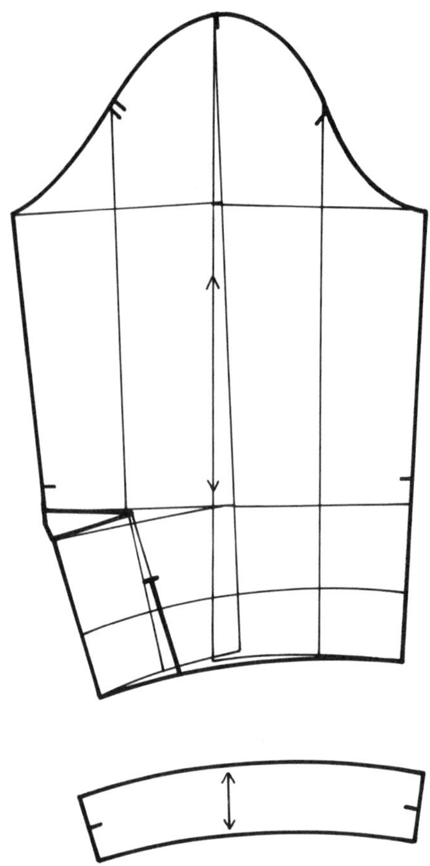

Alternatively it could be made just big enough for your hand to pass through. If a cuff is required as illustrated trace shape from lower edge of sleeve (shown joined at underarm, i.e. sleeve has no opening).

ARMHOLES AND SHOULDER LINES

These two areas are closely related. Even a small change to one necessitates an alteration to the other. There is a variety of sleeve and armhole designs that are around all the time but changes in fashion mean adjustments to the basic block in the shoulder area. It is worth making a set of blocks that include the current feature, especially if it is one that suits your figure. For example, shoulder pads, though not always in fashion except for use in coats, are so good on people with sloping shoulders that they should consider using a block adapted for pads for every pattern.

EXTENDED SHOULDERS

A. Sleeveless. Often called a cap sleeve, the shoulder seam is lengthened but also raised so that the armhole is not reduced in size. If the darts are to be used transfer back dart to neck and bust dart to underarm or waist. A limited extension is advisable unless you want a very full fluted sleeve because the longer the shoulder seam, the higher you must raise the SP.

1. Rule a short vertical line above SP on back and front; raise SP 2cm/¾in. Draw new shoulder seam on back. Extend side seam in a straight line to intersect the new shoulder seam.

2. On front raise SP 2cm/¾in. Rule new shoulder seam equal in length to the one drawn for the back. Place a ruler against side seam and extend to meet shoulder at new SP, adjusting side seam if necessary.

Mark stitching point on side seams 4cm/1½in below original underarm point or seams may split in wear.

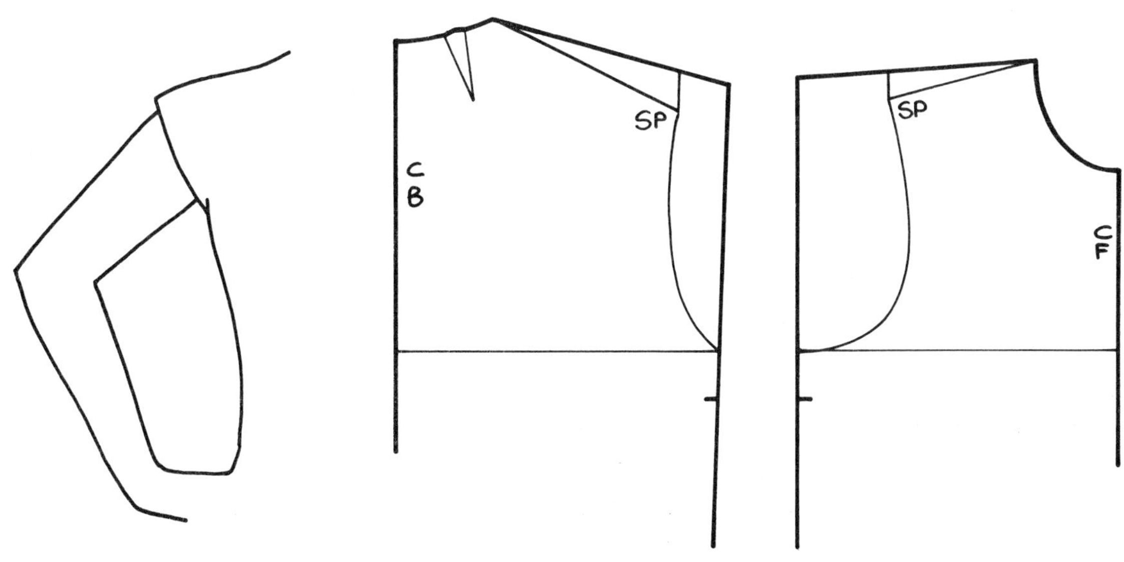

B. With sleeve. The armhole shape is retained but to compensate for the longer shoulder seam the sleeve head and armhole are lowered. The most accurate and logical way to do it is to remove a portion from the sleeve and attach it to the bodice.

1. Outline sleeve block and rule centre line. Draw a new flatter sleeve head from back balance mark to front. Limit the drop at the centre to 3cm/1¼in or arm movement will be restricted. Mark new balance marks across the line. Trace off sleeve head and cut along centre line.

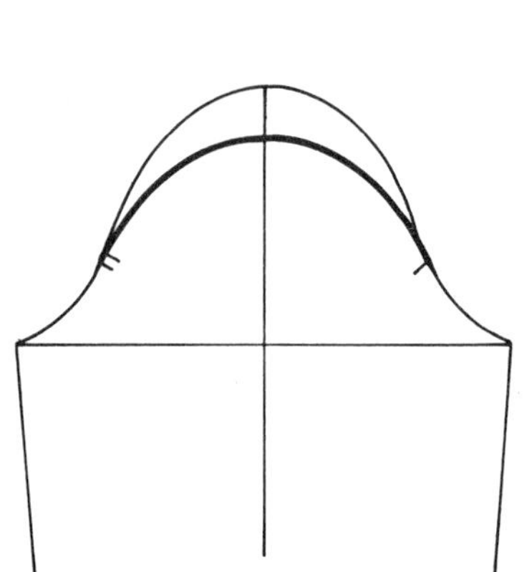

2. Place each traced section against correct bodice armhole with point matching balance mark and with the edge just touching SP of bodice. The curve of the head of the sleeve will overlap the bodice between the two points but this represents the ease in the sleeve head which is not required in a dropped shoulder style.

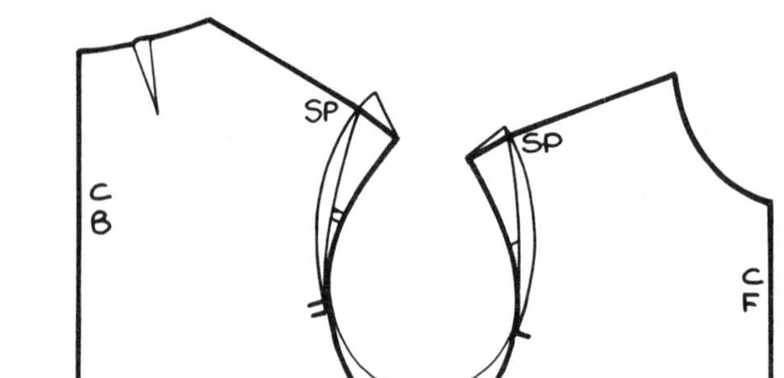

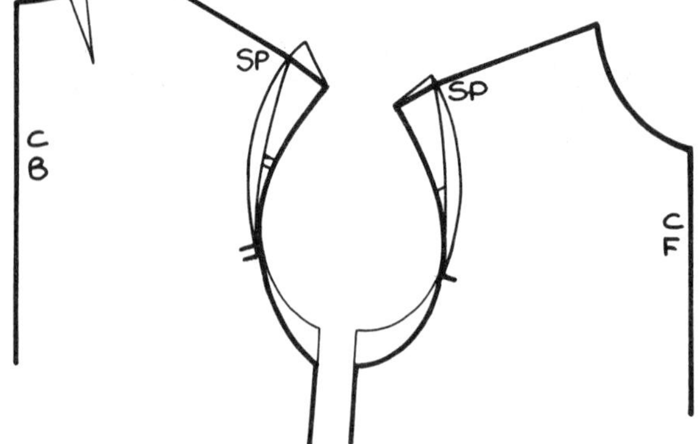

3. Outline bodice, curving shoulder seams slightly.

C. Dropped shoulder. The shoulder seam is not simply lengthened, but shaped to curve over the top of the arm. It gives a closer fit than the previous styles and so SP must be raised to provide a bigger armhole and back and front bodice width is increased a little.

1. On the sleeve block draw sleeve cap curved as shown. This is the new sleeve head edge. Next

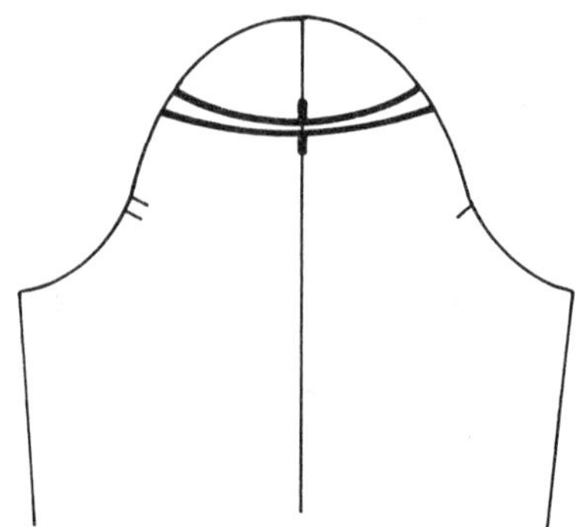

re-draw the curve of the section to be added to the bodice to remove some of the sleeve head ease. Raise the line 13mm/½in on back and front of sleeve. Insert balance marks at centre and trace sleeve head.

2. On back and front bodice raise SP 13mm/½in and rule new shoulder seams. Cut sleeve head tracing along centre line and place sections

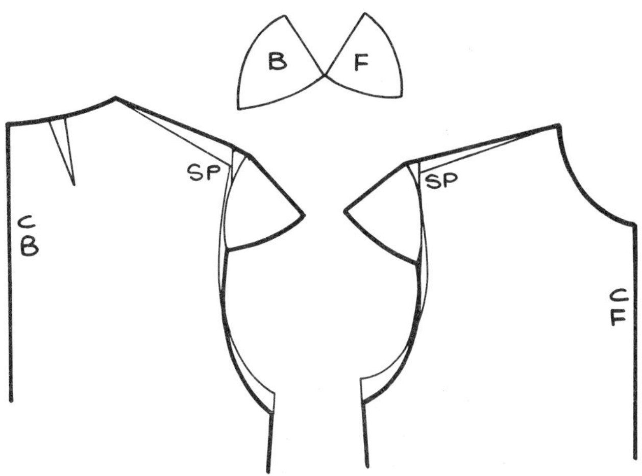

against appropriate armhole. Place sleeve head point 13mm/½in out along new shoulder seam.

3. At the lower point on the armhole arrange a gap of 6mm/¼in; the sleeve head may have to overlap the bodice a little.

4. Curve the new underarm edges, transfer balance marks to new line. Finally draw shoulder seams curved.

D. Dropped shoulder with full sleeve. Sleeve can be flared, with fullness inserted at hem only,

or it may be gathered to fit the dropped shoulder seam.

Follow instructions for dropped shoulder opposite. To make sleeve pattern cut the lower section along all three vertical lines, open at hem only for flared sleeve or open evenly for gathered sleeve. Mark SG and curve hemline and sleeve head.

DEEP AND SQUARE ARMHOLES

These may be exaggerated to emphasize a fashion line, to allow movement in sports clothes or as an accepted classic feature in a shirt where the method of construction also influences the armhole.

A. Shirt sleeve and armhole. This is a small adjustment to flatten the sleeve head and lower

the armhole for a looser fit. The advantage of the less curved armhole and sleeve head is that the sleeve can be attached flat before the side seams are made, using welt seams.

1. Extend shoulder seams on back and front by 1.5cm/⅝in at the same time raising SP by 13mm/½in. Lower armholes by 1.5cm/⅝in. Re-draw armhole curves.

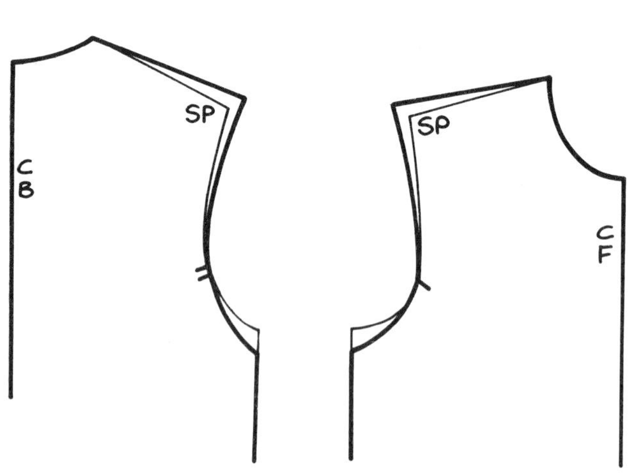

2. On sleeve lower head by 1.5cm/⅝in and curve. Extend width at underarm by 1.5cm/⅝in to correspond with bodice.

3. Finally check sleeve head measurement against armhole. The ease in the original sleeve head was removed by raising SP on bodice so that smooth armhole seams can be made. If there is any discrepancy adjust sleeve pattern at underarm.

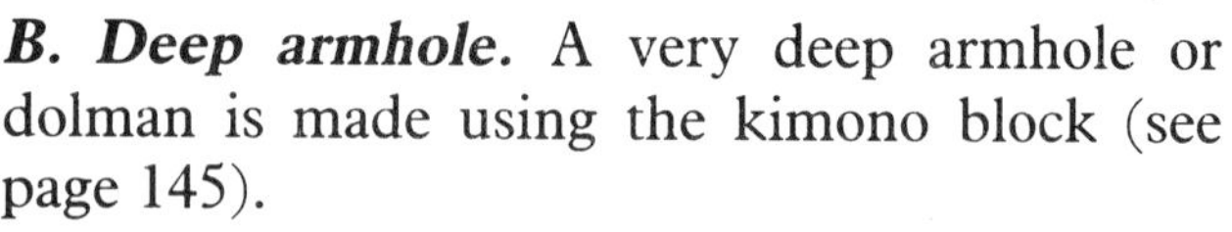

B. Deep armhole. A very deep armhole or dolman is made using the kimono block (see page 145).

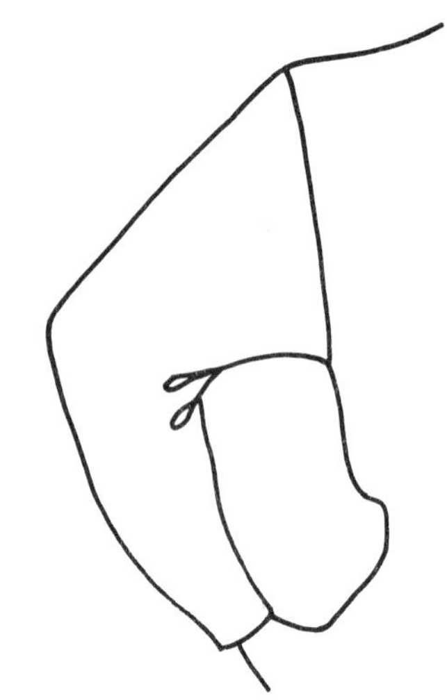

With the less deep armhole shown here, extra width must be added to the bodice so that the waistline is not pulled up when the arms are raised.

1. Outline front and back blocks and rule a line 4cm/1⅝in below the armhole. At underarm

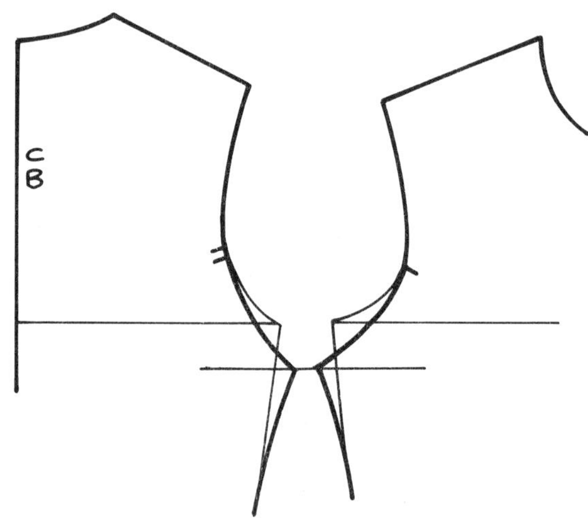

add 2cm/¾in to side seam on the new line. Curve side seams to waist and re-draw armholes.

2. On the sleeve draw a line 2cm/¾in below underarm. Measure out from sides of sleeve 2cm/¾in on this line. Re-curve edge of sleeve. Check length of sleeve head, adjust armhole of

Soft polyester crêpe blouse has double-breasted button fastening and tie neck; bust dart with additional fullness is gathered into a yoke at front and back. The sleeves are smooth at the head and gathered into cuffs.

The swinging A-line skirt in wool crêpe has six gores, a straight waistband and a side zip; it is loose-lined.

Suit in woollen tweed has single-breasted one-button jacket with tailored collar and lapels, wide padded shoulders, patch pockets and two-piece sleeve. The neat knee-length straight skirt has a hemline slit at centre back. The jacket is lined allowing a back pleat for ease and the skirt is loose-lined.

Made in cotton-backed PVC this expensive-looking raincoat features a double-breasted wrap held in place with pearly cap fasteners and a belt with pull-through covered buckle. The classic collar tops wide lapels, there are seam pockets and the bust dart is at underarm. The pattern is from the coat block, slightly flared at the hem.

The sleeves have deep fold-back cuffs and the sleeve head is slightly flattened to eliminate ease and make the PVC easier to handle.

Knitted suit in co-ordinating acrylic fabric. Loose sweater with shoulder tucks into raglan seams; darts over shoulders supported with soft raglan pads. Sporty rib fabric finishes polo neck, cuffs and hip edge. Swirling multi-panel skirt consists of thirty-six equal pieces each hemmed before joining together then alternately edge-stitched on the outside to produce sun-ray pleats.

Left: Natty shorts and top in spotted woven cotton: slightly flared shorts from trouser block, tucks at waist and patch pockets on the hips; the sport shirt has a simple raglan sleeve, bust dart underarm and the scoop neck is finished with a bias strip stitched down on the inside: centre tab is decorative.

Right: The full-length robe made from striped polyester knit is the simplest of the kimono shapes, drawn from measurements and based on a rectangle. The robe has large patch pockets and tie belt and the neckline, front and sleeve edges are finished with straight double bands of fabric.

Left: Blue cotton jersey, lined to the edge with nylon knit; the bust shaping takes the form of gathers in the centre front seam, the lower edge can have elastic attached to tighten it if necessary. The pants have elastic threaded through a casing formed by a line of stitching through fabric and lining.

Right: Spotted bikini, also in cotton jersey has gathers under the bust and is cut away to nothing at the centre front. All edges on top and pants are bound with bias strips of fabric.

Both bras have a length of elastic threaded through the back and are fastened with bikini clasps; the same patterns could be used for lingerie.

The panelled strapless bodice, from the lingerie block, is boned, and self-lined. The full A-line skirt has unpressed pleats at the waist, a zip is fitted in the centre back seam and the skirt billows over a full taffeta lining.

Fitted panel seams run from armhole to waist, the peplum is full and gathered and the long sleeves are puffed at the head. The jacket fastens edge to edge from base of V to waist with rouleau loops and fabric-covered buttons.

Left: Linen suit: the short belted jacket has raglan seams with full sleeves gathered into bands buttoned at elbow. The scoop neck has shaped facings stitched down on the outside and covered buttons are centred down the centre front band. The jacket tops an elegant lean straight skirt.

Right: Soft fine polyester for a Twenties look. The long bodice is gathered on to a shoulder yoke and fastens with ball buttons and rouleau loops; the elbow length puff sleeves have narrow elastic through the hem and wadding supports the sleeve head. The lace collar neckline is finished with a bias strip; the skirt comprises four full A-line panels gathered onto drop-waist.

Made in moss crêpe the bodice has a faced V-neck and gathers under the bust, long fitted kimono sleeve with underarm gusset; at the wrist, ball buttons and rouleau loops. The deep waist yoke spans both front and back. A straight skirt has fullness gathered at the waist and a hemline slit at the back.

Left: Crisp classic shirt in silk shantung; the bust shaping is in waist tucks, the shoulder and sleeve head adapted to shirt-sleeve line and the sleeves fitted with deep cuffs. The long black velvet skirt is cut straight and slit up to knee level at the side. The wide shaped waistband is stiffened and criss-crossed with gold soutache braid.

Right: Simple black georgette camisole has underarm dart and narrow straps; worn with black silk trousers and topped with a gold jersey cardigan with wide sleeves and patch pockets.

Camisole back view shows one-button opening and shaped bound upper edge. The classic straight trousers are fitted with darts at the back and sloping centre back seam of the trouser block; they have seam pockets, front tucks and centre front fly zip.

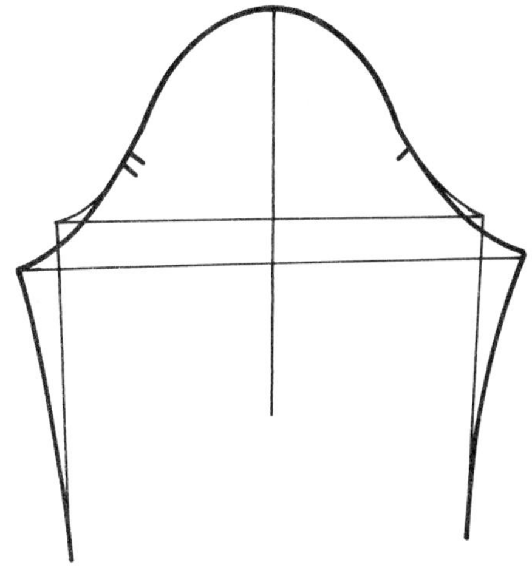

bodice allowing the usual sleeve head ease of 3cm/1¼in which will still be required. Adjust sleeve at underarm if necessary.

C. Loose-fitting armhole. This is probably more commonly used than any of the previous styles because it provides the loose fit and casual look required for comfortable leisure and sports clothes.

The line is achieved by combining the extended shoulder on page 126, design B, with the deep armhole described under B above.

The resulting pattern has a flat sleeve head and underarm with shallow curve and the bodice also has the sharpness of the underarm curve reduced.

Remember that you will require a generally loose-fitting pattern so additional ease may be required on the block.

SHOULDER PADS

There is a wide variety of shoulder pads available. They not only vary in thickness at the armhole edge, but they also vary in style. The correct style – extended shoulder, raglan, for example – should be used to maintain the line of your design. Ideally you should have the pads in front of you when you adapt the pattern so that you can measure not only the thickness but also how far the pad extends into the bodice.

The great advantages of shoulder pads are that the hang of the garment and the set of the shoulders can be established and will remain during wear and also that, to a certain extent, figure problems and imbalance can be corrected.

On a figure with narrow or sloping shoulders it is difficult to make a garment hang and swing from the shoulders but with shoulder pads to raise and widen the point of support, this can be improved. If one shoulder slopes noticeably more than the other, a bigger pad can be used, built up using a layer of wadding, to correct the imbalance.

In addition to a shoulder pad lifting the garment at SP, it fills the hollow between there and the neck. However, the effect of putting pads into a basic fitted shoulder is to shorten the neck. The pattern must therefore be adapted to widen the shoulders as well as raise them. On people with narrow shoulders there may still be insufficient room for the pad, in which case it must be made smaller by trimming the outer edge to reduce the length of the pad.

Fitting shoulder pads

Shaped, soft shoulder pads such as those in the Vilene range will settle to fit most shoulders but those made of foam may need fitting. Place pad on shoulder and see if there is any space underneath between pad and body or between pad and garment being worn. If there is any space, baste a piece of polyester wadding to the pad to fill the hollow to prevent the garment from sliding off the shoulders in wear. If there is a large space or if shoulder pads are being inserted in a loose-fitting kimono style garment, small shoulder pads can be used to fill the hollow.

Covering

Except in unlined garments it is always best to cover shoulder pads if they are not already covered. Use lining, soft cotton lawn, nylon jersey or garment fabric if it is suitable. Cut two pieces at least 3cm/1⅛in bigger all round than the pad. Place pad on WS of one piece and pin. Turn over and pleat the fabric into the hollow. Pin all round. Place second piece of fabric RS up on upper side of pad, pleat over the shape and bring raw edges together. Pin all round. Overlock or zig-zag all round catching in edge of pad for part of the way to prevent it moving, especially when washed. Attach to garment.

Good shoulder pads will have a sleeve head mark or notch on the thick edge; raglan pads will have a line of stitching along the centre. Before you put the pads in the garment make a mark on the edge 13mm/½in further towards the front of the pad and match this to the shoulder seam or sleeve head point. This forward position ensures a comfortable, steady fit and a good line to the garment.

Adapting the pattern

A. Small pads. Small pads are those used in blouses and dresses that have basic armholes and sleeve heads.

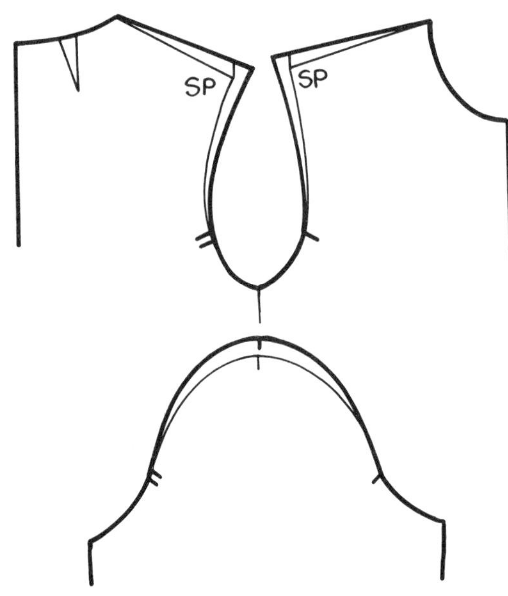

Raise sleeve head 13mm/½in or thickness of pad at centre. Raise SP 6mm/¼in on bodice front and back, or half the amount added to sleeve, and extend shoulder by 13mm/½in.

B. Large pads. Shoulder pads used in outer garments and in other garments with exaggerated shoulder lines are large and the bodice should be adapted as follows.

1. On back and front block rule a line from one-third of the distance from NP to SP, into armhole. Cut and raise at shoulder to insert 1.5cm/⅝in or half thickness of shoulder pad.

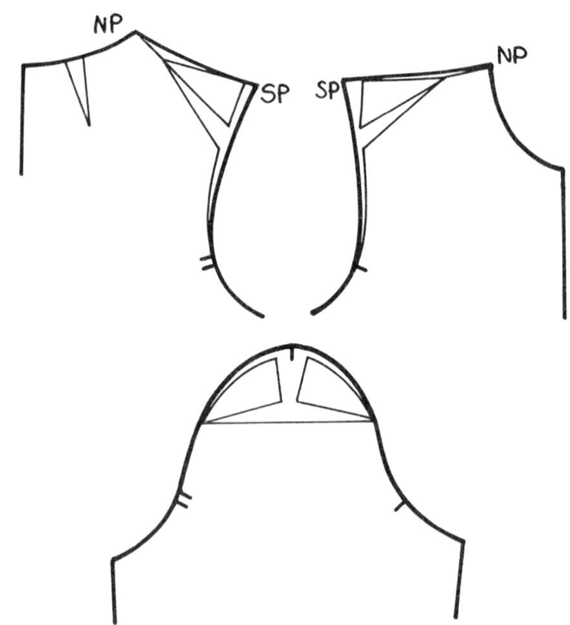

2. On sleeve cut across pattern at corresponding depth, cut vertically from sleeve head and insert an amount equal to thickness of pad i.e. twice that inserted in back or front bodice. Re-draw sleeve head. Extend shoulder seams on bodice by 1cm/⅜in, more if pads are unusually large.
3. The shoulder seam should be redrawn to remove the angle but to retain the curve, as it gives a better fit than a straight seam.
4. Re-draw sleeve head in a smooth curve.

SQUARE ARMHOLE

This adaptation is the opposite of the extended bodice styles. To make a square armhole, a piece

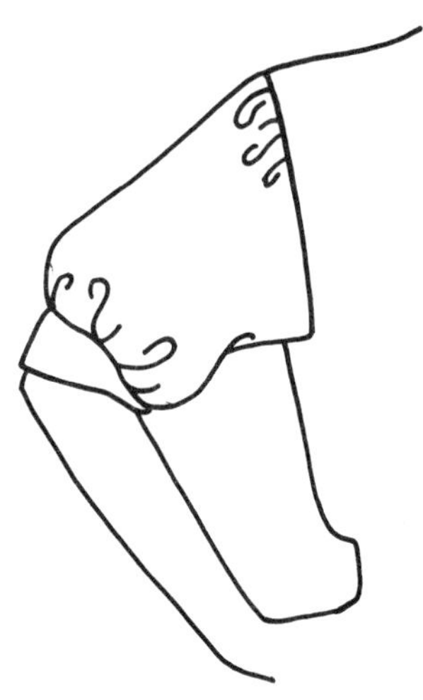

of bodice is detached and added to the sleeve head so that the sleeve will extend into the bodice.

Outline front and back blocks with shoulder edges meeting. Draw shape of square armhole taking note of position of BP; bust dart may be moved into the new seam. Similarly on the back you might consider transferring the neck dart to the seam. Add balance marks; trace armhole section.

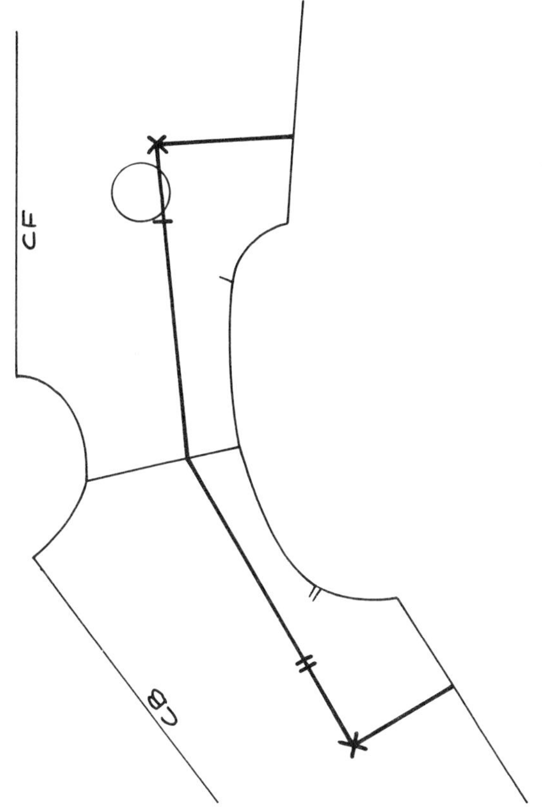

Outline sleeve including underarm line. Rule a line above this and parallel making the distance equal to the depth of the armhole on the bodice.

The traced armhole has now to be added to the sleeve head placing the original armhole edge on the line. Cut across each piece in several places from original armhole edge between balance marks and underarm. Place against appropriate sleeve head matching original balance marks and outlining the section between sleeve head and balance mark. The space between the pieces at sleeve head may be drawn as a seam running from sleeve head to wrist, or as a short curved dart, or it may be gathered to fit the new square armhole.

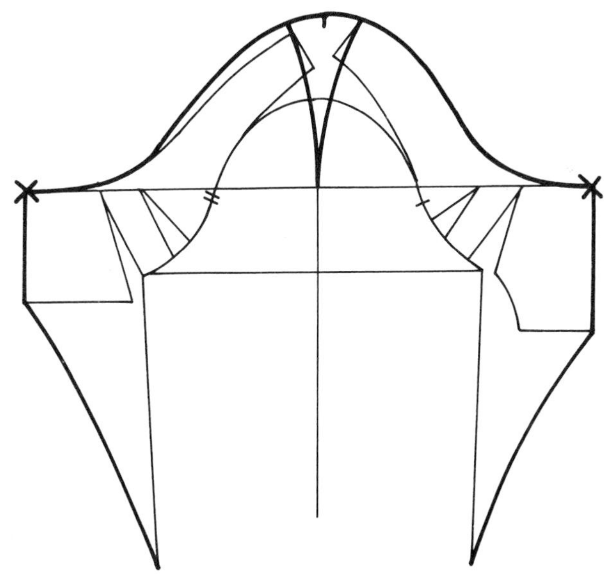

At underarm on the sleeve, open out the slashes and spread the pattern until the inner corners of the square armhole marked 'X' are resting on the horizontal line and the base lines of the armhole are vertical. Outline the sleeve curving from new underarm. Adjust length, fold sleeve and check length and shape of sleeve seam edges.

SEWING TIP

When stitching angled seams press a small square of Bondaweb to WS of angles on bodice to prevent fraying. Place pieces RS together but join one part of the seam at a time stitching from the angle ('X' on the pattern above) to the edge, pressing and snipping the section. With the other section of the seam RS together stitch from the angle to the outer edge, snip and press. This will prevent wrinkles at the corners.

KIMONO, RAGLAN AND BATWING SLEEVES

KIMONO SLEEVES

If the sleeve and bodice blocks are combined and outlined as one piece, the armhole and sleeve head seam is eliminated. This shape, referred to as the kimono, is the easiest of all sleeves to sew. It provides a base from which a wide variety of styles can be made and it is especially useful when loose-fitting clothes are in fashion.

Simple kimono outline

It is worth making a cardboard copy of this shape as it can be used for all types of sports and casual wear as well as housecoats and beach robes.

1. Outline back and front bodice blocks to waist level with plenty of space beyond the armhole. Transfer bust dart to waist on front.
2. Add 2cm/¾in to side seam to loosen the fit. Raise SP 1.5cm/⅝in.
3. Rule new shoulder seam from NP and extend to full length of sleeve block (measure along middle finger line).
4. At wrist rule a line at right angles to shoulder seam. Measure along it half width of basic sleeve block at this point.

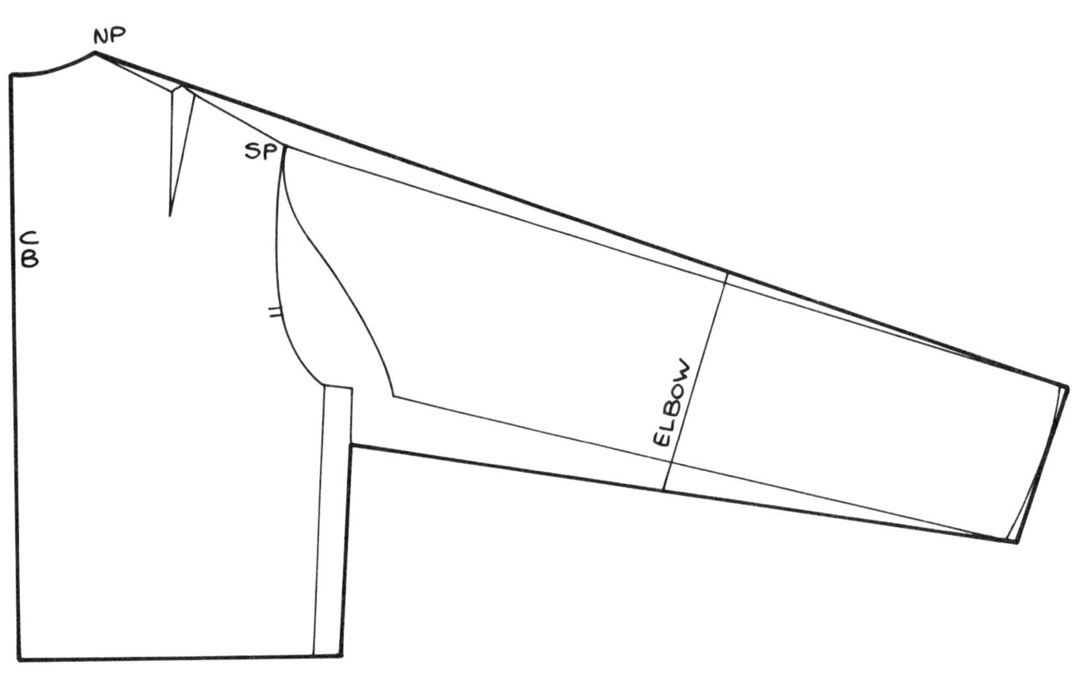

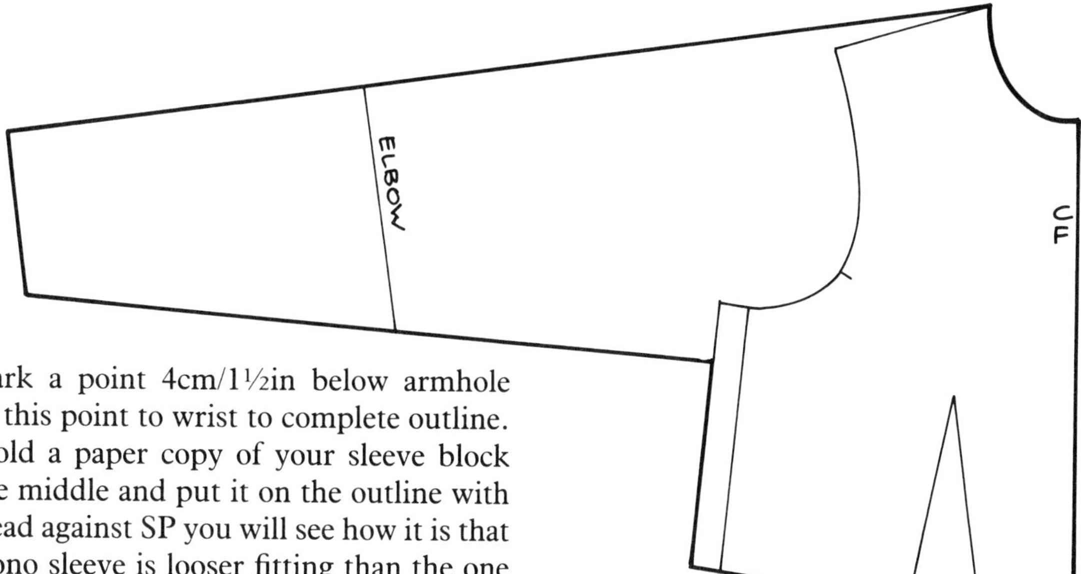

5. Mark a point 4cm/1½in below armhole and join this point to wrist to complete outline. If you fold a paper copy of your sleeve block along the middle and put it on the outline with sleeve head against SP you will see how it is that the kimono sleeve is looser fitting than the one that is set in. SP has been raised and underarm has been lowered to allow more arm movement. Mark elbow line at right angles to shoulder seam; lengthen back underarm seam if necessary.

Kimono sleeve designs

A. Cap sleeve blouse. Outline kimono block; draw new neckline and mark facing width. On

the front rule a sleeve hemline parallel with elbow line on block at required length of cap sleeve. Join sleeve hem to side seam with a curve. Draw new side seam parallel with CF to length required. Draw hem. On back block mark off shoulder seam length to match front, curve underarm and draw side seam equal in

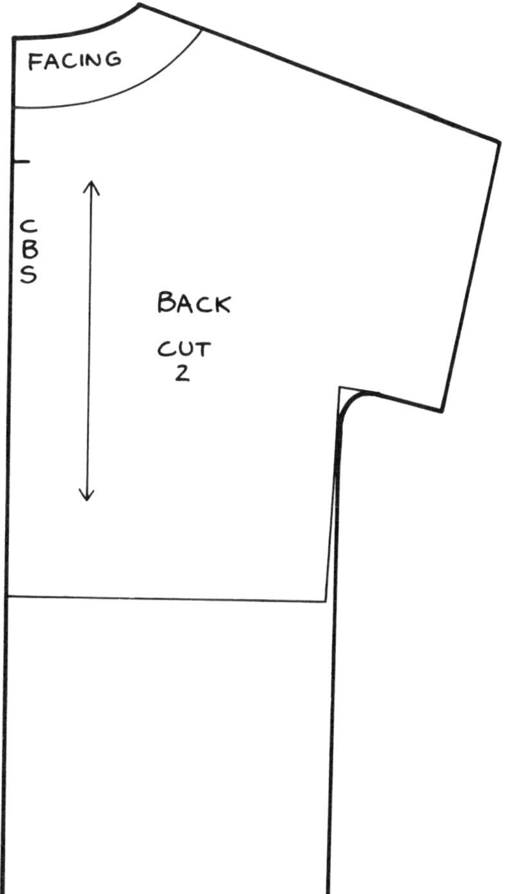

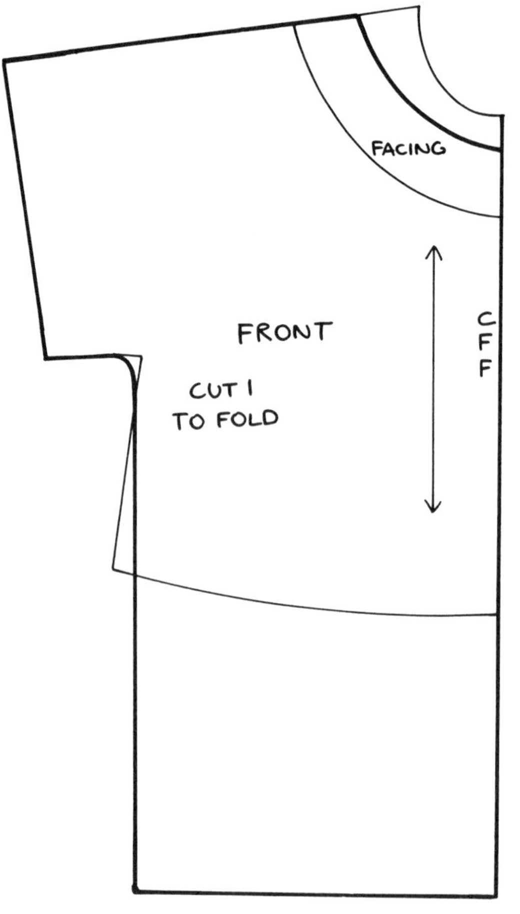

length to front. Draw hem. When seam and hem allowances are added remember to shape the sleeve hem at underarm so that it folds back flat. Mark depth of CB seam opening.

B. Fitted sleeve. The previous kimono design was loose-fitting, with wide sleeves to allow arm

movement. However these can be bulky underarm in some fabrics and sometimes lack the style required in more formal garments. The design illustrated shows a kimono sleeve tight at wrist and fitted with an elbow dart. Room for arm movement is provided by a gusset underarm.

1. Cut sleeve along middle finger line. Place front to front block and back to back block with sleeve underarm point 3cm/1¼in below bodice armhole underarm and with sleeve head touch-

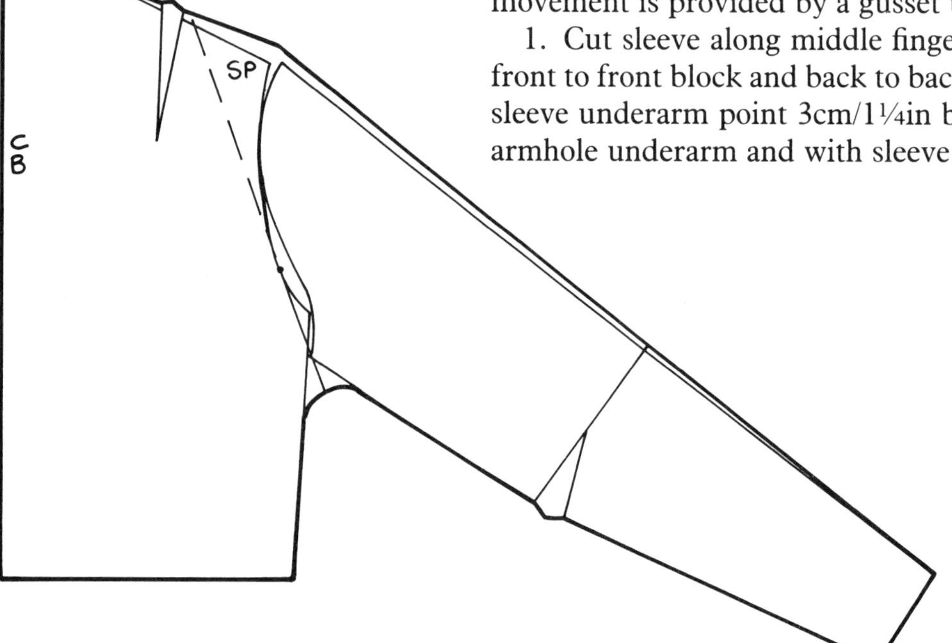

ing armhole higher up. Outline sleeve. From point where blocks meet underarm measure 5cm/2in down side seam and along sleeve seam and draw a curve between these points. Adjust underarms to match.

2. Raise SP on back and front 1.5cm/⅝in and rule new shoulder seam from NP to SP and from SP to wrist.

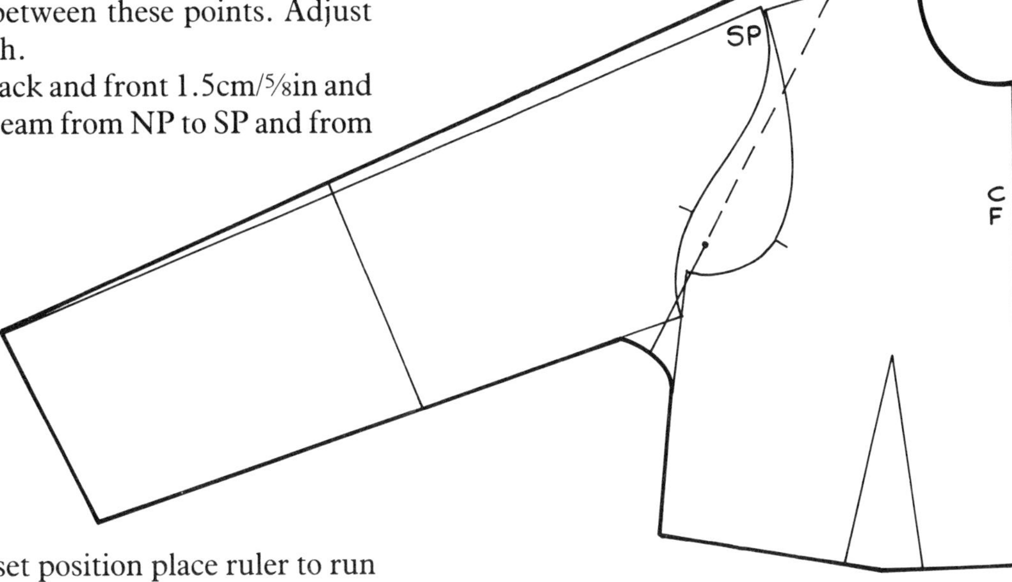

3. To mark gusset position place ruler to run from approximately mid-shoulder to mid-underarm curve and measure 8cm/3⅛in along the line. When making up the garment this line is cut and a square of fabric inserted; two edges joined to front bodice and two to the back. The gusset pattern is therefore an 8cm/3⅛in square.

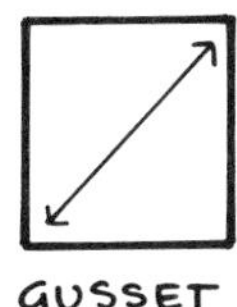

Sometimes the gusset forms part of a bodice panel, in which case only two sides of the square are used. Also, if required the gusset can be a diamond shape, extending further into the front than the back.

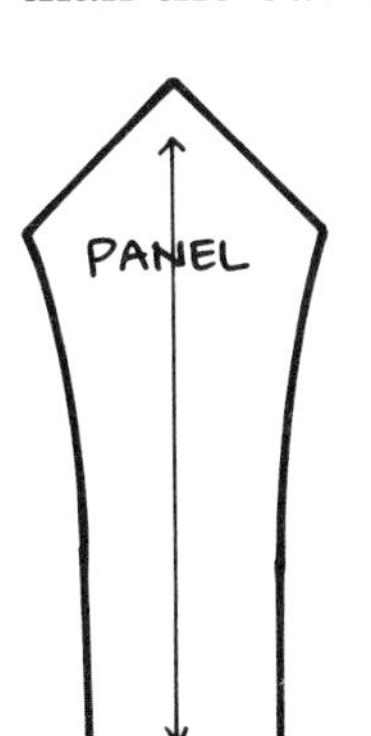

4. To make the pattern for the bodice shown, draw new neckline, folding out 1cm/⅜in at front neck to prevent gaping. Draw shape of waist yoke on back and front. Trace off and close darts. Outline for final pattern. On back bodice close shoulder dart to transfer to waist. Mark gathers or tucks along lower edges. Mark SG and balance marks and outline for final pattern.

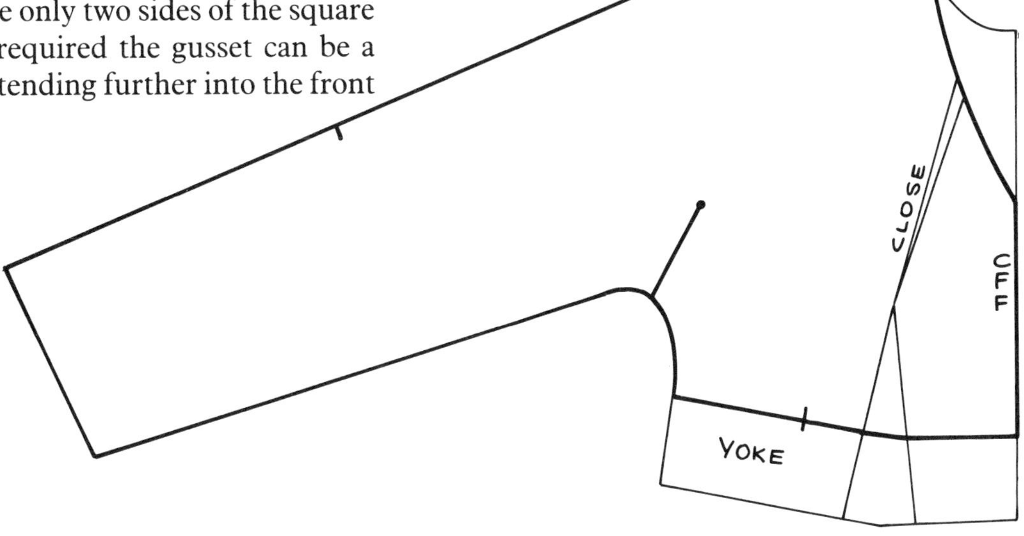

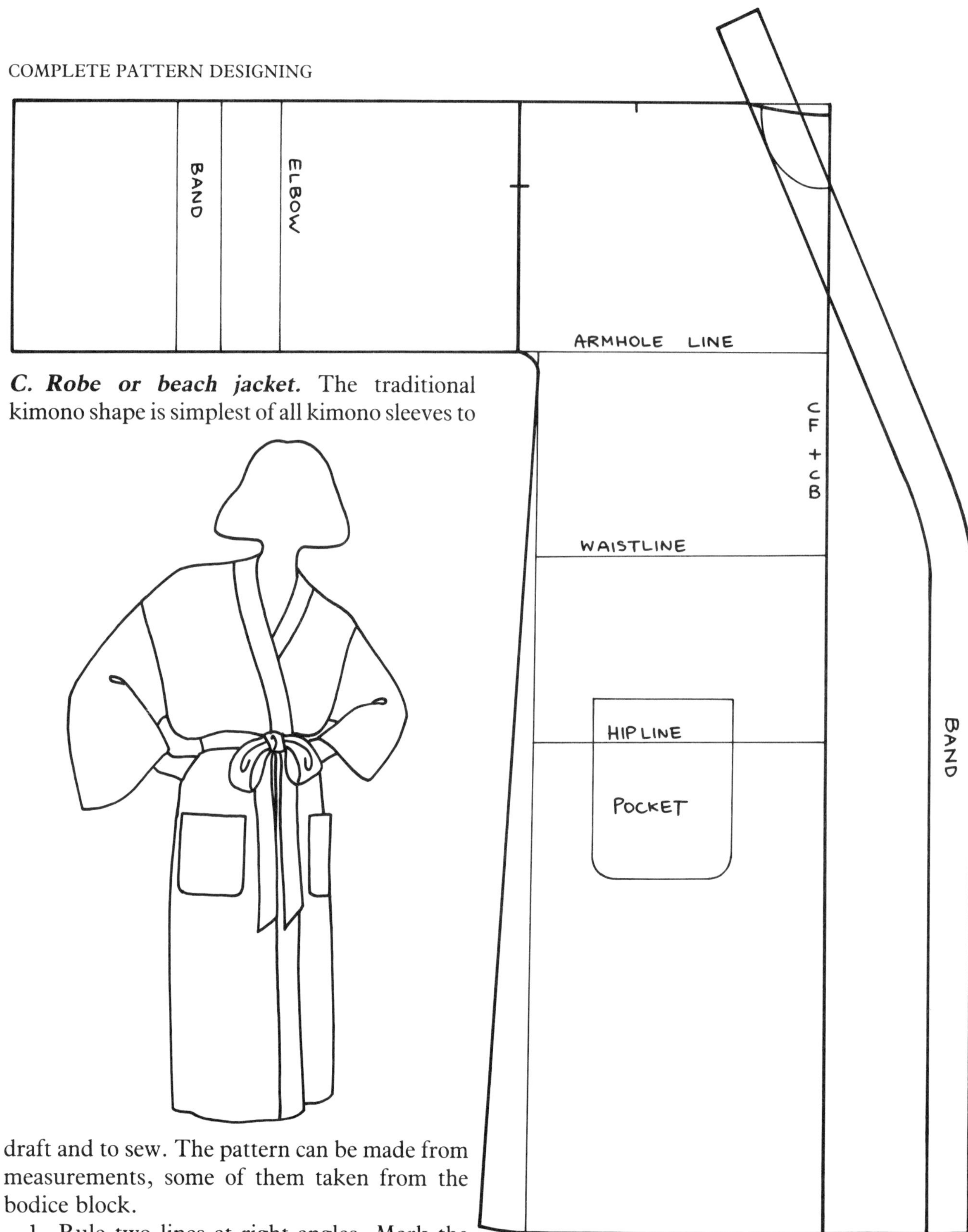

C. Robe or beach jacket. The traditional kimono shape is simplest of all kimono sleeves to draft and to sew. The pattern can be made from measurements, some of them taken from the bodice block.

1. Rule two lines at right angles. Mark the vertical CF and CB and mark the horizontal shoulder line. Draw back and front neckline at the corner taking the size from the bodice block. Measure from neck and mark shoulder point, elbow and wrist length. Measure armhole depth and waist and hip depths and rule horizontals. Extend armhole line and draw wrist line.

2. On hip line measure from CF/CB bodice block hip width plus 2cm/¾in (more for sizes larger than 14). Rule side seam to underarm and

curve at the angle. Extend CF/CB to length, rule hem and complete sloping side seam.

3. For front wrap extend at CF and draw neckline. Add width of band. Adjust back neck width to meet band. Extend band beyond neck sufficient to fit back neck.

4. Trace band and mark cut 4. Trace back and front robe separately.

RAGLAN SLEEVES

A raglan sleeve can be identified by the seam that runs from the underarm or armhole into the neckline. It is a comfortable sleeve because the fitted armhole line has been moved off the shoulder bone and it is easy to sew because there is no sleeve head to manipulate. Originally a man's greatcoat design to slip easily over a jacket, it is used with great effect on all types of clothes. It is particularly useful where a loose fit is important, for example in sports wear, night clothes and baby clothes.

The level of armhole and position of seam in the neckline varies with the design so it probably is not worth making a raglan block in card but the adaptation is quick to do.

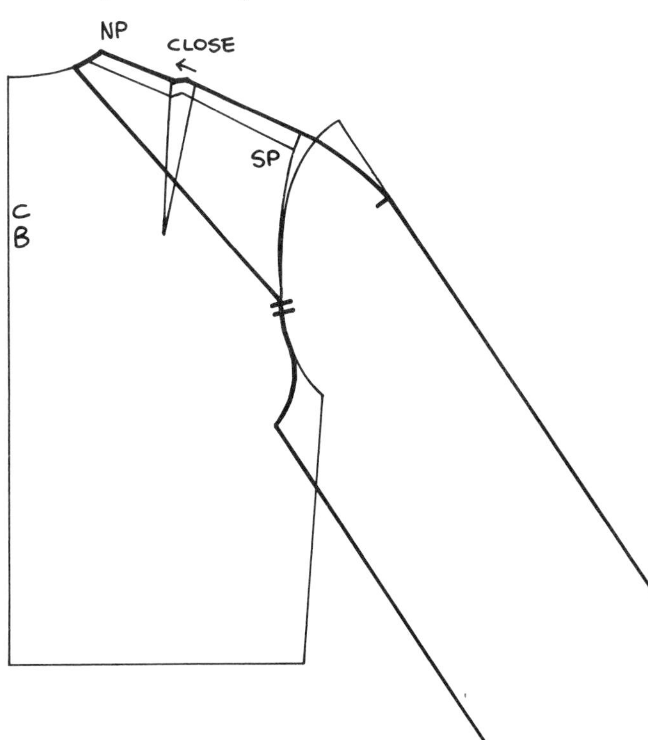

Simple raglan

1. Begin by centralizing shoulder line by removing 1cm/⅜in from front bodice shoulder and adding it to the back. Measure and mark an equal distance round back and front neck from NP. This should be 2.5–3.5cm/1–1⅜in depending on bust size.

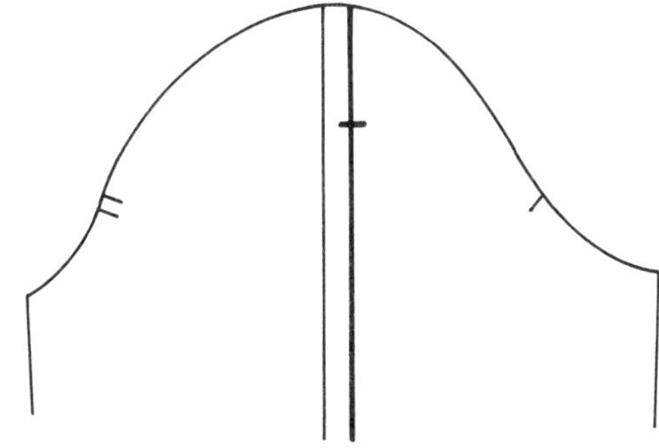

2. Outline sleeve block and move middle finger line 1cm/⅜in towards front. Measure down 6.5cm/2⅝in from sleeve head and mark. Cut out two halves of sleeve along centre line.

3. On bodice and sleeve measure from underarm round armhole 7.5cm/3in and insert new balance marks. On bodice draw raglan lines in a slight curve from this point to marked neck edge points.

4. Place sleeve halves against corresponding bodice armholes matching the new balance

marks. At sleeve head leave a gap of 1.5cm/⅝in between sleeve and SP.

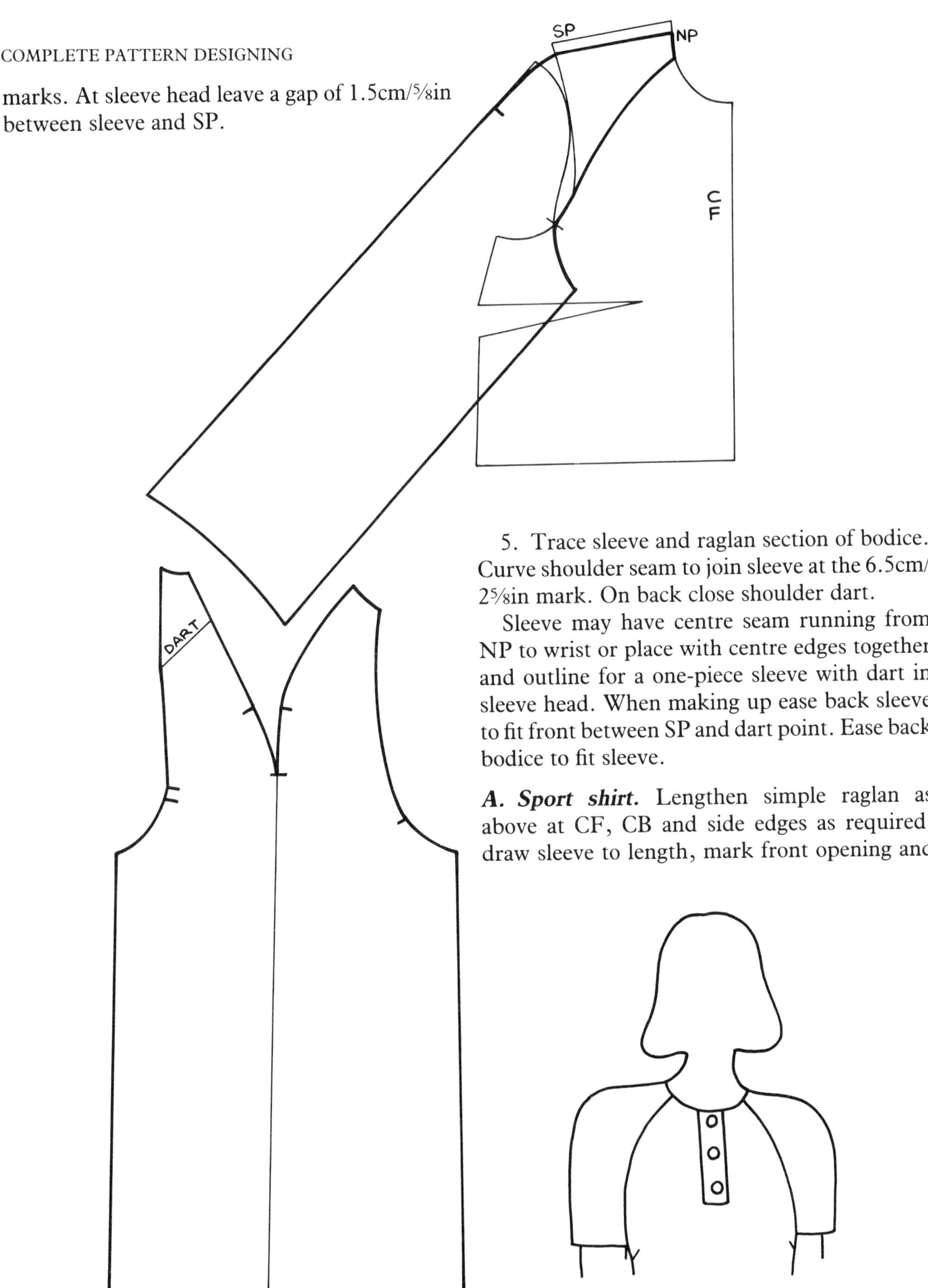

5. Trace sleeve and raglan section of bodice. Curve shoulder seam to join sleeve at the 6.5cm/ 2⅝in mark. On back close shoulder dart.

Sleeve may have centre seam running from NP to wrist or place with centre edges together and outline for a one-piece sleeve with dart in sleeve head. When making up ease back sleeve to fit front between SP and dart point. Ease back bodice to fit sleeve.

A. Sport shirt. Lengthen simple raglan as above at CF, CB and side edges as required; draw sleeve to length, mark front opening and

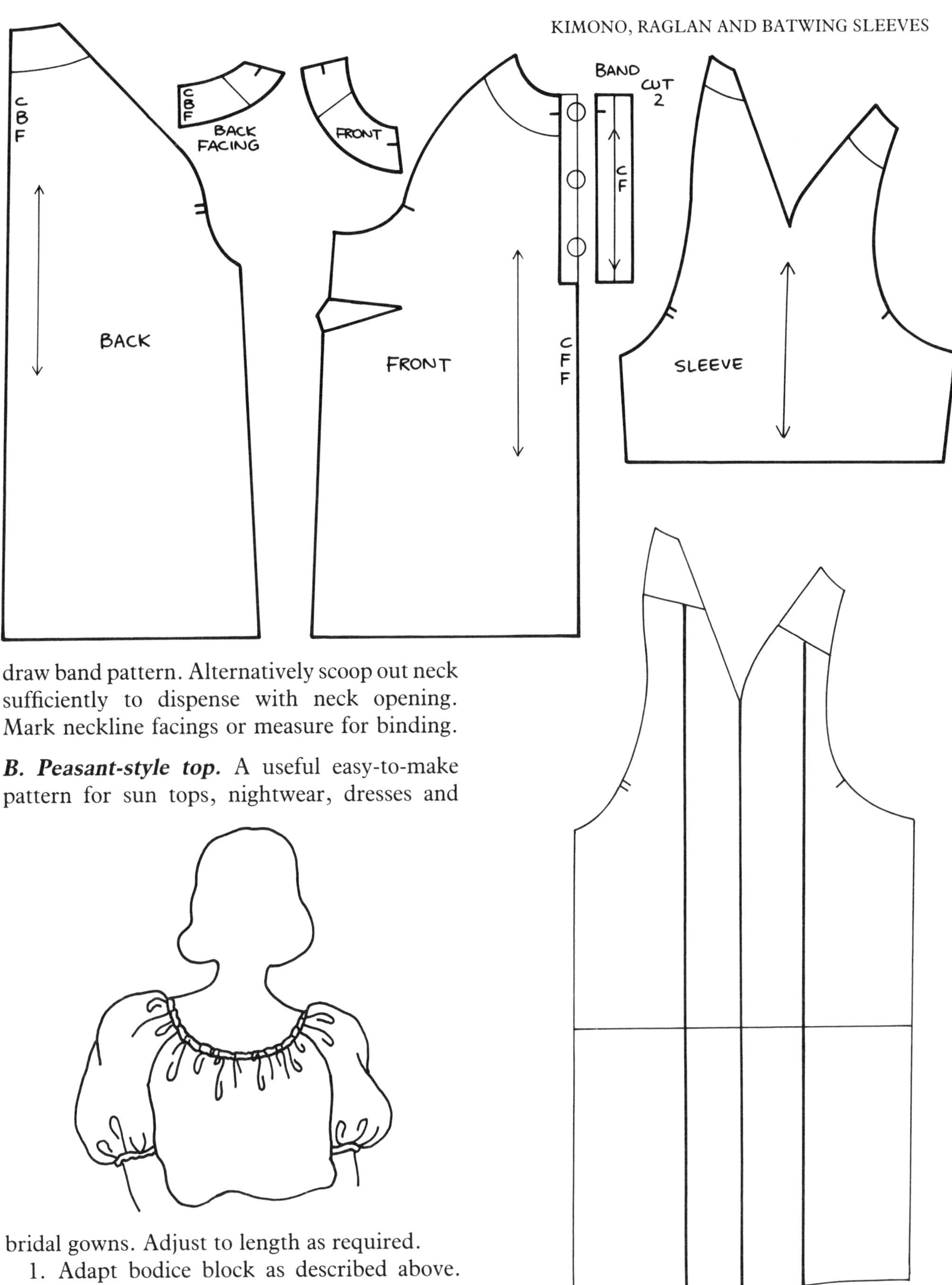

draw band pattern. Alternatively scoop out neck sufficiently to dispense with neck opening. Mark neckline facings or measure for binding.

B. Peasant-style top. A useful easy-to-make pattern for sun tops, nightwear, dresses and bridal gowns. Adjust to length as required.

1. Adapt bodice block as described above. Use straight sleeve block and adapt. Lower

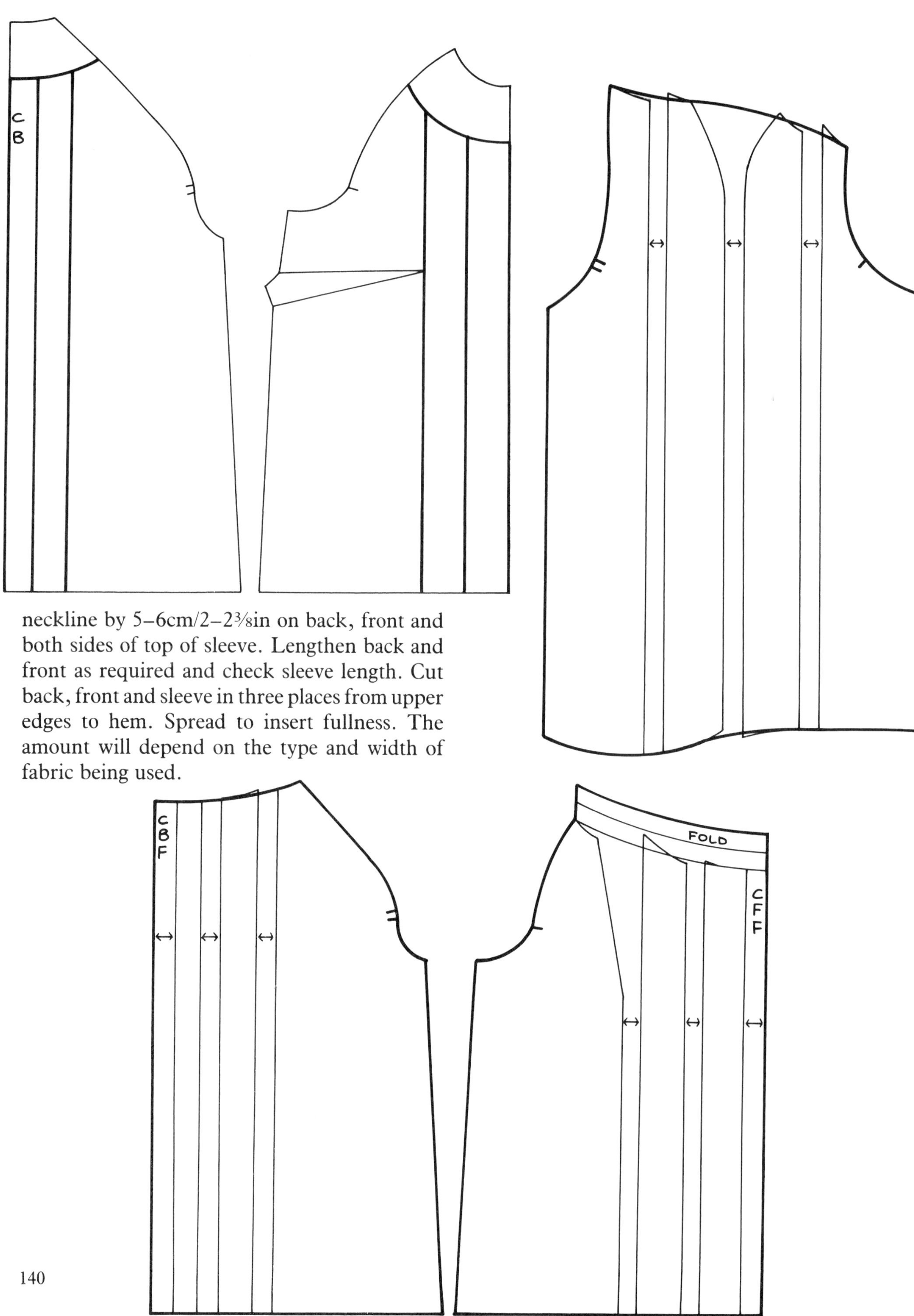

neckline by 5–6cm/2–2⅜in on back, front and both sides of top of sleeve. Lengthen back and front as required and check sleeve length. Cut back, front and sleeve in three places from upper edges to hem. Spread to insert fullness. The amount will depend on the type and width of fabric being used.

2. Outline each piece for final pattern, clipping corners and drawing smooth curves. Measure top and sleeve edges for bias strips for casing or for elastic or drawstring. If there is to be a heading above the drawstring extend edges appropriately. Mark SG and balance marks.

C. Night-dress. Prepare pattern as described for B, lengthening as required and also adding flare at sides.

D. Deep raglan. The raglan seam is so low at underarm that it runs into the side seam. This

involves transferring a bigger section to the sleeve and making an extra adjustment to it but it is nonetheless very logical. Very comfortable and attractive to wear as outer wear, night clothes or sportswear.

1. Construct raglan outline as for simple raglan above. Place sleeve sections together at centre ready to outline. Draw new raglan style lines on the bodice; trace the new shapes from seam line as far as armhole and shoulder but omitting the sleeve. Cut out the sections.

2. Place bodice sections on top of the sleeve at the sleeve head, obscuring the simple raglan lines beneath. Match balance marks and shoulders. Mark balance marks on new raglan edges level with originals.

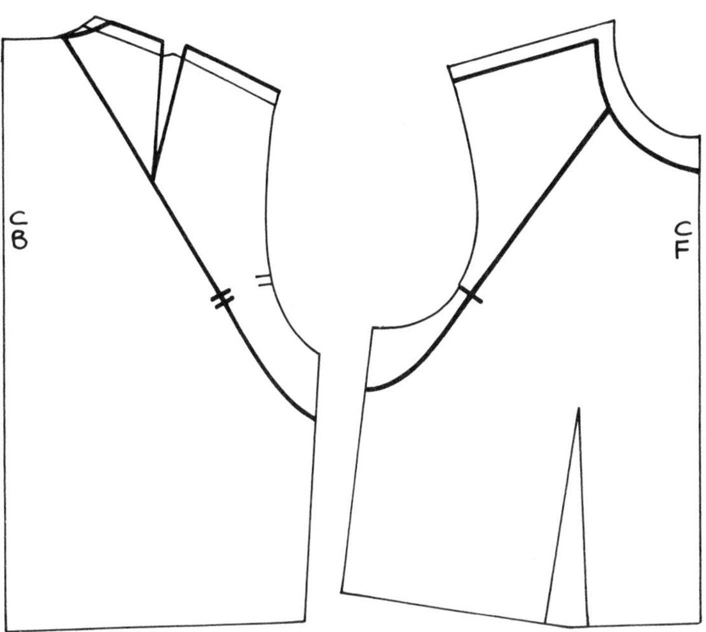

3. Measure down sleeve seam edges half the distance you lowered the armhole on the bodice. Rule short lines out at right angles. Rule a line

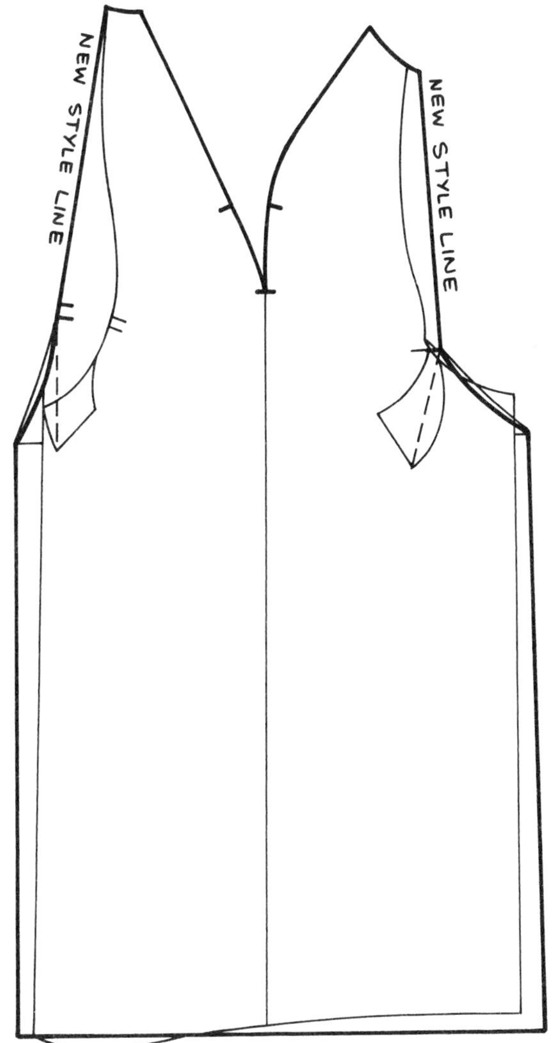

from new balance marks to the corner of the section of bodice that hangs down, so to speak, below the sleeve head. Measure length of line and rule a line the same length from the same balance mark to meet the short horizontal line first drawn at side of sleeve.

Make slightly convex curves of these two lines. Where curve meets horizontal is the new underarm point. Draw new sleeve seam edges to required width at hem (may be wider or narrower than block).

4. There is a final refinement to make to the sleeve pattern. Trace off as far as you have gone and cut out. Cut each side from a point 4cm/1½in below underarm across to a point on the armhole half-way to the balance mark. Swing the section out until you have inserted 6cm/2⅜in in the gap. Draw new curved seam edges from the old underarm point. Adjust length and outline.

E. Belted top. To make the pattern for the tunic illustrated adjust block to deep raglan as

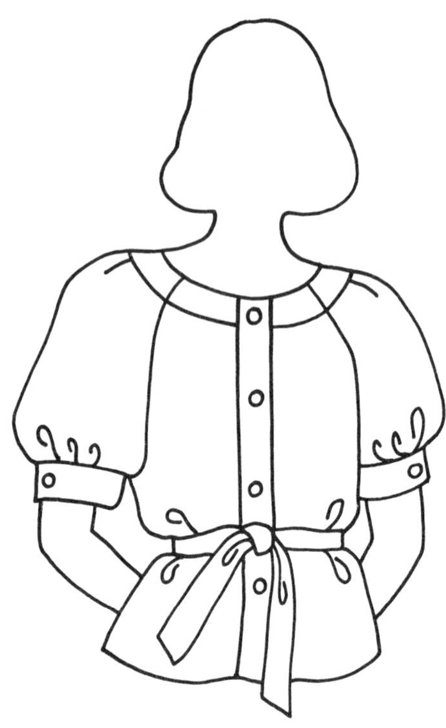

described above. Adjust sleeve length and draw cuff pattern. Lengthen bodice as required, remove a strip from CF twice diameter of buttons and draw band pattern twice that width. Calculate length of tie ends and draw belt pattern. Mark neck facings, trace off and outline with shoulder seams only. Note that the sleeve may have a seam through the centre. It may be more economical in fabric this way and it also gives you the chance of shaping the sleeve if you wish.

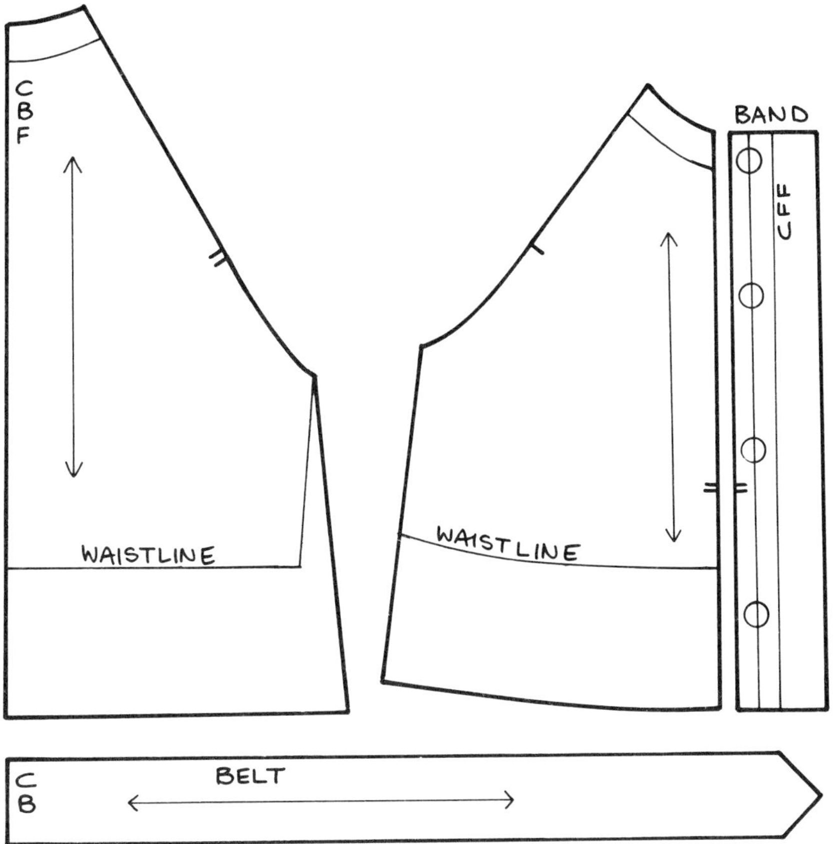

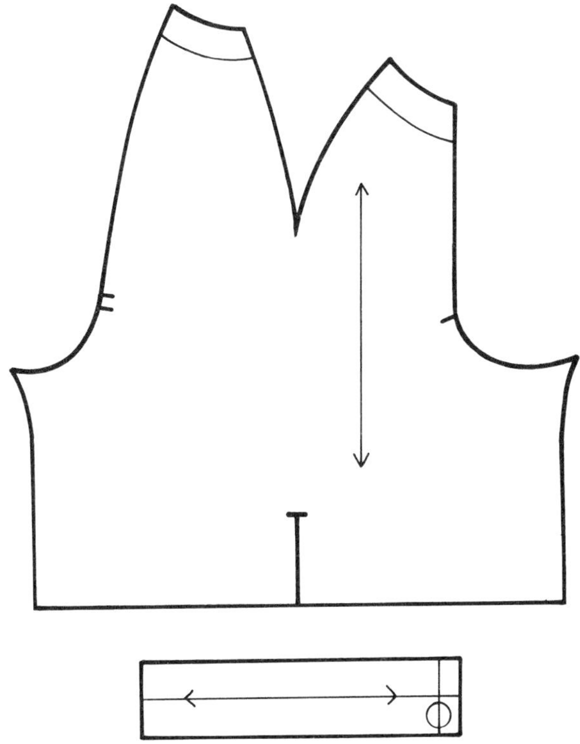

F. It is not always immediately obvious into which category of drafting a design falls. This illustration shows a top with tucks into a yoke but it is in fact a raglan sleeve design.

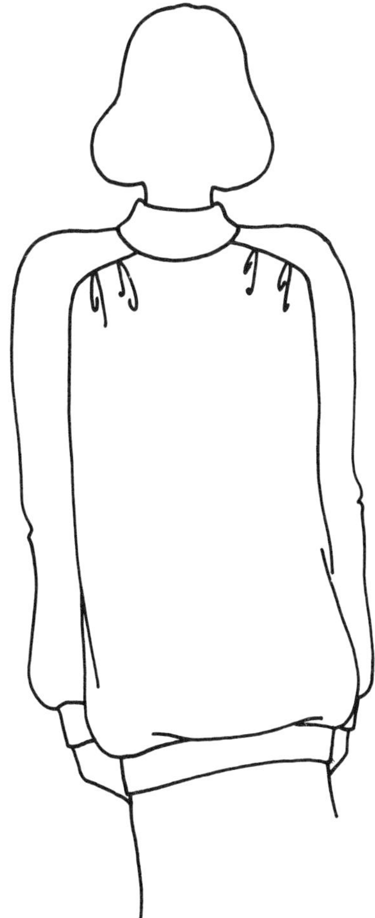

On back and front draw new neckline allowing for ribbed band. Follow steps 1–7, Simple Raglan, page 137, to convert blocks to raglan design. Use straight sleeve block shortened to allow for ribbed cuffs. Cut and spread bodice sections transferring bust dart and back shoulder dart into shoulder pleated area. Lengthen pattern as required and straighten side seams.

Check neck size, mark back neck opening if needed.

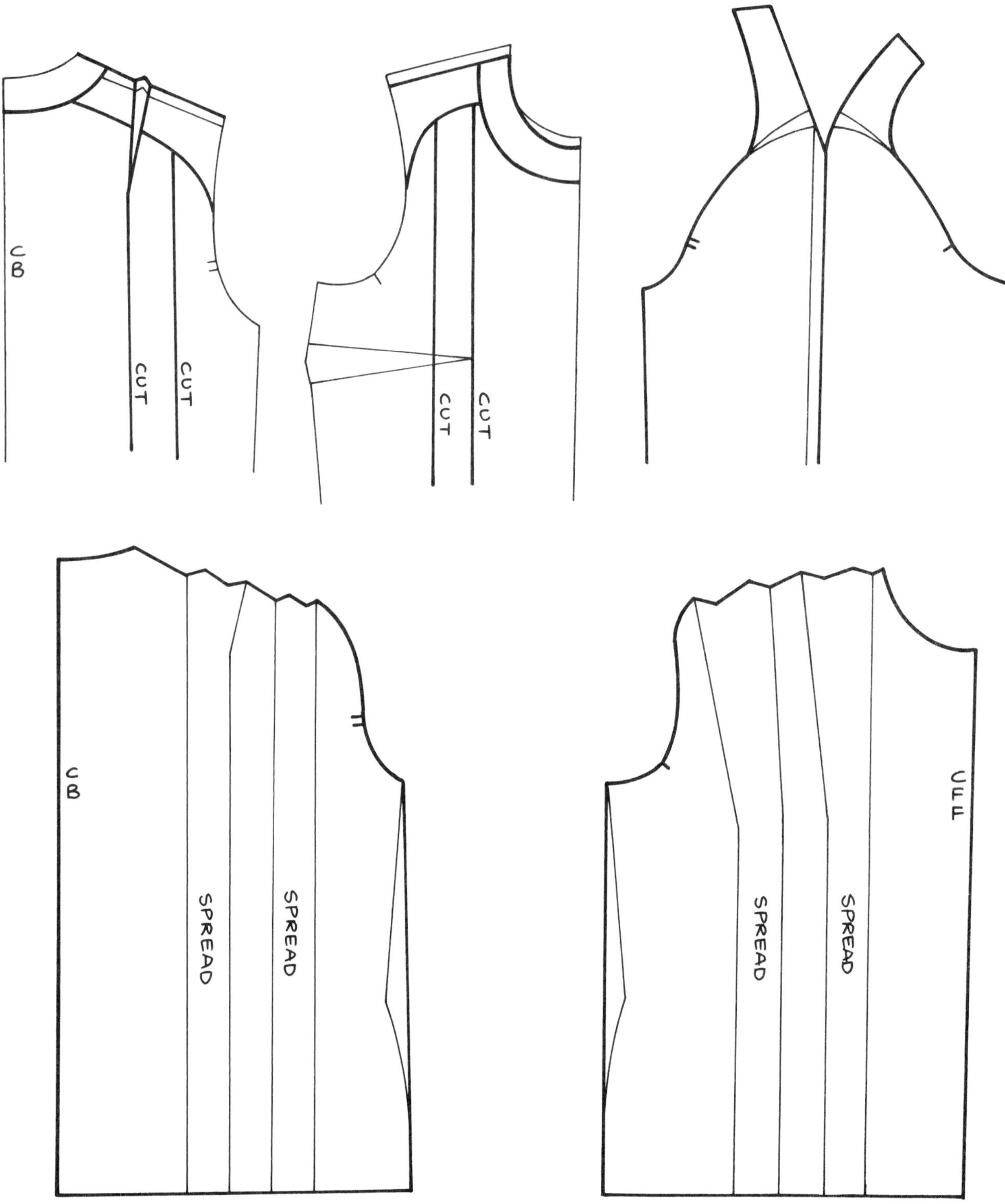

BATWING SLEEVES

Batwing or dolman sleeves are very easy to make and are a development of the fitted kimono sleeve. The underarm seam runs into the waistline. Sufficient room for arm movement is added by cutting and opening the kimono shape between underarm and shoulder. Fabrics should be soft and not too bulky.

Batwing outline

1. Trace back of fitted kimono sleeve, page 134 (B). Replace underarm shape with a new curve between waist and elbow. Rule a line from mid-shoulder to centre of underarm curve. Open paper at underarm to insert 6–8cm/2⅜–3⅛in, depending on fabric.

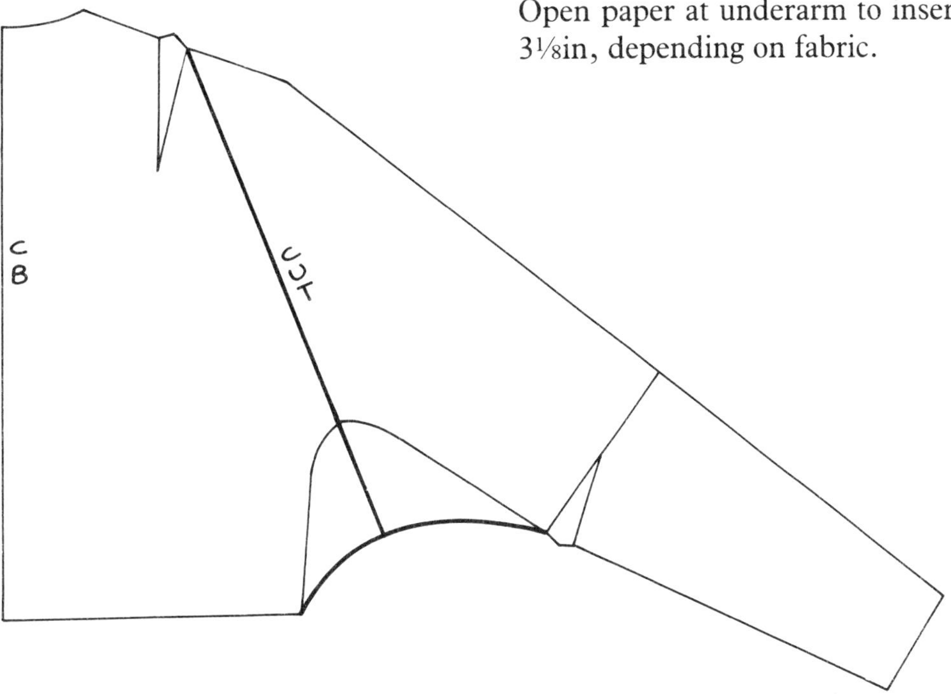

For a straight wide sleeve fold out elbow dart and cut from wrist to dart point.

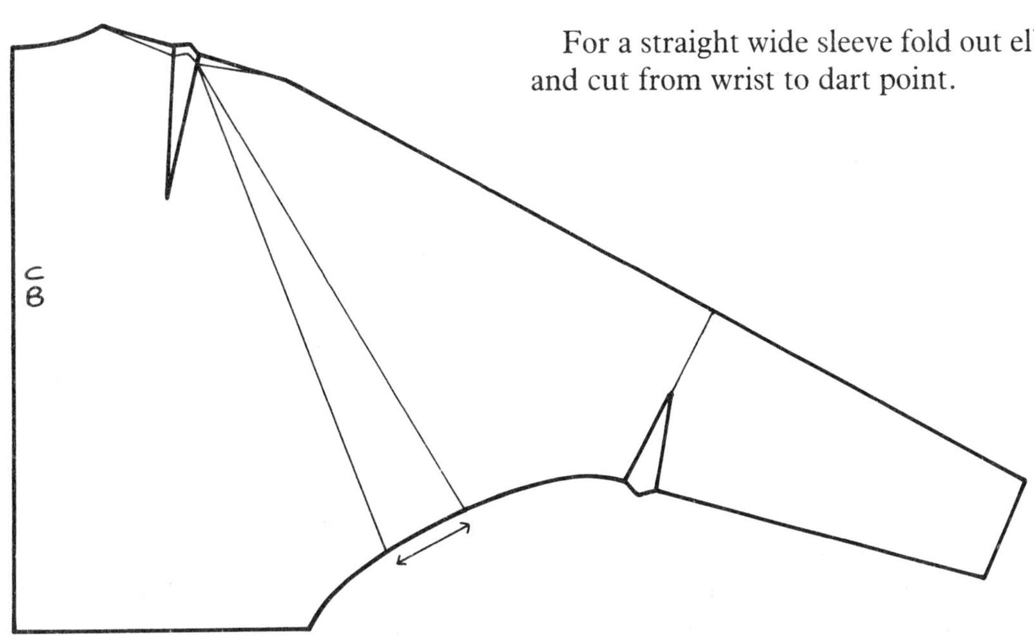

2. Re-draw shoulder seam and underarm to remove angles.

3. Outline kimono sleeve front and adjust in the same way making sure seam edges correspond in length.

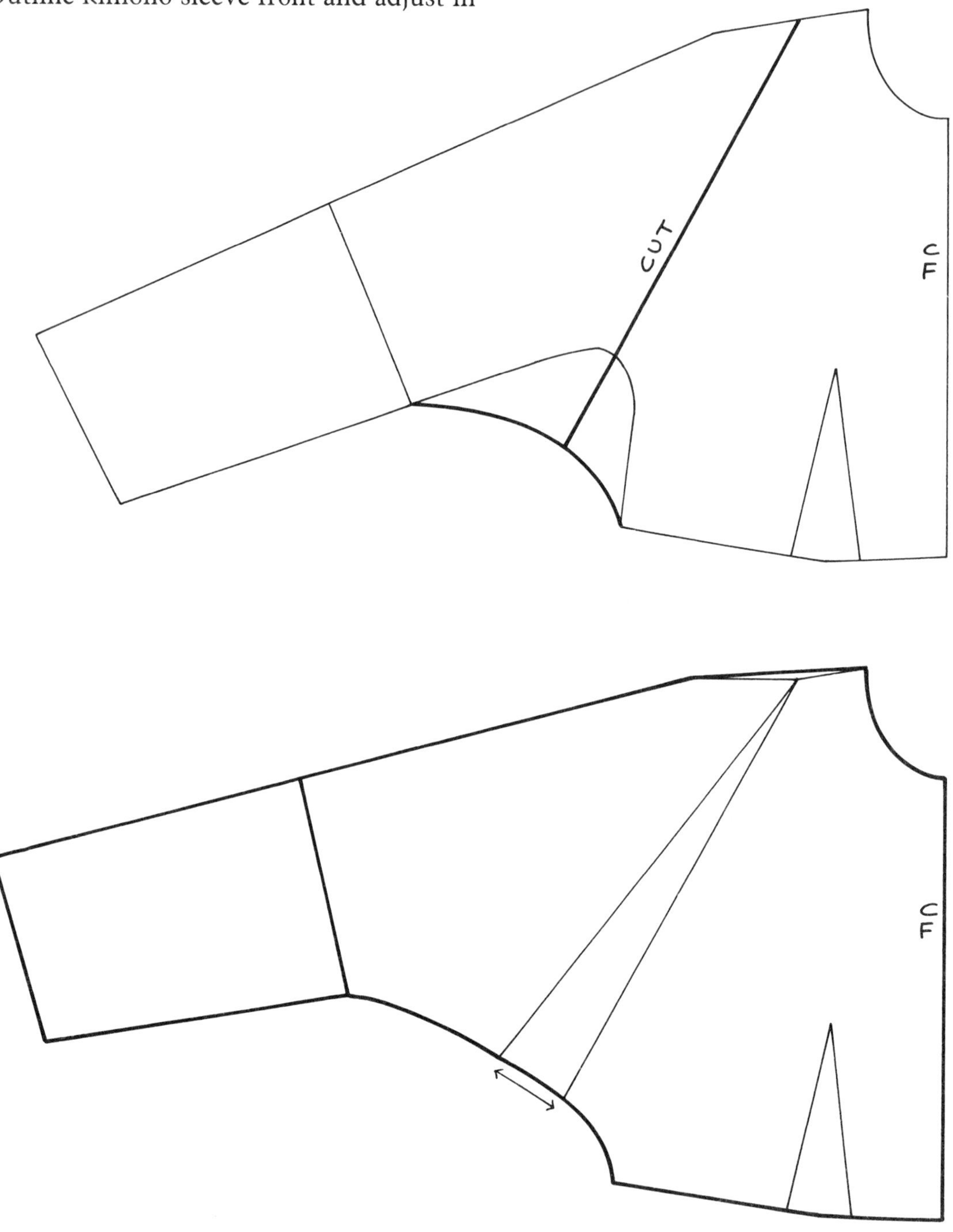

The dart fullness could be gathered at the waist as an alternative on soft fabrics. On the back pattern gather the waist but ease the elbow and shoulder dart to fit front pattern.

The illustration shows a straight sleeve, long and short length. For a sleeve that is shaped at the elbow or wrist, slope shoulder and underarm edges but make sure movement is not restricted.

Batwing sleeve designs

A. Hip length top with ¾ sleeves.

1. Outline back and front batwing sleeve opposite, shortening sleeve to below elbow.

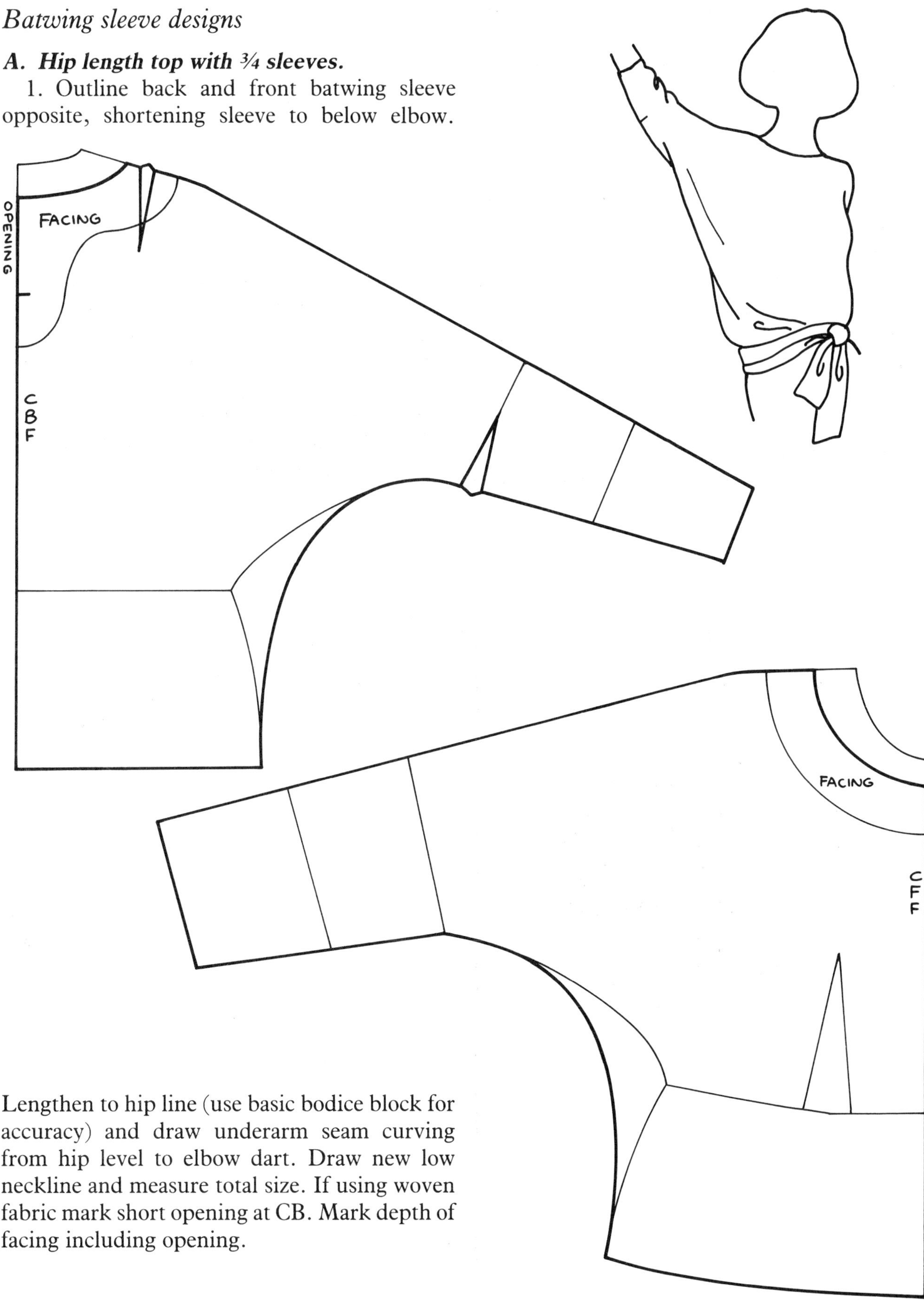

Lengthen to hip line (use basic bodice block for accuracy) and draw underarm seam curving from hip level to elbow dart. Draw new low neckline and measure total size. If using woven fabric mark short opening at CB. Mark depth of facing including opening.

CF + CB
FOLD
BAND

2. Draw hip band with tie ends twice required finished width.

This is an ideal design for making with an overlocker: 6mm/¼in seam allowance would be sufficient and if fabric were suitable facings could be omitted and neck and sleeve edges turned in and topstitched after overlocking.

B. Short sleeves.

1. Outline front and back batwing sleeve above.

SEWING TIP

When making up this type of hip band, tie the cut out band around the figure at required level, i.e. low waist, hips etc., and mark where ends extend. Leave open left side seam of the top for 10cm/4in or so at hem. Gather lower edge and divide into four. Divide band into four omitting tie ends. Matching the quarter marks, pull up gathers until band fits.

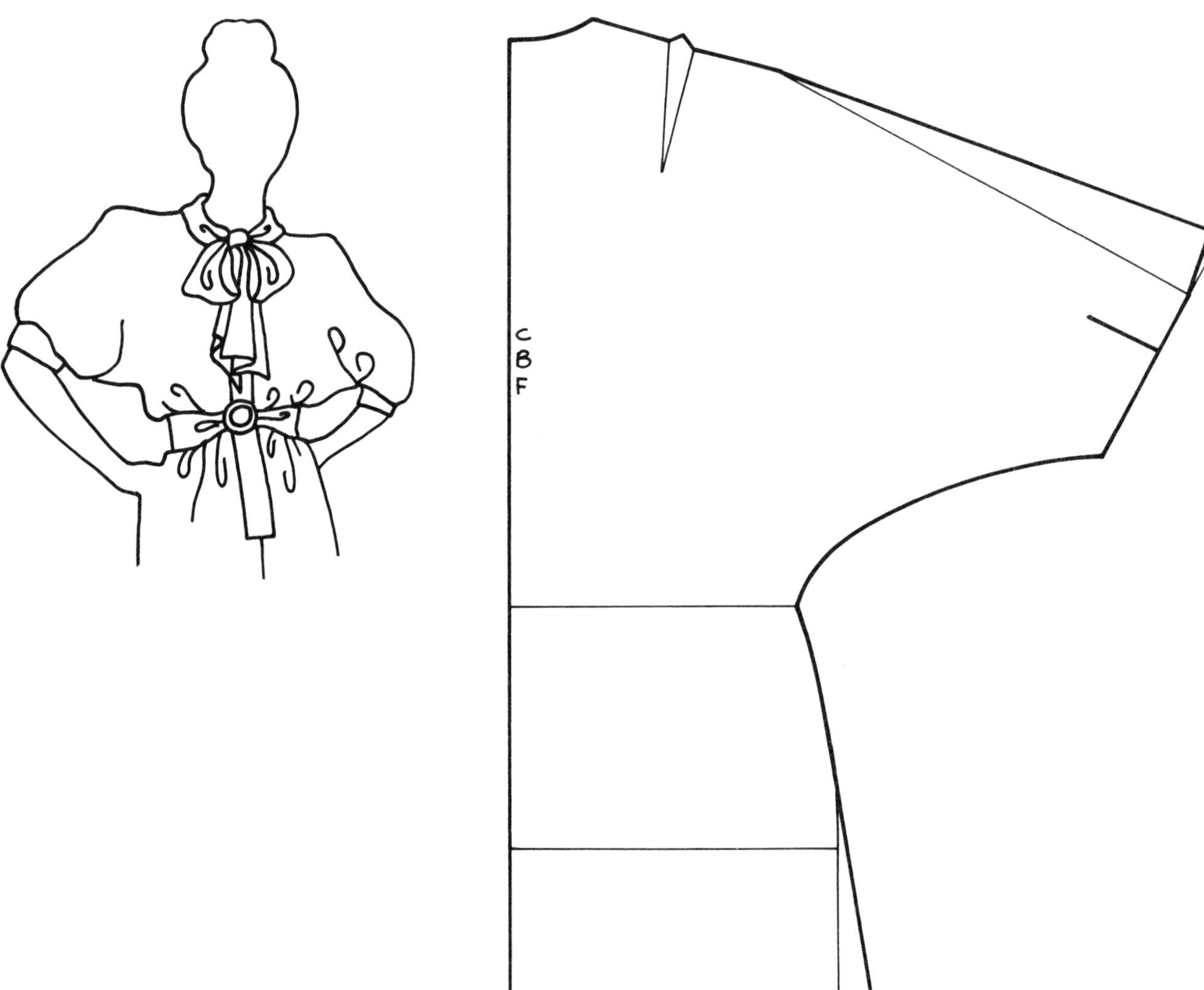

FOLD
CB
CF
TIE
COLLAR

2. Shorten sleeves to elbow length. Add fullness for gathering by extending sleeve hem up and raising shoulder seam by 6–8cm/$2\frac{3}{8}$–$3\frac{1}{8}$in. Curve sleeve hem and mark opening 5cm/2in long.

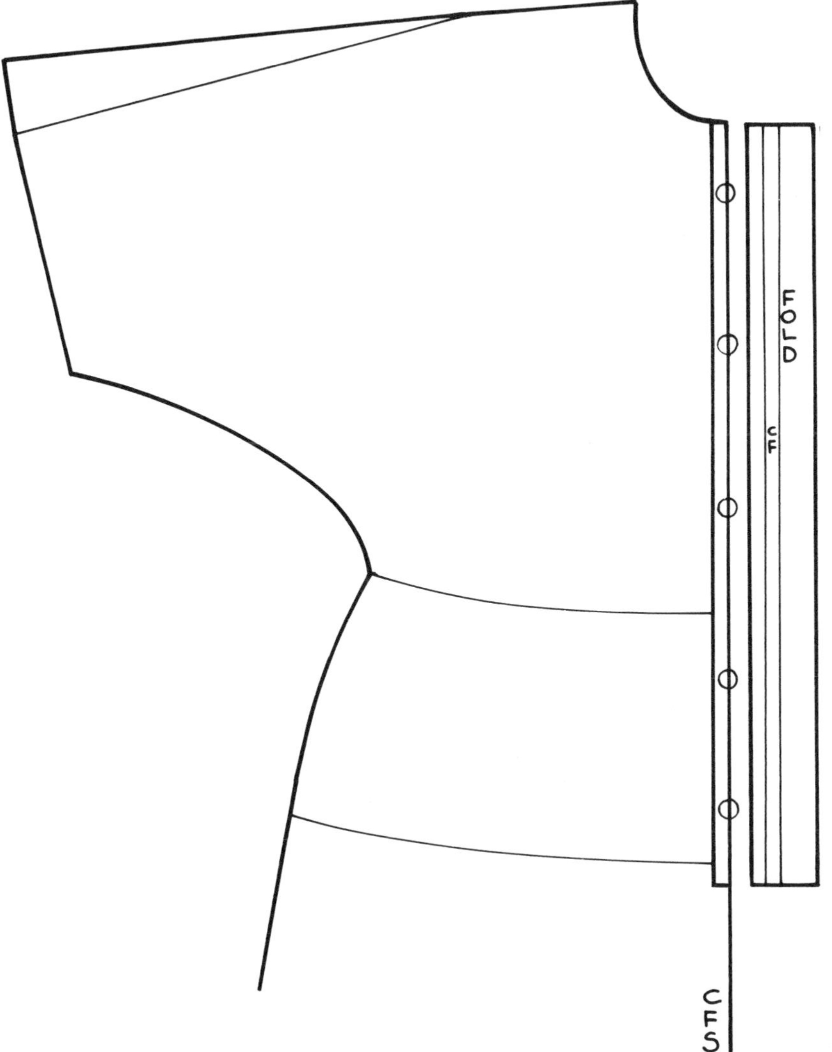

3. Draw cuff pattern to fit upper arm plus overlap.

FOLD
CUFF

DRESS AND TROUSER DESIGNS

DRESS DESIGNS

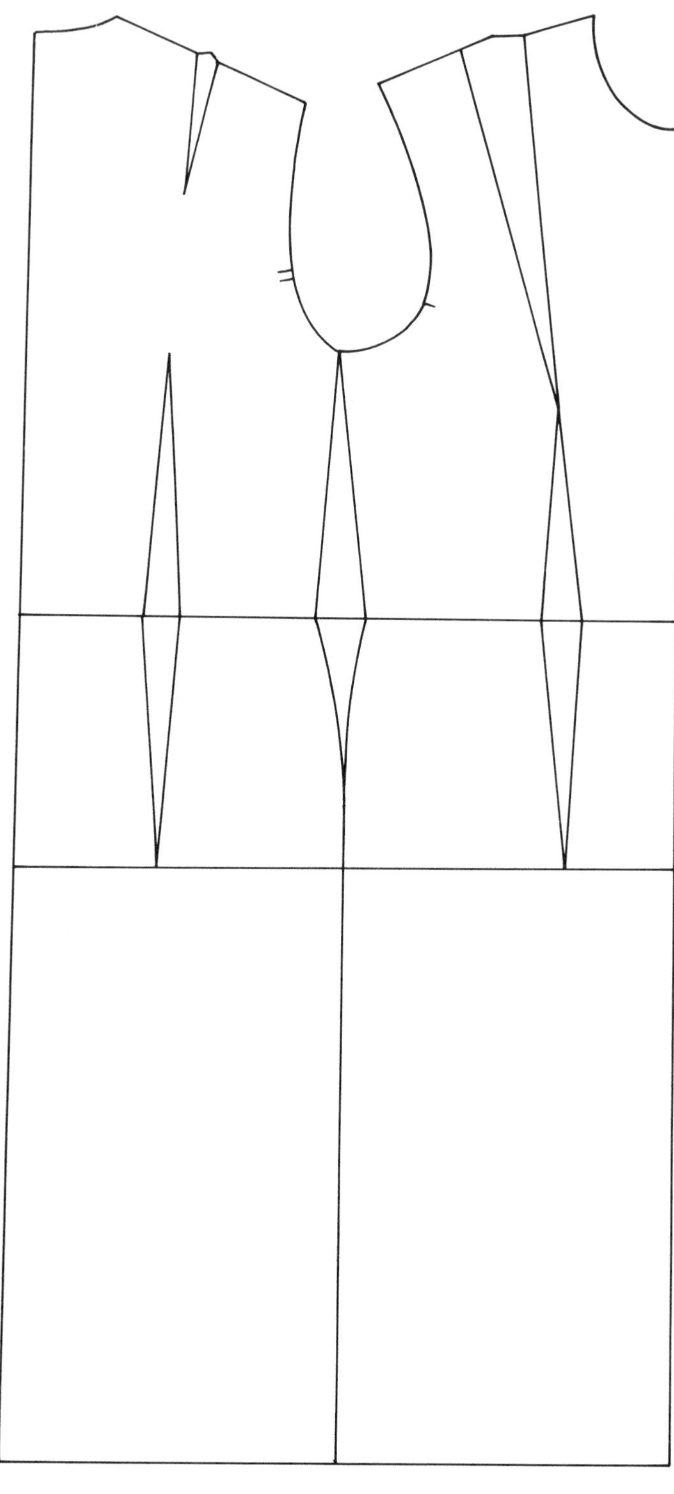

Dress patterns can be made by lengthening the bodice block. One of the advantages of making the original bodice block to hip level is that it is a very simple matter to add the remainder to make it dress length. The illustration shows how this is done but you may feel it is unnecessary to make a full-size dress block for yourself as the bodice can be so quickly adapted each time it is required. With many styles, such as dresses with gathered or circular skirts, the bodice block would be used on its own anyway.

Place the back and front bodice blocks together so that they meet at underarm and hip. Outline to hip length and copy all construction lines, darts and balance marks. Extend CF and CB lines vertically to knee, mid-calf or length required. Rule a perpendicular side seam from hip level to the same length. Rule a horizontal line at hem level. A large hip size may mean that the outlines overlap from hip to hem in which case it will make them more convenient to use to trace off the back and front separately after lengthening.

To use the dress block to make patterns, trace the outline and cut away all darts including side seam shaping. In order to be able to manipulate and transfer the darts cut along waistline from CB and CF as far as the dart. For patterns with waist seams trace bodice and skirt sections separately. After adapting remember to check size of skirt waist against bodice as well as side seam length.

The block outline illustrated is close fitting and the skirt has straight side seams. Remember to add any ease and fullness required for loose-fitting designs. To make the skirt A-line, add extra at side seams and rule new lines from hip to hem. For A-line dresses without a waist seam rule a sloping side seam from underarm to hem.

Adapt the dress block to incorporate your chosen features as described in the chapters on bodice and skirt designs.

A. Drop-waist dress. Outline the back and front dress block, lengthen as required. Add flare to side seams. Draw drop-waist seam at a flattering level for the figure across back and front. Trace bodice section, close bust dart and cut off yoke. Transfer back dart to neckline. Mark CF buttons and loops and measure neckline for length of bias strip.

Cut and spread back and front skirt sections to add gathers. Adapt sleeve to full puff style.

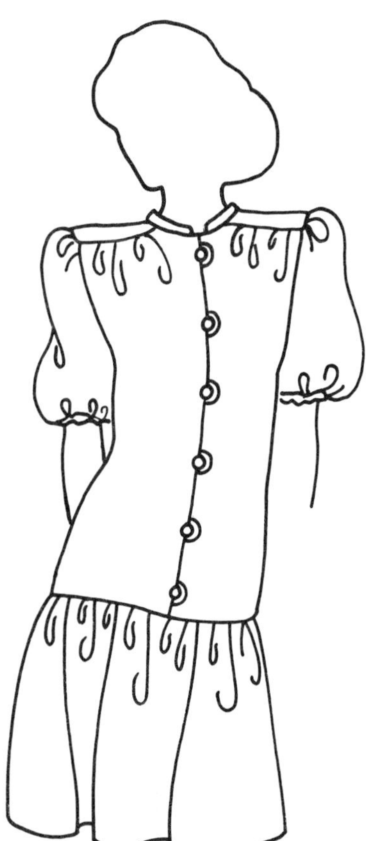

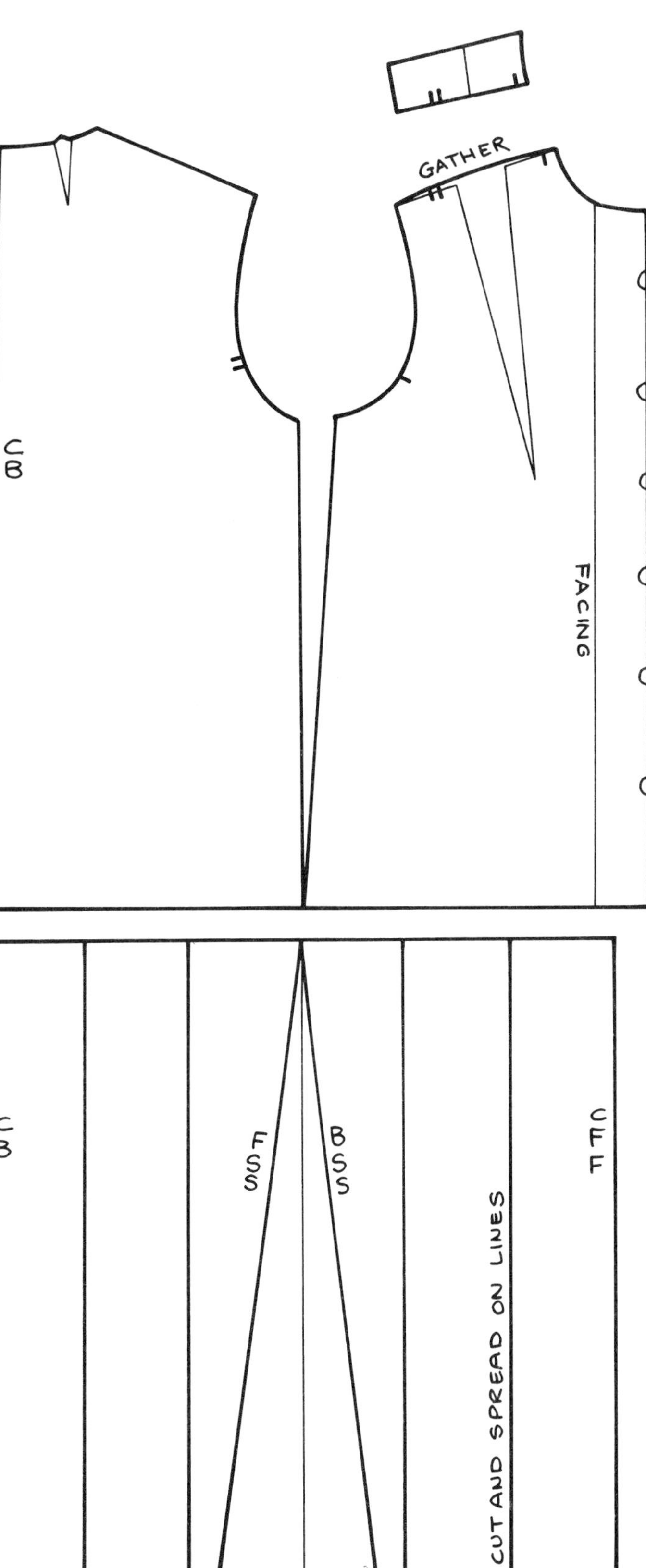

B. Shirtwaister. Outline dress block, lengthen and add slight flare to side seams. Add button extension. On front draw angled seam and false pocket flap; cut to BP. Close bust dart to transfer to armhole.

On back draw corresponding seam and transfer shoulder dart to seam. Draw facing. Construct collar; see page 77. Trace off each section of dress separately.

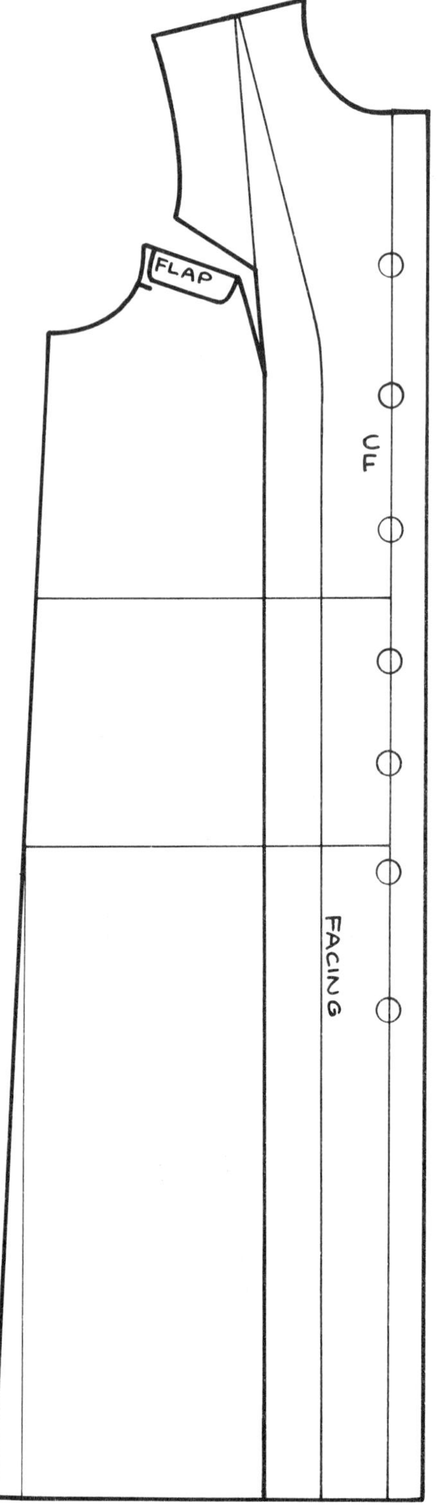

TROUSER DESIGNS

Fortunately, whatever may happen in fashion, trousers remain very much the same shape. The comparatively small adjustments needed to keep in line with current length and width can be easily made and will not upset any careful fitting you may have had to do in the waist, hip and crutch area.

You will find the vertical and horizontal guide lines I suggested for all drafting invaluable when working on trouser patterns.

A. Basic trousers. The block can be made up as it is, without variation and with the addition of a waistband or petersham finish. The zip may be inserted in the side or CF seam.

B. Elastic waist. Outline back and front blocks omitting darts. Rule a vertical line upwards from hip level. Straighten waist level by ruling a horizontal line from CF and CB level with highest part of block. Extend pattern above waist level for twice depth of elastic. Make sure line at CB is vertical so that casing folds down flat. Taper trousers at hemline on outside seam and shorten if desired; mark depth of side slit if required.

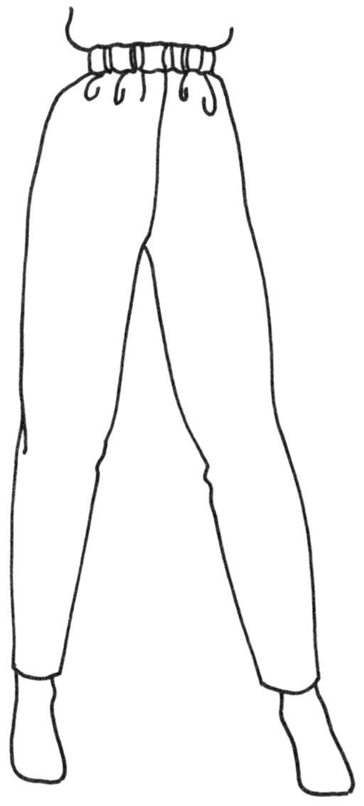

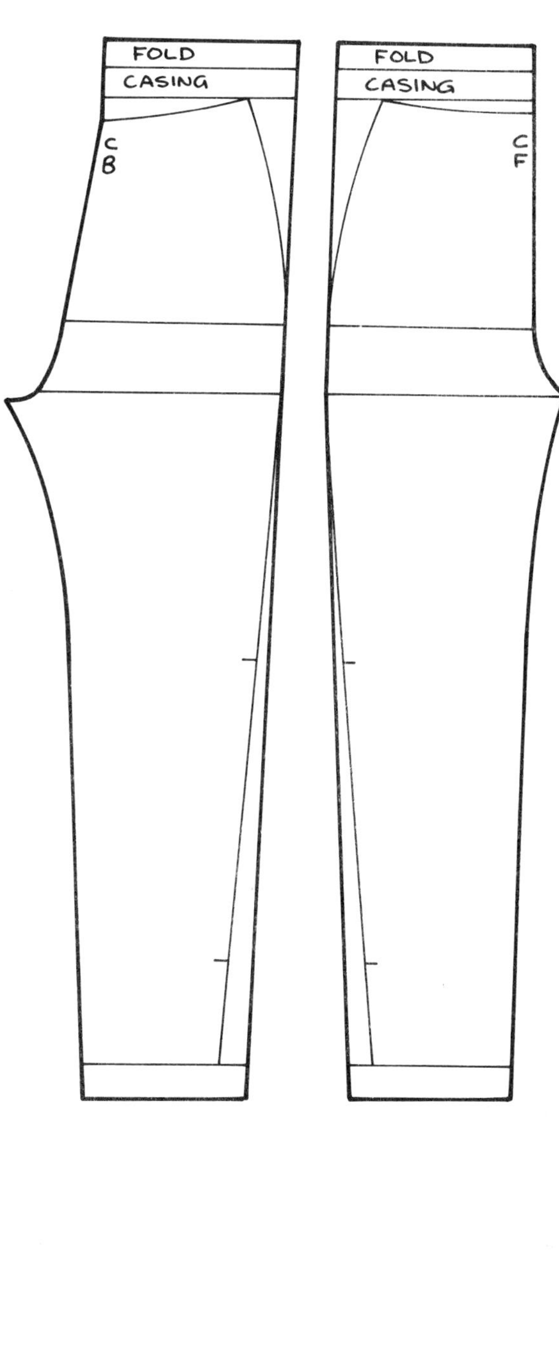

C. Tailored trousers. With fly zip, front pleats and cuffs. Outline blocks marking front dart as a

tuck. Mark zip depth on CF seam and extend for facing. Add extra paper at hems and fold up and back to form cuff finishing with 13mm/½in which will fold up inside the trousers. Cut out pattern with paper folded, open out and rule cuff fold lines along creases. Draw waistband or use a skirt waistband pattern.

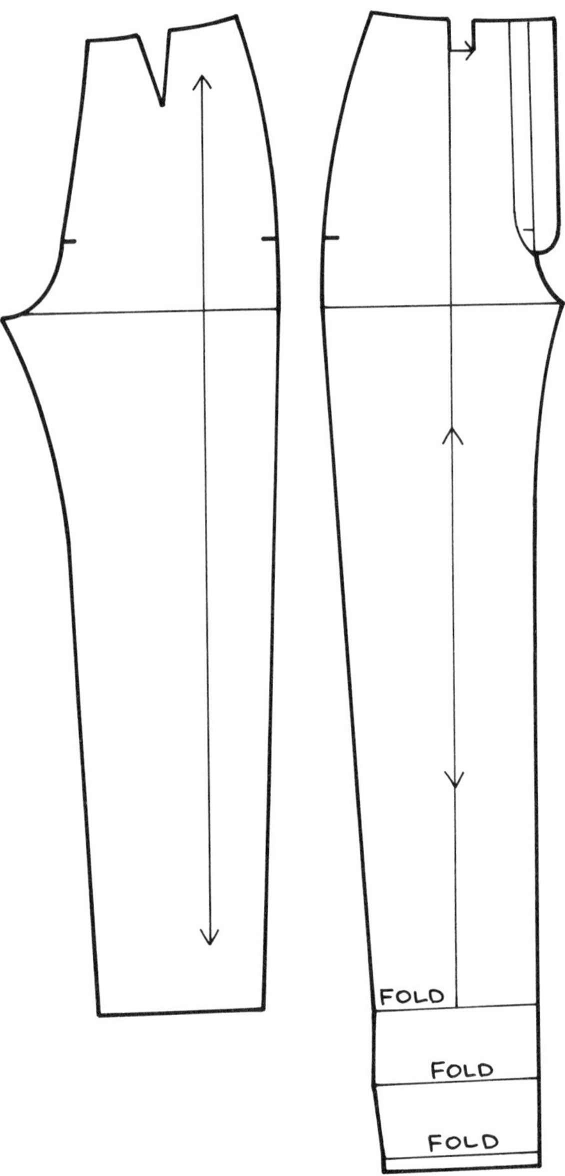

SEWING TIP

For professional-looking trousers construct each leg and press in the creases before joining the crutch seam. Lightly interface WS of edges where zip is to go and secure zip with basting tape instead of tacking stitches. Both these tips make for a perfect zip insertion.

Perfect fitting rests mainly with the crutch seam so make the waistband in two halves and have a seam at CB. Attach each piece of band to waist edge before stitching back crutch seam. Fit carefully, complete seam along crutch and through band then finish inside edge of band.

D. Pleated and tapered. Outline front block and mark size and position of pocket opening

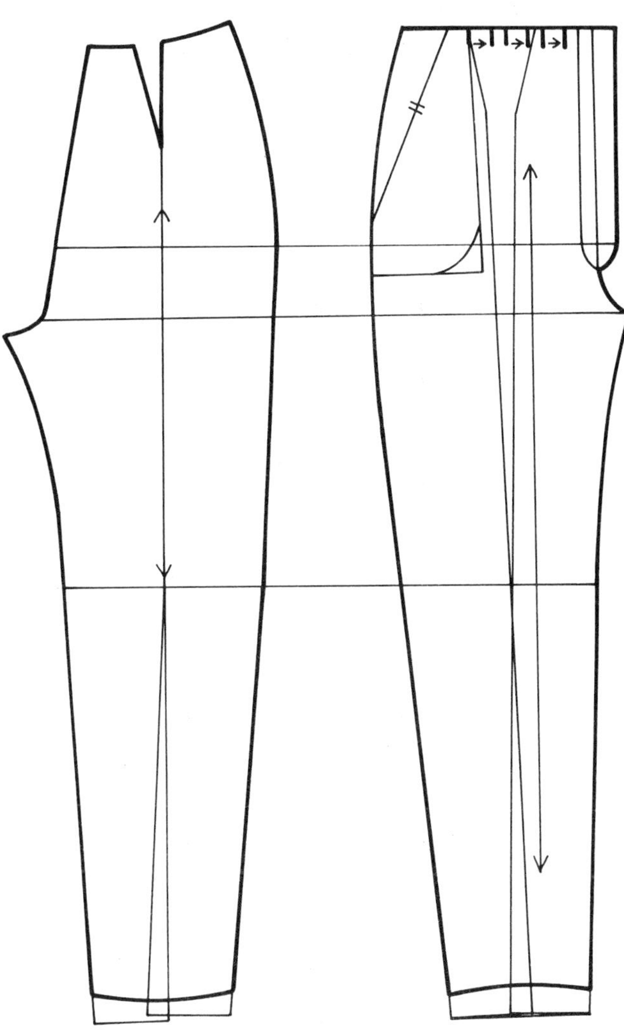

and bag. Add extension for overlapped zip. Cut along crease line and through dart. With paper together at knee line swing out side section to insert extra for waist tucks and at the same time taper the leg. Measure width of dart plus insertion; divide up and mark three pleats.

Outline back block, cut through centre of leg from mid-hem to dart point. Cut out to side at knee level and overlap at hem to remove the same amount as on front leg.

Shorten front and back by amount required, draw new hemline, curved down 3mm/⅛in at back and up 3mm/⅛in at front.

SEWING TIP

The crutch seam must give with every movement: stitch with a triple straight stitch or a slight zig-zag stitch and use a strong polyester thread such as Drima. Reinforce the short section of seam below the zip to prevent stretching with a piece of tape or seam binding.

E. Yoked trousers. Outline back block, draw yoke line and cut off. Fold out dart and outline on double paper, cut out and mark each appropriately: back yoke left or back yoke right. Add extension for fastening at side of left piece. This retains a CB seam in the yoke which is best for fitting. In fact it would be best to join each half of the yoke to the trouser leg before stitching CB crutch seam.

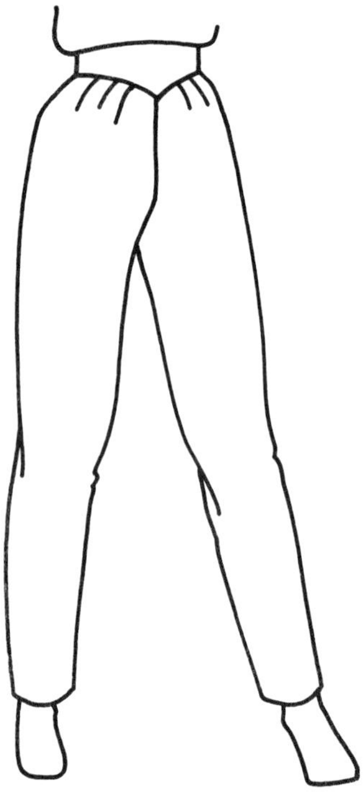

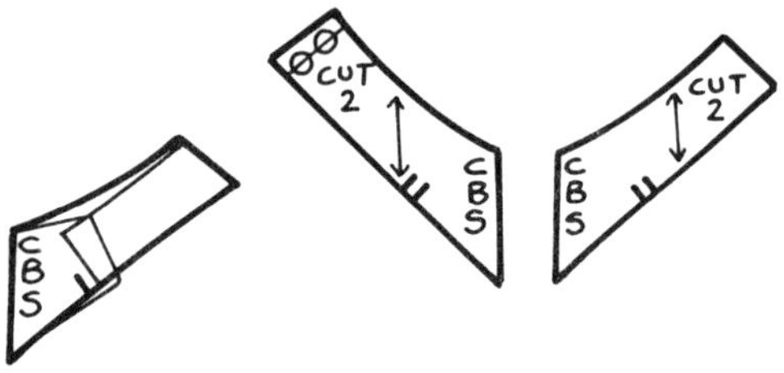

Outline front and detach yoke. Fold out dart and outline against the fold of double paper. Open out and add extension for fastening at left side.

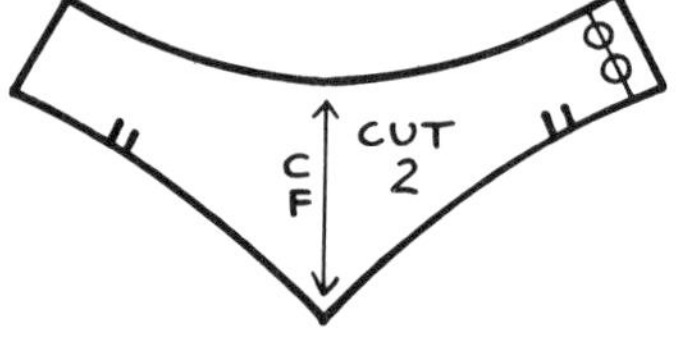

On back and front the dart has been transferred to the yoke seam which will give an excellent fit. To insert the three tucks cut front leg to hip line in two places, open and insert 2–3cm/¾–1¼in keeping CF edge vertical. Outline for final pattern. Taper legs if required.

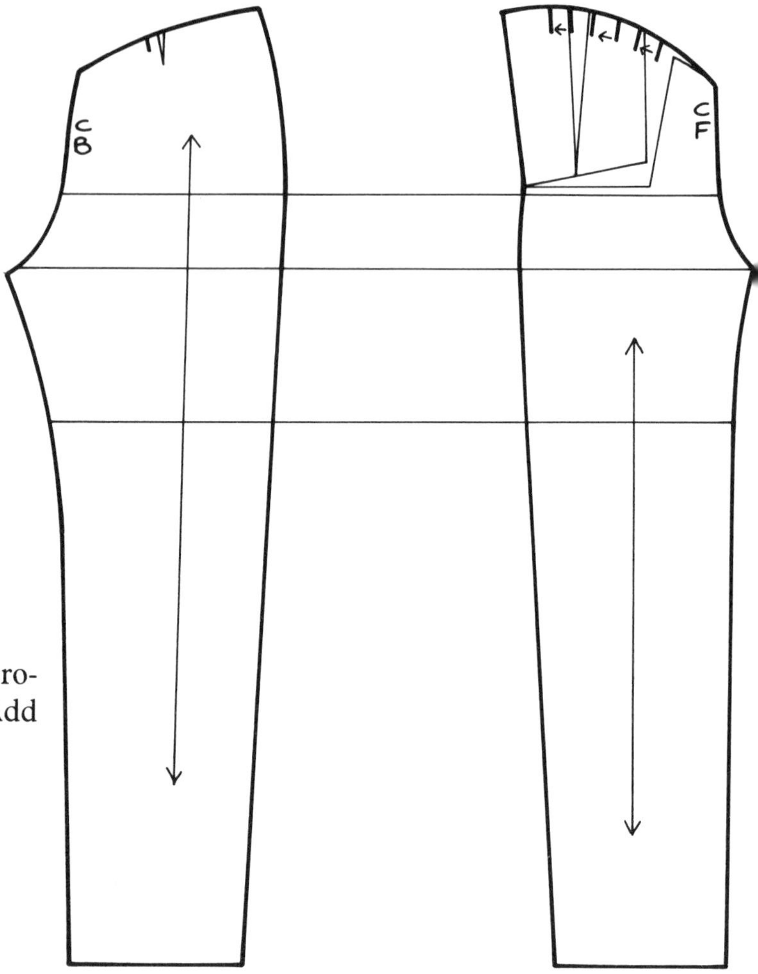

SEWING TIP

Attach iron-on interfacing to WS yoke to prevent wrinkling. A tight-fitting waist will allow very little give when sitting down so remember to check the fit of the crutch seam before finally stitching the waist.

F. Track-suit trousers. Outline block excluding darts, cut front along crease line and again between that point and side seam. Cut back in

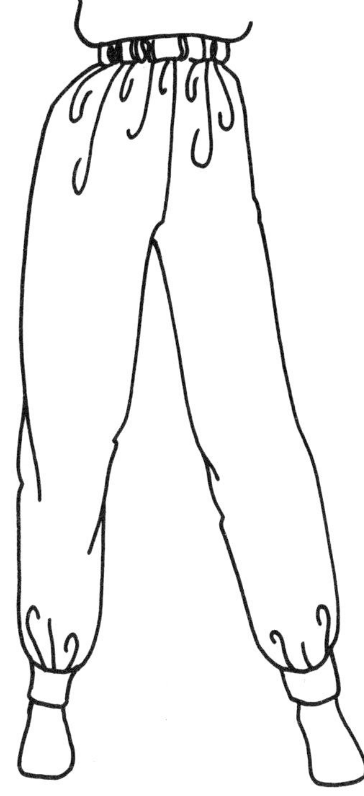

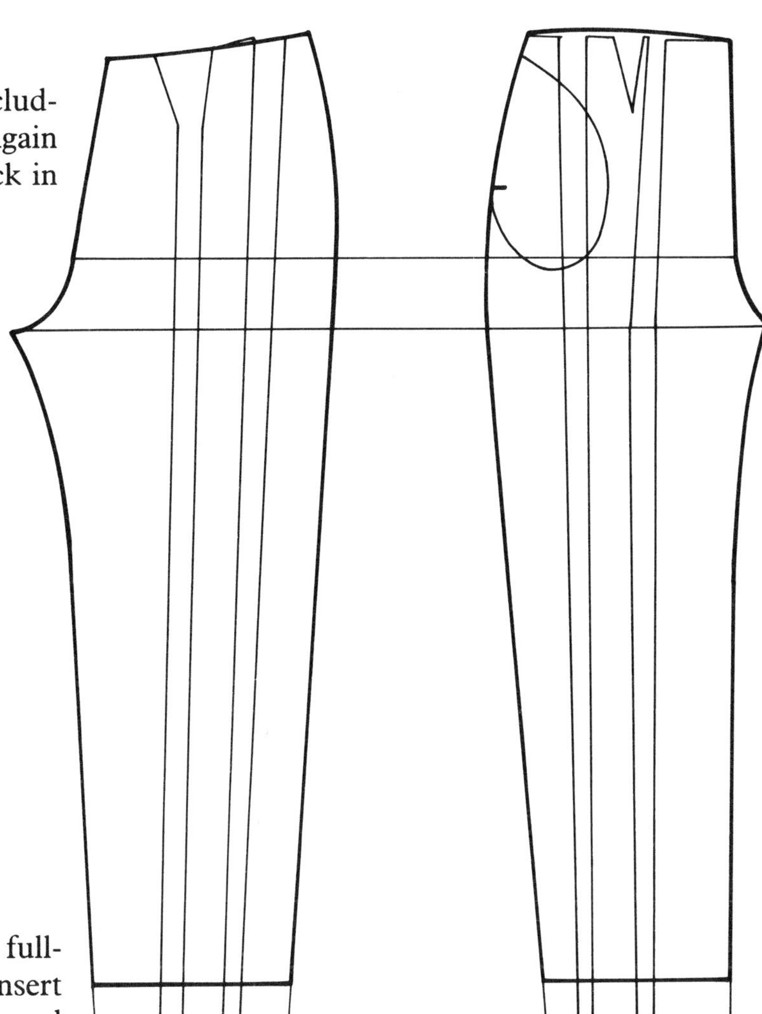

similar position. Spread to insert required fullness at waist to be drawn in with ribbing. Insert less at hems. Lower crutch point on back and front by 2cm/¾in. Shorten legs by two-thirds depth of ribbing. Mark seam pocket. It is better not to include upper edge in waist seam as together with the ribbing it becomes too bulky. Outline for final pattern. Make maternity trousers on the same principle but cutting and spreading front only.

G. Shorts. Most designs are shortened trousers with an adjustment to leg width at shorts hem level. The illustration shows an outline for straight shorts, the pattern raised at waistline for elastic casing. The other outline shows low waist

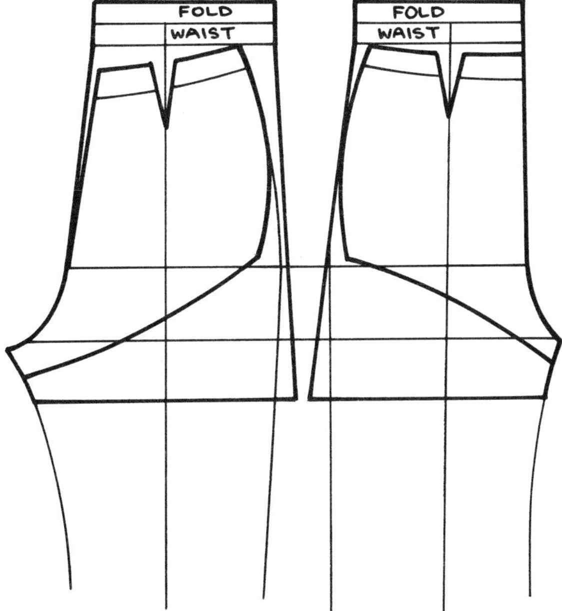

shorts fitted with darts but very short at the side seam and the hemline curved from there to below crutch.

For flared shorts adapt block to length and waist finish. Cut in three places and spread to

add flare at hem. If very full the waistline may be too shaped to have a fold-over casing. In this case attach a folded band of fabric equal in length to shorts waist and thread with elastic. (Front only shown.)

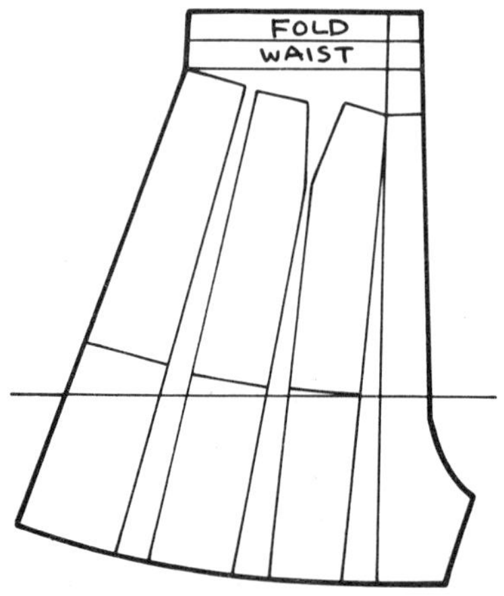

H. Culottes. Adapt a copy of the trouser block to length and widen the leg at the hem. Add pockets, zip position, waist detail etc. For

pleats cut at CF and spread as for a skirt. Straighten inside leg seam. Alternatively adapt skirt block to pleats then add the crutch shape of

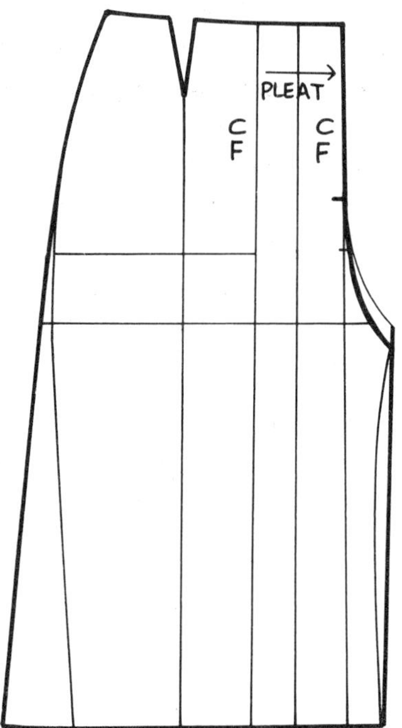

the trousers, tracing it off the block and transferring it to CF and CB edges of skirt. Lower the crutch by 2cm/¾in on all culottes. (Front only shown.)

I. Jumpsuit. Outline bodice blocks to 3cm/ 1¼in below waist. Make pattern for bodice, lowering the neck and adding extension for fastening. Adapt for deep armhole, page 127, C.

Adapt trouser block to gathered waist and outline. Match bodice to trouser at waist, line up CF and CB and extend bodice side seam from underarm to match size of trouser waist.

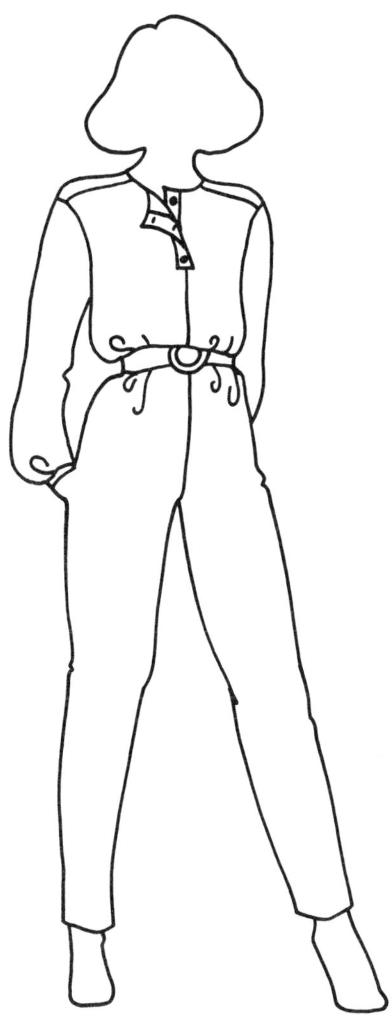

OPENINGS, FASTENINGS AND WAIST FINISHES

OPENINGS AND FASTENINGS

Whenever possible decide on the type and size of fastening before drafting the pattern especially if the opening forms part of the design.

Consider the following points when planning the opening in your design:

1. Decide whether the opening is functional or decorative or both.

2. Is it to fasten meeting edge-to-edge or should it overlap? Edge-to-edge openings are only suitable for the back of a garment or on the front down to just above bust level. The exceptions are lingerie and some evening wear.

3. Length. If an opening is closed at one end, for example if the two parts of the garment do not completely separate, you must ensure that it is long enough. It should be possible to put on the garment without a struggle and without straining the base of the opening.

To calculate length of opening, measure the widest part of the body over which it will have to pass, namely head, shoulders, hips, hand etc., and add 2–5cm/¾–2in ease.

Subtract the size of the permanently open part of the garment – waist, neck, cuff etc. – divide the remainder by two and you have the minimum length the opening must be.

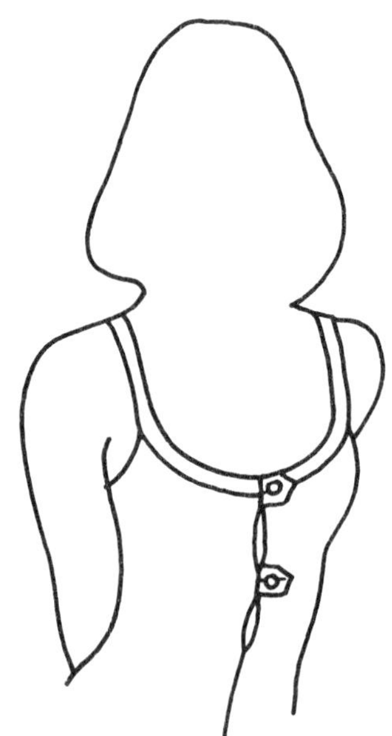

If using elastic the open part of the garment must be equal to the size of the part of the body over which it passes plus at least 5cm/2in ease.

4. Consider the remainder of the design – style lines, pockets and other features. Place buttons and other visible fastenings so that they form part of the design rather than just clutter it. For example, a vertical line of buttons can be slimming but if a button falls level with a horizontal seam it will emphasize that seam.

5. The type of fastening influences the type of opening which in turn affects the design. The type of fabric and its bulk should be considered here too.

Buttons with buttonholes. Must overlap; the bigger the button the bigger the overlap. The edge of the garment must extend beyond the end of the buttonhole by the diameter of the button. This ensures that the underlap will form a backing for the buttonhole slit.

Horizontal buttonholes. The button settles into the end nearest the garment edge.

Vertical buttonholes. These seem to show less; the button settles at the top of the buttonhole. Can be used on a narrow overlap which will limit the size of the buttons. Suitable for strap openings but not for fitted clothes as the buttons may pull undone in wear.

Buttons as a feature. Buttons can be combined with other fastenings such as hooks, press studs or Velcro.

Buttons with loops. May be used on edge-to-edge or overlapped opening. Thread or rouleau loops do not form a firm fastening unless there are lots of them placed close together. Frogs made from braid or cord are also quite loose when fastened. Always add back-up hooks or press studs at each end of the line of loops. A single button and loop is satisfactory at the top of a short edge-to-edge opening.

On a front opening on a fitted garment place a button level with BP to make sure it will not gape.

Hooks. A slightly wobbly fastening but strong. Can be used where there is little overlap. It will be less conspicuous if a thread loop is used rather than a metal one.

Press studs. Can be used at the top corner of openings to keep flat or under a collar or neck bow: less bulky than a button.

Hooks and press studs make a firm fastening if several are used in a line. Consider using those attached to tape, bought by the metre.

Eyelets and lacing. Loose but adjustable. Use on an edge-to-edge opening, remembering to interface firmly.

Flat hooks or skirt hooks. A strong functional fastening for waistbands and belts needing very little overlap.

Velcro. Decide on the quantity required to fasten the opening adequately then choose between Velcro in a strip and Spot-Ons – circles of Velcro.

For example, if there is little strain at the wrist 1cm/⅜in of Velcro or 1 Spot-On could be sufficient to fasten a cuff. One Spot-On would be sufficient as a supplementary fastening for buttons. A longer piece of Velcro, 2.5–4cm/1–1½in would be needed on a waistband or belt. If the opening is to be fastened with Velcro either space out Spot-Ons or cut short pieces of Velcro, which are equally as strong but less bulky than a continuous strip.

Plan the overlap to take the width of the Velcro or Spot-On with 3mm/⅛in to spare on all edges.

Zips. A zip can usually be inserted without an overlap, using the seam allowance to form the double edge. However, for a fly opening or if you want to completely cover the zip with a flap of fabric, extra must be added to the pattern at that point.

Ties and tabs. Loose fastenings for edge-to-edge or overlapping openings. Tabs may be buttoned or secured with press studs, buckles or Velcro.

Adapting the pattern

If the fastening is to be visible – for example, buttons or loops – begin by drawing the position of each one on the copy of the block. They are then your guide to drawing neck shape, overlap and so on.

On a close-fitting garment and on large-size patterns with front openings, place one button (it might be the top one) level with or slightly above or below the bust point. If a garment is fitted at the waist, place one button on the waist line; if not, arrange buttons above and below. On tuck-in blouses, have no more than one button below the waist as they may show.

If the seam is to be stitched, e.g. for a zip, mark the zip length point on the pattern.

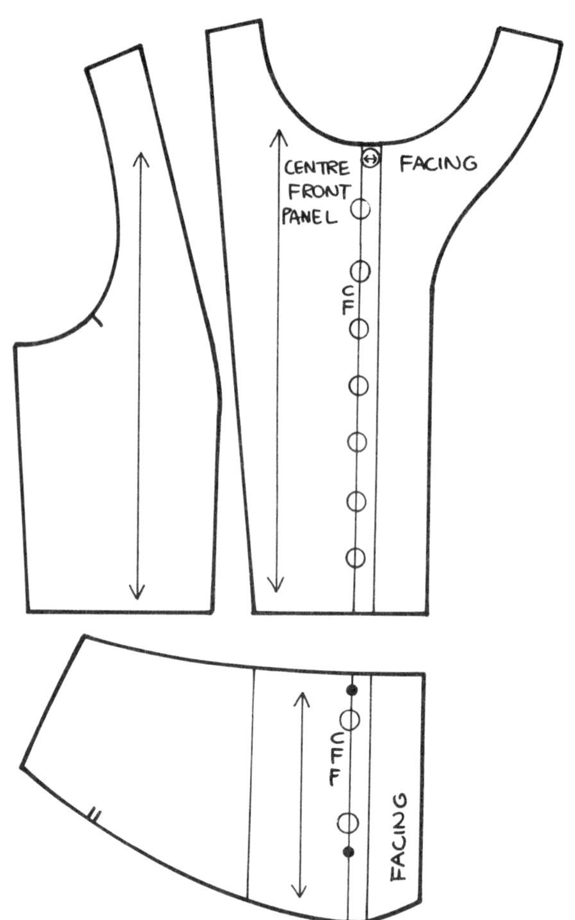

A. Small overlap for small buttons. Facing could be cut in one with centre front panel. Fitted skirt yoke has fewer buttons and may need press studs between.

B. Wider overlap to allow for two lines of buttons with vertical buttonholes. Buttons placed level with top of tucks and waist with one more below to keep in place.

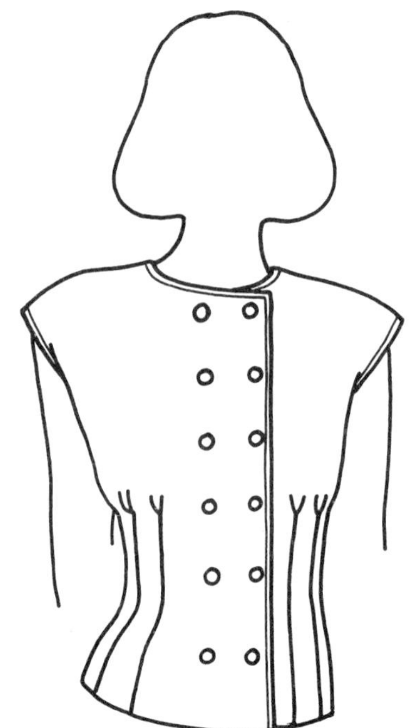

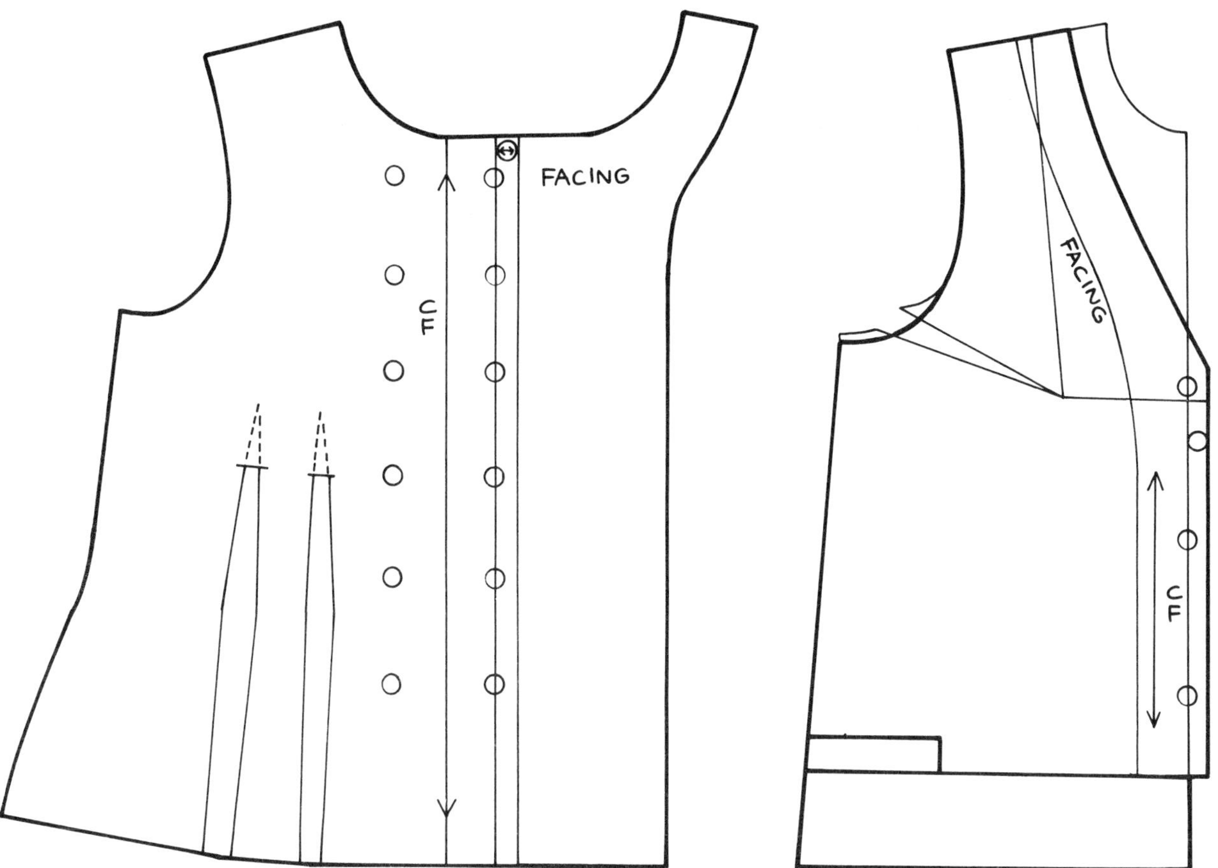

C. Position of top button crucial for neckline depth; bottom button must be a pleasing distance above drop-waist seam but not level with edge of welts.

D. Decorative buttons hold down corner of overlap but press studs or Velcro required above waist and on corner of underlap.

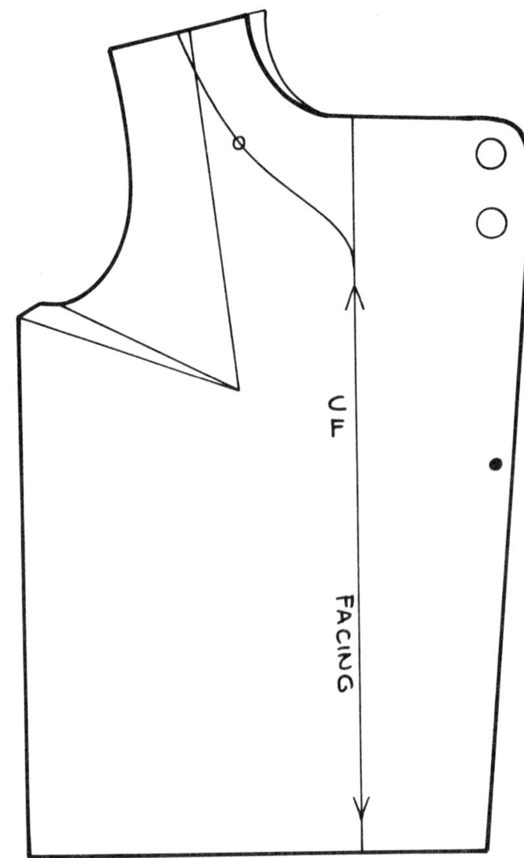

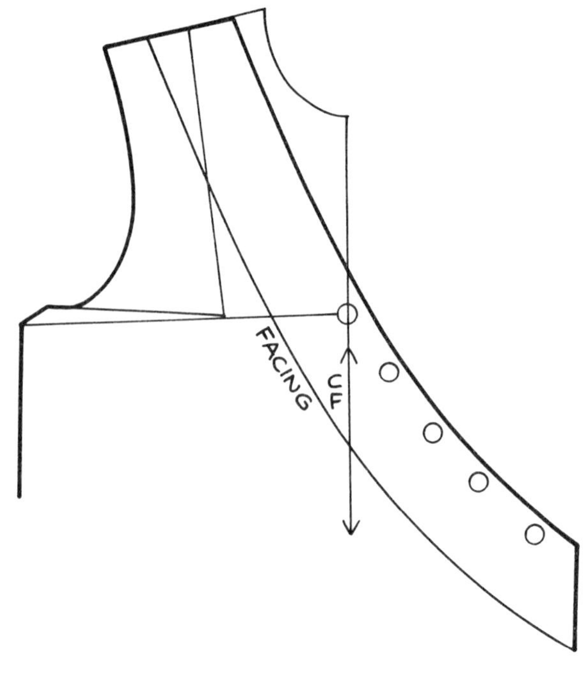

F. Single button and loop requires press studs or Velcro at neck edge but jacket is loose fitting so belt will probably hold remainder in position.

E. Top button crucial to V-neck and start of wrap-over. Loose fitting so vertical buttonholes can be used; horizontal ones would in any case spoil the effect of the top stitching.

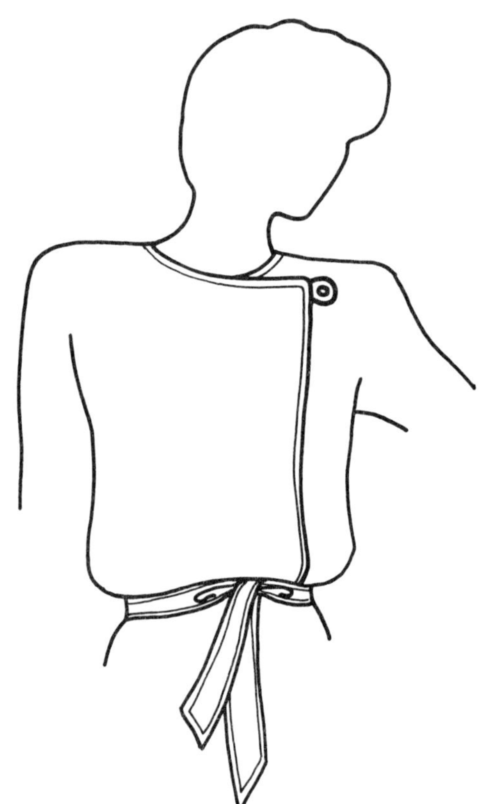

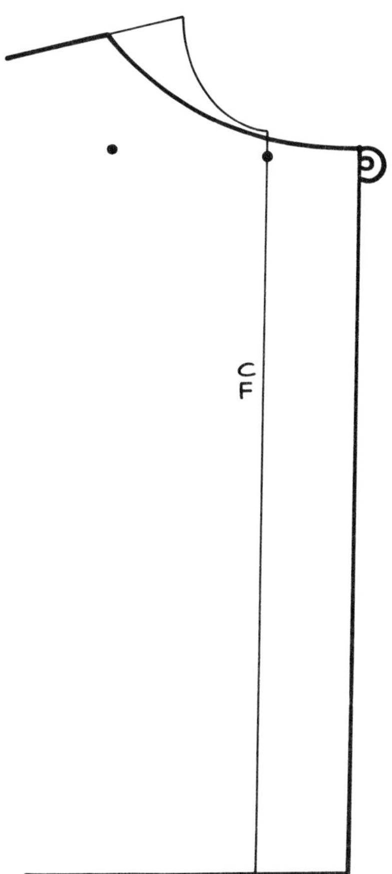

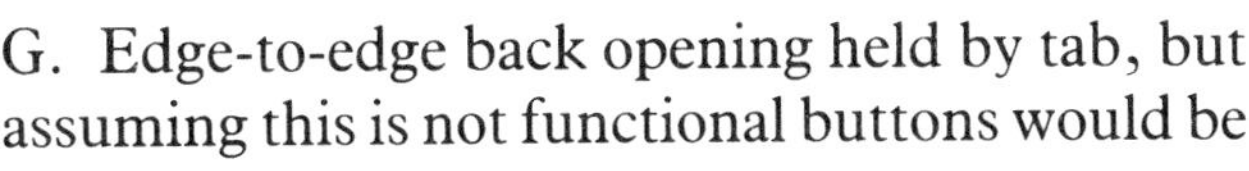

G. Edge-to-edge back opening held by tab, but assuming this is not functional buttons would be sewn right through tab and garment. Additional seam allowance required at CB or a combined facing.

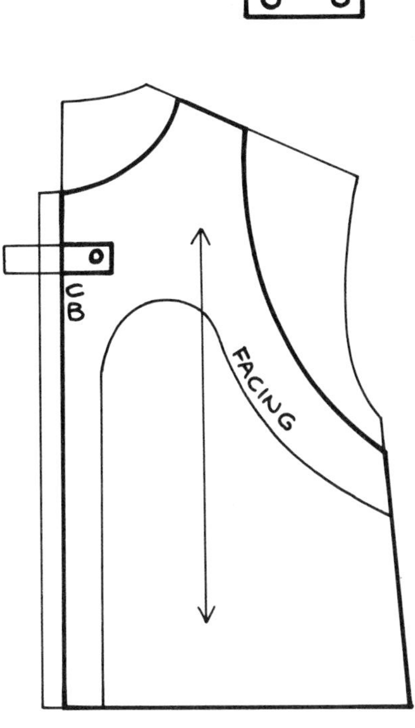

H. Plan pocket first then place tab above to

produce a more slimming line. May need press stud at CF.

not extend beyond CF; second press stud or Velcro can be placed on corner.

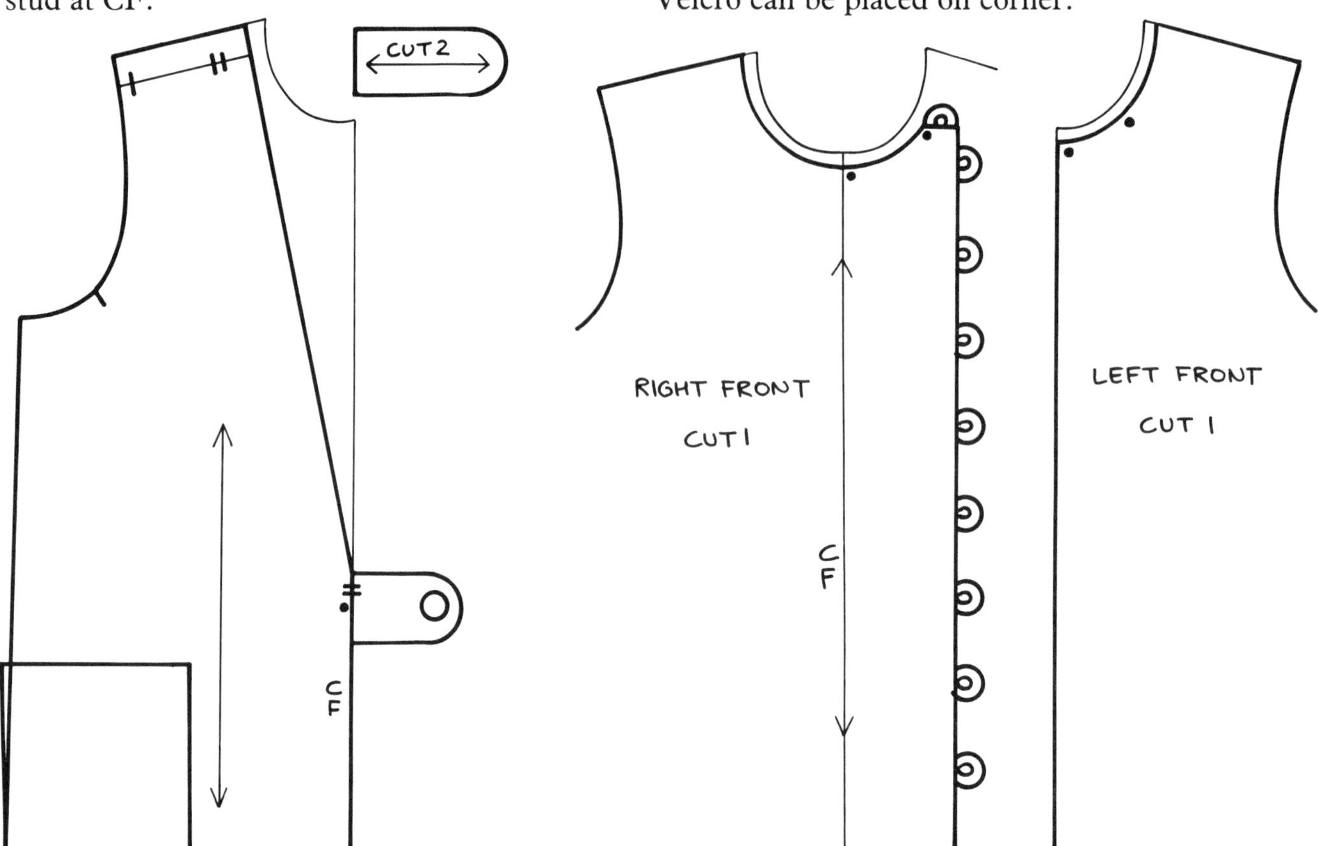

I. Loop is sufficient to hold corner in place but inner edge requires anchoring. Left side need

J. Three frogs insufficient to hold jacket neatly together but design is edge-to-edge. The solu-

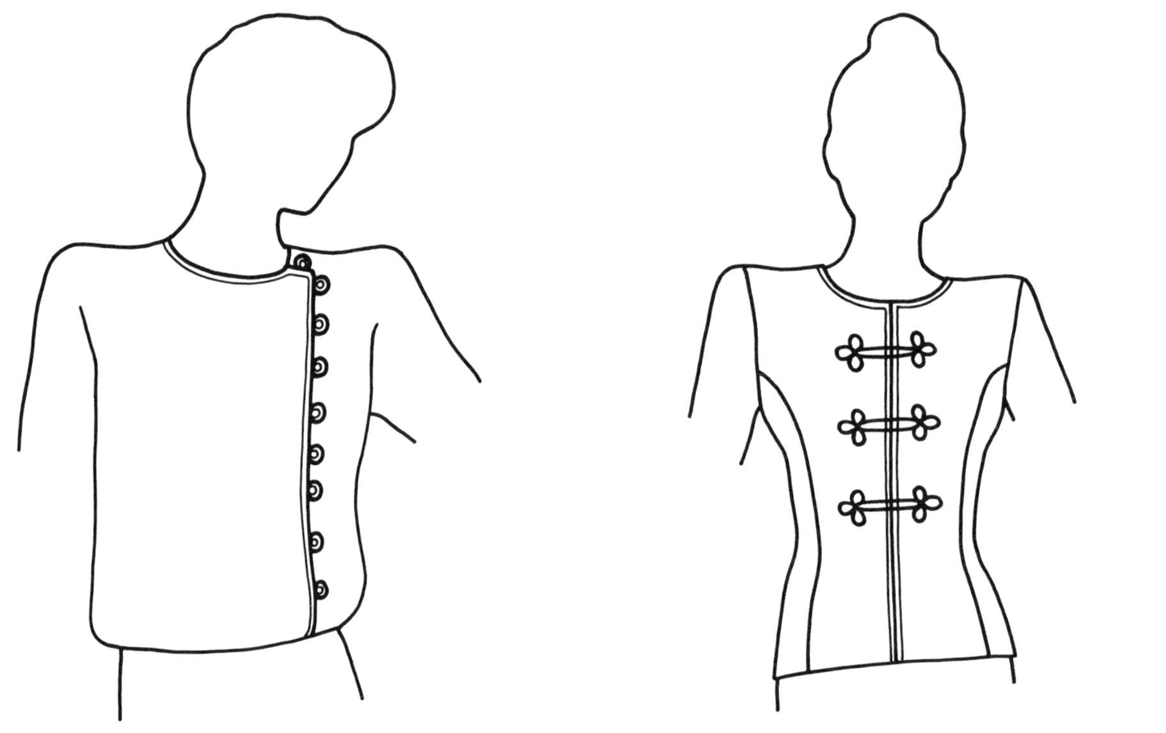

tion is a narrow underlap attached to left side only and press studs or hooks above and below and possibly in between the frogs as well.

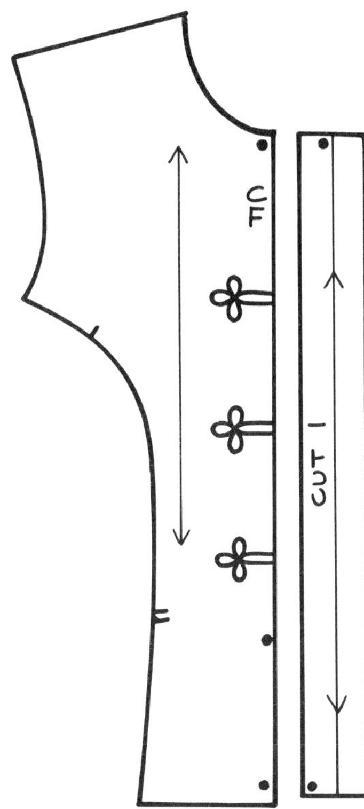

K. No strain or movement but length is critical.

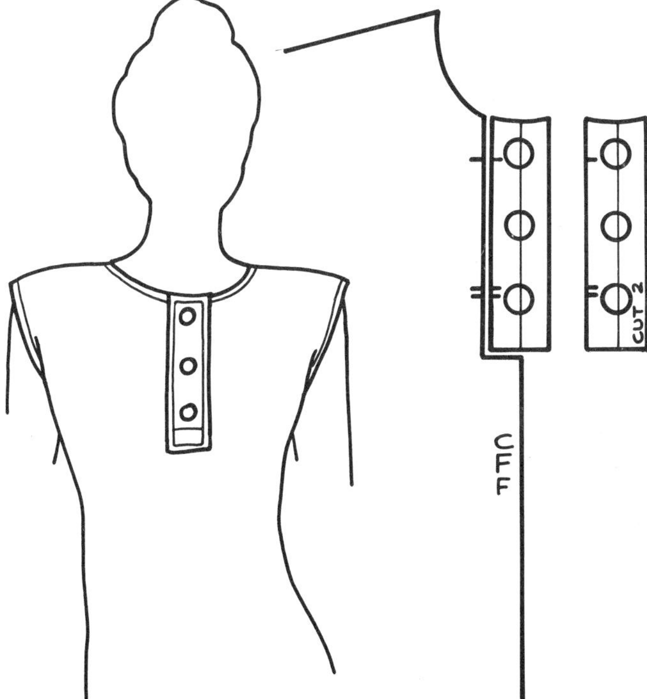

SEWING TIP

Stitch bands from base to neck each side before cutting garment and sew across the bottom by hand for accuracy; top stitch to finish.

L. Zip length is crucial to a close-fitting high-necked dress. Hemline opening can have fold-back facing but make it longer than the opening to help keep it in place.

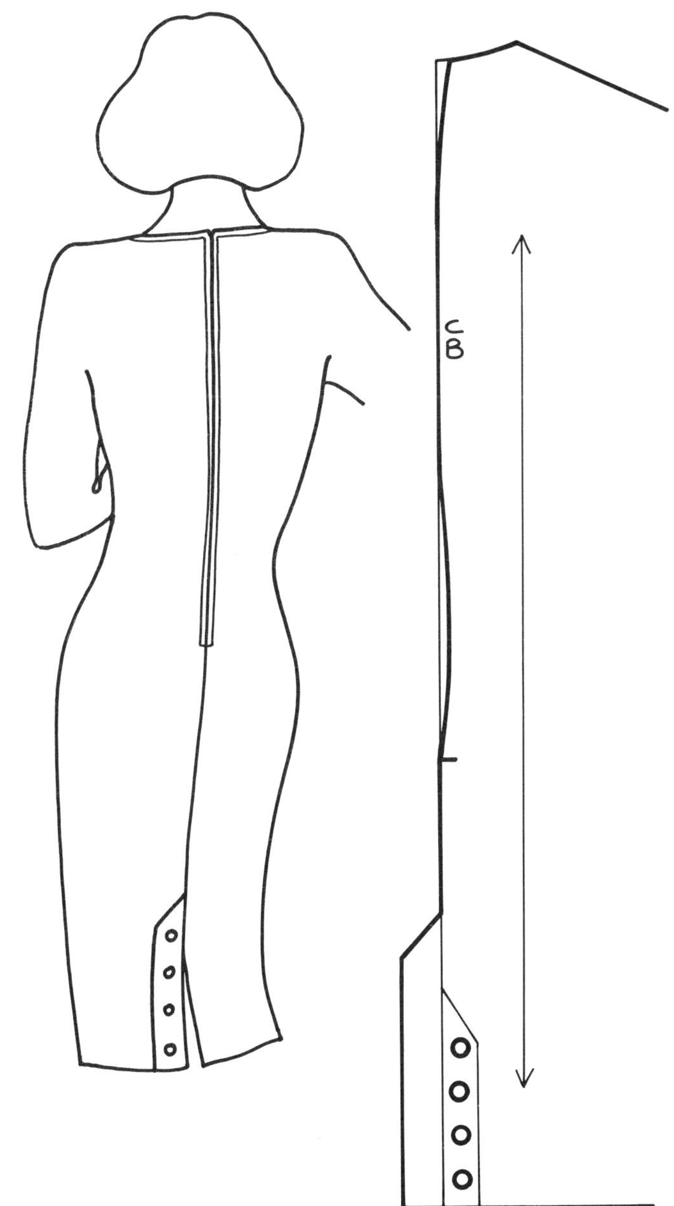

M. Zip requires a flap but not a full fly so a fold back facing is sufficient. Facing should not extend into curve of crutch and zip stitching point should be a little above that.

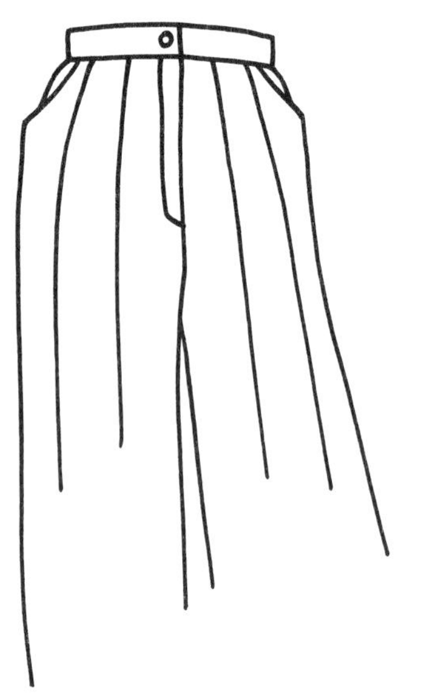

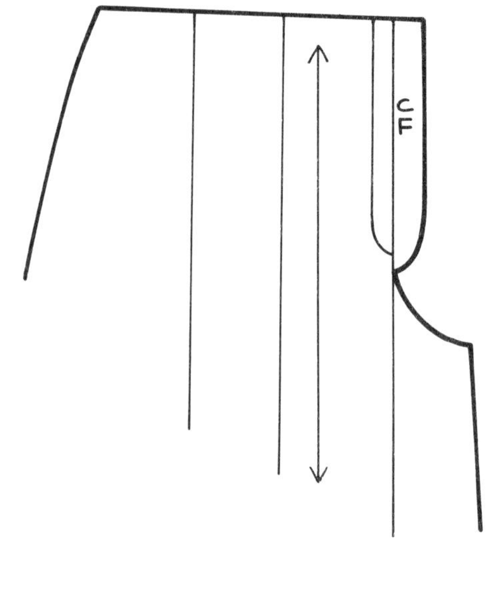

WAIST FINISHES

The selection of a waist finish for skirts and trousers depends on design and personal preference. Choice of fastening depends somewhat on the type of waist finish. If it is at all possible, decide on the fastening to be used while you are making the pattern because each requires different amounts of overlap.

It is not necessary to make a waistband pattern for each skirt and pair of trousers you make unless you want to store one with the pattern. Instead make two patterns, one narrow and one wide, to be outlined directly on to fabric each time one is required.

Waistbands

A. Straight. The conventional method of establishing the length is to measure the waist edge of the skirt pattern holding the tape measure on edge. Use this method as an exercise in pattern cutting or if the wearer of the skirt is not available. However, the following method will provide a more accurate fit. It helps to decide first on the stiffening to be used so that the waistband can be made the correct width. Choose between single width stiffening, such as petersham or

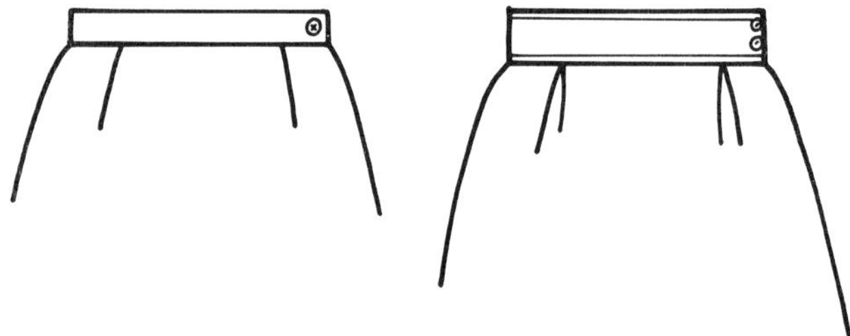

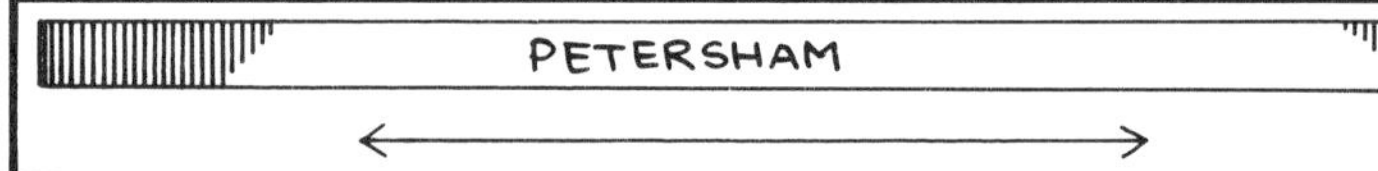

Fold-a-Band which covers the whole waistband.

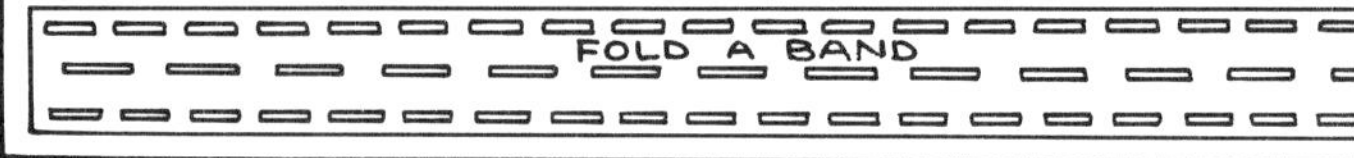

Measure the stiffening round your waist, add an overlap and cut. If the stiffening is not to hand, measure the waist with a tape measure. Rule two parallel lines that length and the width of the stiffening apart. Mark SG along the middle and mark the overlap. If using Fold-a-Band this

forms the pattern. In other cases, fold pattern and cut to make it double the width. Remember to add seam allowances if using petersham or other single width stiffening.

A narrow waistband is one that is up to 2cm/¾in wide; a wide one up to 5cm/2in. If required wider than this it should be shaped. (See below.)

B. Curved. Some people find a shaped waistband more comfortable to wear than a straight one. Make a narrow one as follows.

Use a length of curved petersham cut to length as described above for straight stiffening and outline it on drafting paper. Mark the overlap. Fold the pattern in half matching ends but excluding overlap and cut across. Mark one piece 'front', the other 'back'. Fold each piece end to end to find SG position and label 'Cut 2'.

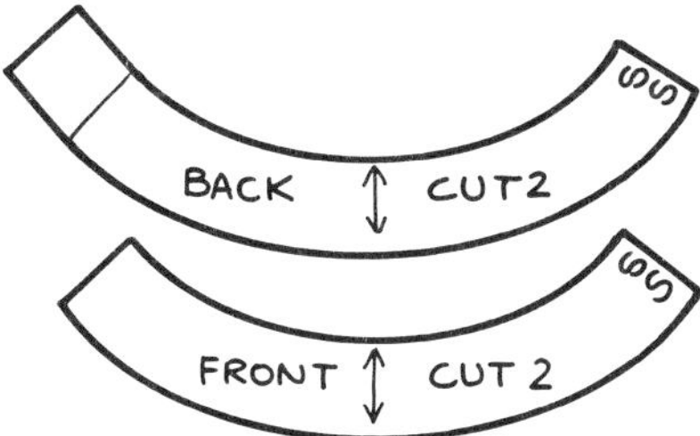

Add seam allowances. When making up join the side seams then place both pieces RS together and join along concave edge. The convex edge is attached to garment.

To make a wider curved waistband, up to about 5cm/2in in width, use the petersham as a guide, outlining it on heavy weight Vilene and increasing the width as required along both sides.

C. Shaped. Sometimes the design demands part of the waistband to be below the waist. Close dart on front skirt block and outline the waist area. Draw shaped seam. Extend CF and side seam above waist and draw upper edge. Trace off for pattern. Draw back band to size of back waist and shape side seam to match front.

D. Wide shaped. A wide shaped band, possibly of a different width front and back, is also made from the bodice block. Also suitable to attach to trousers but adjust waist size if necessary.

Outline front and back waist areas with side seams together. Draw the shape required. Trace the waistband and cut out. Fold out back and front darts and outline again, correcting outer edges if necessary. Mark SG on each piece parallel with CB or CF. Decide on position and type of opening and if an extension for fastening is required, add this to the pattern. Mark each pattern 'Cut 2' to fold; mark back pattern 'Cut 4'. For a close fit round the ribs take in side

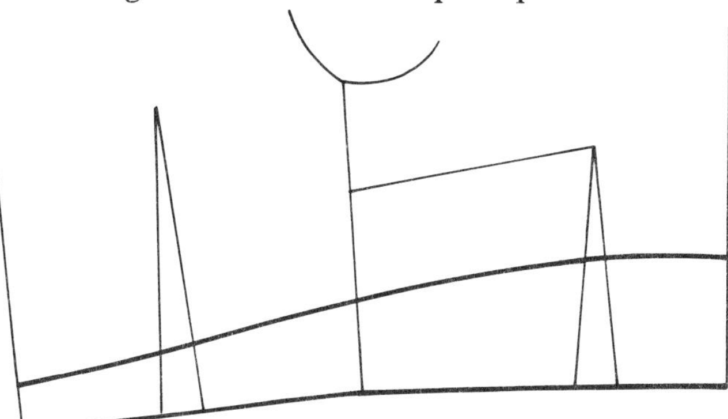

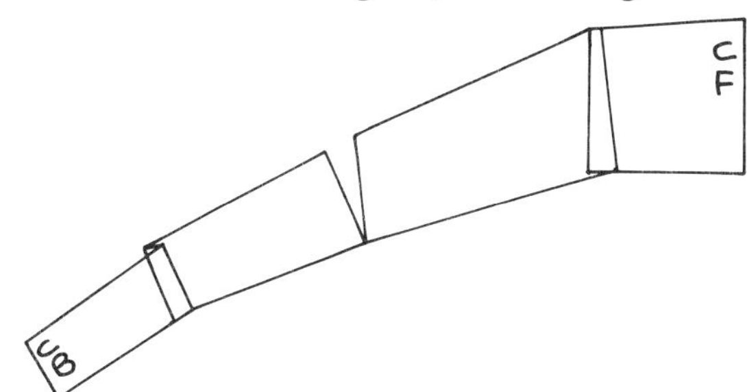

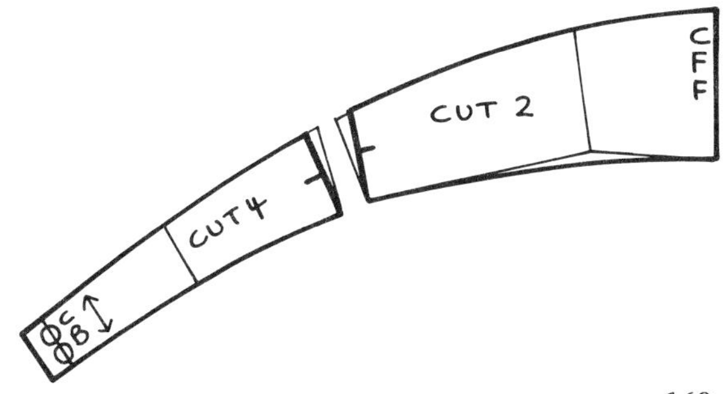

seams a little from nothing at waist to upper edge.

Petersham finish

Curved or straight petersham can be attached to the waist edge of trousers or a skirt and tucked inside. This finishes the waist at a lower point than a waistband which is one of its advantages. No waistband pattern is required and no adjustment to the main pattern is needed.

Elastic waistband

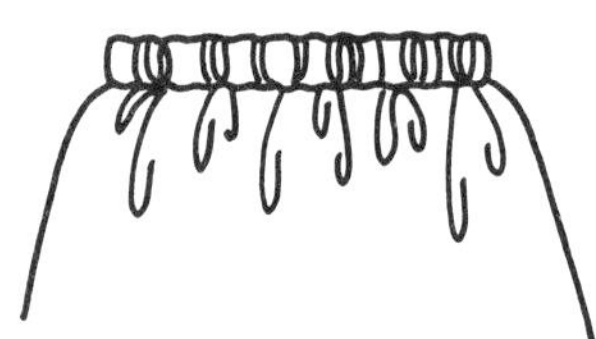

A skirt or trousers in jersey can have the opening and zip omitted and a continuous waistband containing elastic attached to the waist edge. Omit darts in garment and make sure you can get it on. Cut a pattern or length of fabric twice width of elastic plus 3cm/1½in. The length

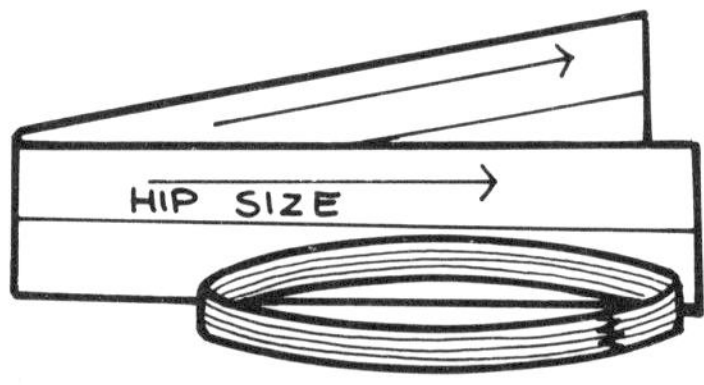

should be sufficient to pass over hips with fabric stretched.

Facing

For a soft finish such as might be required on trousers or a skirt to have belt loops, trace the waist of the back and front pattern to a depth of 5cm/2in. Mark SG to correspond with pattern. Decide on position of garment opening and mark 'cut to fold' where appropriate. The facing pieces should be interfaced. If the garment has a yoke use the yoke pattern for the facing.

Zip positions

Skirt. The zip may be placed in the left side seam using either the edge to edge or the lapped method. Alternatively the zip may be inserted in the CB seam, again by either method. The latter gives a smooth line over each hip but it tends to snake and does not fit well into a hollow back. An advantage, however, is that the zip can be inserted early in construction leaving the side seems to be used as fitting points. The only time a zip is put at CF is in a casual or sporty panelled skirt and in that case the fly method should be used.

Trousers. If the zip is placed in CF seam using the fly or lapped method, a guard is not usually necessary in women's trousers and anyway it adds bulk. A zip in the left seam should be inserted by the lapped method. There may occasionally be a case for putting the zip in the CB seam although it is not a good idea. The zip will prevent the CB seam from giving as the wearer moves and it can be very uncomfortable. Nevertheless if the zip has to go at the back the edge-to-edge method is the least bulky.

Extensions for fastenings

The strength of a waistband depends on the fastening and the way it is sewn, not on the size of the overlap. Too much overlap is unnecessary and bulky. The decision about whether the extension is an over- or underlap depends on style, position of opening and type of zip insertion.

A. One button and buttonhole; CF fly zip: 2.5cm/1in overlap.

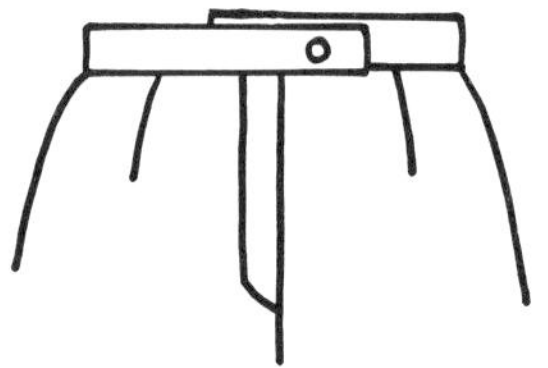

B. One button and buttonhole at side; lapped: 2cm/3⁄4in overlap.

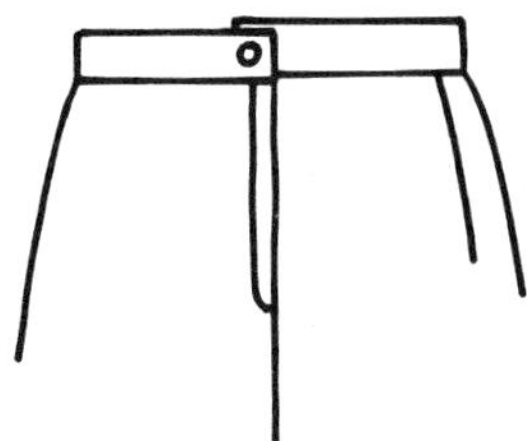

C. Two flat hooks and bars; CF fly: 4cm/1½in underlap.

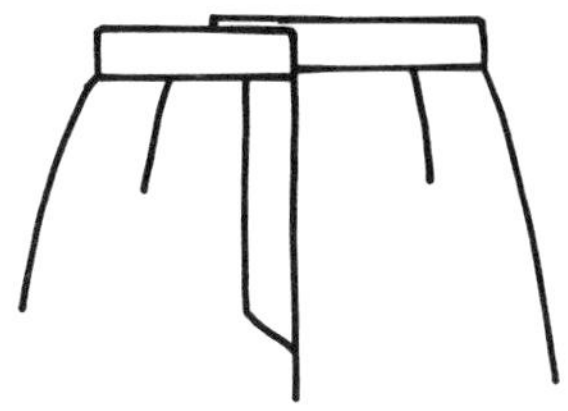

D. Two flat hooks and bars or Velcro; side, lapped: 6cm/2⅜in underlap.

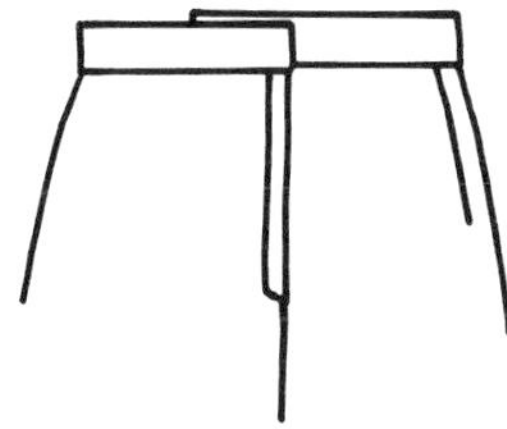

E. One hook, one press stud; side, lapped: 4cm/1½in underlap.

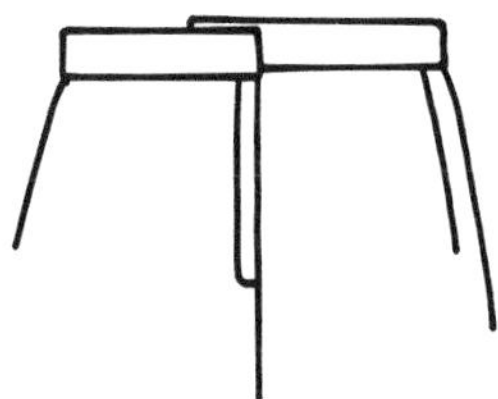

F. Two buttons, one button one hook, or Velcro, front wrap over: 13–20cm/5–8in under and overlap.

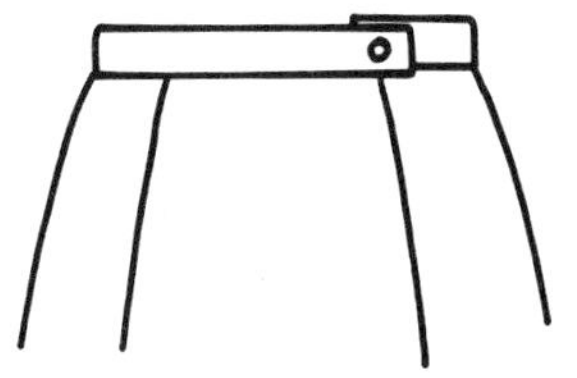

G. Yoke, facing, shaped waistband or petersham: any of these can be fastened edge-to-edge with hooks and eyes, hook and eye tape or a trouser clasp and bar or with an underlap and 3cm/1¼in Velcro.

PATTERNS FROM MEASUREMENTS

There are a number of garments that use measurements rather than blocks as the starting point. This means you have no guiding outline so there are more decisions to be made by you and they are, in the main, relative to the fabric that you are using or plan to use.

There is often no need to make a paper pattern when making up one of these garments in full size; the shape can usually be marked directly on to the fabric. As with everything else you would be wise to practise and learn the principles by drawing them in small scale, perhaps just making notes to refer to when working in full size. When you do reach the point of marking shapes directly on to fabric always remember to add seam and hem allowances to your calculations.

GATHERED SKIRTS

These consist of straight pieces of fabric, joined if necessary and with an opening in the top of the left or CB seam. The grain should always run down the skirt except in the case of border prints or lace flouncing. It will help if you know the width of the fabric in order to calculate whether it will be one, two, two and a half etc., widths that will be required to produce the effect required. Resist the temptation to use full-size widths simply in order to avoid cutting the fabric and possibly wasting a strip of fabric. And never include a strip of fabric on the opposite grain to make a narrow skirt wider.

Simple garments need your skill as a designer just as much as the ones that look complicated. Gathered skirts, probably more than any other garment, can very easily look dreary and lack style. On the whole they look best if they are long and skimpy or full and bunchy. Plan the waistline or waist finish carefully so that it enhances the skirt.

It helps to make calculations and patterns, if any, for single, rather than folded, fabric to avoid confusion. Often the pieces can be torn across the width more accurately than cutting.

A. Long and lean for any soft fabric including

lawn and silk but not for those that are springy.

Rule a horizontal line near the bottom of the paper (fabric) and a vertical line at one end equal to the length required. Measure along the hem

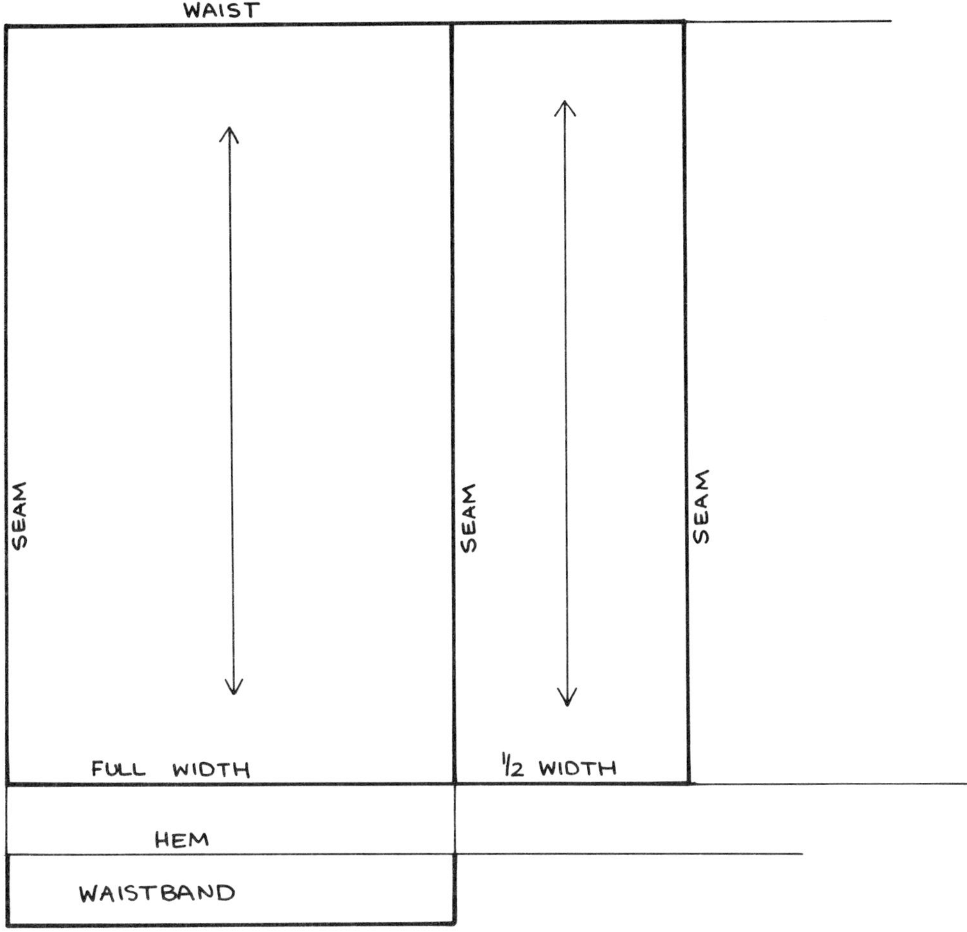

line hip size plus 25–40cm/10–15in ease (more for larger sizes). Complete the rectangle. This is the minimum width for the skirt so next calculate how many widths of fabric will be required. Measure off along hemline 90cm/36in, 115cm/45in as appropriate. If you are short of a very small amount the skirt can be made a little narrower but it would be safest to add another quarter or half width because 1.5cm/⅝in seam allowance will be used up on each vertical edge anyway.

Depending on whether there is a piece to spare along one edge of one of the sections make an allowance for the waistband either there or add extra to your quantity calculation. Remember to add waist seam allowance and hem depth to each of the pieces planned for the skirt whether full or part width.

B. A full gathered skirt can be calculated in the

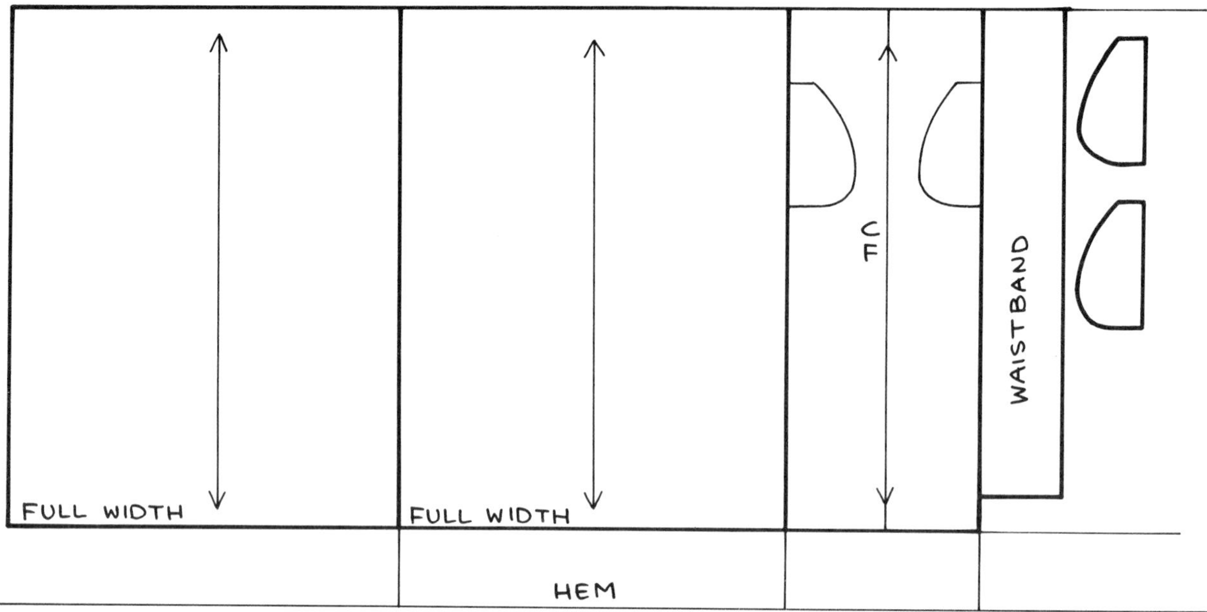

same way as A above, using as many widths as required. Bridal and evening gowns may have 6, 8 or 10 widths.

If seam pockets are included arrange the seams evenly, one at each side, or if a half width is used place it centrally at the front. Cut pocket bags from remaining fabric or use lining.

C. Unpressed pleats give a flatter line but are more difficult to work out than gathers. Mark out a series of evenly spaced chalk or fabric pen marks across the width of the fabric and fold over and pin. Measure the final size after adjusting pleats if necessary or planning whatever design you wish. Calculate how many widths of fabric will be required.

To work out an uninterrupted line of pleats all round, even across the zip, it is easiest to seam up the fabric. Join, say, three widths (more than

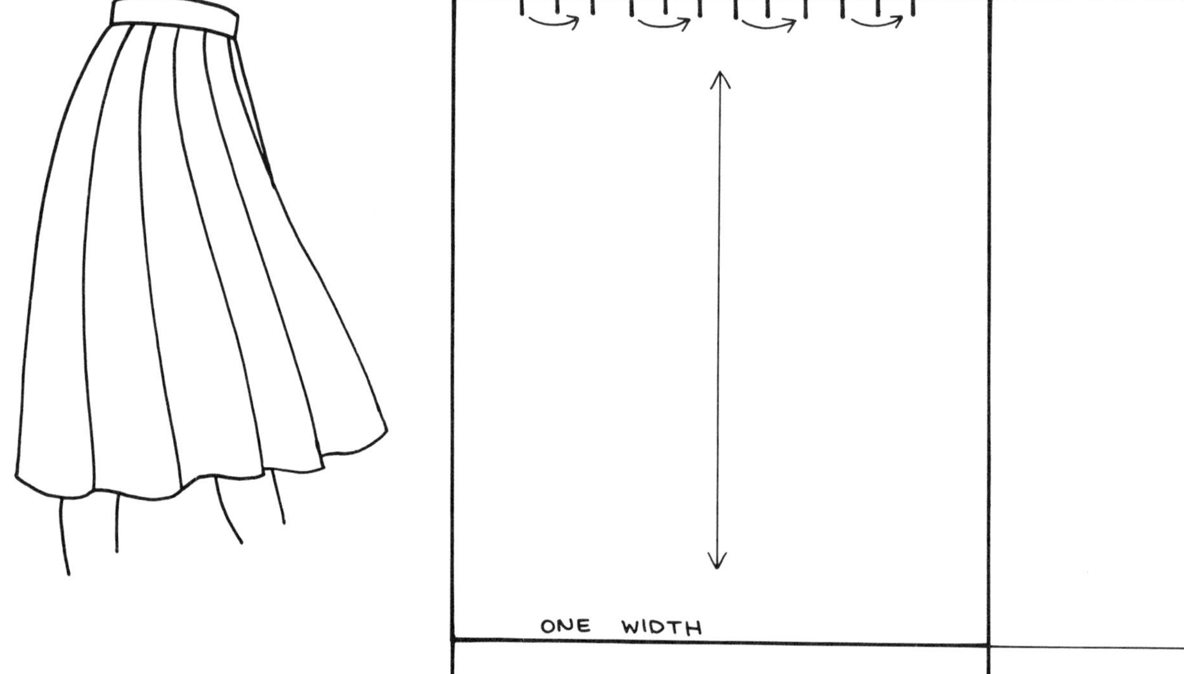

for gathers), leaving one seam unstitched and leaving zip opening in one of the other seams. Insert the zip.

Starting at zip position fold and pin the first pleat to the size required then work from there in both directions inserting remainder of pleats. Join final seam taking up as much as is necessary to keep the pleats uninterrupted.

D. Gathered and shaped. The illustration

shows a gathered skirt on a fitted drop-waist bodice but a hemline much fuller than the gathering suggests. Plan for three or four widths of fabric but shape seam edges a little to reduce bulk at waist.

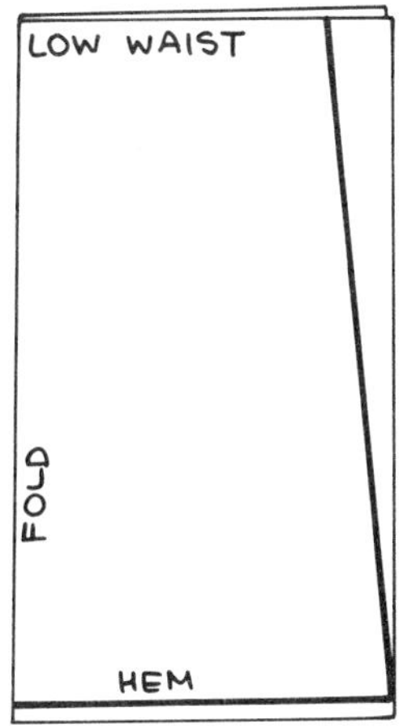

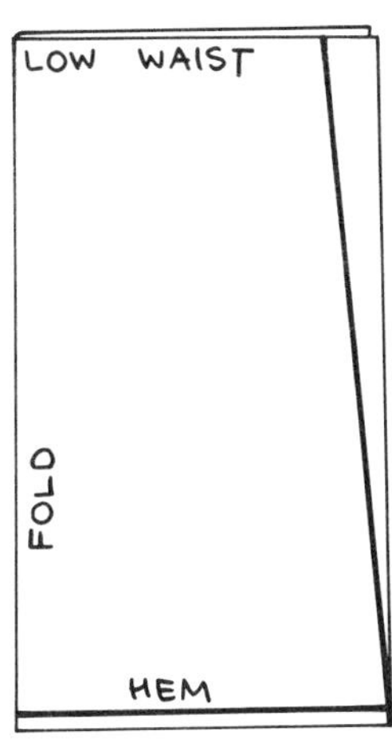

E. Gathered tiers. Plan a good balance with the

remainder of the garment and decide on the proportion of each tier. If the under tiers are to be attached to a straight or A-line base, make the pattern for the base and mark the tier attachment lines first. Decide on depth of top tier.

Work out the width of the top tier first, allowing at least three times the length of the edge to which it will attach. Next work out the depth of the under tier bearing in mind that it may have to extend under the top tier for a short distance. Calculate the number of widths required making it less full than the top tier, say

TOP
TOP
TOP
FOLD
BOTTOM
BOTTOM
BOTTOM 1/2 WIDTH

two and a half times the size of the garment at attachment point.

Finally, add seam and hem allowances to each piece.

If you find the above complicated or hazardous, cut some paper into strips of different widths, mark seams and hems and overlap them. This will at least help you to see how to adjust them in order to make sure the finished length of the garment is correct.

F. Yoke and gathers. Make yoke pattern by

tracing desired shape from front skirt block with

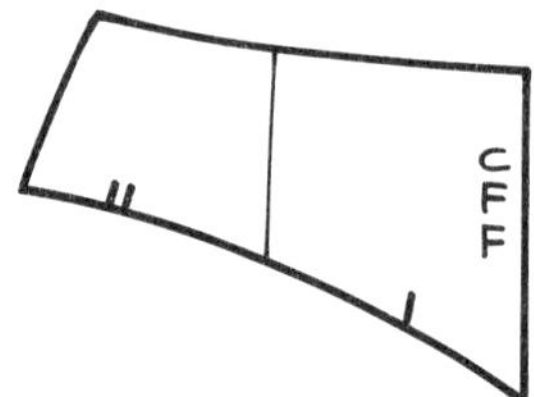

dart folded out. Draw one width of fabric and slope the seam edges. Mark off depth of yoke at side seam and centre seam and draw a gentle convex curve between the two. Make back pattern in the same way.

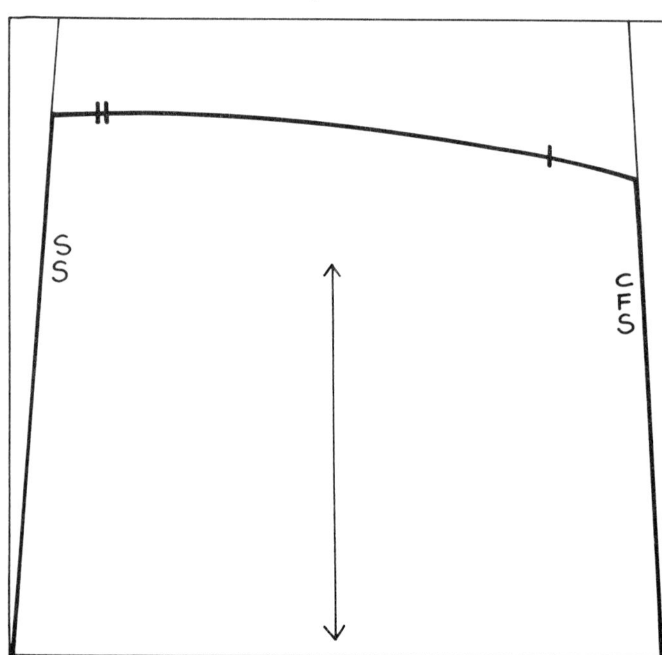

CIRCULAR SKIRTS

A full circle or several circles or even a quarter, half or three-quarters of a circle can be a skirt pattern. The shapes are simple, easy to make up and the results are always attractive. One advantage over gathered skirts is that the waist is smooth and fitted. You need to be slightly more careful with the calculations than for gathered skirts but it is worth learning the principle because circles can be used for other things besides skirts.

Depending on the width of the fabric and the skirt length you may be able to dispense with CF and CB seams on a full circle; it will save some sewing time.

Whatever final result you are aiming for it is only necessary to cut the pattern for or mark out in fabric, one quarter. It is then cut as many more times as required. Remember to add an allowance for the waist join and for a narrow hem.

One quarter can be wrapped right round and

have a CB seam. This is often used for lingerie and night clothes but a skirt looks better if the quarter is divided in half so that there can be two side seams.

A half circle is fuller and is usually cut as two quarters, the skirt being given two side seams.

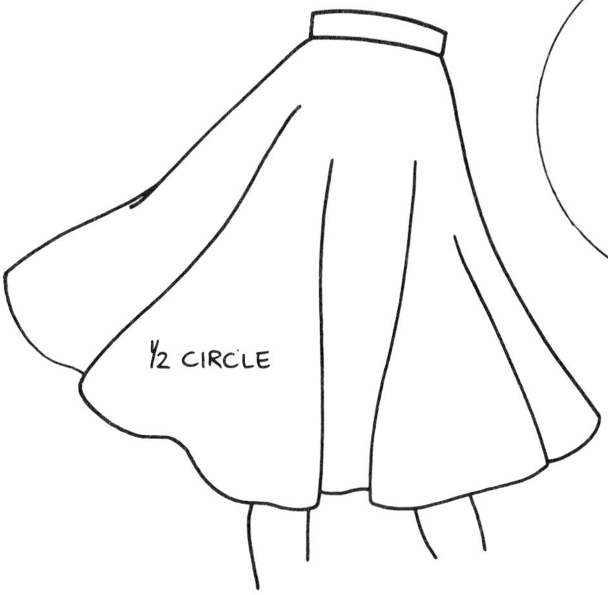

A full circle can be four quarters joined together or two halves (the quarter pattern cut twice against a fold).

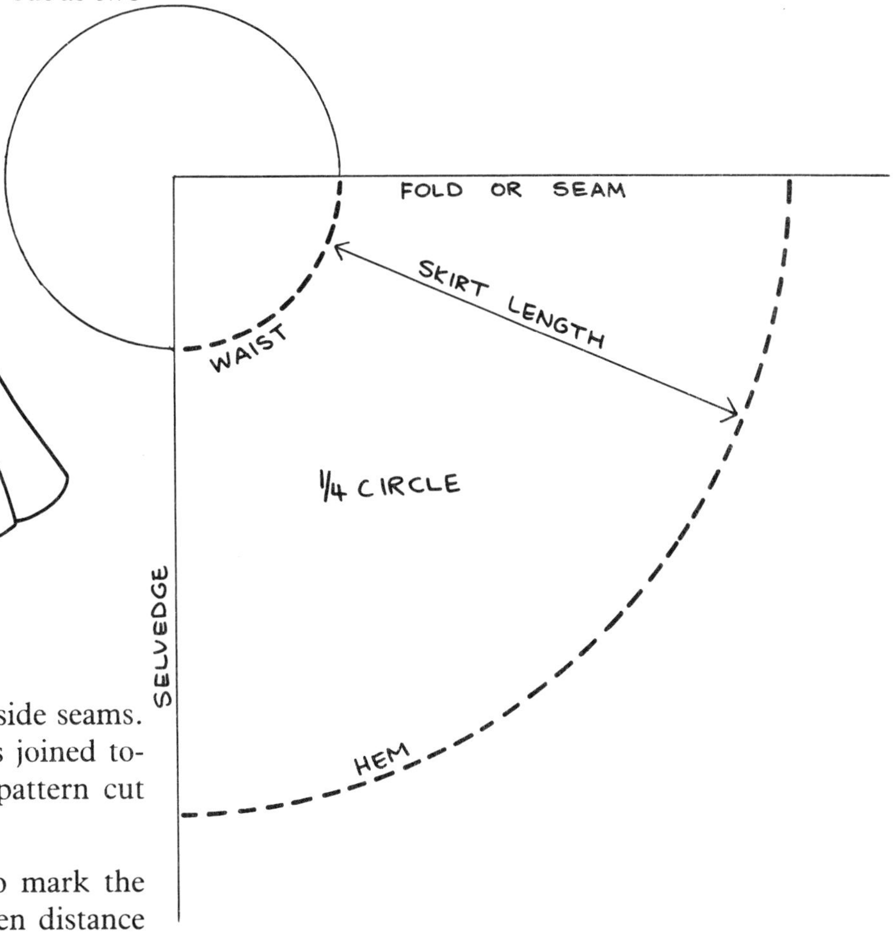

A. The quarter circle pattern. To mark the waist of the pattern measure an even distance repeatedly from the top corner of a piece of paper; the resulting dotted arc represents a quarter of the waist. Measure from that arc the required skirt length then for accuracy measure the total distance from the corner to mark the hemline arc. One straight edge will lie on the selvedge, the other will lie on the weft yarns of the fabric. This could be the fold of the fabric and you would then have half a circle. Repeat this and you have the second half. Remember to add a seam allowance above the waist arc and a hem below the bottom one.

To calculate the correct distance from the corner of the waist arc, to make sure it is exactly one quarter of the waist, visualize the distance as the radius of a circle and the circumference of the circle as the waist size.

Waist size divided by 2 and multiplied by 3.14 = the radius of the circle or the distance to be measured from the corner.

B. The full circle. To calculate the amount of fabric required measure from the corner to the hem including hem allowance and multiply by four. The longer the skirt length, the less likely you are to be able to cut the circle without making a join near the outer edge. However, joins are easy to make and you will not need any additional fabric.

To make joins cut out the quarter circles.

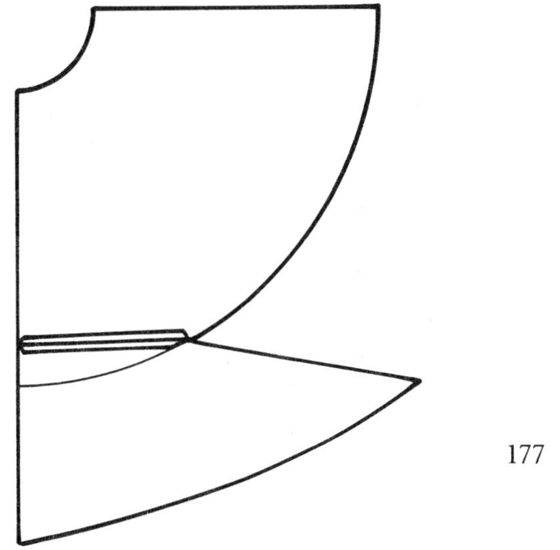

There will be a selvedge or straight edge on one part above the hem. Take one of the spare pieces of fabric and pin to the edge, right sides together and with selvedges level. Join with an open seam and press open. Repeat on all quarters to replace missing sections. Mark remainder of hemline and cut out.

C. Quarter, half and three-quarters. To make a quarter-circle skirt the arc at the corner of the paper must equal the waist measurement. The circumference of the circle, for the purpose of

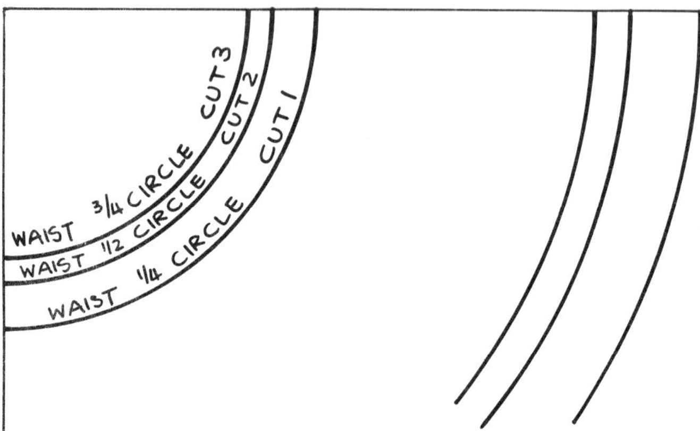

the calculation, must therefore be waist × 4. Two sections will be used for a half circle and three for a three-quarter circle skirt. The waistlines and hemlines are at correspondingly different levels. Remember to add a seam allowance above the waist arc and a hem at the outer edge.

D. Gathered circular skirt. These are easier to make because the waist calculation is less critical; by gathering the waist you are correcting the tendency of the waist arc to stretch and eliminating any measuring errors.

The gathers make the skirt beautifully full but it needs a firm waist finish to hold the extra weight. Wide waistbands, plain or elasticated are suitable. If part of a dress the bodice should be close-fitting at the waist and the seam firmly stitched.

The waist arc of each quarter must be 2 to 3 times longer than for a fitted skirt, depending on the fabric, so increase accordingly the circumference of the circle used in calculations. The hemline will be correspondingly lower. Double circles can also be made gathered if the fabric is fine.

SEWING TIP

The weight of a full skirt may strain the zip especially on evening or bridal gowns. Using a length of tape stitch it to the waist seam allowance all round leaving 30cm/12in ends beside the zip. Alternatively stitch 30cm/12in tapes to edge of waist seam beside zip. When putting on the dress tie the tapes to draw the teeth together and take the strain then pull up the zip.

E. Yoked circular skirts. Using block, fold out

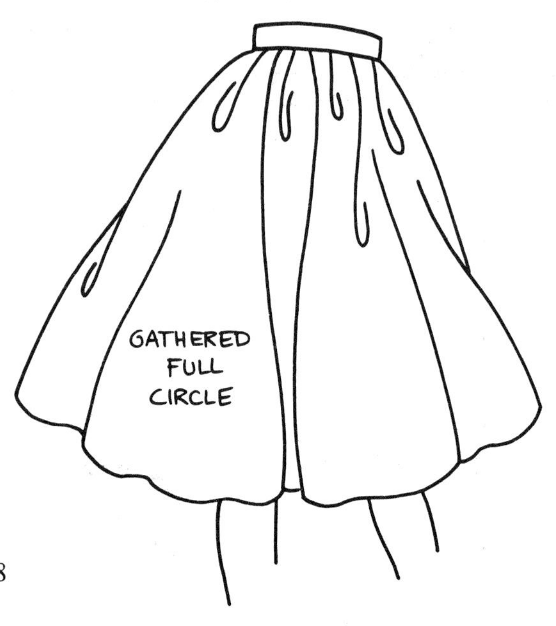

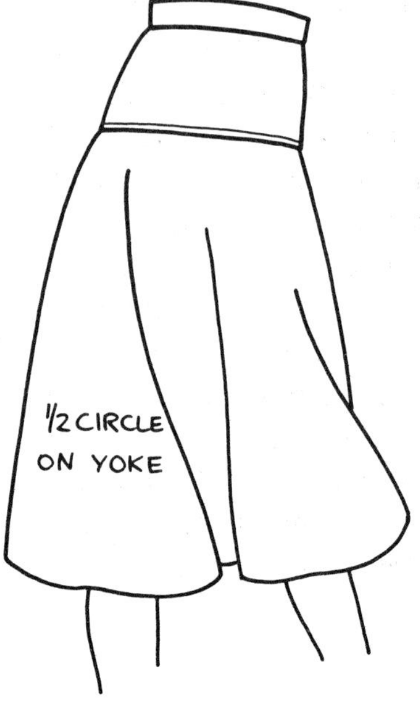

dart on skirt back and outline. Mark yoke and trace. Make back and front to the same depth at side seam. If elastic is to be inserted do not fold out darts. Measure lower edge of yoke and multiply by two for circumference of circle.

FLOUNCES AND FLUTES

Small circles and parts of circles of all sizes make decorative features. To start with you may have to experiment with pieces of fabric but you will soon learn to recognize how to convert a circle to give the effect you want. Most small circles can be cut in one piece or with one join for ease of handling.

A. Hemline circle. Adapt skirt block as required and shorten to length. Measure hem edge of back plus front and multiply by two for circumference of circle.

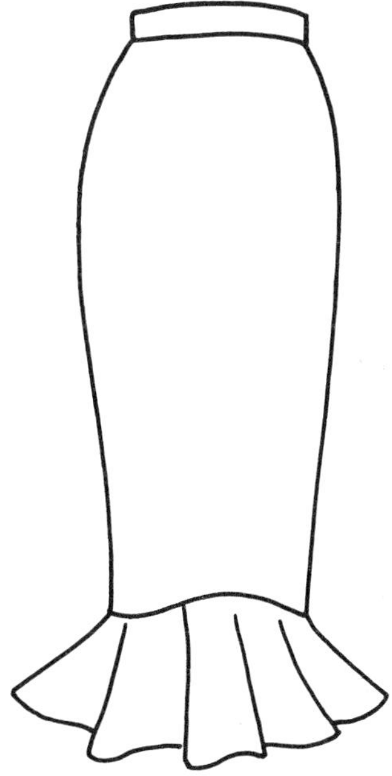

B. Hemline flute. A shaped flute should have seams to match those of the garment so that the sides can be adjusted if necessary.

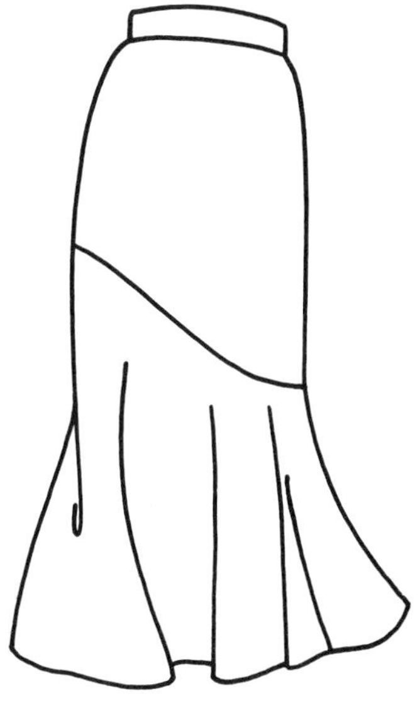

Adapt dress pattern as required and measure width of pattern at highest point; multiply by two and calculate radius.

Draw a half circle for front and one for back to the longest length and draw shape of upper edge of flute.

C. Fluted peplum. Cut patterns for these on the

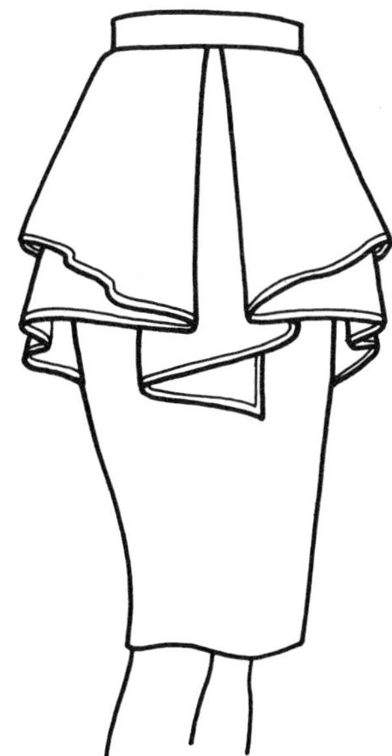

same basis as B above but shaping the circles appropriately and re-positioning CF and CB.

D. Waist peplum. Cut two full gathered circles with seam at CB and at CF or at sides.

E. Inset circle. A half circle with upper arc

equal in length to yoke seam. Shape straight edges to fit and correspond with armhole so flute can be included with seam.

F. Jabot. Two full circles with seam at CF and

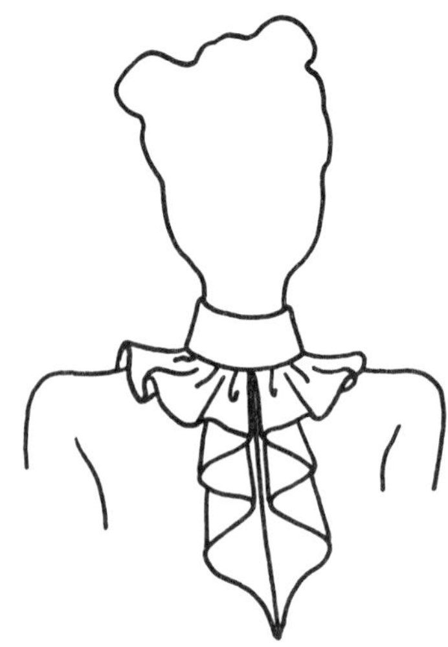

opening at CB. Draw circles initially with radius equal to length of jabot at CF and shape sharply to narrow part.

ALL-ROUND PLEATS

The shape of a pleated skirt or kilt can also be marked directly on to the fabric if you wish. The hemline is straight and the skirt adjusted from the waist if necessary. The fullness of the skirt and therefore the size of the pleats will be governed by the width of the fabric. If you are using tartan or check fabric, the size of the checks will influence the way in which you pleat the fabric, since the pleats must produce an attractive, even pattern. This can only be worked out on the actual fabric although the illustration below will help you to understand

the principles involved. A kilt is often made by cutting the 137cm/54in wide fabric in half along the fold and using it with the warp running round the skirt. The weight of the quantity of fabric, usually 3m/3¼yd, will ensure that it hangs well despite being across the grain. Whichever way you decide to make it cut two, three or four pieces of fabric full width and length required plus waist and hem allowance. Cut the waistband from one piece and a strip to be fringed if required. Join all together with open seams, matching the checks and press. Turn up and finish the hem or at least tack it, and press.

If making a kilt, mark off a flat area at each end equal to the distance between darts on skirt block and mark two waist darts on outer and under flap.

Measure hip depth from upper edge (this may be high or low level according to preference) and pin pleats all the way across to reduce fabric to hip size (minus kilt flap). The quickest way to do this is to divide the fabric into eight and reduce one section, by experimenting, to one-eighth hip size. Baste all pleats from hip to hem and press. Between hip line and waist overlap each pleat a little more to reduce upper edge to waist size.

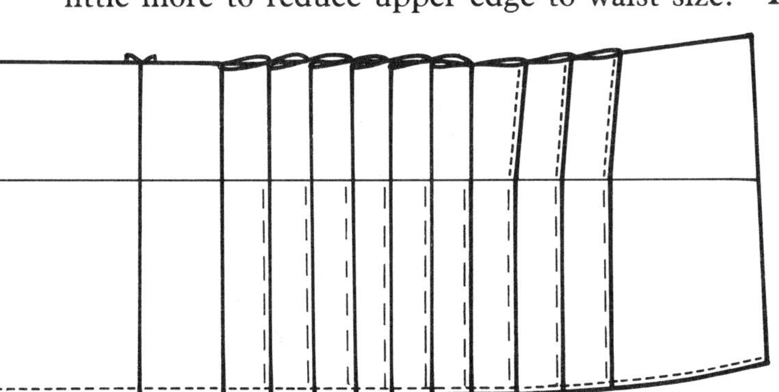

Overlap those at the centre a little more to provide more shape for your bottom. Baste, press and stitch pleats as far as hip line.

POCKETS

Although the pocket pattern depends on measurements, you will also need the garment pattern beside you to get the proportion right.

Most pockets are visible, some are deliberately designed to be decorative and those that are set into seams often only become obvious when they are used.

The type, style and shape of the pocket is a matter of choice but have regard to your sewing skill especially where cut or tailored pockets are concerned. The size of the pocket depends on the position, the size of the pattern piece and the looseness of the garment at that point. Also, from a practical point of view if the pocket is to be used it must be easily reached, have an opening wide enough to take the hand and not be so deep that it requires a contortion to retrieve things.

Always make pattern pieces for pockets; they can usually be fitted into odd corners when cutting out. Areas that are not visible can be made in lining or nylon jersey to reduce bulk. Always interface the open edge to keep it in shape. Soft Fold-a-Band is quick and convenient for straight edges and for welts so allow for the width when planning hems. There is no need to add more than 6mm/¼in seam allowance round outer edge of pockets when cutting out.

Patch pockets

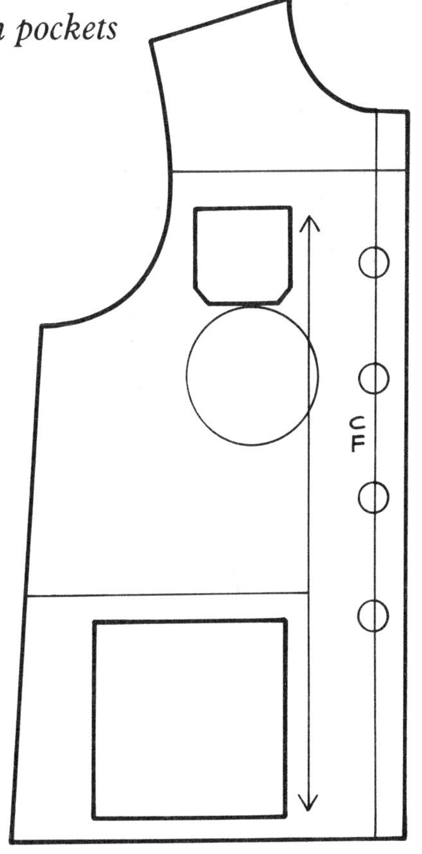

Adapt the block and prepare the pattern for the garment adding all other features then draw the exact shape and size of the pocket on the pattern. Bear in mind the design points made earlier in the book regarding button positions and also the bust point position, waistline and so on. The open edge of pockets that are to be used should equal the measurement across your hand plus 6mm/¼in or more.

Trace shape of pocket, add extra to fold over top edge if appropriate. For shaped pockets fold paper in half and cut outer angle, curve etc. If pocket includes separate flap draw the whole pocket to start with including flap. Trace flap to make separate pattern then lower upper edge of patch section 6mm/¼in. If pocket is to have a poacher's pleat, fold a pleat in a piece of paper, place traced pattern on top and cut round outer edge.

Mark SG to correspond with garment or at 45 degrees, perhaps for stripes or checks. Mark pattern cut two or four, mark which are to be cut in fabric, lining etc. as appropriate and note position of interfacing.

A. Hipline patch pocket.

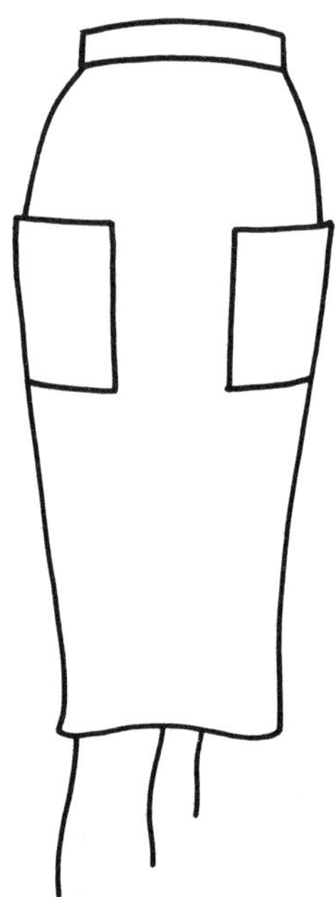

B. Poacher's pocket on loose garment.

C. Breast pocket kept small on fitted garment.

D. Deep hipline pocket, sloped to allow access; side edge included in garment seam.

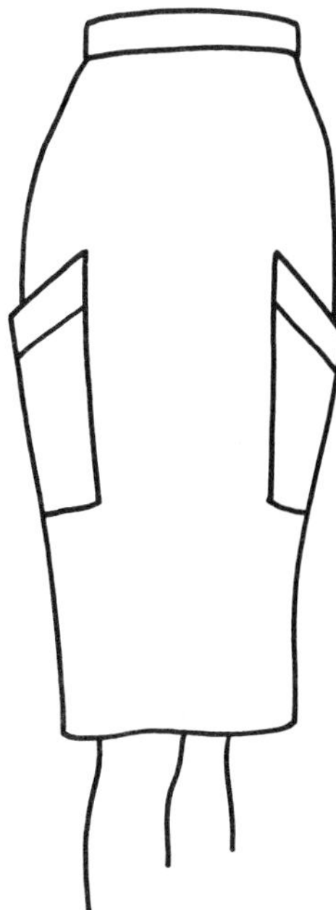

E. Double fabric shaped patch pocket included in waist and side seam.

Cut pockets

Cut pockets and others that require a bag inside the garment should be designed with the same care as patch pockets even though they are less visible.

Draw the size of the piping, welt etc. and also the size and shape of the bag. These pockets

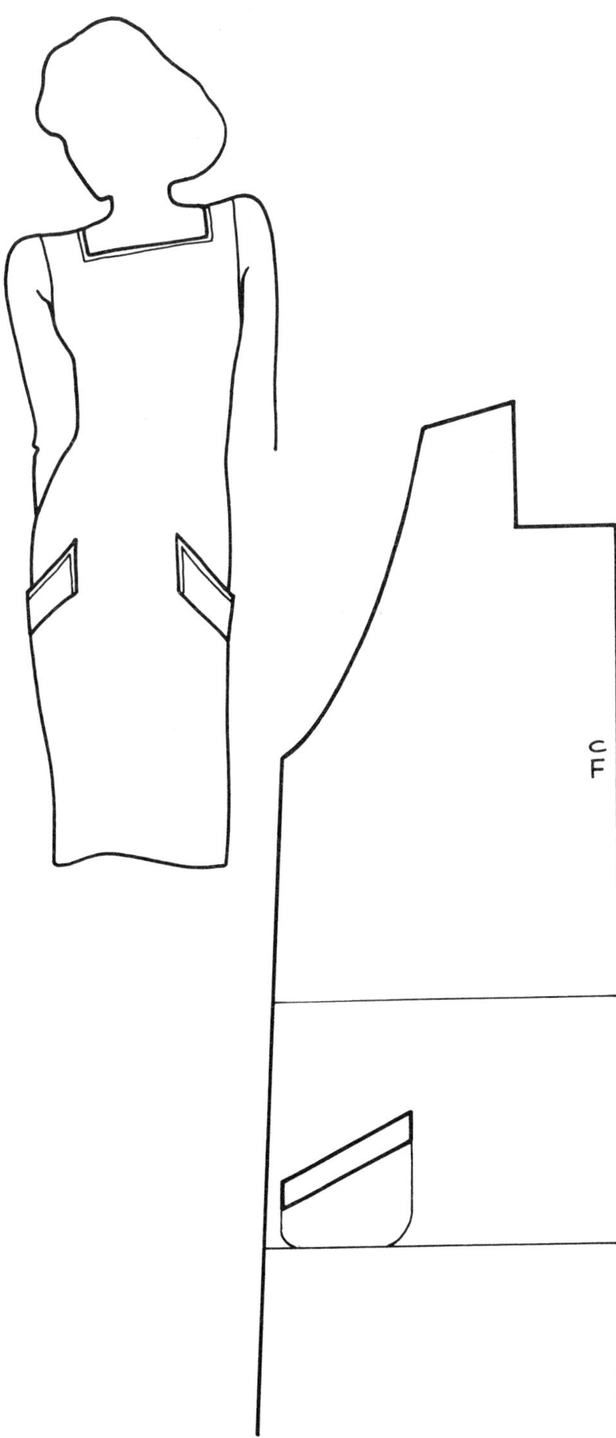

should not be too deep; less than from fingertip to wrist or they are ugly when used. Try to ensure the bottom of the bag will not cause a ridge at hip level.

The depth of jacket pockets may be governed by the length of the jacket. If the bag of a breast pocket is likely to extend on to the bust point it could be made as a decorative welt only.

Trace shape for pattern and mark for cutting out as for patch pockets.

Seam pockets

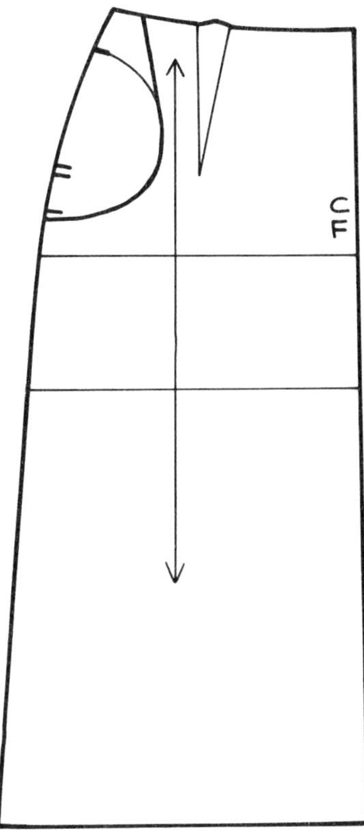

Adapt the pattern then mark off an opening equal to hand width plus 6mm/¼in. Draw a semi-circle making sure it does not extend as far as darts, hip line etc. Outline shape of bag, not too deep and if possible extend it to a seam. This will suspend the pocket and keep it flat inside the garment.

Trace the shape for the pattern, mark grain and cut 2 or 4 etc.

Inset pockets

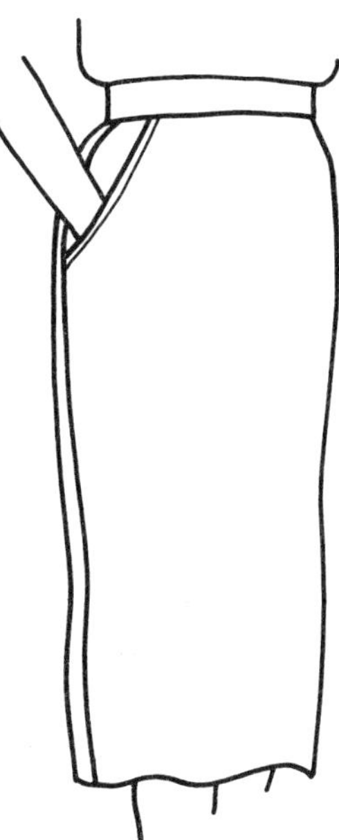

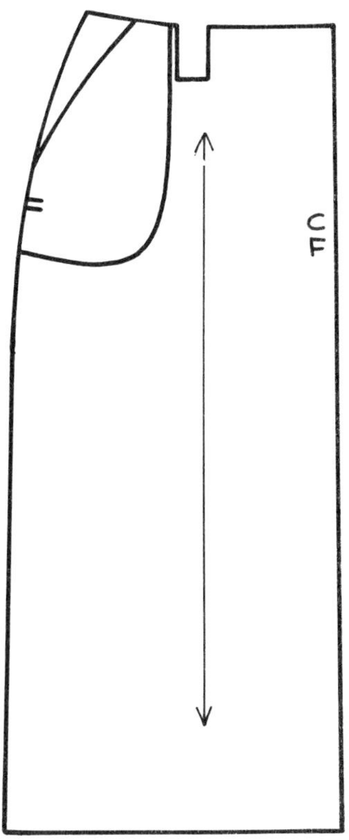

Draw pocket edge on adapted pattern and add shape of bag as for seam pocket. Trace separately outer pocket bag pattern and inner part of bag which includes part of skirt. Outer bag only can be marked to be cut in lining.

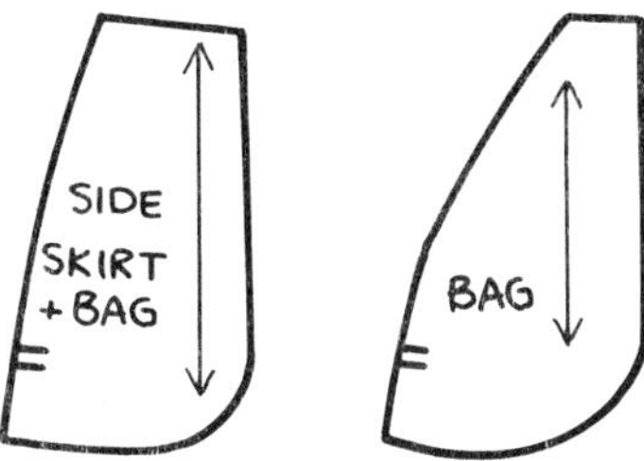

STRAIGHT BANDS

Bands for cuffs and edges that are straight can be cut directly in fabric if you wish although it is sometimes helpful to have a pattern piece to lay out on the fabric.

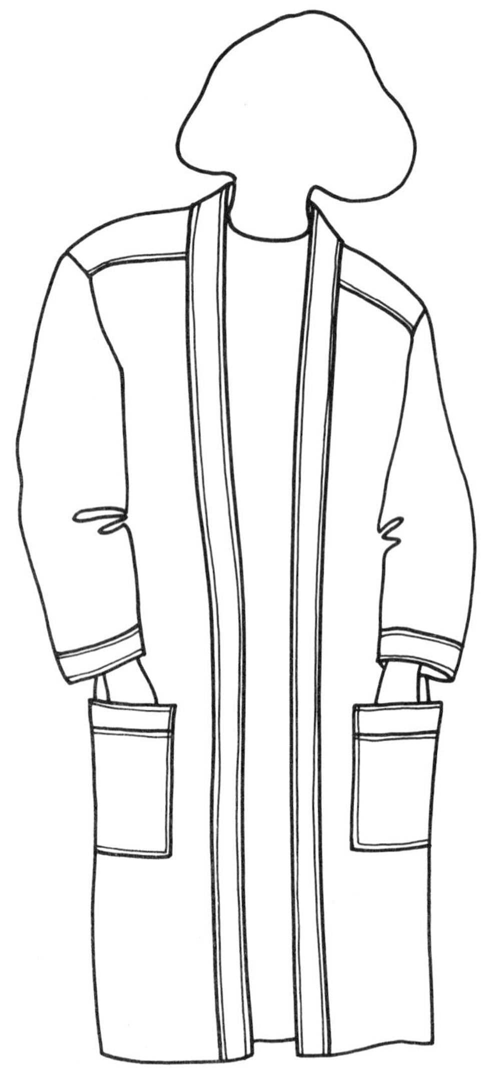

Adapt the pattern to include all other design features then measure the length of the edges to have bands attached. Rule rectangles twice the finished width on folded paper. If a particularly long piece is required simply make a short section and add a note to extend to length when

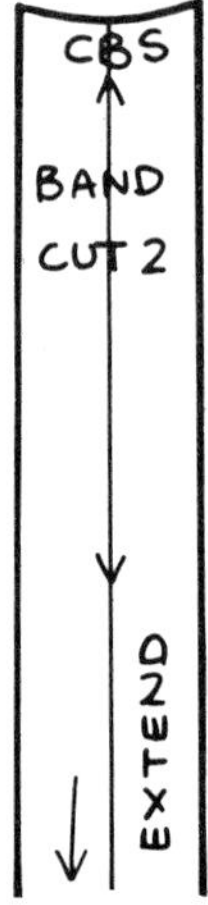

cutting out. Joins may be made at CB or to correspond with garment seams, for economy

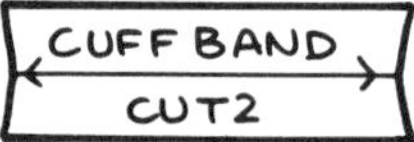

and also so that slight shaping can be introduced if required. Make all similar features such as tabs and pocket tops the same width as the main bands.

Alternatively, instead of cutting a pattern, make the bands the same width as soft Fold-a-Band, simply noting on the pattern the length to be cut.

TIES AND SASHES

With experience you will be able to make a fairly accurate guess as to the length and width of these features. There is no need to make a pattern except perhaps for those that are shaped or cut on the bias, or those that are made double and will therefore require a lot of fabric.

Look at the picture you are copying and decide on the length of the tie ends in proportion to the total length of the garment. Write down twice this measurement. Add it twice more for a bow and once more for a knot. Finally measure the garment around neckline or waist and add to your calculation.

Alternatively use an odd piece of fabric tied around you or the dummy and measure the result.

PATTERNS FOR UNDERCLOTHES, OUTERWEAR, MATERNITY CLOTHES AND SPECIAL FABRICS

PATTERNS FOR UNDERCLOTHES

Lingerie, beach-wear, sundresses and other close-fitting garments without shoulders and worn with nothing underneath require less ease than other clothes. In addition the bust shaping must be more pronounced for a closer fit. The adaptations to the bodice block are quickly done but if you plan to make a lot of these items it would be worth making a lingerie block in card.

Lingerie block

1. Outline back and front bodice block to hip level using shaped side seam.

2. Reduce width at side seam by the following amounts:
Underarm level: 1.5cm/⅝in
Waist level: 6mm/¼in
Hip level: 3mm/$\frac{1}{16}$in

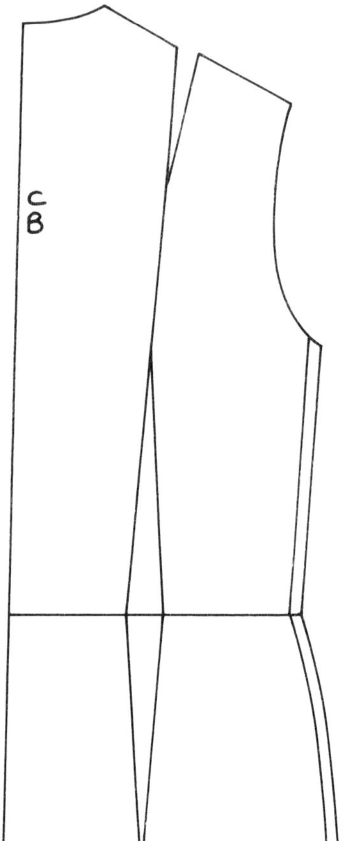

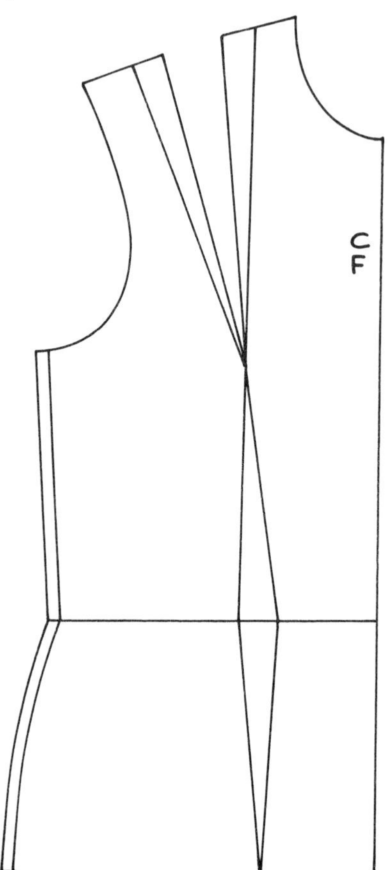

Re-draw side seams.

3. On the front double the width of the bust dart at the shoulder seam by adding half to each side and rule new lines to BP. Use this dart, transferred as required, for bra patterns and other close fitting tops.

The block may also be used for nightdresses with fitted tops but other styles and also pyjamas will require the ease that is included in the basic blocks.

A. Bra. Outline lingerie block and reduce width at side seams by a further 1cm/⅜in. Draw back and trace. Close dart and outline, add extension for fastening or mark for attaching bra fastening kit.

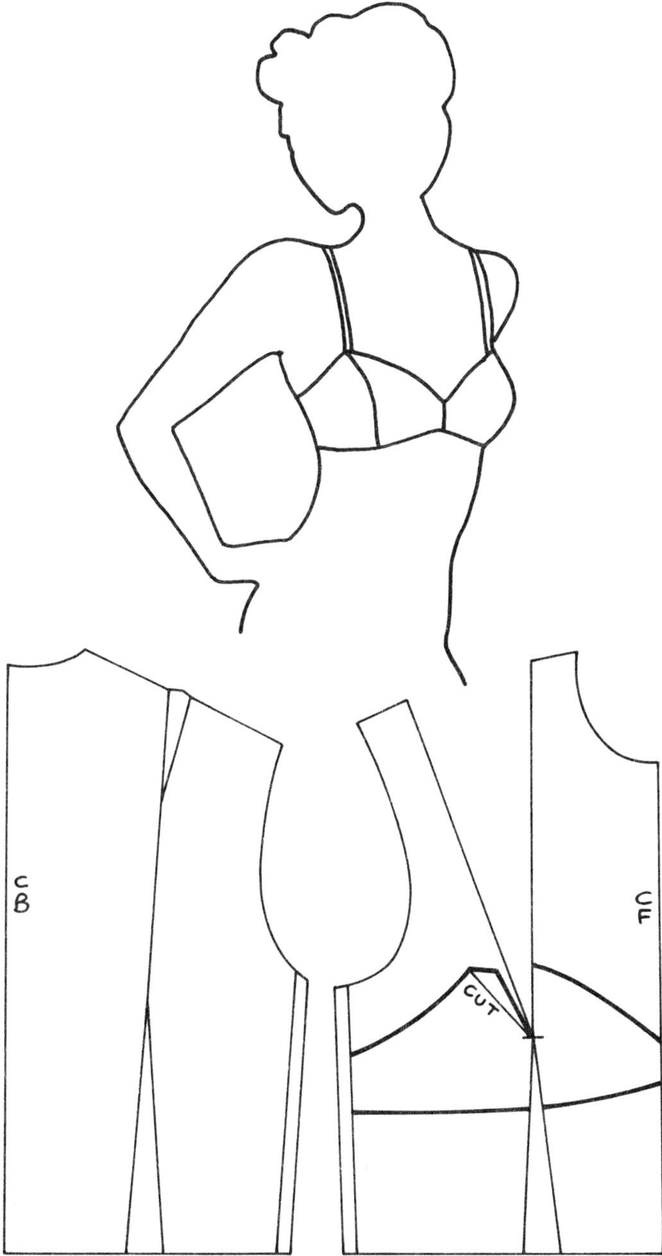

On front draw upper and lower edges, widening dart by a further 1cm/⅜in. Trace sections omitting dart. Measure block for strap length.

B. Bikini top. Follow instructions for Bra but transfer dart to under bust or CF position to be gathered.

C. Camisole. Outline back and front lingerie block to waist level and mark elastic level above waist. Straighten side seams. Draw upper edge and Princess seams. Transfer bust and waist darts to seams. Draw buttons and add extension for fastening.

D. Bikini pants. This pattern is for nylon jersey

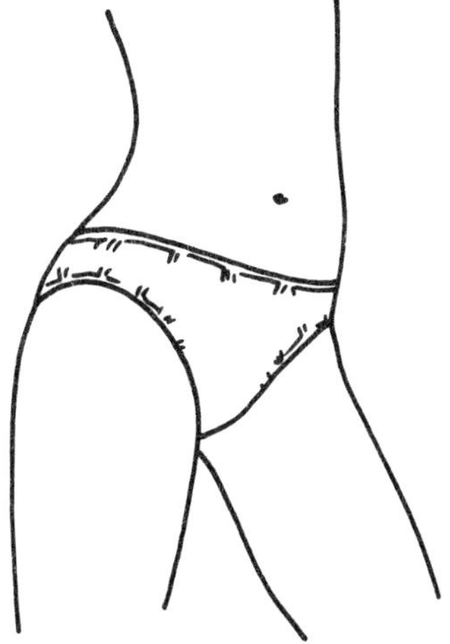

or other fabric with give. If you want to make pants or French knickers from woven fabric use the trouser block (see next page).

1. Rule two vertical lines equal in length to crutch depth measurement; label one CB and the other CF. Rule lines at the top at right angles equal to ¼ hip. Rule verticals 8cm/3⅛in long

parallel to CB and CF. At bottom of CB and CF rule line at right angles 3cm/1⅛in long.

2. Back. Extend CB upwards 2cm/¾in and curve down to SS. Measure 2cm/¾in from cor-

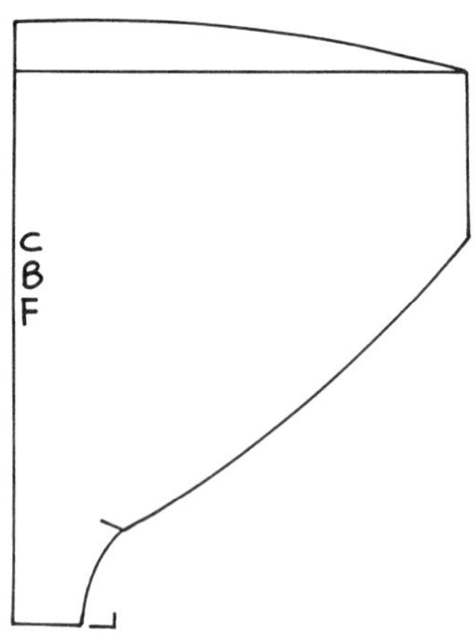

ner crutch and measure up from this point 5cm/2in. Curve the leg edge through this point.

3. Front. Rule a vertical 7cm/2¾in up from crutch line, rule a dotted line to SS. Draw concave leg edge curving it in 3cm/1¼in. Curve down to 2cm/¾in from crutch corner.

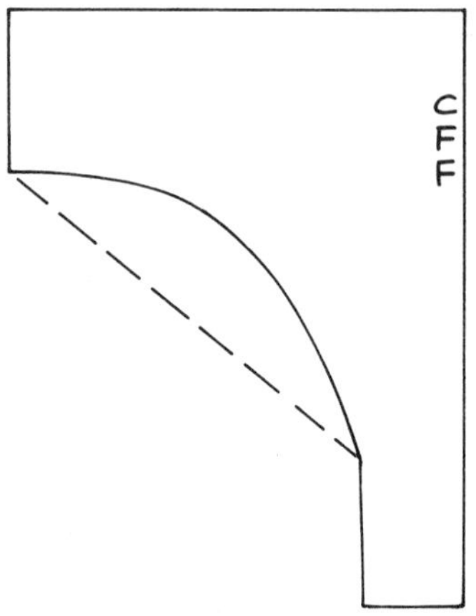

E. Camiknickers.

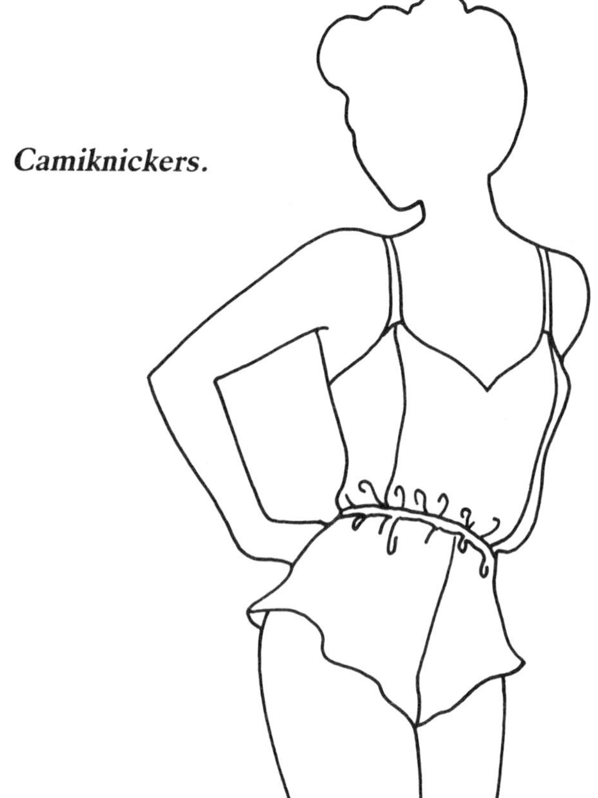

1. Make pattern for bodice as for a camisole top to waist level. Allow for a long opening to hip level.

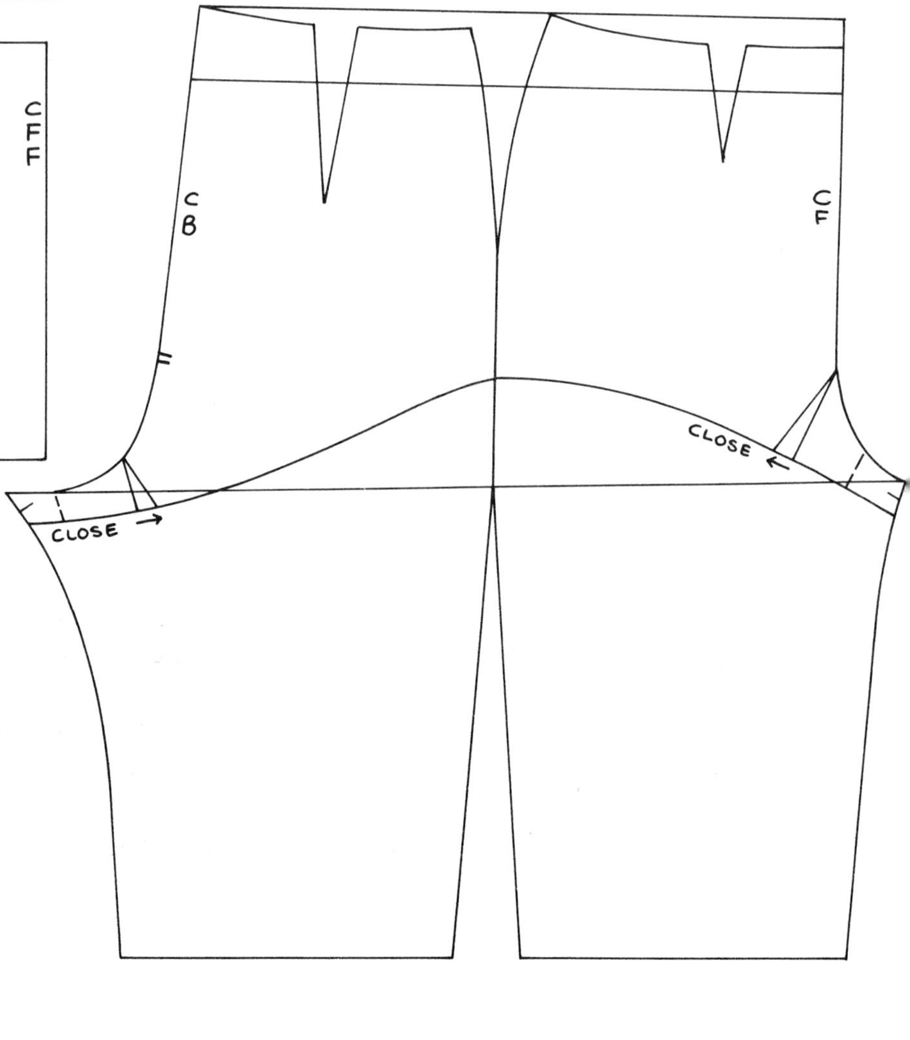

2. Outline trouser blocks to knee level. Draw straight waist edge level with CB.

3. Curve leg edges to depth required at crutch and side seam. Trace in one piece without side seam. Measure 10cm/3½in along leg edge from crutch, cut to crutch seam and close by 13mm/½in to tighten leg edge.

Adjust camisole waist at sides to fit edge of pants. An alternative to a long opening is to have a crutch gusset fastened with buttons or press studs. Trace back and front crutch to dotted line, place pieces with inside leg seam edges together and outline on folded paper. Re-shape outer edges in smooth curves, cut out and mark pattern 'cut 2'.

For wide-legged or French knickers cut legs separately to have a side seam and add flare at side or cut to the waist and spread at hem. These may then be cut on the bias if you wish.

PATTERNS FOR OUTERWEAR

Coats, jackets, anoraks etc. need to be roomy enough to go over other clothes. This entails enlarging the basic bodice and sleeve blocks; once again it might be worth making permanent copies, depending on how much of this type of sewing you do.

Coat patterns generally need to be larger than jackets although this depends on the design. In the following instructions the coat measurements are first with those for jackets in brackets.

The best shape of sleeve for outer garments is undoubtedly the two-piece. Follow instructions below for adapting the block.

Bodice

1. Outline back and front bodice block to hips with straight side seams.

2. On front cut vertically through centre of

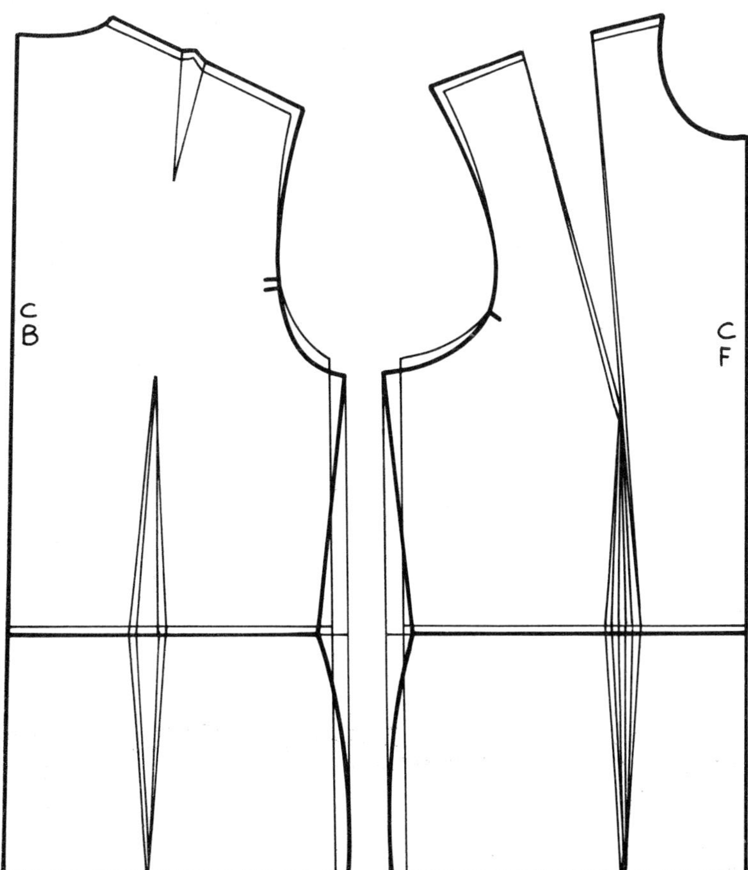

waist dart to BP. Spread sections to insert 6mm/¼in. Mark BP mid-way between sections and re-draw dart.

3. On back and front raise shoulder seam 6mm/¼in. Extend at SP by 6mm/¼in (1cm/⅜in).

4. At armhole lower back and front by 1cm/⅜in (2cm/¾in) and extend the sides by the same amount. Re-draw waist line 6mm/¼in lower. Re-draw side seams curving in to new waist points.

5. At waist line add 6mm/¼in to each side of both waist darts. Re-draw darts. Adjust block to required length when used.

Sleeve

1. Outline sleeve block with sloping seam edges. See page 115, Sleeve Designs. Cut along middle finger line and spread to insert 1cm/⅜in. Lower the armhole each side by 1cm/⅜in and extend seam 1cm/⅜in. Raise SP 1cm/⅜in, re-draw sleeve head curve.

2. Cut round outline and fold so seam edges meet over centre line. Measure in from front fold 4cm/1⅝in and 2cm/¾in from back fold. Rule vertical lines. These are the new seam lines.

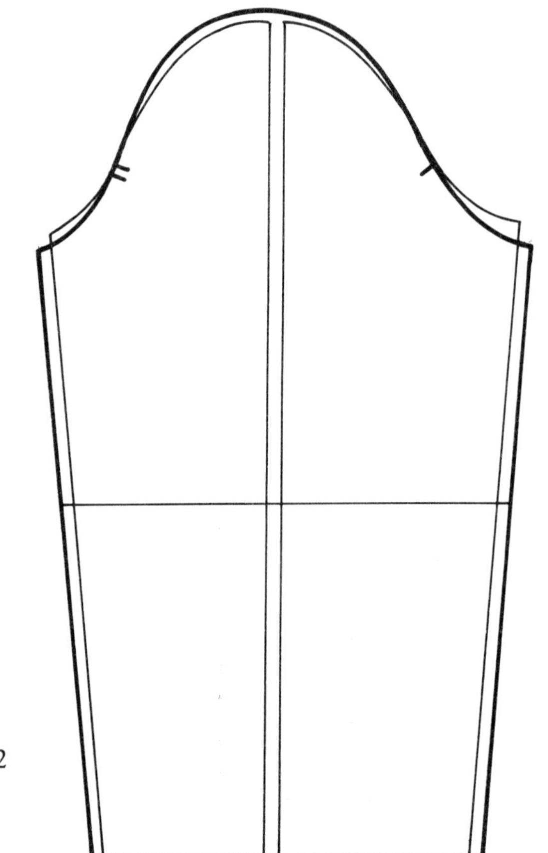

3. To insert elbow shaping cut along elbow

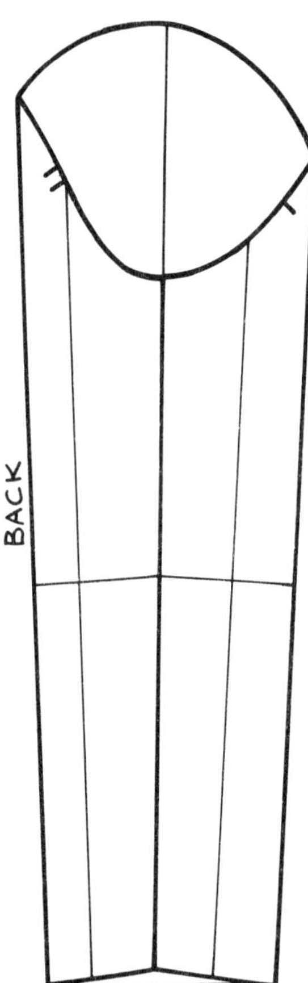

line with sleeve folded and spread to insert 2cm/¾in at back fold.

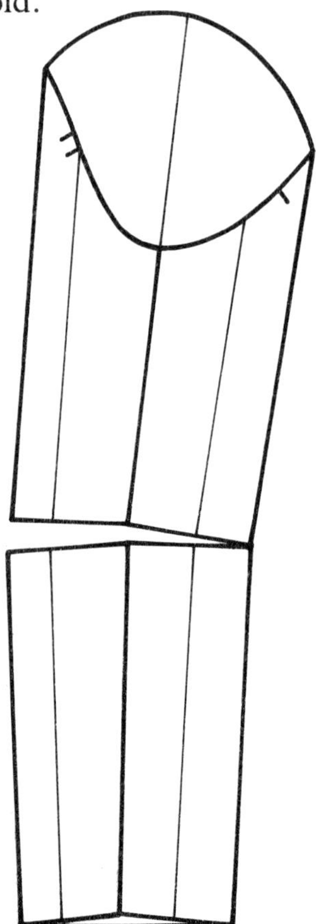

4. Trace underarm section. Shorten front edge at hem to fit corresponding top sleeve edge. Mark underarm point. Open out paper and trace remainder – top sleeve. Add balance marks and SP.

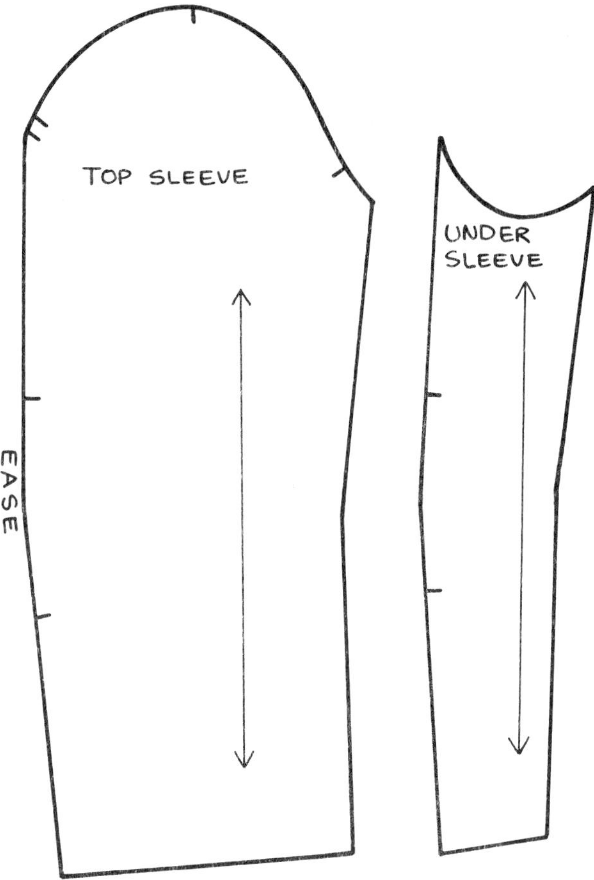

SG will usually run vertically through each piece. When sewing the seam the elbow shaping is eased.

SEWING TIP

For professional results and to extend the life of a coat or jacket, attach a suitable weight of interfacing to WS of entire front section, possibly omitting dart areas. This ensures stable shoulders and armholes and also reinforces the pocket area. Depending on the fabric it often helps to place an additional strip of interfacing along button and buttonhole positions.

A. Loose fitting edge-to-edge coat.

1. Outline sleeve block with straight seam edges. Enlarge as described for coat sleeve, 1, above.

2. Using back and front coat block adapt to simple raglan, see page 137. Extend CF and side seams to length adding flare at hemline (see next page).

Complete sleeve by adding flare at wrist and cut in two sections to give a seam from shoulder to wrist. Mark facing and pocket position.

SEWING TIP

Include a length of seam tape or narrow strip of interfacing with raglan seam stitching. Welt seams, which involve top stitching, will help to stabilize the seams in wear.

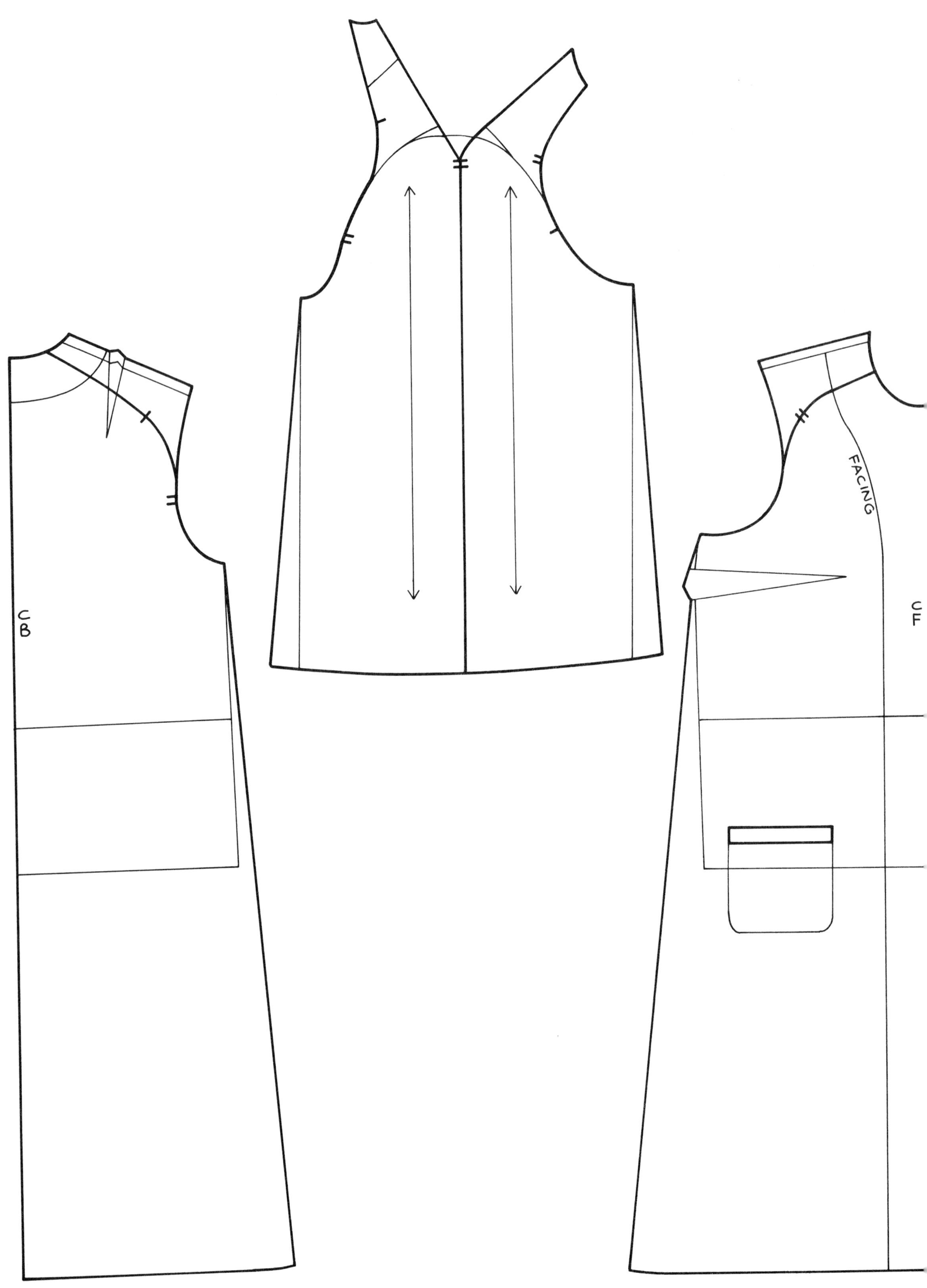
CB
FACING
CF

B. Double breasted jacket.

SEWING TIP

Do not add seam allowances to edges to be finished with folded braid. Bulk can be reduced by cutting the lining with edges level with those of jacket and attaching the braid to enclose both.

1. Outline jacket blocks to length required. Use two piece sleeve pattern, marking cuff opening on outer seam. Straighten side seams of bodice. Draw panel seams from armhole and transfer waist darts to seams, adjusting length. Close bust dart to transfer to panel seam. Add button extension and draw new neck edge. Mark facing and pocket.

2. Place back and front with side seams meeting and trace back jacket as far as panel seam.

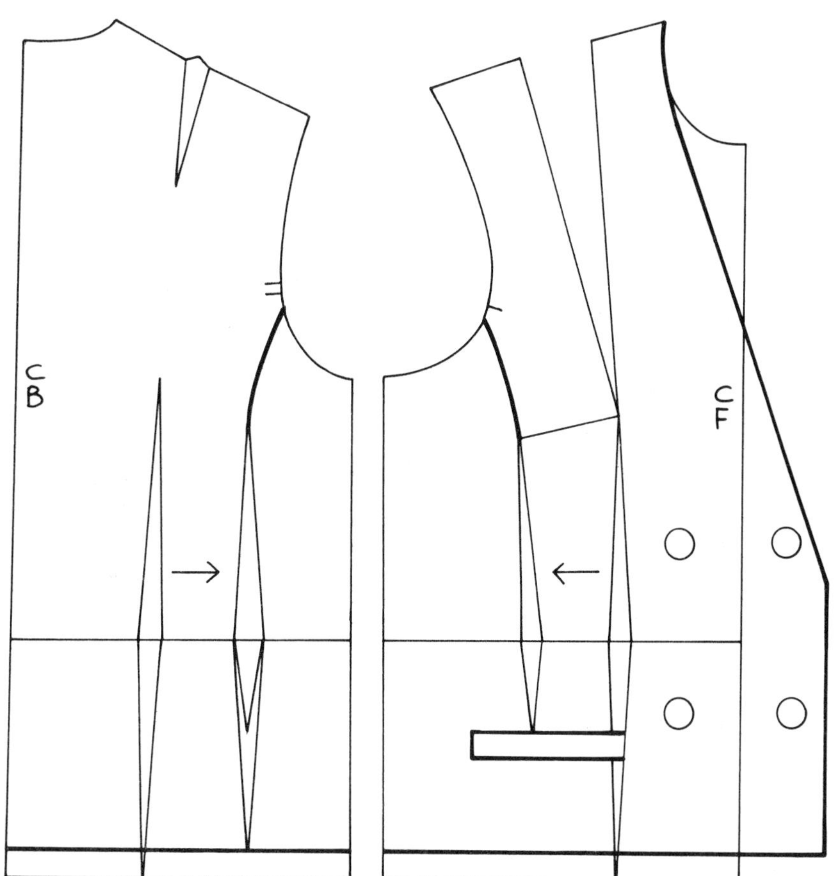

Trace remainder for jacket front and side pattern as one piece.

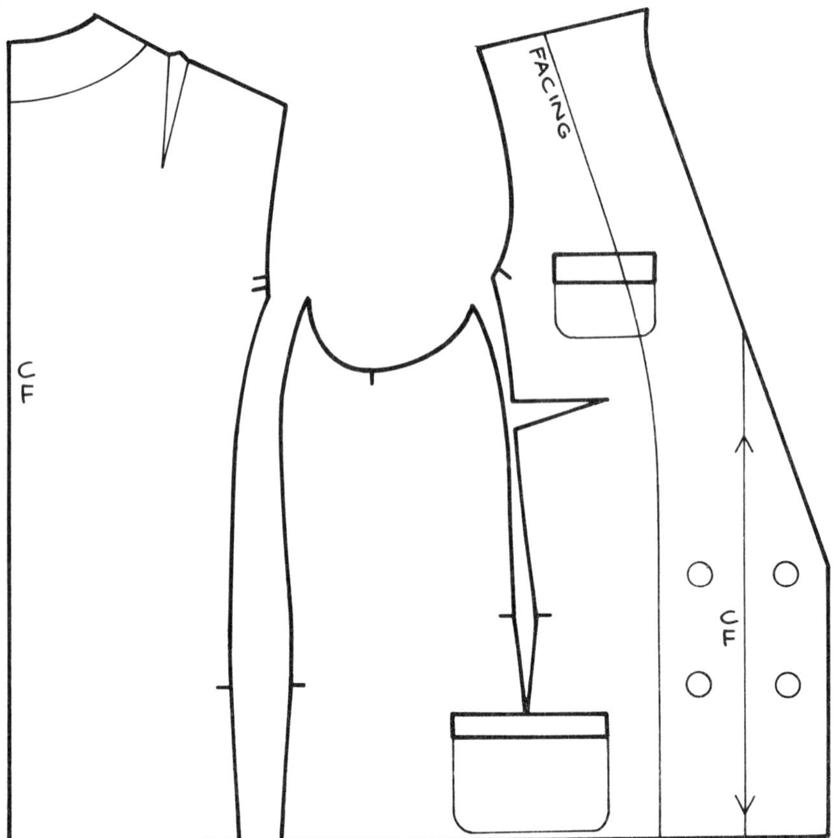

C. Single breasted jacket – classic tailored collar and lapels.

1. Outline front jacket block with straight side seams. Extend CF 6mm/¼in and rule short line at right angles. Add extension for buttons. Extend shoulder seam at NP by 2cm/¾in and join to top of button extension to form the lapel roll line.

2. Extend roll line above shoulder by length of back neck plus 1cm/⅜in. Measure 2cm/¾in towards armhole and rule from that point to end of extended shoulder line. This line is the roll line for back neck of collar. Rule a CB line at right angles to extend 3cm/1⅛in towards armhole and 5cm/2in outwards, making collar 8cm/3⅛in deep at CB.

3. Mark a new neckline with straight lines as follows: Mark 1.5cm/⅝in above horizontal ruled at the start (see 1, above). Rule from original NP to join top of extended CF. Extend beyond CF to shape rever.

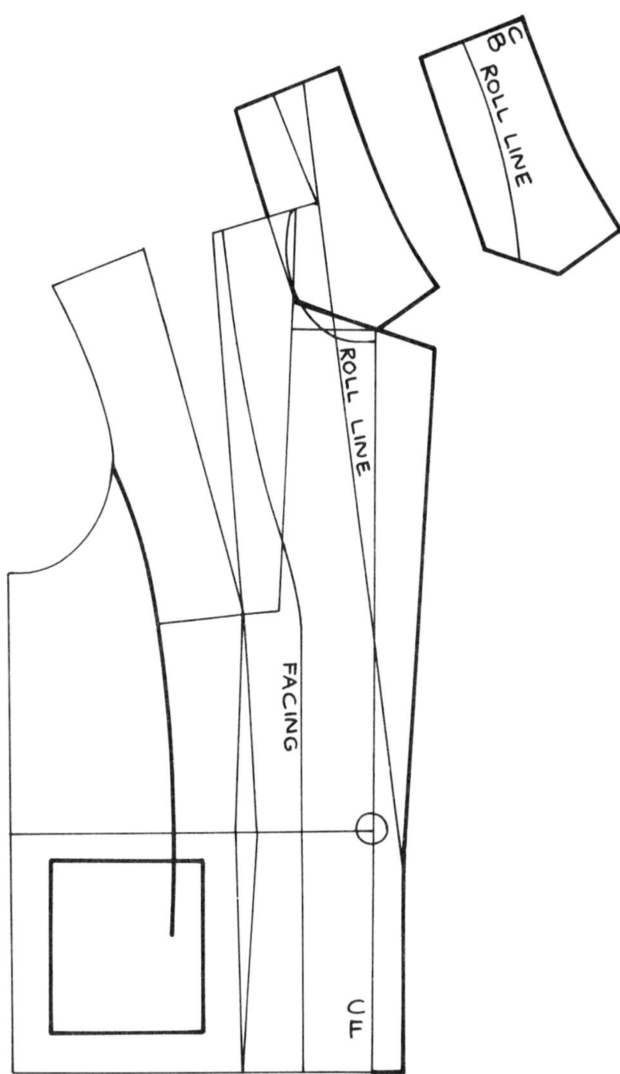

4. Draw the collar neck edge from CB to the same point and draw shape of outer edge. Trace off collar.

5. Make back pattern following instructions for double-breasted jacket, page 195.

6. To complete front pattern mark pocket, draw panel line from armhole to below waist. Cut horizontally from BP to panel line. Cut from point on new neckline to BP. Close bust dart, transfer 2.5cm/1in to neck dart and remainder to panel line. Shorten neck dart a little.

7. Move waist dart to panel line and lengthen the armhole at the panel to give a better seam line. Lower SP by the same amount to keep armhole correct size. Mark front facing. Trace jacket front pattern.

8. Construct two-piece sleeve as page 192.

D. Cape.

1. Outline back and front coat blocks. Draw bust dart to outer circle. Extend horizontal armhole lines beyond block to add ¼ of the CB to armhole measurement. Extend CB to length and rule hemline to hem width required. Rule side seam from hem to extended armhole point.

2. On front extend length and width to match back and draw side seam. Curve both hemlines. At shoulder extend shoulder seam and new side seams to meet. Measure 2.5cm/1in from corner and shape shoulder through the point.

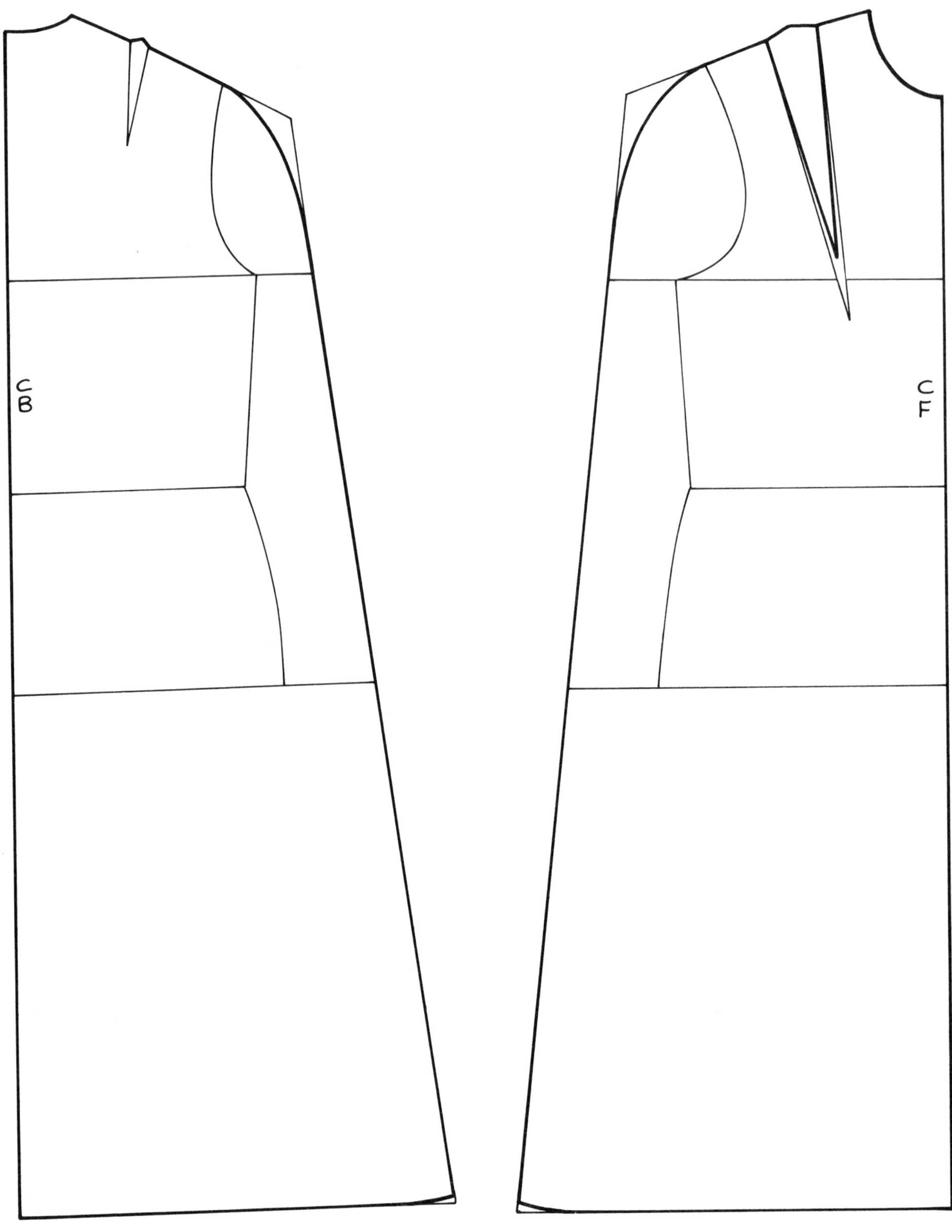
CB
CF

E. Cardigan.

1. Outline jacket block with straight side seams tapered to fit hips. Lengthen as required and draw neckline. Mark buttons, extension for fastening and pockets. Transfer bust dart to underarm and draw dart to outer BP circle. Ignore waist dart. Mark facing.

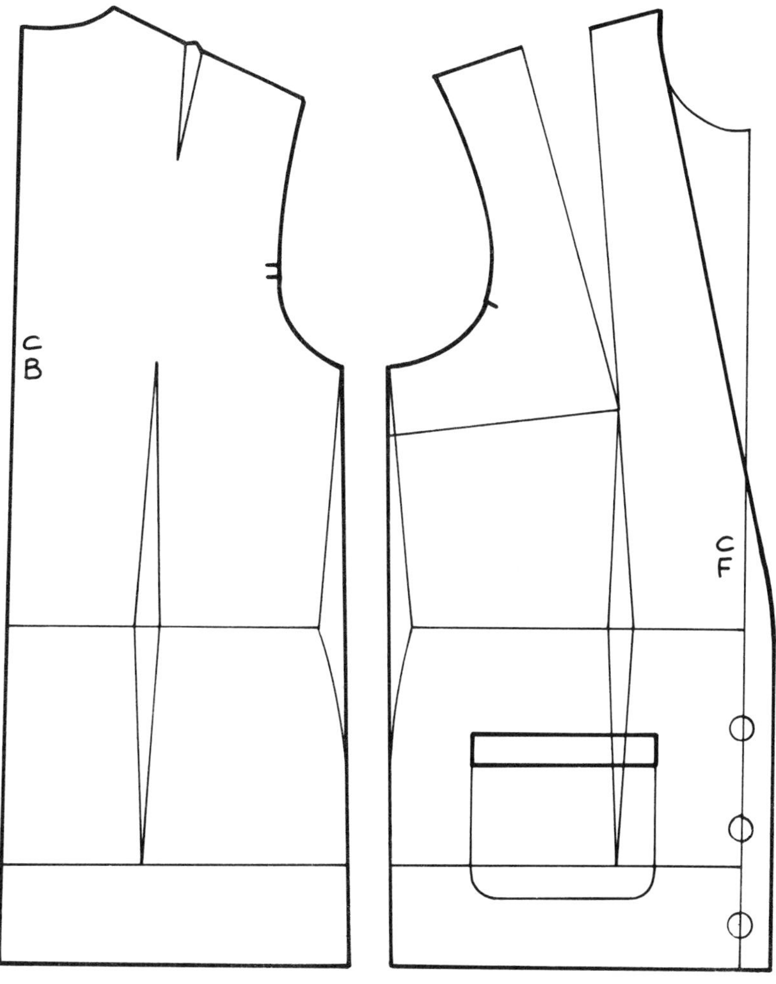

2. Use two-piece sleeve as described on page 192, but straighten the seam edges to increase width at wrist.

F. Raincoat.

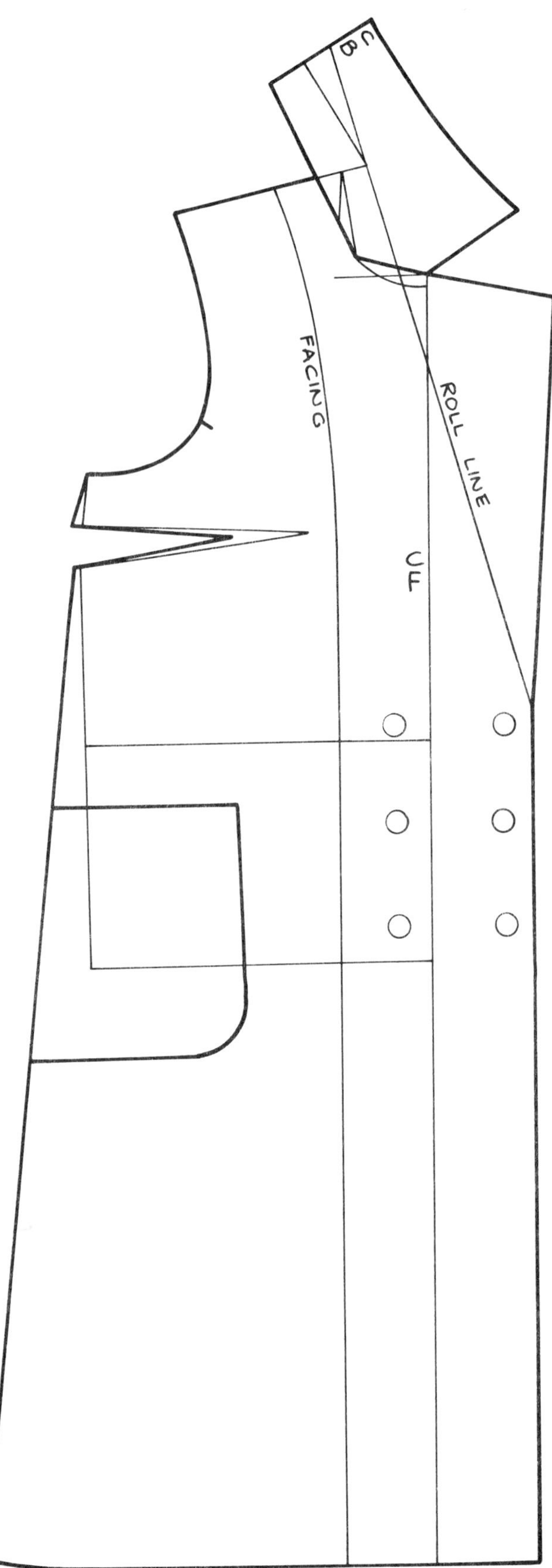

1. Outline coat block with straight side seams. Extend to required length and add flare. Add extension for double-breasted fastening. Shorten bust dart. Adapt to deep armhole, see page 127. Make sleeve pattern from two-piece sleeve and adapt armhole to match bodice.

2. Construct tailored collar and lapel following instructions for C, page 196, but making it longer at CB for a wider collar; draw correspondingly wide lapel.

G. Hood.

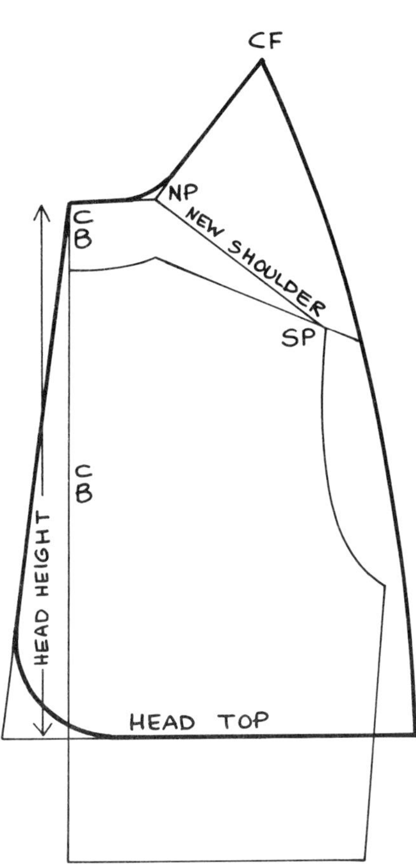

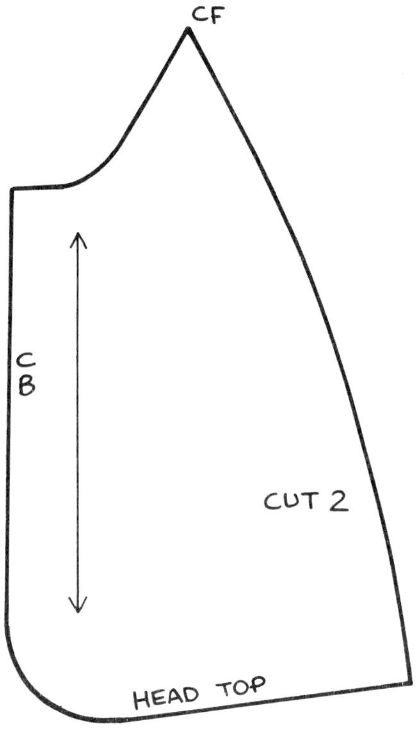

1. Outline back bodice omitting darts. Extend CB above neck 5cm/2in and rule a line at right angles equal to length of back neck. Rule a line from this point to SP.

2. From new raised NP rule a line at right angles to new line equal to length of front neck. Label end of line CF.

3. Measure your head height, measuring at side from shoulder level to top of head. Measure down CB from new raised CB point head height plus 10cm/4in and rule a horizontal 25.5cm/10in long to the right. Extend line beyond CB by 5cm/2in and rule from there to new CB. Measure up 8cm/3⅛in from corner and curve the hood.

4. Extend SP 2.5cm/1in. Complete hood by curving from CF to lower line passing through new SP. Curve neckline angle. Mark pattern cut 2; pattern is a more recognizable shape if turned up the other way.

PATTERNS FOR MATERNITY CLOTHES

For comfort, maternity clothes should be larger all over so start with basic blocks one size larger than usually worn. The adjustments are easy to make, widening the front and also adding length (see next page).

Maternity dress block

1. Outline front and back bodice using straight side seams and extending length to 63cm/24¾in below waist, or whatever length is required.

2. On the front mark bust dart to outer circle. Cut from CF horizontally 10cm/4in below waist and spread pieces to insert 6cm/2⅜in at CF. Lengthen CF to 69cm/27¼in and curve hemline. Check length of back and front side seam edges.

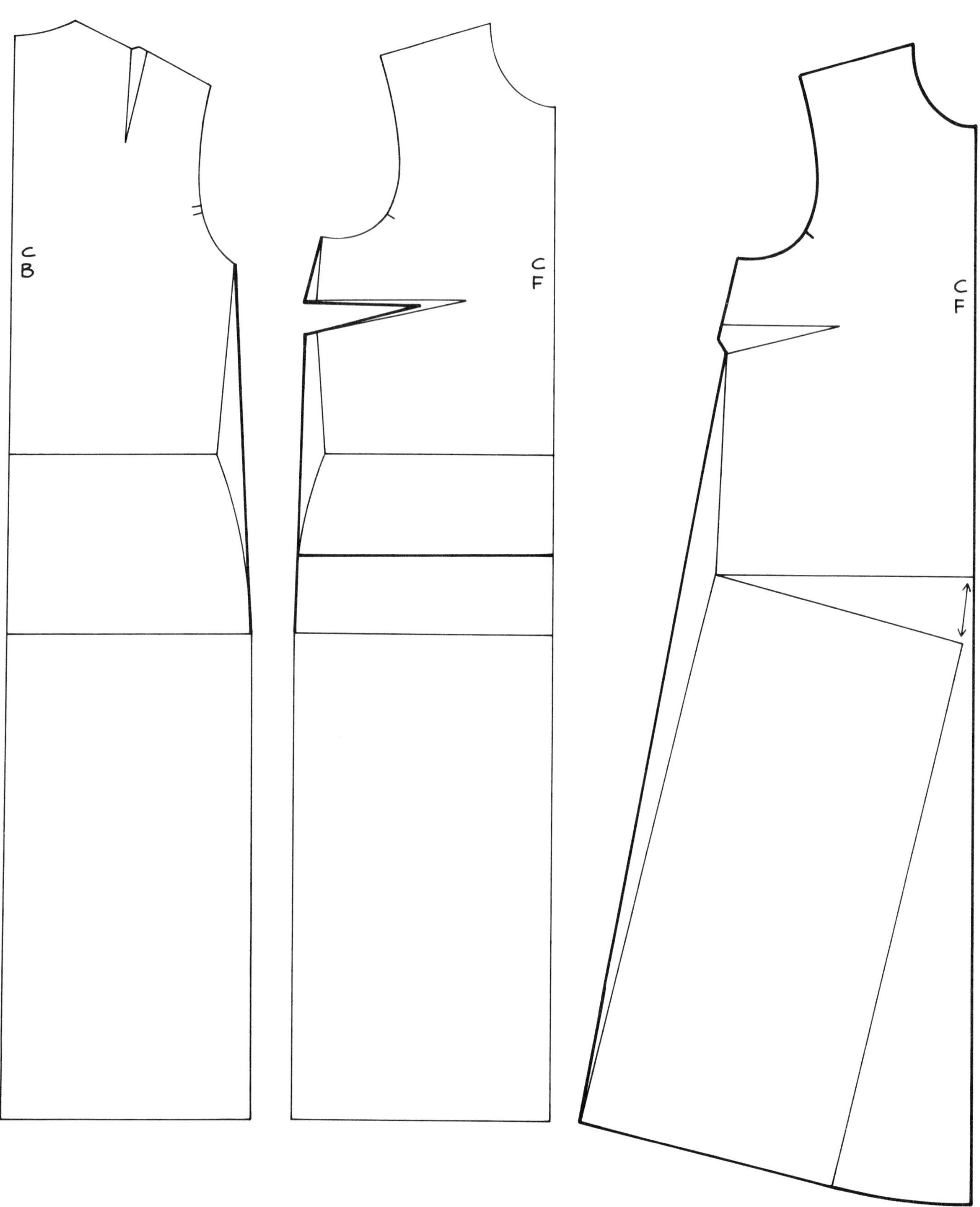
C
B
C
F
C
F

A. Flared top with deep armholes.

1. Outline back and front maternity dress blocks to length required. Draw new neckline and mark facings. Lower armhole by 3cm/1¼in and extend outwards by 1.5cm/⅝in. Re-draw armholes and side seam.

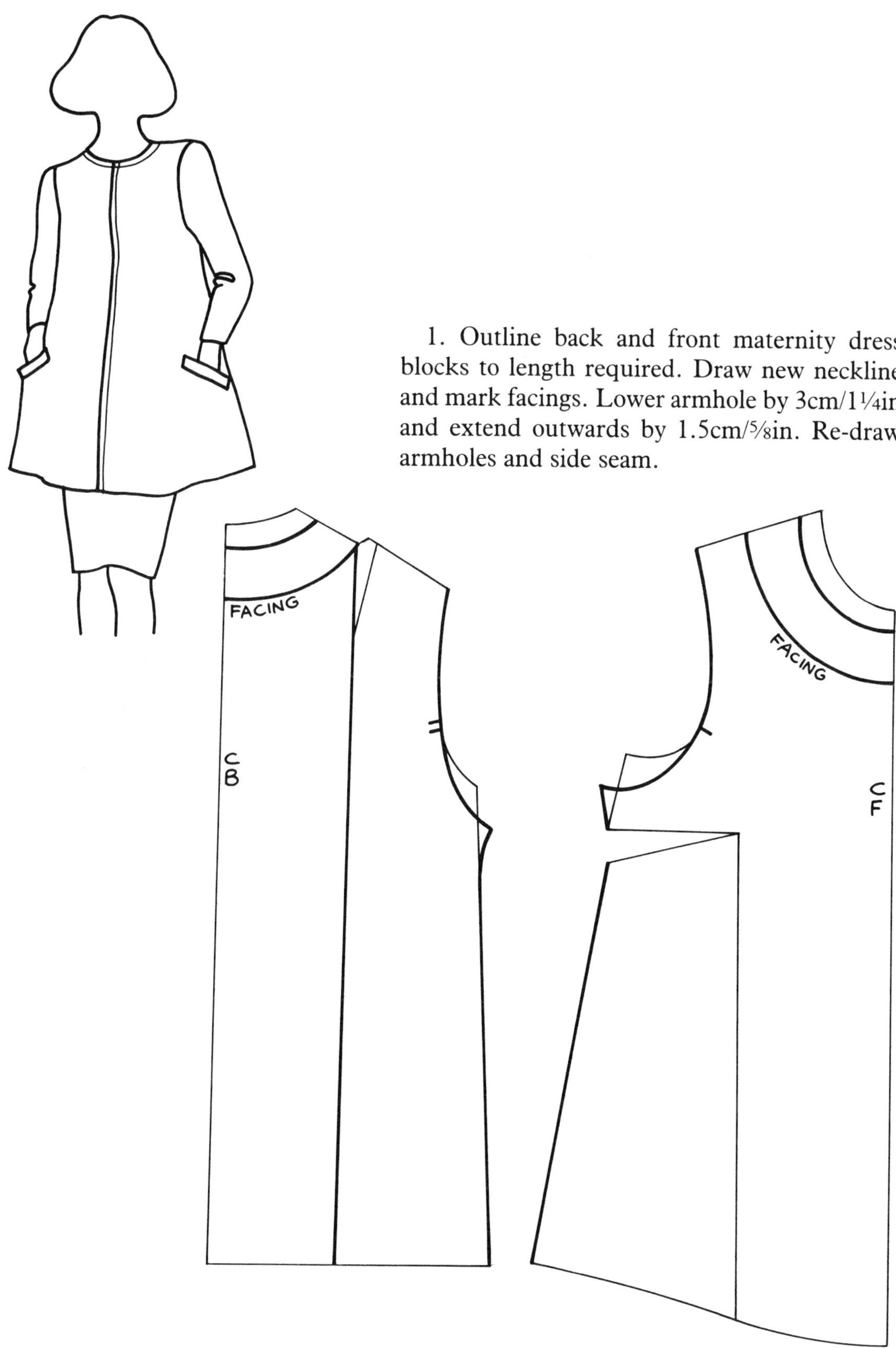

2. On back cut from hem to base of shoulder dart, close dart to add flare at hem. Draw curved hemline.

3. On front cut from hem to point of bust dart to add flare to hem. Draw curved hemline.

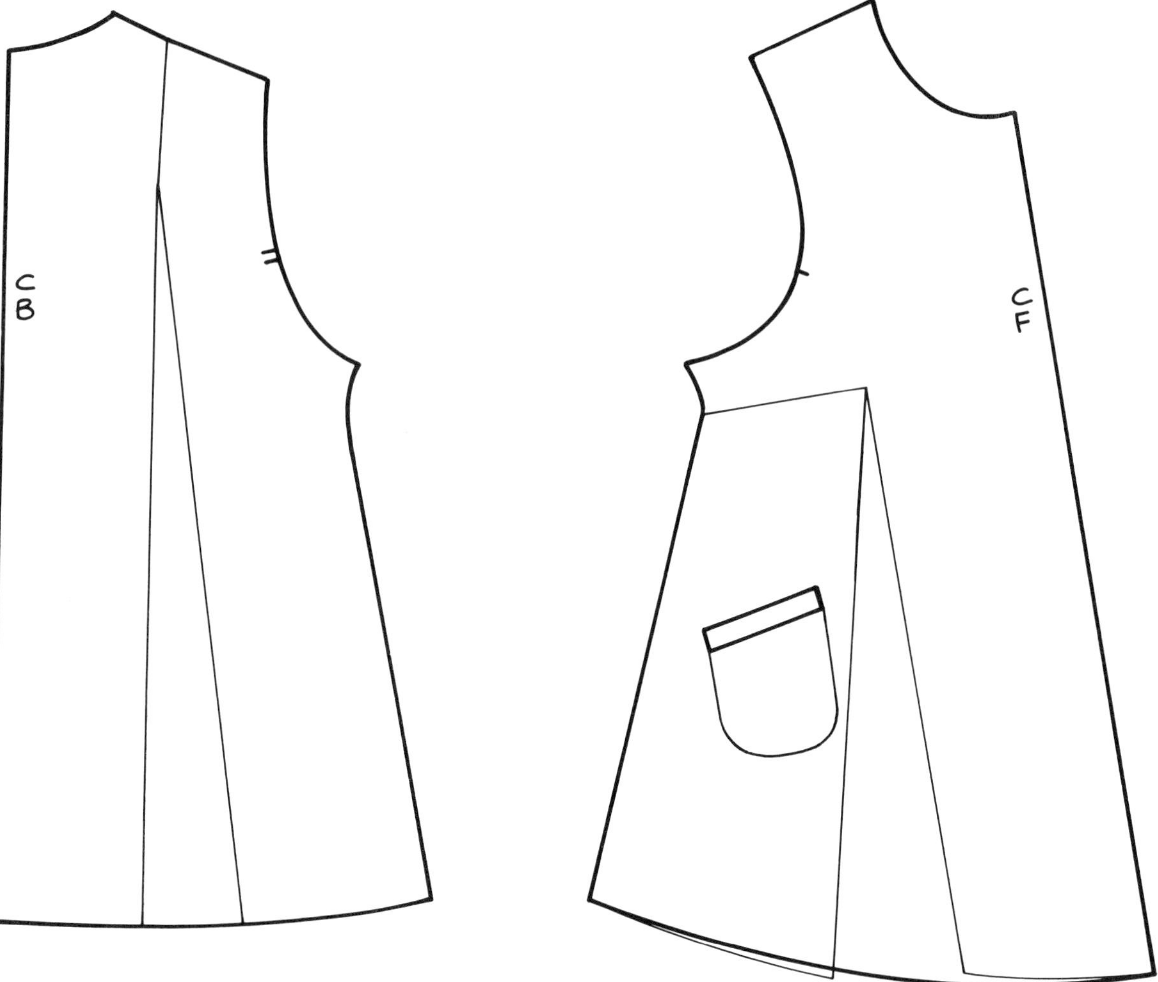

4. Outline sleeve block to length required using sloping seam. Lower underarm by 1.5cm/⅝in and extend outwards 1.5cm/⅝in. Re-draw seam edges to join sleeve at elbow level.

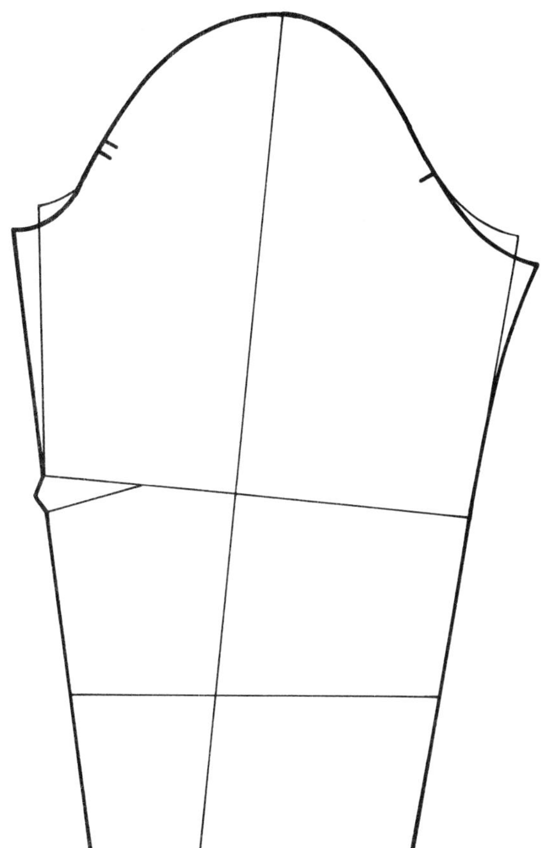

B. Square-neck dress.

1. Outline back and front maternity dress block. Draw yokes and new neckline. Detach yokes, close back neck dart. Add extra flare to side seams. Cut from hem to yoke edge and

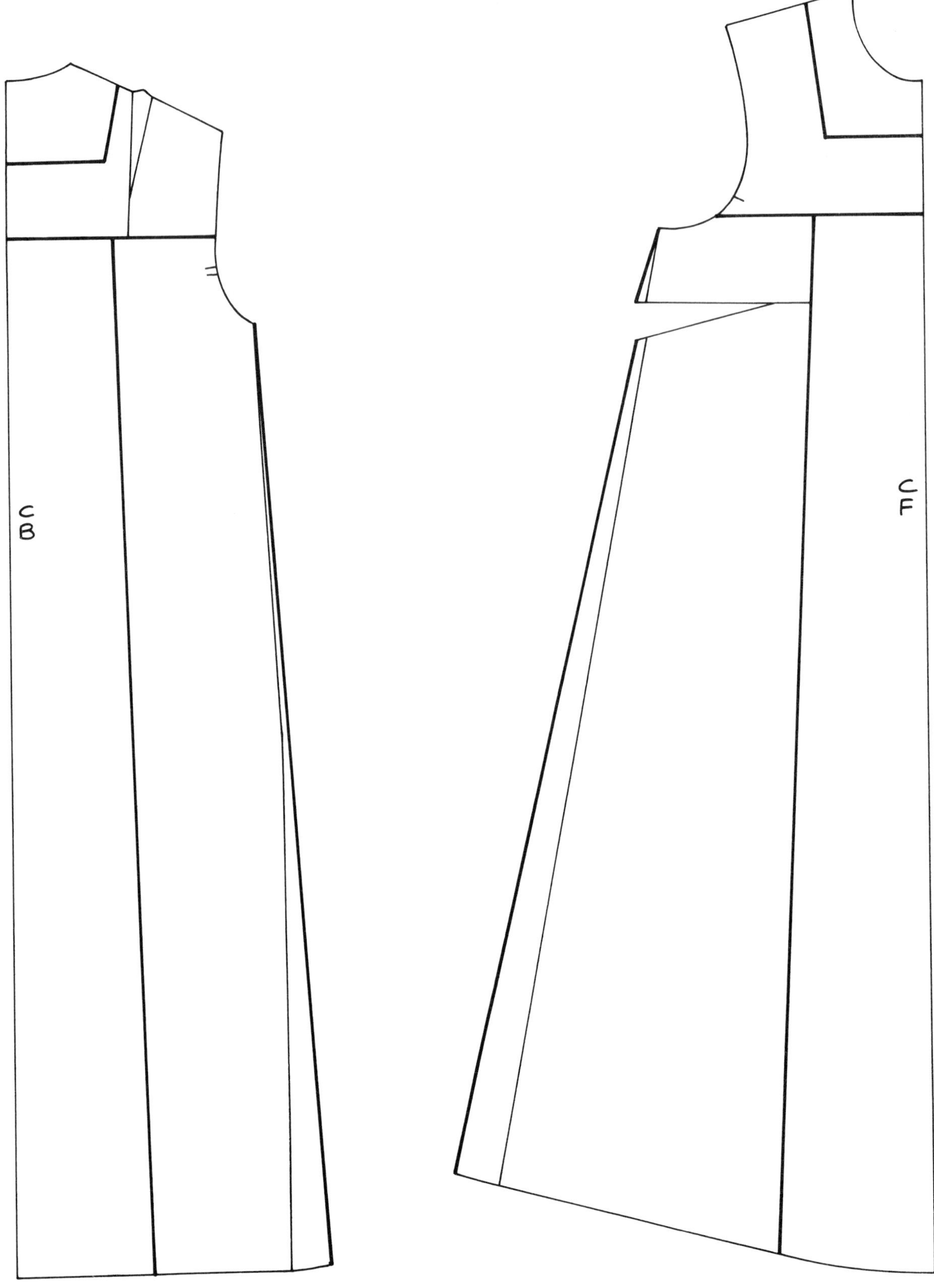
CB
CF

spread to insert box pleat. Close bust dart to transfer dart to yoke edge.

2. Outline sleeve block to short length. Cut on all finger lines and spread to insert fullness.

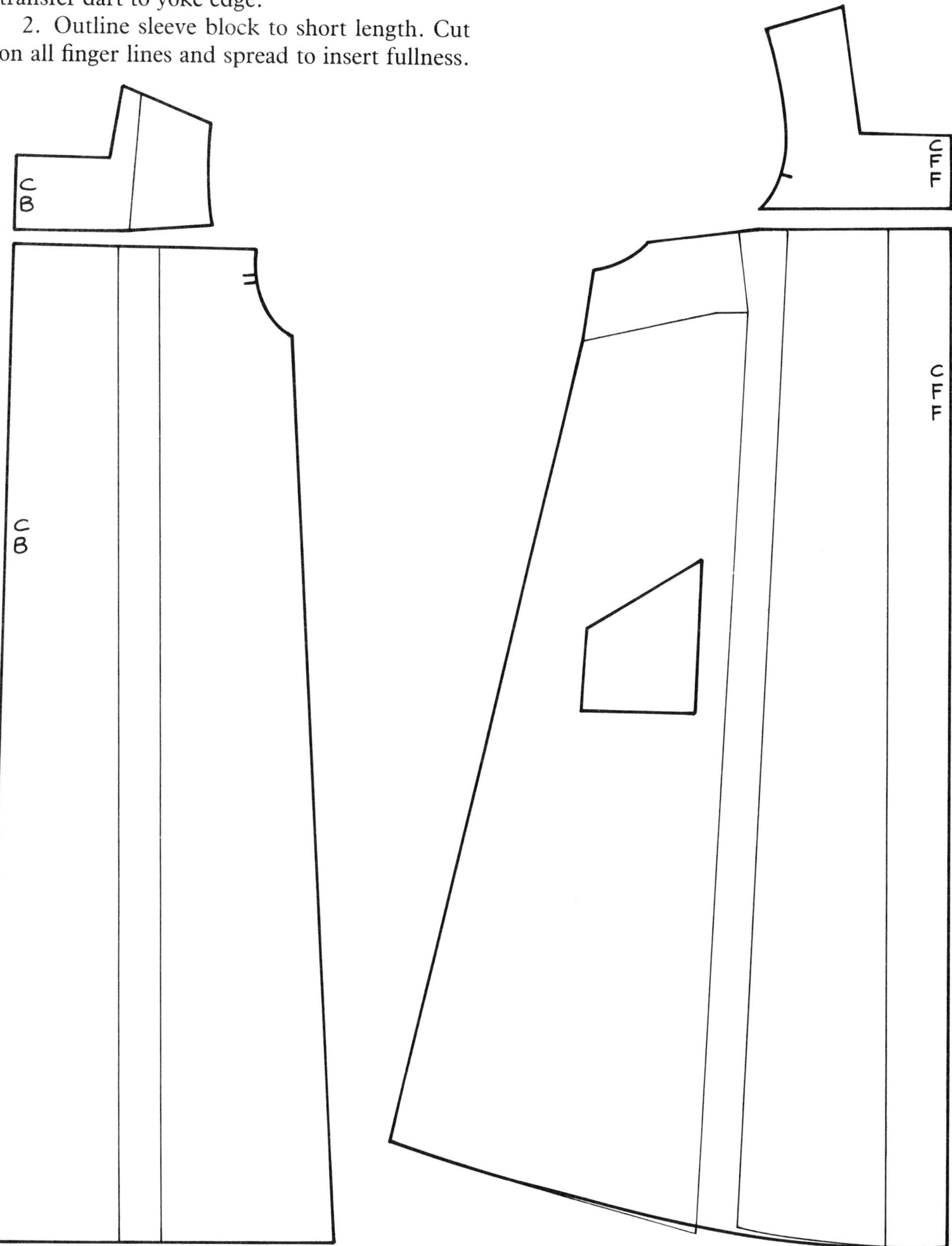

PATTERNS FOR SPECIAL FABRICS

Once you have learnt the main principles of pattern cutting through practice, possibly in small scale as suggested, it is much more satisfactory to design for specific fabrics when possible. Some fabrics require amendments to the pattern and you can save time if you bear in mind the characteristics and possible limitations of the fabric and allow for it from the start. Keep notes of what you do attached to a scrap of the fabric for future reference.

Leather

All skins have thin or marked areas so patterns should be composed of small pieces. The advantage is that there is no grain to follow so pieces can be fitted closely together. Angled seams are better than sharp curves; allow only narrow hems; avoid leather facings, use lining instead. Metal-capped fasteners that are hammered in position are an alternative to buttons.

Small garments are no problem to fit on to skins; if you make trousers or a jacket, plan extra seams and make a feature of them with top stitching.

Velvet

With the exception of panné velvet, which is thin and soft, velvet is at its best when used for plain and sculptured styles. Plan seams rather than darts which are difficult to press at the point. Keep fullness such as gathers to a minimum and avoid bulky openings. With the exception of jacket collars and lapels have the lining extend to the garment edge rather than use velvet facings.

Calculate the quantity of fabric to allow for cutting the pieces lying in one direction only. The most usual way is to have the nap running from hem to neck for a rich effect. Velvet can be made up with the nap running down the garment and with embossed and crushed velvet this shows up the design better but with plain velvet it may be liable to look patchy after sitting down.

Lace fabric or embroidered flouncing

Fabric that has a scalloped edge needs careful planning to ensure that there is sufficient edging for the design.

The scallops may run along one or both edges. Note the width of the fabric and cut the pattern pieces within that measurement. Work out one or two layouts, making maximum use of the edging, remembering that it can be cut off and rejoined. It can be cut following part of the design and overlapped on to another piece and zig-zagged invisibly. If there is to be a draw-string or elastic, make a welt seam to serve as a casing.

Do not add hem allowances to the pattern pieces that are to have scalloped edges. Make the pattern exactly to length and place the hemline on the inner part of the scallop. Lining should also be hemmed at that level leaving the scallop to show off the embroidery.

Border fabric

The printed border will run along one selvedge only and size of the pattern pieces will be controlled not only by the width of the fabric but also by the depth of the design. With a trailing floral you will not have much more than a width of 50cm/20in along one side for cutting a bodice, sleeve etc. You will be able to cut skirts and trousers easily enough with the border around the hem and for the rest it may be best to use a plain contrast.

A striped or geometric border has more possibilities because it can be cut off. The border will usually be deep enough for sleeves, yokes, pockets, waistbands and hembands.

Contrasts

Combining different textures as well as colours and prints can be very effective if thoughtfully planned. Reasons for using more than one fabric can be for figure flattery; for emphasis; for economy; to use remnants or left-over pieces; a heavier fabric or a double band can be used to add weight; the main fabric may be unsuitable for the entire garment so a contrast can be used as a highlight, e.g. velvet collar.

If you are mixing fabrics for economy make sure you make maximum use of each according to its width. It is easy to finish up with large left-over pieces.

If the remnants already exist you will be governed by what is available. After cutting the pattern draw lines where contrast seams will fall and insert balance marks. If you have designed an asymmetrical panel, make a copy of the whole pattern before drawing lines.

Cut off contrast sections, mark SG as on original except where a bias band is to be used. Remember to add seam allowances to both cut edges.

Brocade and taffeta

These and other stiff fabrics are most impressive when used for full skirts, frills, flounces and bows. Keep seams to a minimum and avoid tucks and gathers. Shaped edges such as scallops are effective but on the whole the fabric looks best uncluttered, especially if it has a moiré, embossed or Jacquard finish.

Non-fraying fabric

These include net and tulle as well as plastics. Do not add a hem allowance to the pattern pieces and for net add 1cm/⅜in maximum on seams which should then be overlocked or joined with one row of zig-zag stitch.

Raw edges must be cut smoothly; pinking shears can be used.

Quilting

Plan seams rather than darts which are inclined to poke. The most satisfactory finish for edges is binding which helps to keep the fabric flat and will also contain the lining if any. Do not add seam allowances to edges to be bound. Turn-back cuffs look attractive if the quilting is double sided. Patch pockets can be bulky; a better alternative is to apply them before the main seams are stitched so that the edges can be included in the seams.

Reversible coating

Do not add hem allowances, although turn-back cuffs are an attractive feature. Bind edges with matching or contrast folded braid and bind patch pockets.

Add 2cm/¾in to pattern along seams so that you can make welt seams. If the garment is to be truly reversible make the seams by separating the two layers for 2–3cm/¾–1¼in along the edges. Join two edges right sides together and press open then fold under the two remaining raw edges so that they meet and join with hand slip-stitch.

Fur fabric

Fur details such as collar and cuffs are planned in the same way as for contrasting fabric.

Fur fabric is usually very wide and so can be used economically. Avoid fitted styles. The fabric is bulky so allow plenty of ease on the pattern and add 2.5cm/1in allowance on all seams.

Pressing may not have much effect but edges can be defined with top stitching and leather or plastic or knit trim can look effective.

Stripes and checks

Keep seams to the minimum and where you must have them keep them to the sides. Features such as yokes, tabs and pockets often look best if the fabric is turned 90 degrees or even used on the bias.

Make sure you know what the effect will be by adding the stripes or checks to your preliminary sketch.

After making the pattern, draw the stripes or checks on the main pieces, placing the first one carefully down CF or just below the bust line. Place sleeve pattern beside it and continue lines from main pattern.

The pattern can then be placed on the fabric and you can be confident that the pieces will match perfectly when joined.

Knits

Knitted fabrics vary in the amount they stretch; on the whole those that are ribbed and heavy stretch more than fine silky ones although some cotton knits and T-shirt fabrics stretch a great deal.

Dispense with darts and make patterns smaller to allow for the stretch or you will waste fabric as garments will be too large. It is difficult to be specific about the size of reductions but the following is an approximate guide line:

Most rib knits will stretch by one third across their width i.e. 10cm/4in will stretch to 15cm/6in. You can therefore reduce the width of your pattern by one third. However, this would produce a close fit and should be regarded as the maximum.

You can safely use this guide for edgings on parts of the body that require a tight fit. For example, rib fabric to be attached double to wrists, necklines and waists should be cut two thirds of the measurement of the body at wrist or waist, or, for a neck, two thirds the length of the garment neck edge.

Do not assume that the knit will stretch lengthwise, although some do and therefore drop in wear but can be adjusted. To make a smaller pattern for use with knits outline back and front blocks without darts and reduce the width as appropriate. The following amounts are a guide and refer to an average size 12. For maximum stretch:

Remove 2cm/¾in from CB and CF
4cm/1⅝in from back and front side seam
3cm/1¼in from armhole end of shoulder seam

For minimum stretch the amounts will be:
1cm, 2cm, 1.5cm/⅜in, ¾in, ⅝in

For fabrics in between:
1.5cm, 3cm, 4cm/⅝in, 1⅛in, 1⅝in

Use the above amounts as a guide only: always test a piece of the fabric for stretch before committing yourself. Small sizes may want a tighter fit and therefore a greater reduction, larger sizes may prefer a smaller reduction for a looser fit. Judge each fabric separately.

In each case re-draw armhole and neck curves slightly smaller than originally. Remember to add seam allowances, which can be 1cm/⅜in if garment is to be made on an overlocker.

Lycra

Lycra has a great deal of stretch in both directions which means the pattern length can be reduced as well as the width. Once more you will have to experiment as it is a matter of choice how tight or how loose the garment is to be. Reduce the length by making several small horizontal pleats across a copy of the block.

PATTERNS FOR LININGS

It is seldom necessary to cut a separate pattern for lining because it will always follow the shape of the garment fairly closely. However, the exception might be if you were lining a full or pleated skirt or dress with a straight lining. The straight lining would be less bulky and more economical. Also there are times when it might be desirable for the lining to be a closer fit than the garment to relieve the pressure of the body on the fabric. If you do this remember that polyester or acetate woven linings are not hard-wearing and will easily split. A better alternative is to use nylon jersey if there will be any strain. Nylon jersey is also a good choice for lining knit and jersey fabrics.

Adapting the pattern

There are some alterations to be made to the pattern in order to economize on lining. For example, the lining must be made shorter at the hem.

Mark the alterations on the pattern, possibly in coloured pencil, as a reminder, and also if the lining is not the same width as the fabric make a note of the quantity required.

Seams. If they are to be narrow i.e. overlocked or zig-zagged only, no more than 6mm/¼in need be added to pattern edges when cutting out lining.

However, to avoid split seams add 3mm/⅛in beyond this so that the lining is slightly loose inside the garment.

Any straight seams on the pattern have the possibility of being placed to a fold depending on width of lining.

Darts. Stitch darts 3mm/⅛in shorter than marked on the pattern to retain the maximum shaping. This is especially important on close fitting garments.

Pleats. Where there are pleats, make seams in the lining instead of pleats, stitching to 3cm/1¼ in above the pleat and making a hemmed slit below.

Zip position. Keep the lining clear of the zip teeth by cutting a 2cm/¾in wide strip off the lining for the length of the zip and cutting into the corners at the base of the zip. The lining can be turned under and hemmed to the zip tape or the edge can be overlocked and left free.

Hems. The lining should be finished 2–3cm/¾–1¼in shorter than the garment whether it is to be stitched down or hemmed. If you intend to make a narrow hem on the lining cut out level with the edge of the pattern i.e. without adding a hem allowance. If you prefer a wide hem add the amount you need for it minus 3cm/1¼in.

Sleeve and jacket length. If the lining is to be stitched to the garment hem extra length must be allowed for ease or the lining will pull at the garment. Add an extra 1cm/⅜in at hems, in addition to whatever you calculated under ***Hems*** above.

Trousers. With the exception of length, see ***Hems*** above, use the trouser pattern exactly as it is when cutting the lining.

Centre back jacket or coat. A considerable amount of ease is required across the shoulder blades of a coat or jacket. Place CB pattern 2cm/¾in from the fold of the lining. After cutting out baste the pleat from neck to hem and press to one side. Stitch pleat at top and bottom for about 3cm/1¼in to make it easier to handle at the edges and also stitch it at waist level.

Faced edges. The lining must overlap the raw edge of the facing by 1.5–2cm/⅝–¾in in order to avoid a ridge if the lining is hand sewn. Mark a lining cutting line on the pattern the width of the facing from the edge plus an amount for overlap. A seam allowance is also added.

Lining to edge. If the garment edge is to be bound or bagged out the lining can be cut exactly as garment pattern. Mark pattern appropriately.

Neckline with collars. Use the pattern without alterations and cut the lining right to the neck edge at the back no matter what method of attaching the collar is to be used. Do not use a back neck facing of main fabric; it is bulky and quite unnecessary.

INTERFACING

You will know from your sewing experience which areas of your design will need interfacing. It is not usually necessary to cut separate pattern pieces, instead simply mark collars, cuffs etc., with the word ‘interface’. If a section of a pattern piece requires interfacing, such as the edge of an opening, draw a dotted line on the pattern to mark the extent of the interfacing.

There are many types and qualities of iron-on and sew-in interfacings. They vary in width and some of them, even non-woven varieties, must be cut with the straight grain parallel with that of the garment. Some areas such as collar points may need more than one layer of interfacing and they can be different types, but often you will not know this until you reach that stage of making up the garment.

Vilene alone manufacture a dozen different interfacings including Superstretch for stretch and jersey fabrics. It is important to select the best one for your fabric, even testing several pieces to make sure that the finished garment is as you designed it.

Interfacing should be concealed between two layers of fabric, often a facing forms the second layer. The interfacing can be cut to the line of the facing or 3mm/⅛in narrower for concealment.

Fastenings should have a double, interfaced edge, with the interfacing extending around the fastening to prevent a ridge. The width of interfacing required for a buttoned opening therefore should be three times the length of the buttonhole.

Other materials for interfacing include those that are made in strip form and include petersham and Fold-a-Band for waistbands and belts. If possible have the products by you when making the pattern so that the pieces can be cut to size. Soft Fold-a-Band for cuffs, straps, tabs, buttoned edges, tops of pockets etc., is 3cm/1¼in wide on each side of the central perforations and again it is sensible to cut pattern pieces to size.

When adding hem allowances to your pattern, if you plan to use Wundaweb, remember that it is 2.5cm/1in wide.

HOW MUCH FABRIC?

One of the advantages of cutting your own patterns is that you need only buy exactly the right amount of fabric. This is not to imply that commercial pattern companies are inaccurate but they can only quote an amount for a person of average height. Added to that is the fact that they add an extra 10% or so for what is sometimes termed 'scissor fright'. A definition of that complaint might be an 'inability to close pattern pieces up tight together' or maybe an inbuilt compulsion to add a bit on 'just in case'.

Having made your pattern and knowing it is the right length etc., you work out how much fabric you require but you must then have confidence in your calculation otherwise any economy may be cancelled out.

The very best sequence of events from a creative point of view is to have the fabric beside you while you design and cut the pattern but unless you are using up a piece purchased previously that may be out of the question. The next best thing is to identify the fabric you want, taking note of the width and any particular characteristics such as one-way print, nap and especially size of print and distance between repeats. You can then go home and make the pattern and calculate the amount required. However, if you find the fabric has sold out your calculation may not be correct for a second choice.

The third option is the most convenient. Design and cut the pattern with a *type* of fabric in mind, for example firm woven, silky knit, pile fabric, taffeta, towelling, lace etc. Work out the quantity required for widths of 90cm/36in; 115cm/45in and 150cm/60in. Make a calculation for one-way fabric as well as for fabric on which pieces can be dovetailed. If you decide on a patterned fabric with checks, stripes or print that is to be matched or balanced there is a simple rule of thumb to be followed. In exactly the way that you allow one extra pattern per length of wallpaper, each pattern piece of skirt, sleeve, bodice front, bodice back and so on will require the equivalent of one extra pattern depth. If the fabric is wide enough to take two pieces side by side – both trouser legs or the bodice back beside the sleeves – add one pattern depth only.

How to calculate

The easiest method is to spread out a length of fabric, place pattern pieces in position having regard to notes on the pattern for SG, FOLD, CUT 4 etc., and measure along the selvedge when all pieces are in position. You may like to keep several lengths for the purpose in various widths, and marked every 10cm/4in along the selvedge. Alternatively mark out an old double size sheet, marking across the width as well as the length. A cutting board can also be used to calculate quantities although you will have to visualize the economies that could be made by refolding.

Haberdashery and Trimmings

List all the items needed to complete the garment, including zips, hooks, number of buttons, shoulder pads, length of binding, lace, elastic etc.

SUPPLIES

Pattern drafting equipment including paper available from the following sources:

R. D. Franks Ltd
Market Place
Oxford Circus
London W1
Tel: (01) 636 1244

MacCulloch and Wallis Ltd
25–26 Dering Street
London W1R 0BH
Tel: (01) 629 0311

A GLOSSARY OF TECHNICAL AND FASHION TERMS

A-Line. Originally Dior's description of a new shape. Now used to describe any fitted dress or skirt in which the side seams continue outwards at a slight angle. An A-line skirt is wider at the hem than at the hips but not full enough to fall into folds.

Anorak. Waterproof jacket, often also padded, with elastic or drawstring at the hem and close fitting cuffs. Pockets are zipped, buttoned or fastened with Velcro, the front fastening is often a zip covered by a flap that fastens with Velcro.

Armhole. The seam which joins bodice to sleeve, literally the hole for the arm. A horseshoe shape that tilts towards the front, it is important for the depth and width to be correct for the individual especially when clothes are tight fitting.

Armhole Scye. Term used to describe the scooped out curve of the armhole on a block or pattern.

Bag out. Describes a method of attaching a lining that extends to the edge of a garment so eliminating the facing. Use the same pattern pieces for the lining and the garment so that they are cut the same size.

Balance. Refers to hang and also proportion in garments. Fashion dictates balance to a certain extent, for example long tops over short skirts. Where flat pattern cutting is concerned it is often difficult to judge correct balance until the garment is seen in fabric.

Balance marks. Marks made on edges of pattern pieces that show where they are to be matched. They are a useful construction guide on all seams but where edges of a different shape are to be joined or where one edge is fuller than another, balance marks are vital. In pattern cutting make short pencil marks at the edge of the paper, copying them through all stages to the final pattern. On bought paper patterns balance marks are indicated by triangles and are referred to as notches.

Band collar. Usually quite narrow because it is straight or almost so and it often fastens edge to edge at the centre back. The collar cannot fit the neck closely so the bodice neckline should be slightly scooped or lowered.

Baste. To stitch pieces of fabric together temporarily by hand or by machine so that the garment may be fitted or the seams stitched permanently.

Bateau. A wide shallow neckline often made just large enough so that a neck opening can be eliminated. The pattern should not be cut too wide or the neckline will droop at the centre front.

Battle. The name given to the military battle jacket garment that has a hip band and buttoned cuffs. It can be fastened with a zip or with buttons in a fly opening and it will usually feature patch pockets and shoulder tabs.

Batwing. A bodice and sleeve cut in one with just a shoulder seam but which is cut low and loose underarm, providing room for the arm to be raised to the horizontal position. The underarm seam begins to slope out at waist level and is shaped from there to the wrist or elbow exactly like a bat's wing. (See also Dolman.)

Bell Sleeve. A style that fits smoothly into a basic or cut-away armhole but which is very full and flared by the time it reaches elbow or wrist level.

Bermuda. A style of straight legged knee length shorts.

Bertha. A wide collar with curved outer edge reaching to tip of shoulders or beyond. Often gathered where ends meet at centre front and may have a bow or flower.

Bias. Refers to a line on fabric that runs at 45 degrees to the warp or weft, in other words, exactly mid-way between the yarns. Also used when describing the angle on knit fabric even though there are no crossing yarns.

Bias can also be used to describe lines that are not quite at 45 degrees. If fabric is pulled at 45 degrees or less it will stretch. If maximum stretch is required or if a pattern such as checks or stripes are used then a 45 degree angle must be adhered to especially when cutting out large pieces of fabric. Smaller pieces, including narrow strips to be used as bias binding, need not necessarily be at 45 degrees especially if fabric is short.

Pieces cut on the bias will stretch. This can be used to advantage in lots of ways but it is important to remember that bias skirts and other large pieces will drop considerably; some fabrics being much worse for this than others.

Bias binding. Narrow strips of fabric can be cut and joined and put through a bias binding tool which will fold it ready to apply. When planning a design requiring a lot of binding allowance should be made when calculating the amount of fabric required. The length of bias binding required can be calculated by measuring all the relevant edges of the pattern.

Bias cut. Refers to a garment such as shorts, skirt, dress or underwear, the pieces of which are wholly or partly cut on the bias.

Bishop. A long sleeve that is very full at the wrist and gathered into a cuff.

Blouson. A style of waist on a top, blouse, dress or jacket that is long and loose fitting and then is hitched up with the use of elastic, a drawstring waistband or belt.

Boiler suit. An all in one trousers and top, usually fairly plain or sporty in style. Dressy versions are usually called jumpsuits.

Bolero. A sleeveless jacket finishing above the waist. May be either without fastenings or with edge-to-edge rouleau loop fastenings. Worn over other garments so a pattern should have deep, possibly even square, armholes.

Bomber. See Battle.

Bondaweb. A fine non-woven web on a backing of transparent paper in sheet form. Available in packs and by the metre or yard. It has many uses including appliqué, mending and prevention of fraying.

Bound edge. The edge of a garment finished with bias binding. The binding may be purchased or it can be cut from fabric and folded ready for use using a bias binding tool.

Box or boxy. A word used to describe a coat or jacket that has square shoulders and straight sleeves and a hemline width about equal to the shoulder width.

Breeches. Trousers reaching to below the knee, usually fitted to the leg with a band.

Bridle. A piece of tape stitched along the roll line of a tailored lapel and collar to keep it in shape. The roll line position must always be marked on the pattern and then transferred to the fabric.

Bubble. A skirt which is gathered and pulled in at the hemline. Usually made in stiff fabric, the skirt is longer and fuller than its lining, it is gathered along the hemline and joined to the lining.

Bust point. On some people the bust point is better defined than on others and when clothes are close-fitting it is very important to match the bust point of the garment with that of the figure. The bust point is marked on the bodice block in the correct position for the individual and the bust shaping in all patterns made from the block must be directed towards that position.

Buttocks. The buttocks or bottom vary in shape, size and position on the body and can present a fitting problem particularly if combined with a small waist and especially with trousers. With any garment the pattern must be wide enough at that level, fullness being provided by darts, gathers etc., but then often much of that fullness has to be made to disappear by waist or knee level.

Buttons and buttonholes. Positions of fastenings should be planned and marked on the paper pattern although they can be adjusted when the garment is made. The size of button and direction of buttonhole must be decided early on in the drafting of a pattern so that the necessary extension for overlapping can be allowed.

A button should sit within the edge of the garment by half its diameter when fastened. Use vertical buttonholes on loose garments where there is little strain; the button sits in the upper end when fastened. Use horizontal buttonholes at points of strain; the button sits in the end nearest the garment edge.

Button stand. Also button extension. This is the amount of garment beyond the end of the buttonhole or button at the fastening edge of a garment. The amount varies with the position on the body but is also governed by the size of the button because you have to make sure the underlap extends right under the buttonhole.

Caftan. Also Kaftan. Full length loose garment with wide slit neckline; all-in-one sleeves may be loose or gathered in with elastic or binding. An easy garment to make and an easy first pattern to cut.

Camiknickers. Combined camisole top and knickers. An undergarment or nightwear.

Camisole. Originally an item of obligatory underwear the camisole is now included in lingerie, nightwear, casual and beach wear as well as formal evening wear. It always features shoulder straps, a straight or petticoat-style upper edge and it reaches to the waist or just below.

Cap sleeve. A slightly extended shoulder seam on a sleeveless bodice bringing the edge of the garment on to the shoulder bone or a little beyond. The armhole edge is usually straight from shoulder to side seam. The side seam stitching should not be too high or the cap sleeve is pulled under the arm and is liable to split when the arms are raised.

Cape sleeve. A full, loose circular sleeve usually with a plain ungathered sleeve head and extending to the elbow or a little below. Often used as a decorative over-sleeve.

Cardigan. A collarless jacket of any length from below waist to knee.

Casing. A section of double fabric forming a slot through which elastic, cord or a drawstring are threaded. If the casing comes at a straight edge of a garment the pattern can be extended sufficiently for the fabric to be folded over and stitched down. If it comes in the middle of the garment a separate strip of fabric, possibly purchased bias binding, must be attached.

Bear in mind the fitting point on the garment. The waistline for instance will usually run along the middle of the elastic or cord so from this you can calculate by how much to extend the pattern to allow for the casing.

Cat suit. Also called a jump suit this is an all-in-one top and trouser garment. A cat suit is usually close fitting and made in jersey or Lycra; a jumpsuit is looser and may have decorative features such as gathers or wide legs. A flying suit or boiler suit is another version usually made in a more pedestrian cotton fabric and featuring big pockets, buckles, etc.

Centre back and Centre front. The vertical line that runs precisely down the middle of the figure from the neck at back and front. They are both vital reference lines on patterns and should be marked on the basic blocks and on every stage of pattern cutting including the finished pattern. Most pieces of pattern are placed on double fabric so one edge of some pieces will actually be the centre front or centre back.

Chanel. Coco Chanel, despite all her achievements, is probably best remembered for her short, cardigan-style, braided jackets, still one of the easiest jackets to make without resorting to tailoring.

Checks. More is required if check fabric is used as the design must match horizontally and vertically. Most check fabrics are one-way designs and most are oblongs rather than squares. The bigger and more complex the check the more fabric will be required. If possible find the fabric and measure the checks then draw squares the same size on your pattern pieces with all edges matching. Lay out your pattern and calculate the amount of fabric required.

Cheongsam. A straight close-fitting dress with a mandarin collar, side fastening, ball buttons, piped seams and hemline slits.

Classic. The term that has come to be used to describe any design that has uncluttered, simple lines that do not become outdated. It also seems to indicate dependability and conjures up a picture when prefixing shirt, coat, dress, skirt etc.

Clip. A small snip or cut made in the edge of fabric. All curved edges must be clipped so that the fabric lies flat when final pressing is done.

Coat dress. A garment that is neither coat nor dress but which has features of both. Usually made in dress weight fabric, often buttoned and never fussy in design.

Combined facing. Also called all-in-one or neck and armhole facing. A garment that has neither collar nor sleeves but has edges finished with facings will lie better around the neck and shoulder area if one large facing is cut to extend from neckline to armholes. Bulk is reduced this way and it prevents facings from popping out.

Convertible collar. A basic, pointed collar and revers that can be worn open or fastened up to the neck. Used mainly on coats and shirts which can be single or double breasted.

Corslet. A combined bra and corset although the term is also used to describe a waist length, fitted strapless top.

Cossack. Describes an outfit comprising long belted jacket over trousers, the latter often tucked into boots.

Couture. Used to describe specially designed and often individually made clothes.

Couture hem. A hand finished hem used on dresses, skirts and coats requiring a hem depth of 5–7cm/2–2¾in to weight the garment. This amount should be added to the pattern before cutting out.

Cowl. A draped collar that can be loose or attached to any style of neckline. The cowl is shaped to provide generous folds of fabric at the back or the front of the garment. The pattern is usually cut on the bias so that the fabric falls readily into folds.

Crew neck. The description used for the style of neckline that follows the base of the neck, a term more often applied to knitted garments than those made of fabric.

Crutch depth. The distance from the waist down to crutch level on the figure. The measurement is taken vertically, while seated, down to the chair seat. The measurement is used for checking a trouser pattern. See also Crutch seam length, Crutch point and Rise.

Crutch point. This is where trouser inside leg seams meet the crutch seam. The exact position depends on the figure but the crutch point should be towards the front of the body.

Culottes. A combination of skirt and trousers originally designed as a women's bicycling garment. A skirt pattern adjusted to required length is extended in a crutch shaped curve at the centre front and centre back. Culottes can be short, knee or floor length, plain, gathered or with pleats.

Cummerbund. A wide, tight-fitting belt of pleated fabric which must be shaped to fit the body above the waist and fastened securely.

Cutting board. A specially constructed folded corrugated board which opens out to cover a table or bed to provide a surface on which to cut out or make patterns. One side of the board is marked out in 5cm/2in squares as a grid for cutting and tracing. The most useful cutting board is one that has a multi-size basic pattern printed on the reverse to be traced and used for pattern designing.

Cutting line. The point beyond the stitching line or seam line where the fabric is cut. With patterns that have no seam allowance the cutting line is marked on the fabric using chalk or fabric pen. On a commercial pattern the printed outline is the cutting line for both pattern and fabric.

Dart. A fold of fabric stitched to taper gradually to a point. A bulge of fabric is formed at the end of the dart. Darts form the foundation of the shape of many garments. The length and width at the base varies; the wider the dart the greater the area of shaping it provides. Darts are used as the basic block patterns in all the positions where a bulge or hollow occurs in the figure although they are not all necessarily used in the finished design.

Dart tuck. Dart shaping but with stitching that stops short of the point and appears as a tuck from the outside. It provides general rather than specific shaping so it is often necessary to add more shape in the form of additional dart tucks.

Dior pleat. A false pleat with less bulk and maintenance than a real pleat. Usually found at the hemline of a straight skirt, a slit provides room for movement but it has a rectangle of matching or contrast fabric hanging on the inside, attached to the seam allowances of the centre back seam. Add a wide seam allowance to the pattern otherwise the Dior flap can droop below the hemline.

Direction of stitching. Drag on seams can be eliminated by stitching from the wide to the narrow part of the garment. It is helpful to mark arrows on the pattern edges to act as a reminder. Correct direction of stitching is from hem of skirt or dress to waist, waist of trouser to hem, sleeve underarm to wrist and from neck along to shoulder.

Dolman. A wide loose sleeve cut in one with bodice. The sleeve seam starts at the waistline and curves around to a wrist that is often tight fitting. The long bias seam and the fullness provide room to raise the arms but if it is insufficient a gusset should be inserted under the arm. The gusset can be cut as a panel and form part of the design of the sleeve.

Double breasted. A style of front fastening that wraps over to fasten on the left of the body (or right on a man) instead of at the centre front. If buttons are featured they are arranged in two rows, the inner row being sewn on the outside, without buttonholes.

Double pointed darts. These are used where shaping is required in two places not separated by a seam; for example to shape for the waist on a one-piece dress. The amount of fitting that can be done with this dart is limited, sometimes two parallel double pointed darts of different lengths are required. For a closer fit these darts should be replaced by a shaped seam.

Drafting. The term applied to drawing and cutting a paper pattern.

Draping. A way of obtaining the shape for a garment by pinning a length of fabric on to a dummy and folding and cutting it until the required design results. It is a more experimental method of pattern cutting than flat cutting. Draping is not difficult although the principles of pattern cutting should first be learnt through flat cutting. Cheap fabric such as muslin is often used for draping. The garment fabric itself could be used provided there is plenty of it to allow for experimenting.

Drawstring. To pull in the waistline of a dress, skirt or trousers, or necklines or hems by means of a cord or rouleau. This may eliminate the opening so the garment must be wide enough to put on. In the case of a dress waist, the bodice pattern should be lengthened to allow a little blousing so that the arms can be raised. This should also be done if track suit trousers are to have drawstrings at the ankles. The drawstring is threaded through a hem or applied casing with buttonholes or slots in the seam through which the tie ends emerge. An alternative is elastic; less additional length will be required as the elastic will give. If elastic in trousers or skirts for active wear 'gives' too much a good compromise is to make two casings, one for elastic and one for a drawstring. Do not use drawstrings in children's clothes.

Dropped shoulder. The shoulder seam is extended so far down the arm as to replace the armhole seam with a seam across the arm. The armhole must be lowered, or even filled in and extended outward, to allow room for movement. The sleeve should be made fairly wide.

Duffle. A short or full length casual thick coat, often unlined. A duffle normally features toggle fastenings, hood, patch pockets and welt seams.

Dummy. Dummies, also called dress forms or stands, are available in light or solid construction. Very useful for checking toiles and patterns and they are a help with some sewing processes such as pocket positions, shoulder pad placing, the hang of pleats and the set of a collar. A dummy can only be used for fitting if it conforms to your size. Adjustable types are available and you can also pad out a dummy to your own shape.

Ease. The amount added to measurements so that there is room to move in the finished garment. The amount varies according to fashion: a dress described as 'fitted' in the forties was much tighter than a 1980's fitted dress. The amount of ease required depends on the garment; there would be none at all in a swimsuit but quite a lot in a nightdress. See also Fullness.

Easing. This is needed when joining two edges of different lengths and shape. The longer edge makes a slight bubble of fabric as the seam is made which provides a little room for movement. Often the edge to be eased would have had a small dart in that position on the original block. Examples of easing include sleeve heads into armhole, back shoulder on to front shoulder, back edge of sleeve seam on to front edge at elbow level.

Empire. A high waist seam. The garment can be a dress, tunic or nightdress, fitted over the bust and often with the lower section pleated or gathered into the waist.

Extended shoulder. The shoulder seam is lengthened so the armhole seam slopes outwards and runs across the top of the arm instead of passing over the shoulder bone. The underarm must be lowered to allow room for raising the arm.

Extension facing. See Fold-back facing.

Facing. The piece of fabric, matching or contrast, which is used to finish the edge of a garment. Usually applied to the outside and rolled out of sight inside although for a sporty or contrast effect it may be applied to the wrong side, brought over on to the right side and stitched down. With some designs it is essential to use a facing, for example where loops or ties are planned.

Fall – collar. The part of a collar, shirt style, classic coat collar or any fold-over collar that folds down and covers the neck seam.

Fall – hang of skirt. Used to describe the way in which fullness behaves in skirts, sleeves etc.

Fan pleats. Shaped narrow pleats which run to nothing at the upper edge. Can be used on skirts, on hem and sleeve flounces and on inserts. Also called accordion pleats.

Fichu. The term for a soft draped finish on a neckline. It is an additional piece of fabric often contrasting, that is draped, gathered or folded and often made to hug the shoulders if the dress is strapless.

Flare. Shaped fullness added to a sleeve, skirt etc. The hemline is always wider than the upper edge. When cutting a pattern flare is added by cutting from top to bottom of the basic shape and spreading the pieces at one edge only.

Flounce. A full, often quite deep, circular edging for necklines, sleeves and hems. If a long flounce is required several pieces should be made, cut to the middle and joined end to end. Flounces are easier to attach if they are gathered so allowance for this is required when making the pattern pieces.

Fold-a-Band. Iron-on strip interfacing with central perforations. It makes cuffs, waistbands, welts and tabs much quicker to make so cut pattern pieces to size so that Fold-a-Band can be used. There are two weights and several widths available. The lightweight cuff interfacing can also be used to back pleats and stabilize buttoned edges.

Fold-back facing. This is a way of finishing a straight edge such as the button edge of a blouse, by eliminating the seam at the edge. Add a sufficiently wide extension to the edge of the pattern and attach interfacing to extend over the fold line to provide a firm edge when the facing is folded onto the wrong side. A useful facing on fine or transparent fabrics where a seam would be bulky and visible.

Forearm seam. The seam nearest the front on a sleeve cut in two pieces.

Fork. The point where crutch and inside leg seams meet on trousers. On women's trousers the term crutch point is also used.

Fortuny pleats. Named after a designer, these are tiny knife pleats used in profusion, often crushed and sometimes folded and stitched at both ends, for example at waist and hem, to allow the fabric to billow in between.

Frill. A strip of fabric of any width gathered and attached to a garment as an edging.

Gaucho. Knee length or below, short slightly flared trousers.

Gilet. A brief waistcoat, often straight, sometimes consisting of a front which fastens around the neck and waist with straps.

Godet. A flared or triangular insert in the hemline of skirts, sleeves and trousers.

Gorge line. The short seam that joins the end of a classic collar to its lapel.

Grading-Sizing. Refers to the way that a pattern is adjusted to other sizes while keeping the style. Used in the production of commercial patterns.

Grading-Trimming. This refers to trimming several seam allowances to varying width so as to avoid the possibility of a ridge on the finished garment.

Grain. The direction of yarns in a woven fabric along the length or across the width. In knitted fabric the grain line follows a line of knitting loops. Lengthways grain, following the warp yarns which are strongest, is the best position for the grain arrow of large pattern pieces. It is not usual to place the straight grains across the width as weft threads may stretch although this would not matter on small pieces and it can actually be used to advantage on something like a collar.

Gusset. A small piece of fabric inserted in a seam to allow room for movement. Gussets are most commonly required in knickers, bikini pants and French knickers and also at the underarm in some kimono sleeves to allow arm movement.

Halter. A style of neckline that has a strap or an extension of fabric running from the front near the armhole round the back of the neck.

Harem. Wide full trousers in lightweight fabric, gathered at the ankles.

Hobble. A style of long skirt in which the hemline is gathered into a band, often ribbed, below the knees or at the ankles.

Interfacing. A layer of specially made fabric to stiffen some parts of a garment. Areas to be interfaced should be marked on the finished pattern, often the same pattern piece can be used for cutting the interfacing but if not then separate pattern pieces must be provided. Features requiring interfacing include collars, cuffs, waistbands, belts, pockets and edges of many openings and also if the style and fabric are suitable, pleats, yokes, angled seams and hems. Occasionally whole garments are interfaced.

Jabot. A decorative frilled or circular feature on the front of a blouse or dress. Can be made detachable with the use of Velcro, in which case make separate pattern pieces.

Jodhpurs. Trousers that balloon out at the side at thigh level but which fit closely around the calf.

Kimono. Traditional Far Eastern garment with wide loose sleeves, wrap front and wide sash. A style sometimes adapted as a housecoat or jacket pattern. A kimono sleeve design is one that is cut in one with the bodice. The sleeve may be wide and full or more fitted, with the aid of a gusset. It may even have a cuff at the wrist.

Knickerbockers. Trousers finishing below the knee and gathered into a band that fits around the calf and fastens with a button or Velcro.

Layer. See Grading.

Layered. Co-ordinated garments of varying lengths to produce a 'layered look'.

Marking. Pattern information such as balance marks, fold lines and gathering points must be transferred to the fabric before the pattern pieces are removed. When making your own patterns you have gone to some trouble to get the size correct and when cutting the fabric you have added appropriate seam and hem allowances. It is advisable and logical to transfer as much of this information as possible to the fabric. Although it takes a little time to do it will certainly save time in construction and make for greater accuracy. Marking can be done using tailor's tacks, tacking stitches, with tailor's chalk, chalk pencil or chalk wheel, with dressmaker's carbon paper and a smooth tracing wheel or with a fabric marking pen.

Mid-calf. A skirt length that is well below the knee.

Military. A coat or jacket, even a dress, that includes features such as a convertible or high stand collar and double breasted front perhaps with brass buttons, half belt, shoulder tabs etc.

Mini. A skirt length that is well above the knee, the style may be straight or full and flared.

Nap. Pile, loops or surface fibres on fabrics such as face cloth or velvet which mean that the pattern pieces must lie in one direction or the finished garment will be shaded. Other fabrics that should be treated in this way because they catch the light are satin and knit fabric. Patterned fabrics such as one-way prints and some checks should also be treated as having nap. When cutting a pattern for a nap or one-way fabric it helps to draw the grain line with the arrowhead at one end only as a reminder when cutting out the fabric.

Negligée. A flimsy, feminine dressing gown.

Notch. See Balance mark.

Off-grain. The term to describe fabric in which warp and weft yarns are distorted and not at right angles to each other. Also describes a garment or part of a garment that has been cut incorrectly with the straight grain not accurately positioned for good hang.

Parka. A windproof, lightweight hooded jacket with drawstring hems.

Peasant. A garment or outfit that is reminiscent of Hungarian or Roumanian dress. Garments include blouses with puff sleeves and wide drawstring necks, full gathered skirts, possibly with frills, and ornate sleeveless jackets.

Peg top. Skirt or trousers narrow at the hem but pleated into the waist at the front causing them to almost balloon out. The deep folds at the waist are best held in place with a wide shaped waistband.

Pencil. A tight-fitting straight skirt of any length that is literally pencil slim.

Peplum. A shaped, often stiffened section of garment attached to the waist of a fitted bodice or jacket and extended over the skirt to approximately high hip level.

Petal. A feature that can be incorporated in a sleeve, skirt or cape-collar and composed of separate overlapping pieces of fabric. The sections are lined or self-lined and are usually petal-shaped.

Peter Pan. A collar with curved outer edge which may be in two halves with curved ends meeting at CF or CB or it may meet at CF only. Referred to as a flat collar in pattern cutting terms indicating that it does not stand up at the neck but lies flat over the garment from the neckline. However, a completely flat collar is not very flattering even on children's clothes so the pattern is usually made with a small stand across the back of the neck.

Piecing. Joining fabric before cutting to shape. This is needed when you have a pattern piece too wide for the fabric. Joins should be made on the straight grain.

Placket. Strictly speaking this simply means a functional opening in a garment which is necessary in order to get it on. However the term is now almost entirely restricted to wrap over openings that are finished with a strip of fabric or binding and having press studs or hooks attached for fastening.

Pleat. A fold of fabric. There are several types of pleats and different effects can be created by pressing them in various directions.

Polo – collar. A high collar cut on the cross and standing up at the neck. The garment may have to have an opening at the back with the collar fastening end to end but if jersey fabric is used this is not usually necessary.

Polo – shirt. Sports-style shirt with ribbed bands at waist and sleeves; the neckline usually has a short strap opening and a small pointed collar, often also ribbed.

Poncho. A square or oval shape of fabric with a hole or slit in the centre for the head. Patch pockets can be added and edges can be fringed or bound.

Princess. A garment with vertical seams running from mid-shoulder to hem, usually on back as well as front. Sometimes the seams begin in the armhole but these styles are usually called panel designs. Both princess and panel seams are shaped because they include the bodice darts and they are useful where a close fit is required or where an out-of-proportion figure has to be fitted.

Puff. A short full sleeve gathered into the armhole and into a hem band.

Raglan. Originally an overcoat in which the sleeves and shoulders were cut in one piece. Eliminating the fitted armhole seam in this way loosens the garment and results in a more comfortable fit. Raglan sleeves are easy to sew and can be used in all types of day and night wear including lingerie and baby clothes.

Rever. The fold-back triangular area of a lapel. Revers may be small and short or wide and extending well towards the waist.

Rise. A term normally used in relation to men's trousers it refers to the length of the front part of the crutch seam from crutch point up to waist.

Roll line. The line on which a collar and/or a lapel fold over. The roll line is established when the pattern is made as it influences the style of the collar as well as the fastening of the garment. In tailoring a line of stitching is made on the roll line to ensure that the collar and lapel retain their original shape.

Rouleau. A narrow tube of bias fabric used for ties, bows, straps etc. Small amounts can be made from left over fabric after main pattern pieces have been cut. If a large amount is required allow additional fabric when calculating quantities.

Ruffle. A narrow gathered or pleated frill.

Saddle. A one-piece yoke that extends from the join with the back bodice over the shoulder to the front. When cutting the pattern for a saddle yoke simply put the back and front together to eliminate the shoulder seam.

Safari. Casual, loose jackets with four big patch pockets, collar, revers, front buttons and belt. Usually designed to be made in cotton, drill, linen etc.

Sailor. Style of collar that meets in a V at the front, widens over the shoulder and extends over the back to finish square across the shoulder blades.

Scye. See Armhole Scye and Armhole.

Seam allowance. The amount of fabric beyond the seam line of a pattern. On commercial patterns this is a standard 1.5cm/⅝in but one of the advantages of cutting your own patterns is that for accuracy you work without seam allowances and then when ready to cut out the fabric you add only what is necessary. For example, up to 2cm/¾in on main seams so the garment hangs well, 1cm/⅜in or even less on necklines, collars and other tight curves and the right amount for the hem depending on the fabric being used.

Separates. Tops and bottoms such as blouses and skirts or shirts and trousers or even three or four items, which are planned to be worn together. The main design features should occur on each garment.

Selvedge. The finished lengthways edge of fabric parallel with the warp yarns. Although it can be used as a straight guide it is best not to use the selvedge in a garment as it is often tight and may even shrink.

Set-in-sleeve. This refers to any style of sleeve that is attached to a basic armhole.

Shaped facing. A piece of fabric used to finish the edge of a garment, usually a shaped edge such as neckline or sleeve edge and the facing has one edge shaped to correspond. The facing shape is obtained by tracing the garment edge; seams in the facing usually match those on the garment. Self fabric can be used, the facing may contrast or it can be lining fabric.

Shawl. A square of fabric, often fringed, that is worn round the shoulders.

Shawl-collar. A one-piece collar on a V-neck or on a front fastened garment, that extends from base of neckline over the shoulder and round the back neck.

Shift. A simple straight dress of any length, usually sleeveless and with a slashed or boat neckline.

Shirt sleeve. Usually pleated into a cuff this sleeve is quite flat at the head often in a low armhole with extended shoulder.

Shirt waist. Refers to a style of dress that has the basic features of a shirt above the waist such as buttons, collar, revers and possibly yoke.

Shoulder pads. A variety of sizes and styles of pads are available including those for raglan sleeves, extended shoulder lines and cut-away necklines. Most are made of foam or wadding but Vilene make a particularly good range of soft washable pads. Allowance must be made for shoulder pads when cutting a pattern so it helps to have an idea of what type you might use.

Shrinkage. This is less of a problem than formerly although jersey fabrics should be washed before cutting as the knitted loops tend to close up. Also all wool should be pressed using a damp cloth. However, play safe by washing or damp pressing any inexpensive or un-named cotton or viscose fabric. Shrinkage is rarely so severe as to affect the amount of fabric required for a design.

Sleevehead. The top part of a sleeve, the part that is convex, between the balance marks. The shape of the sleeve head varies according to style, for instance a shirt sleeve has no fullness and is not very curved, therefore hardly any sleevehead at all, whereas a full, high, puffed sleeve has a very high, exaggerated head in order to include enough to gather.

Square neck. A neckline may be square at front or back or both. Difficult to wear for people with sloping shoulders as the narrow amount of shoulder seam tends to slip off the shoulders. Keep the neckline fairly shallow so that it does not gape and do not make it too wide or shoulder straps may show.

Stay. An extra piece of fabric such as tape, seam binding or interfacing, stitched into a seam that might be liable to stretch or lose its shape. When cutting a pattern it helps to indicate where a stay might be required.

Stay stitching. A line of medium to large machine stitches placed within the raw edge of pieces of cut-out garment. The stitching prevents stretching or distortion during handling or fitting and should be made immediately after cutting the shapes. Edges that are liable to stretch and should be stay stitched are necklines and bias edges of shaped or angled seams and yokes.

Step. The angle between the end of the collar and the upper edge of the lapel in a classic tailored rever style.

Stock. A wide piece of fabric, sometimes attached to the neckline of a blouse, wound twice round the neck and tied loosely. It looks best if the fabric is cut on the bias.

Sweetheart neck. Similar to a square neck, shaped, usually at the front only, curving to a V. This neckline fits best if little or nothing is taken off the shoulder seam when cutting the pattern.

Tabard. A short straight garment usually tied at the sides and worn over other clothes, often as an apron.

Tailored collar and lapels. The classic narrow collar and open lapels that are the hallmark of men's and some women's coats and jackets.

Taper. To gradually reduce without changing the shape too violently, for example, on patterns for trousers.

Tent. The overall silhouette of a dress or coat that is fitted at the shoulders but the side seams slope straight out so that the garment does not touch the figure elsewhere. A useful maternity style but it is also used for concealing figure problems.

Toile. An experimental pattern but one made in muslin, calico or even old sheeting, that you can try on or put on a dummy to check the balance and position of style features etc. The toile can be taken apart and used as the pattern or the adjustments can be transferred to the original paper pattern.

Top collar – upper collar. The upper section of a conventional collar when it is in its worn position. When marking patterns for jackets, coats and other items to be made in medium or heavy fabric a separate pattern piece should be cut for the top collar, larger than the under collar, to allow for folding along the roll line.

Tracing wheel. A small serrated wheel with a handle used for copying patterns. As a quick alternative to tracing put the new paper beneath the pattern you wish to copy and run the tracing wheel along the lines to perforate the sheet below. Use a ruler to keep the wheel straight on straight lines. The tracing wheel obviously also perforates the pattern you are copying so its use is limited to the intermediate stages such as copying a yoke prior to removing the dart.

Trumpet sleeve. A style of sleeve that is wide and loose at the wrist but fits smoothly into the armhole at the sleeve head.

Tucks. Folds of fabric, often parallel and stitched so the fabric is raised on the outside. Wide or flat tucks must be included in the shape of the pattern piece, in the same way as pleats, and their width and position marked. Pin tucks are very narrow so it is best to cut the pattern piece to finished size, pin tuck a piece of fabric and then pin on the pattern to cut out.

Tulip. A wrap-over gathered skirt or sleeve that is narrower at the hem than at the top.

Tunic. A simple short sleeveless garment worn over other garments. A tunic dress is often worn over trousers, loose or belted.

Turtle neck. This describes a loose stand or roll collar.

Under collar. The under section of any collar that folds or rolls. Patterns for tailored collars are distinguished by the fact that a separate smaller pattern is provided for the undercollar. See also Top Collar.

Unpressed pleats. Folds of fabric that are stitched across the end but which are not pressed below that point.

V-Neck. A neckline shaped to a V at front, back or both. The depth of V depends on the garment. When cutting a pattern make the V fairly conservative in depth; it can always be made lower.

Vent. A slit in the back hem of a jacket which allows it to move when wearer bends, sits or uses a pocket, without pulling the jacket. Vents in skirt hems are usually called slits.

Warp. Yarns in woven fabric that run for the entire length of the roll or piece. In the main the straight grain on a pattern piece should lie along the warp or lengthwise grain although there are exceptions for small pieces, for striped and border fabric etc.

Weft. Yarns in woven fabric that run across the width. Also called filling yarns, the weft is often a weaker yarn than the warp.

Welt. A narrow ridge of double fabric. The word is used to describe a strip of fabric finishing a pocket or a particular type of ridged seam.

Wrap-over. The term applied to a style of blouse, dress, skirt, coat etc. with one side overlapping the other and often unfastened except for a belt. Such designs are extravagant of fabric especially if right and left halves of garment are the same size; often the under section can be smaller.

Yokes. A small flat area at the waist of a skirt or trousers or at the shoulders of a blouse or dress. The yoke line may be emphasized with stitching, ribbon etc. but the functional purpose of a yoke is that it provides a horizontal seam where shaping can be introduced.

INDEX

armholes, 30, 31, 125–31, 214
  depth, 25, 26
  deep, 71, 127–9, 203–5, 217
  gaping, 108
  sleeveless, 64
  square, 130–1

back, 25, 26, 29, 30, 39, 94, 165
backing fabric, 23, 49
balance marks, 18, 20, 21, 214
bands
  collar, 89, 214
  front edge, 93–4, 136–7, 185–6
  hip, 66, 96, 97, 148
  necklines, 79, 90, 92–4
  placket, 167
  shaped, 92–4
  with ties, 79, 148, 187
  see also: cuffs; Fold-a-Band; waists
belts, 13, 212
bias, 23–4, 106, 209, 214
  binding, 90, 94, 214
  collars, 68–70, 78–9
bikinis, 189–90, 218
binding, 90, 94, 209, 214
blocks, 7, 19, 20, 22, 27–36, 37–43
  bodice, 29–31, 39–40, 104–5, 150
  lingerie, 188–9
  maternity clothes, 201–2
  skirt, 7, 27–9, 38–9
  sleeve, 20, 32–4, 40–1, 114–24
  trouser, 34–6, 41–43
  small-scale, 22
bodice, 13, 62–72, 191–2
  block, 29–31, 39–40, 104–5, 150
  see also: armholes; bust; collars; darts; necklines; raglan; seams; swathes; yokes
Bondaweb, 87, 131, 214
border design fabrics, 23, 208
bows, 10, 11, 13, 187, 209
bra, 189
braid finish, 94, 195, 209
bridal gowns, 23, 112, 139, 178
bust, 8, 9, 10, 11, 12, 24, 26, 39
  feature placement, 161, 162, 182
  point, 14, 15, 24, 16, 31, 214
  shaping, 14–16, 31, 62–71, 92–3, 94, 108
buttocks, 24, 214
buttonholes, 161, 164, 193, 212, 214
buttons, 14, 161, 214
  decorative, 102, 163
  hemline opening, 167
  interfacing, 193, 212
  and loops, 13, 151, 161, 164, 166
  neckline, 167, 164
  overlaps for, 161, 162, 170, 171
  placement, 161, 162, 163, 164, 182

camiknickers, 190–1, 214
camisole, 65, 189, 214
capes, 81, 197–8
cardigans, 199, 216
checks, 180, 209, 216
coats, 108, 186, 191, 193–4, 200, 209, 211
collars, 73–90
  bands, 89, 214
  contrast, 81, 85, 208, 209
  cowl, 68–70, 216
  draped, 78–9
  flat, 73, 74–6, 81, 214, 219
  fluted, 79–81
  interfacing, 74, 84, 89, 211
  jackets, 86–7, 90, 208
  Mandarin, 77–8
  Peter Pan, 73, 74–5, 219
  points, 74, 86, 89
  revers, 82–3, 85–6, 220
  shawl, 81–8, 220
  shirt, 89–90
  stands, 76–9, 81, 89–90, 101–2
  tailored, 196–7, 221
  ties, 75, 76, 79, 89, 187
contrast, 8, 9, 10, 12, 208–9
  collars, 81, 85, 208, 209
  godets, 59
  necklines, 10, 11, 90
copying styles, 13
cuffs, 21, 23, 114–15, 119–20, 122, 124, 185–6, 209
culottes, 158, 216
curves, drawing of, 20, 22
cut and spread, 16–17

darts, 13, 217
  armhole, 71
  back bodice, 30, 31, 62, 92–3
  bodice without, 62, 71–2
  double pointed, 217
  ends, 16, 21
  larger sizes, 71
  linings, 211

moving, 14–18, 57, 58, 62–71, 92–3, 94, 108
neckline, 90
skirt, 28
underarm, 31
waist, 30, 108
velvet, 208
see also: bust; shoulder; sleeve
dolman styles, 128, 217
drafting, 14, 19, 20, 22, 214, 217
drapes, 13, 112–13, 217
dresses, 98–9, 106–7, 109–11, 139, 150–2, 167, 216
maternity, 201–2, 205–7
dressing gowns, 81, 84, 136–7, 219
dummy, 20, 37–8, 217

ease, wearing, 37, 217–18
edge finish, 90, 211, 212
bands, 93–4, 136–7, 185–6
binding, 94, 209, 214
braid, 94, 195, 209
see also scallops
equipment, 20, 22, 214, 217, 221
evening gowns, 23, 108, 113, 160, 178

fabric
amounts, 23, 210–11, 213
choice, 22–4, 48–9, 81, 210
special, 208–10
facings
combined, 81–2, 216
eliminating, 214
fold-back, 218
hemline opening, 167
necklines, 84, 90–2
patterns for, 21, 90
shaped, 220
skirt waist, 170
zip flap, 168
fall of fabric, 23, 218
fastenings, 14, 161, 162–8, 170–1
see also individual types
fitting, 37–43
flares, 18, 58, 158, 203–5, 218
flounces, 179–80, 208, 209, 218
fluting, 13, 79–81, 179–80
fly fronts, 154, 170
Fold-a-Band, 102, 168–9, 181, 186, 212, 218
Franks, R. D., Ltd, 214
frogs, 161, 166–7
fur fabric, 209

gaping, 64, 90, 108, 161
gathering, 13, 20
bodice, 16, 66–8, 99–100
darts replaced by, 16, 62
edges; shaping, 16
peplum, 111–12
see also: skirts; sleeves; yokes
godets, 59, 109–11, 218
grain, 20, 23–4, 94, 209, 218, 219
skirts, 56, 172, 181
gussets, 134–5, 218, 219

height, illusion of, 8, 9, 10, 11
hems
bias, 23–4
features, 52–4, 167, 179
couture, 216
cutting allowances, 19, 20
linings, 211
Wundaweb, 212
hipline
bands, 66, 96, 97, 148
measuring, 24, 26
pockets, 8, 10, 11, 182, 183–4
wide, 8, 9, 10, 11, 13, 39
hood, 201
hook fasteners, 161, 171

illusion, lines of, 8–12
interfacing, 14, 74, 211–12, 219
armholes, 64
buttoned openings, 193, 212
knits, 211
necklines, 64
outerwear, 193
seam reinforcement, 87, 131, 214
for soft line, 84
zips, 154
see also: collars; pockets; yokes

jabots, 180, 219
jackets, 191, 214, 220
cardigan, 199, 216
collars, 86–7, 90, 208
edge-to-edge, 93–4, 165–7
kimono, 136–7
linings, 211
peplum, 111–12
pockets, 184
tailored, 108, 195–7
jumpsuits, 158, 214, 216

kilts, 180–1
kimono styles, 136–7, 218, 219
knickers, French, 189, 191, 218
knit fabrics, 23, 209, 210, 211

lace fabric, 208
lacing, 161
large sizes, 64, 71, 104
leather, 208, 209
lingerie, 160, 176, 188–91, 218
linings, 23, 208, 210–11, 214
lop-sided figure, 38–9, 41, 129

MacCulloch and Wallis Ltd, 214
maternity clothes, 157, 201–7
measurements
body, 8, 24–6
patterns from, 7, 172–87

nap, 208, 219; *see also* grain
neck, styles to flatter, 8, 12, 129
necklines, 10, 14, 30–1, 90–4
bands, 79, 90, 92–4
binding, 90, 94
bows, 10, 11, 79
button placket, 167
facings, 90–2
gaping, 64, 90
gathered, 66–7
linings, 211
ribbed, 210
scooped, 91–2
square, 64, 98–9, 205–7, 221
tie, 79, 187
V-neck, 8, 9, 75–6, 79–81, 90–1, 92–3, 163, 164, 221
wide, with front folds, 70–1
see also collars
net, 209
nightwear, 137, 139, 141, 176, 189

openings, 14, 70, 160–8
see also fastenings
outerwear, 191–201
see also coats; jackets
overlaps, 161, 162, 170–1
overlocker, 210

patterns, 14–18, 19, 20–1, 22
see also: blocks; measurements
peasant styles, 139–41, 219
peg top styles, 46–7, 219
peplum styles, 111–12, 179–80, 219
petersham, 168, 169, 170, 171, 212
petticoat, 106
plackets, 167, 219–20
plastic materials, 209
pleats, 20, 48–54, 180–1, 218, 220
all-round, 180–1
backing of, 48, 49
box, 50–1, 205–7
Dior, 217
knife, 51–2, 53–4
linings, 211
sleeveheads, 120
trouser waists, 155
unpressed, 55, 174–5, 221
yoked bodice with, 101–2
pockets, 13, 181–5
breast, 182, 184
cut, 183–4
false, 152, 184
grain direction, 23, 209
hipline, 8, 10, 11, 182, 183–4
inset, 185
interfacing, 181, 193

jacket, 184
patch, 181–3, 209
in seams, 183, 184–5, 209
straight skirts, 48
welts, 23, 152, 184, 186, 209
press studs, 161, 163, 164, 166, 171

quilted fabric, 209

raglan styles, 70–1, 130, 137–44, 193–4, 220
revers, 82–3, 85–6, 220
reversible coating, 209
ribbing, 157, 210

sashes, 186–7
scallops, 91–2, 111, 208, 209
seams, 13, 17–18, 104–12
allowances, 19, 20, 37, 94, 195, 210–11, 220
angled, 87, 131
clipping, 216
eliminating, 18, 94, 108, 211
panel, 104, 108–12, 152
pockets in, 183, 184–5, 209
Princess, 104–8, 189, 220
welt, 127, 193, 209, 222
see also: raglan; trousers (seams)
shape, 8–12, 13
shirts, 89–90, 120, 127–8, 152, 220
shorts, 157–8, 214
shoulders, 30, 31, 39, 125–31
darts, 30, 92–3
dropped, 126–7, 217
extended, 13, 71–2, 125–7, 218
flattering, 8, 9, 10, 11, 13, 129
fullness in, 62, 63–4
length, 25, 26
pads, 13, 129–30, 220–1
see also under yokes
sketching, 14, 209
skirts, 13–14, 44–61
A-line, 28–9, 39, 54–61
blocks, 7, 27–9, 38–9
border design, 23, 208
circular, 176–9, 214
darts, 28
flared, 58, 98
fly fronts, 170
gathered, 45–6, 47, 59–61, 151, 172–6, 178, 209
gores, 56–8
length, 24–5
multi-panel, 61
panel over hip, 59–61
peg top, 46–7, 219
soft waist shaping, 45–7
straight, 28, 44–54
tiered, 175–6
tucked waist, 45
wrap-over, 55–6
yoked, 61, 171, 176, 178–9
zip positions, 170
see also: godets; hems; pleats; pockets; waists
sleeves, 114–24
batwing, 145–9, 214
block, 20, 32–4, 40–1, 114–24
cap, 125, 133–4, 216
cape, 216
combination full and fitted, 118
darts, 116, 117, 118, 122, 124, 134–5
dolman, 128, 217
dropped shoulder, 126–7
fitted, 40–1, 115–18, 119–20, 124, 134–5
gathered, 13, 114–15, 116–17, 118, 119, 121, 123, 127
keyhole, 122
kimono, 132–7, 218, 219
linings, 211
pleated, 120
puff, 123, 151, 220
seam length, 25
set-in, 114–24, 220
shirt, 120, 127–8, 220
short, 120–3, 148–9
three-quarter, 123–4, 147–8
tight, 116–17
tucked, 114–15, 117, 121
two-piece, 191, 192–3
see also: armholes; cuffs; raglan; shoulders
sports wear, 129, 137, 138–9, 157–8, 170, 214
square figure, 10, 11, 13
strap fastenings, 13, 97, 102–3, 106–8, 109–11, 161, 164
stretch fabrics, 23, 209, 210, 211
sun tops, 139
swathes and drapes, 112–13

tabs, 13, 161, 165–6, 186, 209
table, working, 22
taffeta, 209
tall figure, designs for, 13
tapes
basting, 154
seam, 48, 155, 178, 193
thighs, 8, 9, 10, 24, 39
ties, 13, 122, 148, 161, 186–7, 209
under collars, 75, 76, 79, 89
toiles, 39, 40, 41, 42, 43, 221
trousers, 153–9
block, 34–6, 41–3, 153
crutch, 25, 26, 216
culottes, 158
front crease line, 34
jumpsuits, 158, 214, 216
linings, 211
maternity, 157
measurements, 25, 26
peg top, 219
pleated, 155
seams, 34, 36, 42, 43, 154, 155, 218
shorts, 157–8
tailored, 154
toile, 42, 43
track-suit, 157
see also: waists; yokes; zip
tucks, 13, 16, 20, 62, 221
dart, 217
sleeves, 114–15, 117, 121
tulle, 209

Velcro, 55, 75, 102, 161, 163, 166, 164, 171, 214
velvet, 208, 209
Vilene, 48, 73, 74, 84, 98, 129, 211

waists, 8, 9, 13, 168–71
bands, 23, 168–71
drop, 108, 112, 151, 163, 175
elastic, 46, 96, 97, 153, 160, 170
faced, 170
fasteners, 162, 163, 170–1
flattering styles, 8, 9, 10, 11, 12
fullness above, 15, 30, 62, 66, 108
interfacing, 168–9, 212
inset, contrast, 12
measuring, 24, 26
peplum, 180
pleated, 155
pocket placement, 182
ribbing, 157, 210
skirts, 38, 45, 39, 172
trousers, 153, 154, 155, 156, 157
yokes, 99–101, 156
warp yarns, 23, 222
weave, 23
weft yarns, 23, 222
welts, 23, 152, 163, 184, 186, 209
wrap-over designs, 55–6, 164, 222
wrists, 25, 26, 33, 210
Wundaweb, 48, 84, 212

yokes, 94–103, 222
contrast, 8, 9
grain direction, 23, 94, 209
interfacing, 98, 156
saddle, 220
shoulder, 97, 98–9; gathers, 63–4, 94, 95, 96, 102–3, 151; pleats, 101–2; tucks, 143–4
skirt, 61, 171, 176, 178–9
trouser, 156, 171
waist, 99–101, 156

zips, 20, 154, 161, 162, 168, 170–1
dresses, 167
linings, 211
trousers, 154, 168, 170